Outposts and Allies

Other works by James A. Huston

Combat History of the 134th Infantry (1948)

Biography of a Battalion: Being the Life and Times of an Infantry Battalion in World War II (1950)

Across the Face of France: Liberation and Recovery, 1944–1963 (1963)

The Sinews of War: Army Logistics, 1775–1953 (1966)

Out of the Blue: U.S. Army Airborne Operations in World War II (1972)

One for All: NATO Strategy and Logistics, 1949–1969 (1984)

Counterpoint: Tecumseh vs. William Henry Harrison (Historical novel) (1987)

Outposts and Allies

U.S. Army Logistics in the Cold War, 1945–1953

James A. Huston

Selinsgrove: Susquehanna University Press
London and Toronto: Associated University Presses

© 1988 by Associated University Presses, Inc.

Associated University Presses
440 Forsgate Drive
Cranbury, NJ 08512

Associated University Presses
25 Sicilian Avenue
London WCIA 2QH, England

Associated University Presses
P.O. Box 488, Port Credit
Mississauga, Ontario
Canada L5G 4M2

The paper used in this publication meets the requirements
of the American National Standard for Permanence of Paper
for Printed Library Materials Z39.48-1984.

Library of Congress Cataloging-in-Publication Data

Huston, James A. (James Alvin), 1918–
   Outposts and allies.

  Bibliography: p.
  Includes index.
  1. United States. Army—Supplies and stores.
2. United States. Army—Procurement. 3. World
politics—1945–1955. I. Title.
UC263.H87   1988   355.4'15'0973   86-43218
ISBN 0-941664-84-8 (alk. paper)

PRINTED IN THE UNITED STATES OF AMERICA

Contents

Preface	7
1 In the Wake of World War II	13
2 Cutting Off the Tap—Termination of Lend Lease	54
3 Housekeeping and Preparedness	67
4 Rebuilding Forces in Europe and North Africa	87
5 Foreign Military Aid	128
6 North Atlantic Treaty Organization and Aid to Western Europe	160
7 U.S. Military Aid in the Near East	177
8 Military Assistance in the Far East: China and Korea	200
9 Defense Assistance to the Philippines, Indochina, Japan	233
10 Western Hemisphere Defense	256
Glossary of Terms and Abbreviations	318
Bibliography	323
Index	341

Preface

Logistics comprises the time and space factors in war—equipping, supplying, moving, sustaining armies in battle. Or as the Army's *Field Service Regulations* (1949) put it: "Logistics is that branch of administration which embraces the management and provision of supply, evacuation and hospitalization, transportation, and service. It envisages getting the right people and the appropriate supplies to the right place at the right time and in the proper condition."

For a military organization in times of peace, strategy and tactics are reduced essentially to planning and training exercises, but logistics goes on forever. Troops have to be fed and housed and clothed and provided arms and ammunition and transportation whenever they are in being, whether in war or peace. And reserves of matériel have to be maintained to support possible expansion in mobilization. Clearly applicable at all times are all the aspects of logistics summarized in the 1957 *Dictionary of United States Military Terms for Joint Usage* that defined logistics as follows:

In its most comprehensive sense, those aspects of military operations which deal with: (1) design and development, acquisition, storge, movement, distribution, maintenance, evacuation and disposition of matériel; (2) movement, evacuation and hospitalization of personnel; (3) acquisition or construction, maintenance, operation, and disposition of facilities; and (4) acquisition or furnishing of services.

In times of "cold war" the logistic activities of establishing and maintaining bases overseas and of supplying matériel to friends and allies around the world may approach the intensity of those activities in war itself. Here our effort is to relate, in some detail, those activities during the period of the "Cold War" from 1945 to 1953, i.e., from the end of World War II to the end of the Korean War. Logistic support for the Korean War per se is another story, to be told elsewhere, but that complicated the simultaneous efforts that continued in maintaining major forces in Europe, building airfields in the Arctic and in North Africa, and providing military assistance to the Near East, Southeast Asia, East Asia, the Western Pacific, and Latin America, as well as to the North Atlantic Treaty countries.

The reader may protest that he really is not interested in knowing the forty-six steps involved in getting approval for a construction project in Alaska—or the further complications in Morocco where the Moroccan and French governments are involved. All he needs to know is that we had bases there, not how they got there. But the *how* is the essence of logistics. How forces are established and how they are supported is what logistics is all about.

Surely one may feel a sense of tedium in approaching the ponderous mechanics of administrative procedures, congressional appropriations, international agreements, and military implementation. What are the reasons for bureaucratic red tape? Complications of politics and diplomacy often may be present. But bureaucratic red tape exists mainly to guard pennies and to disperse responsibility. Any agency charged with administering public funds lives in constant dread of some critical exposure or accusation by the news media, congressional committees, the General Accounting Office, or aspirants to public office. And with any hint of waste or extravagance or corruption, the pressure is on for yet stricter accounting, more reviews, more reports. At the same time, multiple concurrences by other staff sections and other agencies and approvals by layers of officials and officers above and below relieve the individual of full responsibility when something goes wrong. And when something does go wrong, the pressure is on for more concurrences, more approvals, more inspections, more reviews, more reports.

But with all the ponderous machinery and political accountability, the eight years after World War II were years of bold imagination and remarkable military achievement in making effective the totally new course in world affairs upon which the United States had embarked. We need to take note of how that was done. Details of how the United States went about adjusting its military programs to the post–World War II era are instructive in any attempt to understand all that has followed. What has followed have been, in large part, efforts to build upon and adapt from policies and programs of those years of imagination and creativity.

For the United States—in those years of transition from a leading participant in the greatest of all world wars to leadership of the "free world" in a cold war of unprecedented proportions—two basic laws of history, as always, were at work. Opposing each other, yet merging with each other like the yin-yang symbol on the Korean flag (and the blue and gray patch of the 29th Infantry Division) were the law of continuity and the law of change. Nothing is completely new, and nothing is completely different. As the old French saying puts it, *plus ça change, plus c'est la même chose*. But now the ball of the yin-yang was turned more in the direction of change.

For assistance in the preparation of the manuscript and seeing it through publication I am indebted to many persons at many places. First of all I would like to thank Dean James F. Traer and the Committee on Faculty Research and Development at Lynchburg College for their support. For assistance in reseach I would like to thank the staffs of the General Reference Branch,

Office of the Chief of Military History/Center for Military History; the National Archives, the Army Library, the library of the Army Logistics Management Center, and Mary Scudder, Julie Beamer, Deborah Beckel, Carol Pollock, Marjorie Freeman, and Linda Harwell of the Lynchburg College Library. For assistance in the typing and reproduction of the manuscript I want to thank Doris Collins, Joyce Good, Lois Daniel, Shirley Moore, and Phyllis Lane.

A special note of appreciation is due David N. Wiley, director of the Susquehanna University Press, whose encouragement saw this project through, and to Beth Gianfagna, managing editor of the Associated University Presses and Cynthia Perwin Halpern, copy editor, for their expert guidance and great care in getting this into the proper form. Any remaining errors and of course all statements remain my own responsibility.

And for continuing assistance and support in so many ways, I am deeply indebted to my wife, Anne Marshall Huston.

The photographs of the construction of a NATO pipeline are by courtesy of the NATO Information Service, Brussels; all other photographs are from the Still Pictures Branch (NNSP) of the National Archives in Washington.

Outposts and Allies

1
In the Wake of World War II

> One of the fallacies of our time is the notion that now the war has ended, an era quite different will begin—that we shall be able to return quickly to the "good old days."
> —S. McKee Rosen in the
> Introduction to Harold D. Smith,
> *The Management of Your Government* (1945)

Introduction

Chastened by the experience of going through a Second World War only twenty years after the triumphal conclusion of the First, Harry Truman and the American people were determined to face their responsibilities for world order in the 1940s and 1950s rather than walk away from them as they had done in the 1920s and 1930s.

With unmatched industrial capabilities and with a monopoly on the atomic bomb, the United States, now demonstrably the leading power in the world, stood in a unique position to influence world affairs. This was the period of the great transition from wartime involvement to the peacetime support of overseas forces and allies with a view to maintaining world order. It was something altogether new for the United States. For the first time the United States was maintaining large military forces outside its own territory for a prolonged period of time; for the first time the United States was providing large-scale military matériel assistance to foreign powers in peacetime; for the first time, except for the French alliance during the Revolution, the United States was willing to enter into formal alliances for mutual defense, and to do so in peacetime.

At the outset the demobilization of the World War II armies turned out to be, predictably, a race between getting the boys home and maintaining a semblance of defenses in Europe and Asia. The disposal of surplus property was a race between assistance for allies and national security on the one hand and private profits on the other.

After what some leaders, particularly in allied countries (except for China where an exception was made), regarded as an overly hasty termination of the wartime Lend-Lease program, other programs for supplying military supplies

13

and equipment soon appeared. At the same time the United States was taking steps to build new bases and to supply its own forces abroad.

In earlier times there had been occasions when a state of affairs returned more or less to its previous pattern, before some violent interruption. Thus after the Stuart restoration in England in 1660, conditions in a way returned to what they had been before the interregnum. At various times European wars ended in peace settlements that restored the status quo ante bellum. Not so the Second World War. The postwar world of the 1940s and 1950s was a new world, and the place of the United States in it was, for this country, unique. It was unique for the times, but it set the direction of the United States in world affairs for decades to come.

Now, far from a retreat to the isolationism of the 1920s, the United States found itself thrust to the center of the world stage, in competition with another super power that to some appeared to threaten world domination. Actually, in those first few years after World War II, the United States was the dominant power in the world. Then, as Soviet power grew, a strained relationship developed into what came to be called the "Cold War."

The United States assumed leadership of what its leaders called the "free world." In a contest for security in a "free world" the United States shored up its own defenses, sent forces to outposts in Europe and Asia, to the torrid tropics, and to the Arctic wastelands. Foreign military assistance and multilateral military cooperation became continuing policies for a nation bent on meeting the challenges that lay ahead. In doing so it affected the policies of scores of other nations with whom it became involved in mutual defense treaties, base agreements, and programs of military assistance. Its old world of neutrality and isolation and noncommitment would be no more.

Relief from the perils and tensions of all-out war that comes with the ending of conflict brings with it a hope—and an assumption—that, as in the ending of a novel or of a play, the major problems at hand have been solved. Bright hopes for a brave new world outshine the awareness of the continuing nature of those problems. Actually the military problems that followed in the wake of World War II combat operations were, in some ways, even more difficult than those of warfare itself. They were more difficult in at least two respects: (1) the abrupt change from all-out mobilization and build up to all-out demobilization and liquidation; (2) concurrently, the necessity of backing up foreign policy in times of rapidly changing conditions and opposing pressures.

Many logistic problems—and with a termination of strategic and tactical operations most problems that remained were logistic—were if anything greater than before. The American army had been deployed over the globe during the course of four years. People demanded its return in a few months. Mountains of equipment had grown as war industry hit its peak in 1944 and 1945. Now that equipment had to be disposed of. The national economy had been geared to full war production. Now the call was for rapid reconversion to meet growing shortages in civilian goods. Beyond the immediate problems of liquidating the war effort and cleaning up the battle areas, it would become increasingly clear in the years following that problems now assumed to be purely political would have their military facets. American foreign policy commitments would be effective only to the extent that a military establishment was at hand to support them.

The ragged ending of World War II left without precise definition the beginning of the postwar period. The worldwide extent of the war, the apparent necessity for maintaining certain legal fictions in order to continue controls over the domestic economy, and the play of international politics resulted in a graduated termination of the conflict. For certain purposes—such as the beginning of limited demobilization, industrial reconversion, and the suspension of lend-lease shipments to those allies participating only in the European war—World War II ended on V–E Day, 8 May 1945. For certain other purposes—such as the cancellation of war contracts—the war ended with the Japanese acceptance of surrender terms, 14 August 1945. For some purposes—such as general demobilization and industrial reconversion, and the termination of lend-lease—the war ended on V–J Day, 2 September 1945. For still other purposes—such as the duration of the Surplus Property Act and other matters generally relating to domestic policy—the war ended with the president's proclamation of the cessation of hostilities, 31 December 1946. The war ended officially with Italy, Bulgaria, Hungary, Romania, and Finland when peace treaties with those states became effective on 15 September 1947. The war with Germany officially ended with the Joint Resolution of Congress approved 19 October 1951. Finally the war with Japan came to an official end on the date that the Treaty of Peace with Japan came into force, 28 April 1952.[1]

The years between V–E Day and the Japanese peace treaty saw perhaps the greatest "peacetime" build-up in history. Almost from the start new tensions had begun to replace the old ones. Demands, first for husbanding resources and then for rebuilding, soon would overtake those for continued reduction. In his final report as chief of staff of the army in 1948, General of the Army Dwight D. Eisenhower wrote:

> In the fall of 1945 our military forces in Europe and the Orient were still formidable; our network of bases and depots was global in extent; vast stores of armament and supply were maintained across the world. Since then, the manpower of the wartime Army has been returned home to be replaced fractionally by postwar volunteers; all but critically important bases have been evacuated; surplus property has been turned over to appropriate government agencies for disposition. But the peace has not become the peace of which war's victims dreamed.[2]

Demobilization—Men and Matériel

"With victory, a stampede for demobilization swept over the country."[3] Long-absent soldiers and anxious relatives and friends brought understandable pressure on government officials for a quick return of troops from overseas and for them rapid discharge from the army. Clinging to the traditions of Cincinnatus and the Minute Men, Americans could not bring themselves to the admission that a large postwar military force might be necessary. The only misgiving that they felt toward immediate and rapid demobilization seemed to be the possibility of widespread unemployment during the period of readjustment, but even those doubts soon dissipated.[4] As it turned out, the rate of troop returns bore little relationship to considerations of changing foreign commitments and responsibilities or to the supply missions that remained. The only real limitation on demobilization during the months immediately after V–J Day was the availability of shipping.[5]

Even as demobilization was being accelerated signs appeared that raised serious doubts as to the wisdom of that policy. As early as 16 October 1945 Secretary of War Robert P. Patterson, Secretary of the Navy James V. Forrestal, and Secretary of State James F. Byrnes could agree upon the inadvisability of continuing the rapid demobilization. Within six weeks of the final victory, Russian intransigence had made it clear that difficult times lay ahead. Yet the secretary of state counseled against making public the details of Soviet diplomacy on the ground that this might provide the Russians with an excuse to claim that provocations had justified their actions.[6] Meanwhile, the rate of returning troops from overseas continued to accelerate.

Troop movements of unprecedented scope had been underway for over three months when the Japanese capitulated. During that period the redeployment of forces from Europe to the Pacific had been the first priority, but demobilization of the troops that would not be needed in planned operations against Japan began simultaneously. When the surrender came with unexpected swiftness, all efforts turned toward demobilization. The five million men who had gone overseas during a period of four years were to be brought home within fourteen months. Target dates called for the return of all troops except occupation and garrison forces of 370,000 in Europe, 400,000 in the Pacific, and 100,000 in other areas by the end of June 1946. In Europe a close-out force of 300,000 men, charged with looking after excess property, was to be returned before the end of January 1946. Between V–E Day and 2 November 1945 nearly two-and-one-half million soldiers returned to the United States from overseas theaters. By November and December they were returning at a rate nearly three times the rate of departures for overseas destinations during the peak war month of January 1945 when 238,000 had embarked. Over 550 ships, including battleships, air craft carriers, and hospital ships as well as transports and cargo vessels—and the British liner *Queen Mary*—were in troop-carrying service during this period.[7]

The return of overseas troops to the United States and the movement and discharge of men was in itself a gigantic logistic undertaking. But perhaps more significant was the effect of the rapid demobilization of personnel on the handling of the vast quantities of matériel that remained. The army's point system, under which a soldier accumulated credit toward his discharge on the basis of length of service, overseas service, campaign stars, decorations, and dependent children,[8] bore no relationship to the integrity of units and little to the needs of the army.[9] Infantrymen in combat had taken a large percentage of the war's casualties; this had limited their opportunities for winning campaign stars, decorations, and often shortened their overseas service. As a result, service troops found themselves with a relatively high point credit, which made them eligible for early discharge. This meant the loss of skilled technicians and the disintegration of essential service units at the very time that the army was facing what were, in some ways, its greatest logistic problems of the war.[10] "Only those present in the units at the time will know the disastrous effect of the demobilization program on supply and maintenance activities. Before we were through officers were performing the duties of mechanics and everybody was doing what they could to save the situation."[11]

Japanese acceptance of United Nations surrender terms on 14 August 1945 caught the army without systematic plans for the types and quantities of matériel that should be returned to the United States. When the chief of staff shortly after the capitulation indicated an intention toward more rapid demobilization than had been previously considered, Army Service Forces was just beginning a study of the question of returning supplies and equipment.[12] This left theater commanders in a difficult position. If they proceeded to ship out supplies immediately, without further instructions, they were likely to tie up valuable shipping with cargo not needed in the United States; if they waited on the completion of the ASF study, outloading activities in Europe would be practically suspended from about 15 September to some time in November, while troop strengths—and thus the capability for handling the matériel—would be rapidly decreasing.

Already troops were being moved out of the European and Mediterranean theaters faster than were supplies and equipment. Continuation of these rates even until October would leave 70 percent of the supplies in the Mediterranean theater still to be disposed of, with only 30 percent of the theater's troops strenght remaining to do the job. Ships arriving in the Mediterranean Theater of Operations (MTO) to pick up civilian-type supplies would have to return to the United States practically empty except for pierced steel plank—used principally as bottom cargo—during the latter half of September and most of October unless the War Department could give additional instructions. As of August 1945 total stocks in the MTO amounted to an estimated five million tons, while those in the European Theater (ETO) amounted to about twenty-four million tons. About one million tons a month could be shipped out from European ports. But by the spring of 1946 ETO forces would be down to occupation strength, concentrated in Germany far from the major ports where outshipments could be handled.[13] In the Pacific an ambitious "roll-up plan"—intended to gather up supplies scattered over the Pacific islands and bring them in to bases near service units and close to civilian markets—began in July 1945. Armed with lists of civilian-type goods most needed in the United States, teams set to work on Guadalcanal and New Caledonia; later they moved up to New Guinea, the Philippines, Okinawa, Iwo Jima, and finally to Japan. During the first five months of 1946, 289 ships arrived at the San Francisco port of embarkation with cargoes of equipment—mostly ordnance—from the Pacific. But here too the depletion of units overtook the collection of matériel, and little could be done just then to salvage great quantities of goods left behind.[14]

In the task of undoing its gigantic mobilization, the army had an undertaking in defiance of the proverbial warning, "You can't unscramble a scrambled egg." But the problems had not been unconsidered. The Baruch-Hancock Report on War and Post-War Adjustment Policy, made public 15 February 1944, recommended advanced planning and well-defined procedures for the cancellation and settlement of war contracts, for rapid clearing out of war goods from industrial plants to make room for return to civilian production, and the setting up of a surplus property administration.[15] As early as April 1943 Donald Nelson, chairman of the War Production Board, had assigned Ernest Kanzler the task of studying the whole problem of reconversion. In November 1943 the Truman Committee and the George Committee of the United States Senate had urged greater attention to problems of contract termination, reconversion, and surplus property disposal. But that was the period when most emphasis was on getting greater, not less, production.[16]

At war's end, the residue of the American "miracle of production" that had loomed so large in winning the conflict lay in supply rooms, warehouses, and outdoor dumps scattered the world over—largely unwanted by those who had it, but wanted very much by many who lacked it.

Disposal of Surplus Property Overseas

Responsibility for the disposal of surplus property of the American Expeditionary Forces after the Armistice in November 1918 had fallen to Brigadier General Charles G. Dawes as purchasing agent of the AEF. Under the supervision of an Advisory Board of Liquidation appointed 27 November 1918, Brigadier General Charles R. Krauthoff, as general sales agent, assumed management of disposal activities three weeks later. His job was to supervise all direct sales made by AEF, to help the various services in disposing of property in their custody, and to sell property himself when that would be more advantageous than sale by the service having charge of it. In February 1919 the War Department created the United States Liquidation Commission, and this commission began operations in Paris the next month as the overseas disposal agency.[17]

The World War II approach to the disposal of overseas surplus property began about where the post–World War I procedures ended. Disposal of surplus was not, of course, a purely postwar problem, for certain amounts and types of property had become surplus—for reasons of changed plans or conditions, obsolescence, over supplying, miscalculations, or other circumstances—while the war continued. This guaranteed at least some consideration of the problem before the cessation of hostilities. A year before V–J Day plans and policies were assuming the creation of a special agency to handle the disposal of surplus property overseas. But it was not clear whether that agency would function under the War Department or under some other office or department of the government.[18]

Initially the solution was to adopt something of a modified and greatly expanded version of the World War I plan. A regulation of the Surplus Property Board in December 1944 left responsibilites for the disposal of surplus property outside the United States in the hands of the owning agencies. The secretary of war and the secretary of the navy that same month established a joint agency, the Office of the Army-Navy Liquidation Commissioner, and delegated their foreign surplus property responsibilities to it. The commissioner would carry out his functions through field commissioners set up in key locations abroad, and he would deal with them directly rather than through military channels.[19] On matters pertaining to the War Department, the commissioner was to report to the under secretary of war. The chief of staff was to designate a general officer as deputy commissioner who would serve as commissioner until that office should be filled, and would then assist the commissioner and act in his absence.[20] Major General Donald H. Connoly received this appointment, and on 15 April 1945, Thomas B. McCabe assumed office as army-navy liquidation commissioner. Disposal of property in foreign areas inevitably raised questions relating to foreign policy. Moreover, military control of disposal activities invited criticism from those who thought that complete control of those activities should be in civilian hands. Within a few months, therefore (on 27 September 1945), the president transferred the responsibility for foreign disposals to the State Department, and the Office of the Army-Navy Liquidation Commissioner became the Office of the Foreign Liquidation Commissioner.[21] McCabe and his whole organization came under the State Department, and continued much the same functions as before. An executive order of 31 January 1946 transferred to the State Department the regulation-making authority relating to surplus disposals abroad that had previously been the prerogative of the surplus property administrator. An amendment to the Surplus Property Act of 1944, approved 1 August 1946, gave statutory confirmation of the transfer of responsibilities, and further provided for a program of foreign scholarships to be financed out of proceeds from surplus property disposals in foreign currencies.[22]

Scarcely a year after OFLC began to function as a State Department agency, word came to the under secretary of war of suggestions that the responsibility for foreign surplus disposal should be returned to the War Department, perhaps under an Army-Navy Liquidation Commission type of organization.[23] A draft letter prepared for Under Secretary Royall expressed the view that "in the present world atmosphere of tenseness and suspicion the explosive possibilities of having the armed forces dealing directly with various foreign governments for the sale, terms and delivery of surplus property are distressingly evident."[24] Much of this would have to be under State Department control in any case—a situation that could lead to the misunderstandings and controversies common to any division of responsibilities. Further reasons for withholding agreement to any such change was the opposition of congressional committees to "military personnel controlling the strategy and tactics of actually selling surplus."[25] The Meade Committee had expressed these sentiments in these terms:

> The Office of the Foreign Liquidation Commissioner is a civilian agency; however, its personnel is overwhelmingly military. For example, in the Washington Office of the Foreign Liquidation Commissioner there are 149 Army and Navy officers, and 36 key civilians. Overseas there are 306 Army and Navy officers and 56 key civilians. Except for the field commissioner, himself, practically all of the high-ranking position in the Paris office are filled by military personnel. The military personnel are still on the pay rolls of the War Department and the Navy Department, respectively. The committee believes that a merchandising function is essentially a civilian rather than a military function, and that it should be discharged by civilian personnel acting under civilian procedures rather than through Army and Navy officers still on War and Navy Department pay rolls, whose training and experience would naturally lead them to think and act along military lines.[26]

Sometime later, OFLC did issue regulations approving the disposal of surplus property directly by owning agencies in those areas where the foreign liquidation commissioner determined that disposal by his own organization would be uneconomical. Whenever the total acquisition cost of property at any one location exceeded $50,000, however, proposed disposition was to be referred to OFLC for review.[27] Theater commanders continued to have complete responsibility for sales or other disposal, as well as for handling of surplus property in areas where no foreign commissioner had been appointed.

How much of the total inventory of supplies in any theater might become surplus depended upon War Department policies and commitments for the postwar period. At first much of the emphasis was on the return of property to the United States. Officers facing the difficult problem of surplus disposal in the United States itself, however, soon came to doubt the wisdom of bringing back more property without first considering its future use.²⁸ In general, the theater commander could determine what property was excess in relation to the needs of the theater and report that determination to the Army Service Forces, or, for property pertaining to aircraft, to Army Air Forces. Property previously classified obsolete by ASF or AAF could be declared surplus without further reference, and this same procedure held for perishable subsistence and for certain classes of items that the commanding generals, ASF or AAF, might list from time to time. Other instructions called for the immediate return to the United States of certain classes of supplies whenever they were found to be excess to theater needs.²⁹

Theater needs represented the sum of various factors that the War Department directed should be taken into account. These included allowances for occupation troops under tables of organization and equipment, tables of allowances, special lists of equipment, and equipment modification lists. Allowances for other troops in the theater were to be somewhat less than for those designated for occupation duty. In addition, stock levels of not-to-exceed-sixty-days' supply would be maintained, special supplies needed for the occupation and supplies to fill replacement requirements during the anticipated period of occupation would be held, and property for certain projects or missions would be saved. All other property would be considered excess. Instructions issued in September 1945 used the date of 15 August 1948 as the limiting date for the policies announced; changes issued in February and August 1946 extended that date to 30 June 1949; by October 1946 it was being assumed for planning purposes that the occupational period would continue until 30 June 1951.³⁰

How much property of commercial value or civilian usefulness ought to be returned to the United States was a continuing question. To some extent it no doubt represented a tug of war between those anxious to bring in supplies to fill civilian shortages and those who feared that the return of large quantities of surplus goods might depress domestic markets—the Surplus Property Act of 1944 had in fact prohibited the reimportation into the United States of any surplus property sold abroad. In January 1946 the secretary of war directed that all items, excepting those of a purely military type, beyond the needs of occupational forces through 30 June 1949 should "be declared surplus and disposed of as quickly as practicable."³¹ The intent of the policy was to obtain liberal declarations of surplus and to prevent the return to the United States of any items of potential civilian use until after the OFLC had had the opportunity to attempt its disposal. Special instructions would make provisions for the use of the available property for aid to the Philippine army, to the Chinese army, and for prisoners of war and displaced persons under the direct care of the army in Europe.³² Revised lists of property which should be returned automatically to the United States continued to go out.³³

In part the reduction in the number and type of items being returned to the United States was due to the cost involved. In November 1946, Supply,

Service, and Procurement estimated that it was costing $45 million a year to return property from overseas.[34] Responsible commanders had pleaded lack of funds and, in consequence of the precipitate demobilization, lack of men to handle surplus property since the beginning of major disposal operations.[35] The Mead Committee, however, was unimpressed by attempts to justify quick sales of property at great sacrifice on the ground that otherwise it would be necessary to keep soldiers overseas a long time to look after it. The committee reported that as of 28 February 1946 Army Service Forces depots were employing a total of 109,530 persons; of these 100,157 were civilians, 5,437 were prisoners of war, 2,662 were officers, and 1,274 were enlisted men. Most of the officers were working at managerial assignments, and the troops were being used not for warehousing, nor for guarding property, but mainly for guarding prisoners of war.[36]

Aside from the return to the United States of certain stated categories of surplus property, overseas commanders might dispose of their surpluses by: (1) declaration to a disposal agency—usually OFLC; (2) sale for the local production of matériel for the use of United States forces; (3) sale as scrap or waste, or (4) destruction or abandonment. Except for supplies being transferred or sold to friendly foreign governments for their military forces, all combat matériel had to be demilitarized—by such expedients as breaking or bending gun barrels, mutilating parts, or crushing whole articles—before disposal could be made. In the absence of special instructions, captured enemy equipment would be handled in the same manner as other army property. Property that had been donated by the American Red Cross was not to be disposed of without consultation with the Red Cross, and if requested, it might be returned to the Red Cross. Property that had been returned to the military commander by OFLC for disposal could be donated to nonprofit educational and charitable organizations.[37]

The foreign liquidation commissioner left to the army the authority for disposing of most salvage, scrap, and waste materials in foreign areas. Some scarce metals and other items were on the lists for prompt return to the United States. Otherwise this property was subject to local disposal.[38] Careless segregation of scrap materials from usable parts resulted in a certain amount of loss in these items. At one place inspectors in the United States found several carloads of material that had been returned from overseas as scrap that consisted almost entirely of major unit assemblies declared economically unrepairable by ordnance representatives; they found good machine tools standing in salvage yards; at other places they found transmissions, transfer cases, axle assemblies, cylinder clocks—and even bearings, gears, and connecting rods still in their original wrappings—which had been taken from cargoes of scrap.[39]

Surplus combat aircraft could be salvaged or scrapped automatically. Parts needed in the theater, or parts requested by a field commissioner of OFLC were to be removed and the residue turned over to a salvage officer for disposal as scrap or waste. Monthly reports of such disposals were to be forwarded to Army Air Forces.[40]

By the end of 1947 theater commanders had declared to disposal agencies surplus personal property having a total procurement cost of $5.498 billion. Of this, $128 million worth was transferred to sixteen foreign governments before OFLC began operations. Thereafter, the foreign liquidation commissioner effected the transfer of $2.9 billion worth of army technical service supplies to foreign governments.[41] Additional declarations, less withdrawals of previously declared surpluses, brought the total of these surplus property declarations in overseas commands to $5.81 billion as of 31 December 1949.[42]

Disposal of Property in the European Theater

Largest of the bulk sales was that to France, signed 28 May 1946, which involved the sale of property having an estimated original cost of something over $1.13 billion. Terms called for payment of $275 million in dollars over a period of thirty-four years; $15 million in real estate, and $10 million in local

A thousand acres of surplus vehicles, from jeeps to $7\frac{1}{2}$-ton trucks, on sale at U.S. Army Depot, Marseilles District.

A few of the thousands of U.S., British, and Canadian trucks assembled at Le Havre for sale to the United Nations Relief and Rehabilitation Administration for Czechoslovakia.

currencies for educational programs and for further real estate improvements.[43] This policy of disposal by bulk deals, in which all property remaining in a country or in a certain area went to the country where the matériel was located without recourse to the segregations and classifications necessary for sale of specified items followed a precedent set in the sale of World War I surplus to France.

The bulk sale to France did not include nondemilitarized combat matériel, nor did it include railway rolling stock.[44] Those kinds of items were subject to separate negotiations and sale on the basis of the French requirement list for the purpose of building France's postwar military force. In this connection the question of the use or destruction of captured German war matériel led to conflict between the State and War Departments. The State Department wanted to hold up on the destruction of that matériel in order to meet French desires for obtaining such equipment to make up shortages in available American property for its rearmament program. The War Department, on the other hand, urged the speedy destruction of captured matériel in order to be relieved of the responsibility for guarding and handling it, and in order to speed up the repatriation of soldiers to the United States. The result was a freeze order on destruction of equipment of possible use to France.[45] By September 1946 the bulk sale had been completed, and by then the problem had passed.[46]

A separate sale signed with France in July 1946 disposed of all surplus ammunition remaining in France plus 50,000 long tons to be shipped from Germany and 2,500 long tons in Belgium, which had been declared surplus specifically for the purpose of balancing the French rearmament requirements. This practically completed sales operations with the French government.[47]

Previously a bulk sale to the United Kingdom, including army surplus hav-

Spare tires—40,000 of them—at the Ordnance Collecting Point, Leghorn, Italy, December 1945.

ing an original cost of about $238 million had been concluded on 6 December 1945.[48] Similar sales followed in Belgium, Italy, and, finally, in Germany.

The arrangement with Belgium had this important difference: instead of an outright sale on the basis of an established price, this was a transaction in which the Belgian government accepted custody of the property, and then sold it on the basis of a 50 percent share of the gross proceeds. The total amount of army property involved was nearly as great as that in the United Kingdom. Because of difficulties in keeping records and in making payments, an outright sale to the receiving government probably was more satisfactory for most bulk disposals, but in this case the arrangement proved to be quite a satisfactory one. Careful accounting, monthly reports, and prompt payments brought agreeable results.[49]

As in other Eurpoean areas, most of the surplus property in Italy finally went to the Italian government by bulk sales. In this case there were two bulk sales. The first, signed 9 September 1946, excluded fixed installations, scrap, and salvage, and property of lend-lease origin. Sales of this property to private individuals or to other agencies continued, but it soon became evident that unless the remaining surpluses could be sold quickly, the army would simply have to abandon great quantities of it. The OFLC field commissioner in Rome, therefore, negotiated a second bulk sale with the Italian government on 21 July 1947. This deal included lend-lease property amounting to about $100 million in original cost, which the British had left in Italy, as well as approximately $84 million worth of army and navy property. This property went for ten cents on the dollar. However, realization on overall disposals in Italy amounted to 23.9 per cent.[50] Total Army surplus property in the two Italian bulk sales amounted to $263 million at original cost.[51]

Sales of surplus property in Germany fell into two categories: (1) Supplies located in Germany but sold to governments and other customers outside Germany, and (2) supplies transferred to the German economy. Early in 1947 army authorities in Europe agreed to arrangements whereby surplus property in Germany was concentrated in major disposal centers where the Office of the Foreign Liquidation Commission could conduct on-the-spot "site sales," and where prospective buyers operating through the central field commissioner's office in Paris could inspect the property. After the army had declared property at a given location to be surplus, in bulk, OFLC depot teams, with the assistance of army personnel, then had to classify, segregate, inventory, appraise, price, and finally issue sales catalogues. For readily salable goods, it took an average of about three months from the time it was declared surplus by a technical service until its sale had been concluded. After certain quantities of property remained unsold for a considerable period of time, the central field commissioner in Paris listed them in competitive invitations to bid. Surplus property credit agreements, making available additional credits of $15 million in addition to $15 million previously granted to the government of Hungary, $10 million to the Netherlands (making a total of $30 million to that government) and $10 million to Denmark expanded the market for this matériel.

One especially difficult problem connected with the site-sale program in Germany was that of transportation. Here, as elsewhere, the purchaser was supposed to accept responsibility for transportation. But occupation policies denied to outside buyers any method for employing German transportation facilities on their own account. The general procedure, therefore, was for the army to deliver the property by rail to a German frontier point where the customer could pick it up. Some relief from this burden came with arrangements for Dutch barges to take on cargoes of sold property at bargeheads located near depots up the Rhine River and to carry it to major ports in Holland and Belgium.

Of some $500 million worth (at original cost) of property listed on master declarations at twenty-six site-sale depots in Germany, OFLC had sold, by the end of 1947, $168 million worth for a return of $42 million. Obviously large quantities of surplus property remained to be disposed of in Germany.[52]

In August 1946 the German states in the American zone of occupation—Bavaria, Baden-Württemberg, and Hesse—with the encouragement of army

Surplus armored vehicles at the Boblingen Ordnance Depot, Württemberg, Germany, November 1945.

occupation authorities, organized a public corporation to accept and dispose of all captured enemy matériel that the U.S. army should release to it. Bremen, which later became a part of the American zone, joined the organization in 1948. The states owned the stock of the corporation, which was called STEG (Staatliche Erfassungs-Gessellschaft fur offentliches Gut m. b.H.). When the European Command later decided that STEG should handle not only captured enemy equipment but all other matériel released to the German economy by the U.S. army as well, it meant that STEG was responsible for accepting and disposing of vast quantities of goods coming to it under four distinct arrangements. These included (1) captured enemy matériel, known as the CEM program; (2) army surplus goods turned over piecemeal under what was referred to as the quantitative receipts program; (3) a second part of army surplus sold under the bulk sales program, and (4) the surplus incentive matériel (SIM) program.[53]

General Joseph T. McNarney, commanding general, United States Forces, European Theater (USFET), saw the possibility of transferring quantities of army surplus goods to the German economy in order to meet serious shortages of food, clothing, medical supplies, and other essential items. Holding that such action was necessary in order to prevent the spread of disease and unrest, he found a precedent in the policies that General Douglas MacArthur was at that time carrying out in Japan. General McNarney decided to transfer surplus goods to the German economy in return for quantitative receipts signed by the minister-presidents of the German States for which the military government would record the value in dollars as a future obligation to the United States to be paid from profits of German exports whenever a favorable balance of trade might be restored. This procedure brought objections from both the Treasury and the State Departments. The Treasury Department maintained that such arrangements were beyond the authority of the military commander, for this in effect amounted to the extension of a loan to Germany and to supplementing the congressional appropriation for the occupation. The State Department objected that the army was disposing of surplus in violation of the Surplus Property Act, which assigned this function to the Office of the Foreign Liquidation Commissioner. Added to that was a War Department decision that quantitative receipts did not constitute valid credit vouchers for relief from accountability for the property so transferred.[54]

Ironically these difficulties arose chiefly because General McNarney and Lt. Gen. Lucius D. Clay, the military governor under his command, sought to obtain some obligation for repayment to the United States for property being transferred to the Germans.[55] Technically, they could have held that the property was not surplus at all. Since it was needed for carrying out the occupation mission, it was not "property in excess of theater requirements." Actually this was the position that USFET assumed when Maj. Gen. Carter B. Magruder, G-4 of the European Theater, notified the central field commissioner of OFLC in Paris that the establishment of a self-supporting economy in Germany would be given priority over the declaration of surplus "under any circumstances."[56] For a while the War Department considered advocating a policy that would assign to USFET the responsibility for disposing of all surplus property in Germany, but dropped the proposal when USFET objected to that additional burden.[57] By the end of 1946 the army had transferred property having an original cost of $115 million for use in preventing disease and unrest,[58] and this total reached $238 million in 1948.[59]

Inasmuch as occupied Germany had no central government of its own, a bulk sale of the kind negotiated with the United Kingdom, France, or Italy did not at first appear to be feasible.[60] But when General Clay, anxious to free military forces from the duties of guarding, handling, and transporting military property, gave his strong support to proposals of the foreign liquidation commissioner to arrange such a bulk transfer, plans proceeded directly to the conclusion of a sale agreement. The contract was between the government of the United States and the Bizonal Economic Council acting under authority of the United States and the United Kingdom Military Governments. Indirectly the army had a role both as seller and as buyer, but if something of a "borrowing from Peter to pay Paul" transaction seemed evident, it was nevertheless highly important in the mysterious ways of government appropriations.

Signed by the central field commissioner for Europe and the chairman of the Bizonal Economic Council on 23 January 1948, the contract became effective at midnight 31 January 1948. It provided for the transfer to the German economy of all surplus in Germany that had been declared to OFLC and that remained unsold on 1 February, together with whatever additional surplus in Germany the Army should declare by 30 September 1948. Designated as the agency to accept and dispose of the property, STEG was to take title to it "as is, where is, without warranty except as to title" at a price representing 21 percent of the estimated original acquisition cost. The purchase price would be a deferred charge against future proceeds of German exports. The contract excluded nondemilitarized combat matériel, air navigation equipment, lend-lease materials, and certain other property. Motor vehicles and accessories, in contrast to the food and clothing of earlier transfers, were the major items in the bulk deal. A supplementary Memorandum of Understanding (28 February 1948), and a Standing Operating Procedure (5 March 1948), both agreed to by the European Command, the Office of the Foreign Liquidation Commissioner, and STEG laid down the specific responsibilities of each agency and subordinate elements in effecting the transfer of property.[61]

According to the estimate given in the contract itself, the total amount of property transferred under the bulk agreement would be approximately $875 million worth at original cost. Actually the amount of property turned over was less than half that. This sizeable reduction could be attributed to several factors. In the first place, sales to outside customers, which continued on a "first come, first served" basis until 31 January, were much greater than had been anticipated. Secondly, the occupational troop strength remained higher than had originally been planned, so that less of the property on hand became surplus. Finally, increasing amounts of property were returning to the United States to go into reserve stocks.[62] Rising international tensions were adding to the army's own supply requirements. On 1 May 1948 the logistics division of the army general staff called for a sixty-day suspension of turnovers of depots to the German economy in order to give representatives of the technical services an opportunity to inspect the property for items needed in the United States. In contrast with earlier demands for quick disposal of surplus, the new policy was to retain all supplies and equipment needed "to meet known and anticipated requirements" under an accelerated military program, except (1) those that would deteriorate beyond economic repairability before use, (2) those requiring prohibitive in-storage maintenance, and (3) those for which storage facilities were lacking.[63]

Actual transfers to the German economy ended about February 1949.[64] Later, changing international conditions would raise serious questions as to the methods by which the property was handled, and as to whether much of it should have been sold at all. Those considerations hardly could have been given full weight at the time of sale. But the policy of the United States would remain firm on the matter of payment for the property sold. When a debt settlement conference met in London in the spring of 1952 to consider the outstanding obligations of the German Federal Republic, the United States would ask for 100 percent payment for surplus property (i.e., 21 percent of estimated procurement cost).[65]

A special customer for army surplus equipment was the United Nations Relief and Rehabilitation Administration (UNRRA), which began its relief activities in Europe shortly after the cessation of hostilities. Both President Truman and Secretary of War Patterson urged special efforts to meet the UNRRA requirements.[66]

A staff officer noted in August 1945, "Judge Patterson wants the humanitarian needs of liberated countries alleviated expeditiously by breaking loose surplus government property so that UNRRA can carry out its mission."[67] This use of surplus property offered advantages to both parties. For UNRRA it meant equipment readymade and available in Europe (and the Pacific) near the areas where it was needed at a price considerably less than it would have been for similar equipment ordered new and shipped to those areas. For the United States it meant a buyer for goods that could not be reimported into the United States and it meant the fulfillment of a certain part of the obligation it had assumed toward contributing to the support of UNRRA by what amounted to a bookkeeping transaction. Maj. Gen. Donald Connolly, deputy army-navy liquidation commissioner, and Karl Borders, chief of the UNRRA bureau of supply, headed a mission to Europe in August 1945 to set up surplus property procurement offices in France and in Italy. In making its purchases, then, UNRRA dealt through the field commissioners, first of the Office of the Army-Navy Liquidation Commissioner, and later of the Office of the Foreign Liquidation Commissioner. As in other surplus property operations, the demobilization of the army and the deterioration of equipment, as well as changing policies of the liquidation agencies, interfered somewhat with the prompt meeting of UNRRA needs. The relief agency had arranged to apply some $150 million of its funds toward the purchase of surplus supplies in Europe. However, delays in congressional appropriations and the unavailability of some needed items reduced this amount to $85 million. Most of this went for trucks and railway rolling stock.[68]

Disposal of scrap in Europe, as elsewhere, continued to be a direct army responsibility. At first the collection of scrap was mainly for the purpose of turning it over to local manufacturers for use in making items for the occupation forces. Soon it developed into sales on the basis of bids from scrap dealers from all parts of the world. As iron and steel scrap became short in the United States, demands for the return of that kind of material from Europe increased. Insofar as reduced troop strengths and facilities permitted, teams policed the battlefields and supply dumps for knocked-out tanks, junk vehicles, and deteriorating weapons. By late 1948 two companies—Purdy Company and Canterbury Corporation—were shipping ferrous scrap to the United States at the rate of 20,000 tons a month. The Canterbury Corporation ran into some trouble when it began delivery of scrap it had purchased to Turin, Italy, where the Fiat company was to process and ship it. Most of it never got through, for Italian industry needed it too badly for itself. This had to be settled by an arrangement under which Canterbury Corporation received authority from the Italian government to buy scrap in Germany against an Italian allocation there in return for the Canterbury scrap in Italy.[69]

Return of scrap from Germany carried with it some danger of creating a vicious circle at a time when the United States was undertaking a program seeking to encourage European economic recovery. In discussions with Paul G. Hoffman, economic cooperation administrator in May 1948, officials of the United States Steel Corporation had agreed that in the interest of the European Recovery Program and of the steel industry itself, it would be foolish to pay the transportation and handling costs for returning scrap to the United States, and then ship steel back to Europe if that same scrap could be used to make additional steel in Europe itself. Their recommendation at that time was that steel scrap in Germany should first be applied to the German economy to the extent that that would help production there; next it should go to industries in Western Europe, including the United Kingdom, and any quantities beyond those should be returned to the United States.[70]

Final close-out of the Paris office of the Foreign Liquidation Commissioner came on 15 May 1949. Remaining unsold property that the army had declared to OFLC went back to the army as unsalable. The heads of the various military missions in Europe received instructions on handling any inquiries arising from the operations of OFLC. One major account remained open. An amendment signed 12 May 1949 extended the 1946 agreement with Belgium, under which that government accepted surplus property for resale on the basis of a 50 percent share of the proceeds, to 1 July 1951. By that time the principal interest of the United States would be not in the sale but in the recovery of some of the huge stocks it had disposed of in Europe.[71]

Liquidation in the Pacific and Far East

Although property left over after the battles in the Pacific and the Far East was less abundant than that in Europe, it was far more scattered, and much more difficult to get to. When V–J Day came, huge quantities of supplies and equipment had been stockpiled on Guam, Saipan, Iwo Jima, and in the Philippines to support the planned invasion of Japan. Other quantities remained behind in earlier battle and staging areas from Hawaii to Guadalcanal and from New Caledonia to Australia. Then came demobilization. The lack of experienced men was more serious here than in Europe, because the battle against deterioration was more intense. Tens of thousands of trucks and thousands of artillery pieces, as well as tanks, ammunition, accessories, and supplies simply had to be left behind. The jungle rot of the tropics and the curiosity of the natives soon set about patiently eating away the complicated machines that they suddenly found at their complete disposal. Other quantities of supplies were declared to the Foreign Liquidation Commissioner (to the Surplus Property Division of the Department of the Interior in the case of Hawaii and Alaska) and sold; some went into reserve stocks of the Far East Command; some went to the relief of distress both in liberated and in occupied areas, and some was returned to the United States.[72]

As in other areas army forces had the responsibility for guarding, maintaining, accounting, inventory, and tallying out the property scheduled for sale. In the western Pacific area alone, the estimate was that these functions would cost $18 million for fiscal year 1947, and another $6 million for the next year. The continuation of these activities and responsibilities beyond that time would result in disproportionately greater costs.[73] Stevedores shifted from one island to another in the South Pacific area in order to ship out property, and by July 1946 that area was being closed out. Then property from the outlying Hawaiian Islands, from the Gilberts, and from the Marshalls had to be brought in to Oahu.[74]

While not always the most profitable, bulk sales certainly were the most convenient, and often, when time was short and personnel lacking, it was the only practicable method of selling large quantities of surplus property, and the Office of the Foreign Liquidation Commissioner resorted to this expedient in negotiating major sales to India, China, and the Philippines as well as smaller sales to Australia and other countries.[75]

After V–J Day a representative of the U.S. army signed an agreement with the government of India by which supplies and facilities that India had previously furnished as reciprocal aid should now be paid for in cash by United States forces there. This agreement was consistent with the termination of lend-lease aid to India, and the Foreign Economic Administration had given its approval. On 15 April 1946 the Assistant Secretary of State, W. L. Clayton, requested the army to hold up on payment of bills owed to India for goods and services furnished between 2 September 1945 and 31 March 1946. This was to enable the State Department to take this into consideration in negotiating for the settlement of lend-lease and for the sale of army surplus property in India.[76] As regards the amount owed through 31 May, came to about $39 million.[77] As a result of the negotiations, India finally agreed to the cancellation of this charge with the intent that it be treated as a lump-sum initial payment for surplus property. For the remainder of the $618 million worth of property of all kinds transferred to India, the United States was to receive 50 percent of the proceeds of sales over $50 million after the payment of Indian customs.[78] Under this provision the United States had received as of 30 June 1948 an additional $13 million.[79]

A letter to the Mead Committee calling attention to the destruction of certain air forces property at Karachi, India, brought a special investigation. The report of investigation acknowledged that beacon lights, pistons, aircraft instruments, generators, starters, and some coil springs had been mutilated by sledgehammer or by fire, but the report stated, "There is no evidence that any steam roller was used in this process."[80]

An agreement concluded with Burma 28 February 1947 provided for the transfer of locomotives, railroad cars, jeeps, generating plants, and construction machinery, which originally had gone to Britain under lend-lease, to the Burmese government in return for payment of $5 million over a period of twenty years with interest at 2 3/8 percent.[81]

Most of the remaining surplus property in the Pacific area went to China and the Philippines in bulk transfers. Earlier the army sold to China in November 1945 some 65,000 long tons of property valued at $62 million plus 9 billion Chinese dollars for a sales price of $23 million plus 9.278 billion Chinese dollars.[82] Negotiations for the bulk sale to China went on in Washington, Nanking, and Shanghai during the spring and summer of 1946.[83] A preliminary agreement with T. V. Soong, Chinese premier, on 21 June 1946 set up the basis for the sale. The transfer was to include all surplus property, including scrap, in the China and Pacific theaters, with the exception of fixed installations, property already sold or under contract when the agreement was made, property to which the Philippines were entitled under the Philippine Rehabilitation Act, aircraft and parts, and ships and marine equipment. Some of this latter equipment did in fact come under other programs. The property included supplies on insular possessions of the United States in the Pacific with the exception of Hawaii and the Aleutians.[84]

A number of problems had to be met before negotiations for the Chinese

Surplus heavy equipment at the engineer subdepot, Manila, January 1947.

bulk sale could be completed. The Philippine government objected to having Chinese come in to pack and load property located in the Philippine islands; the Chinese would not be able to find water transportation to move out the equipment that they had bought unless they had some assistance; the prior claim of the Philippine government to $100 million worth (at surplus sale price) of surplus property located in the Philippines would delay operations there until the Philippine government chose the items it desired.[85] Obviously, American military services would have to give considerable assistance if the Chinese were to collect the material being made available to them.

Signed 30 August 1946, the bulk sale contract with China brought the total amount of surplus property made available to the Chinese, including previous sales of all types, to approximately $824 million worth in original cost.[86] Recognizing the difficulty the Chinese would have in taking possession of property located on Guam, Saipan, Tinian, Okinawa, and other islands, army and navy representatives in Shanghai agreed to cooperate fully in helping to set up and operate work camps that the Chinese would establish near the sites where property was to be recovered. This help included utility service, tentage and shelters and space for storage and operations, loans of transportation and handling equipment, fuel and lubricants, arms and ammunition for Chinese guards, existing communication facilities, and, when available, motion pictures and other recreation facilities.[87] Military representatives cooperated directly with the OFLC field commissioner in Shanghai in making arrangements for the transfer. The War Department warned that close coordination was necessary to prevent the Chinese from playing off one service against another.[88]

At the request of General Marshall the War Department and the Office of War Mobilization and Reconversion had agreed to stop shipments of civilian-type items from the Pacific to the United States, effective 30 June 1946, so that the material would be available for the Chinese sale.[89]

Actual removal operations got off to a slow start. The Chinese contracted two American engineering firms to handle classifying, packing, and stevedoring, while a third American firm accepted a contract for shipping. One of these, The Vinnell Company, signed a contract with China on 29 November 1947 to act as their exclusive sales agent for a period of ninety days, subject to renewal, for the sale of all property, excepting scrap, which the Chinese had acquired on the islands of Guam, Saipan, Tinian, Eniwetok, Marcus, Kwajelein, Ulithi, Majuro, Makin, Peleliu, Iwo Jima, and Wake. It may or may not have been significant in this connection that the FLC regulations specifically excluded "Guam or other Pacific insular possessions" from foreign areas from which sold surplus property could not be imported into the United States.[90] In any case, the Chinese were more interested in earning dollars in the export market than in using much of the surplus property for themselves, and they undertook a vigorous sales campaign toward that objective. They sold most of the metallic scrap to the General Commodities Corporation, a firm incorporated in Hawaii, which in turn sold the scrap to the Bethlehem Steel Corporation for return to the United States.[91] They sold some 100,000 measurement tons of scrap on Tinian, Saipan, and Peleliu to the Lipsett Pacific Corporation and the Oceanic Trading Company.[92] Why it would not have been as well for the Foreign Liquidation Commissioner or the army and navy to have engaged the American firms for removal operations and to have sold the material directly to companies in the United States is not clear.

The Philippine Rehabilitation Act of 1946 provided for the transfer to the Philippines of surplus property located there aggregating up to $100 million in "fair value" as estimated by the Foreign Liquidation Commissioner.[93] The army surplus transferred under this program and under earlier bulk sales totalled $765 million in original cost.[94] Engineering items comprised the most important category of equipment involved, in terms of value, and medical, quartermaster, signal, ordnance, and transportation equipment followed in value in that order.[95] While it was relatively easy to transfer most of the surplus property to the Philippine government and its agencies because it was located in those islands, a major difficulty did appear in connection with that property turned over on a "take away" basis. This happened in areas where the army was not yet ready to evacuate, though it did have surplus material on hand that was to be transferred to the Philippines. The Philippine authorities could take custody of property left in evacuated areas simply by posting guards around it, but lack of transportation made it impossible to carry away all the surplus property in areas where army units remained. The solution was to extend the area turnovers in order to reduce what had to be moved.[96] A special sale transferred to the Philippine government all surplus army ammunition located in the Philippines for demilitarization and salvage. That government then contracted with an American salvage company to handle the project, and return the metallic scrap to the United States.[97] Some years later a congressional investigating committee was told that importers brought into the United States whole shiploads of surplus property that had been transferred to the Philippines for their rehabilitation.[98]

In Japan, General MacArthur avoided some of the grief that came to General McNarney in Germany in transferring surplus property to the civilian economy. First of all he obtained War Department approval with the concurrence of the Foreign Liquidation Commissioner in March 1946 for retaining, without declaring them as surplus, items needed for civilian supply in Japan and Korea until the War Department had approved civilian programs for those countries. Then he arranged for the Foreign Liquidation Commissioner, with the approval of the National Advisory Council, to sell surplus property in Japan to the Japanese. This approval actually came in two parts. The first was limited to items considered essential for the prevention of disease and unrest and for the occupation mission. On 22 November 1946 the Japanese government, with the approval of the supreme commander for the allied powers, entered into a contract with OFLC for the purchase of surplus property having an original cost of $50 million at 30 percent of cost. The second part of the program was the sale of the residue of surplus remaining in Japan. In January 1947 the National Advisory Council gave its approval for sale of this property, not exceeding $20 million in original cost, to the Japanese government, and OFLC completed the sale.[99]

Other surplus supplies went to Korea. The United States military government in Korea signed a contract on 22 January 1947 for the purchase of surplus property having an original cost estimated at $25 million. This included some property already in Korea, about 100,000 tons in the Philippines reserved at the time of the bulk sales, and about 100,000 tons in Hawaii; most of the remainder came from Japan.[100]

As in Europe, the United Nations Relief and Rehabilitation Administration contracted with the Office of the Foreign Liquidation Commissioner for surplus property in the Pacific area. It placed orders for over $40 million worth in sale price of surplus property of all types through offices in New Delhi, Shanghai, Manila, and Honolulu.[101]

After 15 May 1949 when OFLC closed out its combined Shanghai-Manila offices—located then in Manila—the responsibility for the disposal of its surplus in the Pacific area returned to the army.[102]

Sales in Latin America

The Latin American area entered the surplus property picture in two ways. A relatively small quantity of surplus property resulting from the army's defense and air operations in the area, chiefly in the Caribbean and Brazil, remained there for disposal. In addition a question arose in connection with providing surplus property from other areas for Latin American countries under the Western Hemisphere Defense Program. Most of the surplus remaining in Brazil went to that country in a bulk sale.[103]

In the matter of shipping surplus equipment to the Latin American countries, sharp differences of opinion arose regarding prices and regarding the diversion of materials for which there was a civilian demand in the United States. Representatives of the army, navy and the Office of American Republics Affairs of the State Department agreed that principal stress should be put on carrying forward the program, rather than upon financial returns. If necessary, they would have been willing to see the material go for its scrap value plus handling charges. But the Assistant Secretary of State, Dean Acheson, ruled that when alternate markets existed that would bring higher prices, the material would have to be priced at a "fair value." In this case it was the military who were urging "intangible political advantages" as the reason for furnishing arms to Latin American countries, while the State Department sought a return comparable to what could be obtained in another market.[104] Similarly, Under Secretary of War Royall thought that the War Department might be subject to a great deal of criticism if it held items for the Latin American nations that were in great demand in the civilian economy in the United States, but General Maxwell thought that the advantages the United States would receive from Latin America would outweigh the disadvantages to the domestic economy resulting from the transfer.[105]

Error is bound to creep into transactions so complex and so widespread as those involving the sale of surplus property. The Caribbean area offered no exception to this rule. Early in 1946 the H. V. Grosch Company of San Juan, Puerto Rico, bought a large lot of white powder packed in cases labeled "bleaching powder." When the company tried to sell it, however, it found it practically insoluble in water, though the label did show a content of 14.5 percent active chlorine. The company inquired how the powder could be used, and whether it was suitable for water treatment. Actually the stuff was a secret decontamination agent. The War Assets Administration could not have accepted it for sale in the United States because it could not have advertised its composition. But now the formula had been compromised anyway. Army Service Forces directed the commander of the Antilles Department at

San Juan to replace the decontamination powder with an equal poundage of chloride of lime bleaching material, or if that were not available, to cancel the contract and refund the payment to the buyer. It was possible to make the exchange for 27,000 pounds of the decontamination agent that the H. V. Grosch Company still had in storage, but 22,000 pounds had been sold to the French Public Health Service and shipped to Guadeloupe. However, the French Public Health Service reported that they had not been advised that the decontamination powder was not giving satisfactory results.[106]

Domestic Disposal of Surplus Property

At home, as abroad, haste was the greatest enemy of an ordered demobilization and of an economical disposition of surplus property. Blame for loss and waste was abundant enough to be shared liberally. Some of the blame should go to the army for its hurry to get rid of the surplus material. Some of it should go to the disposal agencies for their sales in "bargain lots" to close out their accounts quickly. Some of it should go to Congress, both for urging the haste and for failing to provide funds for storing and caring for the property so that it could be held longer.

Out in Portland, Oregon, Herbert A. Jones, Jr., was anxious to get a couple of jeep motors. When he went around to the local WAA office he found that two jeep motors were in fact available, but they were tied to a lot of unsold residue in an "all or nothing" offering. Jones worked the price down from two or three hundred dollars to $75, and accepted. When he picked up the property he found that for his $75 he had bought, in addition to the two jeep motors, the following: 1 dump truck body, 12 brass plug coils, 104 king pins for trailer hitches, 2 Norgren lubricators for circulating pumps, 240 miter gears, 2 chess wagons, and 4,824 marine universal gear joints. The universal gear joints alone had cost $66,000, and their value even if reduced to scrap was $2,250.[107]

In Des Moines, Iowa, eighty-two-year-old Alfred W. Lawson had set up a "University of Lawsonomy" to teach his theories of "penetrability" in relation to economics, physics, and other subjects. His "school" obtained a quantity of surplus machine tools and other equipment in 1947 for $3,681, which it sold to private buyers a few years later for $120,000.[108] Fortunately such laxness in disposals as these transactions indicated seemed to be more the exception than the rule in the overall disposal operations.

Pressure for rapid disposal of surplus property tended to follow the property itself. Thus in 1945 most of the pressure was against the army for being slow in declaring its surplus, while by 1946 the pressure was being shifted to War Assets Corporation (later to WAA) for being slow in disposing of what had been declared.[109] But this shift in attention did not relieve the army of considerable criticism, and the declaration of property to the disposal agency did not relieve the army of a great many custodial and coordinating responsibilities in the United States any more than it did in overseas theaters.

The War Department was glad enough not to have the full responsibility for the disposal of surplus property, but officials were sensitive to the criticism that continued to come to the army. They sought to meet this criticism to some extent by launching a publicity campaign to acquaint the public with the magnitude and complexity of the task involved. It was noted that a factual statement of the amount of surplus property the War Department had disposed of, and how much WAA had disposed of, should be given, but that "WAA should not be too severely criticized since it would be an added incentive to WAA to have the disposal job pushed back on the War Department."[110]

Factors ordinarily influencing the determination of surplus—requirement of the army in meeting changing strengths and changing missions, obsolescence, repair capacity, and return of property from overseas—were in themselves subject to such variation that their specific application to actual conditions was difficult enough. But now an additional factor, the demand for the release of goods to the civilian economy, imposed further complications. Under instructions from John Steelman, the successor to John Snyder as director of OWMR, the War Department during 1946 turned over many items that were in short supply in the civilian economy.[111] But in doing so, Lt. Gen. LeRoy Lutes, director of Service, Supply, and Procurement (SS&P), (successor to ASF and G–4), made it clear that these items were *not* actually surplus, and it might be necessary to rebuy some of them on the market at some later date.[112] The whole matter of gearing military requirements to civilian needs, and of making strict differentiations in surplus property between civilian-type and military-type goods, depending upon whether or not it had a useful civilian application, added to the difficulties of supply planning and disposal operations. The Plans and Operations Division of the General Staff was becoming concerned about the effects that such disposal policies were having on potentialities for mobilization.[113]

In order to eliminate the categorization of property according to civilian usefulness, and to permit the retention of additional items considered critical, SS&P proposed a new policy stated simply in these terms: "The disposal level for military property in the Zone of the Interior is the sum of all demands as set forth in the current Supply Supplement to the War Department Troop Program."[114] After thorough consideration by all the technical services, army air forces, and other staff agencies, this did become the War Department policy.

Disposition of surplus property was a continuing activity, both during war and during peacetime operations. But the magnitude of the problem that fell to the army after V–J Day brought about a number of changes in procedure. First was the decentralization of authority to act at local depots and stations. Further, the demand for speed reduced the use of the earlier procedure of circularizing other services to find out if they needed a particular item before it was declared to the disposal agency.[115]

This led to one of those obvious difficulties that the army dreaded most—the likelihood that one service would go out to buy items in the market while another service was disposing of the same type of items as surplus, and, even worse, the possibility of the army's buying back some of its own surplus. Procurement regulations did lay down the rule that technical services should offer their excess property to other services, and stipulated, "care will be taken to avoid purchasing property obtainable through disposal agencies from commercial sources."[116] Army air forces suggested that a clause should be inserted in procurement contracts that would require a cost breakdown to show any use of surplus property. The chief of the Readjustment branch, SS&P, doubted the legal right to do that, but he thought it might be possible to demand a statement that any finished item obtained from a contractor was not one that the contractor had obtained from the government. He suggested that the only sure way to prevent the conditions to be avoided would be to insist upon a thorough screening of all items before they were declared surplus, though it might help for WAA to require all buyers to certify that what they bought would not be resold to a government agency.[117]

On the face of it, these suggestions seemed to be examples of what a junior officer often learned early in his career—that sometimes in the army, the paper is more important than the deed, that some commanders are more anxious to protect themselves by requiring a bundle of certificates than they are from actually doing the things to which the certificates purport to testify. Here it was a case of committing a second error to cover up the first. It appeared to be more important to avoid criticism than to get equipment at the lowest price. If the same quality item could be had from a surplus property dealer at a lower price than from anyone else, why should it not have been preferable to buy the article from him? The answer of course was that these staff officers had learned the overriding importance of maintaining the confidence of the Congress and of the public, and in order to keep ammunition from the hands of critics whose principal purpose in life seemed to be to undermine that confidence, whether or not the criticism was justified, it sometimes was more important to avoid the appearance of extravagance than to avoid extravagance itself—sometimes, indeed, even at the expense of what would actually have been greater economy.

Depot commanders could report all items that were no longer standard items of issue in the army directly to the disposal agencies without reference to higher authority. Other items were reported as surplus only when directed by the chief of the technical service having jurisdiction.[118]

At stations having surplus property on hand, the station commander appointed a surplus property officer to look after surplus disposal. This officer assumed direct responsibility and accountability for surplus transferred to his custody by station supply officers and the post engineer. It was his duty to set up and maintain a surplus property stock record account, and, within five working days after receipt of accountability for the surplus property, to edit and dispatch completed surplus declaration forms to the disposal agency. He was responsible for the storage and warehousing of surplus property moved from station stocks to designated warehouses and areas, and for packing, crating, and shipping the property on instructions from the disposal agency.[119]

Pressures for speed, both in declarations to disposal agencies and in its own direct disposal activities, continued to mount against the army. Regardless of the technical divisions of responsibility, many people continued to associate military property with the army, and for them, the army continued to be the first point of inquiry or demand whenever their hopes to buy surplus property—even though sale of the property might be entirely in the hands of WAA—were frustrated. A caustic note on the subject, hand written on a letterhead of the Services of Supply, United States Forces China Theater, and signed simply, HSA (apparently Maj. Gen. Henry S. Aurand who had been commanding general of the SOS in China), came to General Eisenhower, chief of staff. Before forwarding copies to staff divisions, General Eisenhower attached this notation: "While I assume that some of our difficulties arise out of existing law, I think the attached paper is worth reading. If you pass it along to any of the staff please have it typewritten with no marks remaining on it that could give any indication of its origin. D.D.E." The note, dated 30 December 1945, said in part:

> In accord with its policy of ducking Congressional, radio commentator, newspaper columnist, and other editorial criticism, the War Department has attempted to shift its surplus property burdens and problems to other agencies. It is hoped that these agencies will get the criticism. Anyone who either went through the disposal of surplus property last time, or can see through it this time, will tell you that this shift of responsibility cannot be made. The present arrangement is doomed to failure primarily because the agencies to whom the job was shifted have neither the organization nor the physical means to do the job in time. Only the Army possesses both.
>
> Also, the Army has retained the job of determining what property is surplus, in what quantities, when and where. It seems that the Army has woven the rope to hang itself by passing the surplus disposal jobs to other agencies without the organization or means to handle them; and then has helped the hangmen by putting the noose around its neck in keeping in its own hands the surplus determination. The hangmen—the members of the great American public—long ago constructed the scaffold, and are anxiously awaiting the opportunity to spring the trap.
>
> Regardless of what method is utilized, it has become imperative that prompt action be taken to dispose of this property at home and abroad. Prompt action means decentralized action. Authority, complete and full, must not only be given by the WD to its subordinate agencies to declare property surplus; but the disposal agencies must likewise give full and complete authority to their subordinates for disposition. It takes no clairvoyant to see that this job must be complete before June 1946.[120]

A committee of educators in December 1948 objected to the system whereby only property classed as salvage was available for donation to educational institutions. Property desirable for educational use was thus being classed as salvage or junk. The educators found that sometimes it was necessary to take a lot of undersirable junk in order to get the few items they needed in order to maintain "proper working relationship with the salvage or disposal officers."[121] With emphasis being placed on cash returns, salvage officers in many instances were reluctant to contribute property to the donation program which otherwise they would be able to sell.

Time after time letters came to the War Department from persons either bogged down in unsuccessful attempts to get items they wanted from WAA, or thinking that the logical place to get surplus army goods was from the army. A lady in Glen Rose, Texas, was trying to get furniture and dishes for a community center. A former mathematics instructor of General Eisenhower wrote from California in an effort to get some equipment for the Boy Scouts in his area. The 4–H clubs wanted some equipment. A local agency wanted some X–ray equipment. Many of the inquiries came to members of Congress who passed them on to the War Department for explanations. Each time, staff officers patiently explained that the army sold only small lots of surplus, scrap, and salvage. For items coming within those categories, the property disposal officer of the field army within whose area the community was located could give more information. For other surplus property it would be necessary to go to WAA.[122]

Other quantities of correspondence resulted from reports of the destruction of property in various places, and always the letters of protest would receive careful attention and thorough replies. A woman in Minnesota reported that house guests had told of being ordered to throw overboard quantities of clothing when they were returning from overseas. A woman from Boston wrote general Eisenhower that she was "apalled" by reports of the wanton destruction of property in France so badly needed by the French people.[123] The War Department replied to both that such reports usually were exaggerated, and that members of the Mead Committee recently had completed a trip around the world to check on the handling of government property, and so far they had reported no improper destruction except for minor incidents.[124] An investigation at Anderson, South Carolina, proved a local news report of wanton destruction of army property to be based on hearsay. Aroused by a radio broadcast purporting to expose army wastefulness in February 1946, a man in New Mexico who described himself as a "poor farmer" sat down and pencilled a letter to General Eisenhower about the situation. His letter went to the office of the chief of staff. From there it went, under a disposition form, to G–4, where a staff officer prepared a one-and-one-half page reply explaining how surplus property was handled, prepared a memorandum for the record, attached a G–4 slip, and sent it to the assistant to the deputy assistant chief of staff, G–4. Finally it went to the Projects Branch and to the Mobilization Reserve Section.[125]

Disposition of surplus army property included not only gigantic quantities of supplies classified as personal property, but real estate—command installations, civil works projects, industrial properties—as well. Many of the buildings and storage areas containing surplus personal property became surplus themselves once that property had been removed. Total space occupied by the technical services reached its peak in October 1946,[126] which testified to the way in which logistic activities increased rather than decreased immediately after the cessation of hostilities. Total leased storage space amounted to $17\frac{1}{2}$ million square feet as of V–E Day; by 31 July this had been reduced to $5\frac{1}{2}$ million feet.[127] By 31 May 1947 the space occupied by surplus property in technical service depots had been cut to nearly half of what it had been the year before.[128] As of May 1947 the War Department had declared to WAA, or disposed of directly, surplus real properties numbering 2,027, with a value (acquisition cost plus construction costs) of approximately $3.674 billion.[129] As with other types of property, the wisdom of holding real estate for possible future use was difficult to ascertain. Perhaps it would have been well to have retained a considerably greater proportion of warehousing and storage space. This might have made it possible to have saved more surplus personal property for the war reserve and for the army's requirements beyond June 1949; made it possible to hold property that was being sold at sacrificial prices until demand created more realistic prices, and made available these facilities for a future emergency when, it could be anticipated with little doubt, construction costs would be high and the time would be short.

Recognizing that the cancellation of production orders would result in some unemployment, the War Department announced immediately after the Japnese capitulation that its policy would be to make a prompt return of industrial facilities to civilian production. The army turned over its war-built plants to private concerns both through WAA and through its own channels. Strings had to be attached to many of the plants so that they would be available for reconversion to war production in the event of another emergency. A number of key plants were leased to private operators under strict restrictions against alterations that might change the basic purposes for which those plants could be used. The army followed the lead of WAA in disposing of its surplus factories in order to avoid "giving away" a duplicate of a plant that had cost private enterprise millions of dollars to build.[130] Total disposition of surplus command and industrial facilities through 15 May 1950 involved 4,383 properties valued at $4.5 billion—of which 75 percent of the value was in command installations and 25 percent in industrial real estate.[131]

The estimated cost value of the excess and surplus personal property of the army that was processed within the continental United States during the period from 1 June 1944 to 30 April 1947 totalled $21.3 billion. Of this total, the army moved property having an original cost of over $7.6 billion through direct sales, salvage turn-ins, transfers to other government agencies, and donations.[132]

Conclusions

When, later in 1947, new declarations of surplus to disposal agencies dwindled, and the emphasis shifted to direct disposal, it was clear that the great disposal job for war-generated surplus was about over.[133] Army declarations of surplus to WAA ended about March 1948, and an act of Congress approved 29 June 1948 made the termination of declarations permanent. After that the army had to dig up an old law of 1842 for authority to begin direct sales of surplus in addition to small lots, salvage, and scrap.[134] Between September and December 1948 declarations of surplus in the various overseas theaters to OFLC ceased, and the Office of the Foreign Liquidation Commissioner closed on 30 June 1949.[135] Anticipating the termination of the Surplus Property Act by its provision that it was to remain in effect only for three years after the formal cessation of hostilities, Congress early in 1949 replaced that law with a permanent, general statute that did not depend upon the existence of any emergency—the Federal Property and Administrative Services Act of 1949. Effective 1 July 1949, the "functions, property, records and personnel" of the War Assets Administration were transferred to the General Services Administration. Thereafter the administrator of General Services was to have supervision and direction over the disposition of all surplus property in the United States. Important exceptions were that the secretary of agriculture, if he deemed it necessary for the price support program, was to have supervision over the disposition of surplus foods and agricultural commodities, and the U.S. Maritime Commission continued to dispose of ships of over 1,500 tons.[136]

Disposal of surplus property in foreign areas remained in the hands of the owning agencies; that is, the army continued to dispose of its own surplus property abroad. Those disposal operations were, however, to "conform to the foreign policy of the United States." The secretary of state still had the authority to use foreign currencies earned in the sale of surplus property for the financing of scholarships abroad.[137]

Glenn Wolfe, formerly assistant deputy administrator of WAA, told a congressional investigating committee that he believed the Federal Property and Administrative Services Act of 1949 to be a big step in the right direction. A bill similar to it had been introduced in 1944, but instead the Surplus Property Act had been passed with such conflicting priorities and demands as to make an effective disposal job nearly impossible. Wolf said:

> My experience in War Assets taught me one thing. It taught me that if there ever is another situation where we have to dispose of vast quantities of surplus materials, the laws, the rules, the regulations of disposal must be established early, preferably before the end of that conflict. I can't think of anything that was more difficult to do than establish plans and policies for War Assets Administration with conflicting pressures, rules, regulations, from all sources—sell the property, be rid of it as quickly as possible, get

the most money for it, don't worry about how much you can get for it, just get rid of it; another pressure—get all you can for it.

As a veteran, I think I can be critical of that. I took two days from War Assets one time to try to buy surplus property myself, just to see how out plans and policies were working. Frankly it was impossible. I never could do it.[138]

By July 1950 the problem of surplus property was not to dispose of it, but to find out what could be recovered for war purposes. Then those who had been demanding four years earlier that the army quickly put its surplus property on the civilian market without taking the time to check it carefully or to get adequate prices for it would be demanding explanations of why the army now was buying back at a premium property it had sold so cheaply.[139] Of course no one could have foreseen the demand for such property that would suddenly appear in June 1950; yet the international tensions of the cold war were developing early enough to have suggested that it might have been wise, at a time when diplomacy apparently was being based more than ever upon the number of divisions that could be made available to back it up, to have saved that property for the war reserve. To say that future uses for surplus equipment could not be foreseen was like saying that a future use for the army itself could not have been foreseen. And if mobilization should become necessary, the matériel aspects of it would, if anything, be slower and more difficult than any other. It was at least as important to have had a matériel reserve as to have had reserves of trained manpower.

In general the reasons for later purchase of types of items disposed of as surplus in the period between 1945 and 1947 could be summarized in these terms: (1) the difficulties of estimating accurately the army's future requirements; (2) the lack of funds to maintain much of the property, had it been saved, in serviceable condition; (3) the demands and pressures for the quick release of civilian-type items for civilian use; (4) and finally, it actually was more economical in some cases to dispose of and buy later certain items than to store, handle, service, and maintain them.

When the fighting ended, the war industries still were near their peak productions. As long as they continued in operation thereafter they would be adding to the great quantities of surplus that immediately had begun to accumulate. To avoid that unnecessary production, to reduce military expenditures as much as possible, to supply badly needed civilian goods, and to overcome threats of unemployment during the period of readjustment it was necessary to settle war contracts as quickly and as expeditiously as possible, and to get the plants back into civilian production.

Disposal of surplus war property had important relations to matters of military security, foreign policy, and economic policy. Yet advance planning was able to give little weight to the important policy factors involved. Individuals concerns seemed to focus more on avoiding criticism for returning unwanted items to the United States, and for incurring extravagant losses, rather than on supporting foreign and military policies overseas. Nonetheless the sale of this property to foreign governments and to foreign and international agencies undoubtedly made a significant contribution to the relief of local economic distress and military insecurity.

Notes

1. 50 U.S. Code Annotated Sec. 1.
2. Final Report of the Chief of Staff United States Army to the Secretary of the Army, 7 Feb 1948.
3. *First Report of the Secretary of Defense, 1948.*
4. Additional Report of the Special Committee Investigating the National Defense Program (Mead Committee), 22 March 1946, Investigations Overseas—Surplus Property Abroad, Senate Report 110, Pt. 5, 79th Cong., 2nd Sess., 21.
5. *Biennial Rpt. of the Chief of Staff of the United States Army, 1 July 1943 to 30 June 1945, to the Secretary of War.* Hereinafter cited as General Marshall's Report.
6. James V. Forrestal, *The Forrestal Diaries*, edited by Walter Millis with the collaboration of E. S. Duffield, (New York, 1951), 102; James F. Byrnes, *Speaking Frankly*, (New York, 1947), 94–109.
7. General Marshall's Report, 115; "Bringing 'em Back," *Army Transportation Journal* 1 (January 1946) 3.
8. General Marshall's Report, Biennial Report of the Chief of Staff, U.S. Army, 166
9. Additional Report of the Special Committee Investigating the National Defense Program (Meade Committee), 22 March 1946, Investigating Overseas—Surplus Property Abroad, Senate Report 110, Pt. 5, 79th Cong., 1st Sess., 21.
10. Major John C. Sparrow, *History of Personnel Demobilization in the United States Army*, (Washington, D.C. 1951), Office of the Chief of Military History, 369–91.
11. Maj. Gen. J. M. Gavin, Spl Questionnaire, 24 Jan. 51. Quoted in Ibid., 391.
12. Memo, OPD 400 ETO (24 Aug. 45), Lt. Gen. J. E. Hull, Assistant Chief of Staff, Operations Division, for ACofS, G–4, 24 Aug. 45, sub.: Disposal of Supplies in USFET and MTO, G–4 400.703.
13. Rad CM–IN 4010, CG United States Forces, Mediterranean Theater of Operations, to WD, 5 Sept. 45. G–4 400.703; Memo, Col. Joseph F. Prola for ACofS, G–4, 24 Aug. 45, sub.: Disposal of Supplies in USFET and MTO, G—4 400,703 (3), (Minutes of Conference called by Planning Branch, 23 Aug. 45).
14. Capt. James W. Hamilton, "Operation Reverse," *Army Transportation Journal*, Vol. no.? (Sept. 1946), 20–21; Department of State, *The Printed History of Foreign Surplus Disposal*, vol. 3, pt. 1, ch. 6. Quoted in Sparrow, *History of Personnel Demobilization in the United States Army*, (1951), OCMH, 372; Hearings Special Committee Investigating the National Defense Program, U.S. Senate, 79th Cong., 2d Sess., Pt. 36, 19800. Quoted in ibid., 371.
15. Herman Miles Somers, *Presidential Agency; The Office of War Mobilization and Reconversion* (Cambridge, 1951), 176. See Bernard M. Baruch and John M. Hancock, *Report on War and Post-War Adjustment Policy* Senate Document 154, 78th Cong., 2d Sess., February 1944.
16. Somers, *Presidential Agency*, 175.
17. *A Calendar of Documents Pertaining to Disposition of Surplus Property Abroad After World War I*, prepared in Historical Section, Army War Colleqe, by 1st Lt. Harry K. Burmeister, Aug. 44, photostat copy. G–4 400.703 (1); Benedict Crowell

and Robert Forrest Wilson, *Demobilization* (New Haven, 1921), 287–314; Senate Report 110, Pt. 5, 22 Mar. 46, 79th Cong., 2d Sess., 34.

18. War Department Circular 379, 19 Sept. 44, Section 6: Property, par. 5.

19. Additional Report of the Special Committee Investigating the National Defense Program, (Meade Committee), 6 July 45, Investigations Overseas, Senate Report 110, Pt. 2, 79th Cong., 1st sess., 21; WD Memo, 700–45, 9 May 45, sub: Disposal of Property Overseas, par. 2–4; TM 38–420, Sept. 45, 41; WD Memo 700–45, 11 May 45, sub: Responsibility for Overseas Property Disposal, par. 1; TM 38–420, Sept. 45, sub: Disposition of Excess and Surplus Property in Oversea Commands, 9.

20. WD Memo, 850–45, 27 Jan. 45

21. Executive Order 9630, 27 Sept. 45; Dept. of State, OFLC, *Report to Congress on Foreign Surplus Disposal*, July 1949, 5.

22. 50 U.S.C.A. Append Sec. 1641.

23. Memo, Brig. Gen. Donald P. Booth (Exec. to USW), for Gen. Lutes, 16 Sept. 46, carbon, G–4 400.703.

24. Draft Ltr., USW, to FLC, n.d. (about 16 Sept. 46), carbon. G–4 400.703.

25. Ibid.

26. Senate Report 110, Pt. 5, 22 March 1946, 79th Cong., 2d Sess., 16.

27. Ltr, Maj. Gen. Clyde L. Hyssong, FLC, to Maj. Gen. Daniel Noce, Dep. Dir. Log., 1 Dec. 48, G–4 400.703 (11 Jan. 49). G–4 Records Br; Amendment 3 to FLC Req. 8, 1 Oct. 48. (Mimeographed copy in G–4 400.703 (28 Jan. 49).

28. Memo, Col. Joseph F. Prola, for ACofS, G–4, 24 Aug. 45, subject: Disposal of Supplies in USFET and MTO, (Minutes of Conference called by Planning Br., 23 Aug. 45), G–4 400.703 (3).

29. WD Cir. 379, 19 Sept. 44, Sec. 6: Property, par. 5.

30. Memo, Lt. Col. Arno J. Jewett, (no addressee), 28 Aug. 45, sub.: Meeting of Overseas Surplus Disposal Committee, 24 Aug. 45, mimeographed, G–4 400.703 (3); TM 38–420, Sept. 45, 13; TM 38–420, Feb. 46, Cl, 7 Aug. 46; TM 38–420, Cl 7 Aug. 46; For Record Only, Lt. Col. Cross, 7 Oct. 46, sub.: Levels to be Used in Determining excess Military Property, carbon, G–4 400.703.

31. DF, WDGDS 8167, ACofS, G–4, to CG's AAF and ASF, 10 Jan. 46, sub.: Return of Civilian Type Items from Overseas, carbon comeback copy, G–4 400.703 (4).

32. Ibid; Ltr., Brig. Gen. Donald P. Booth, Spl. Asst. to USW, to Sen. James M. Mead, 23 Jan. 1946, carbon comeback copy, G–4 400.703 (4).

33. TM 38–420, Feb. 46 Cl, 7 Aug. 46, 7, 9; Memo, Lt. Col. M. H. Clark, for ACofS, G–4, 6 Dec. 45, sub.: Conference with USW, ms, G–4 400.703 (4); Ltr, TAG to CG's Overseas Cmds., 30 Aug. 46, sub.: Return of Military Property from Overseas, mimeographed, G–4 400.703.

34. Summary Sheet, WD GSP/Dl 400, prepared by SS&P, for US/W, 26 Nov. 46, sub.: Disposal Levels for Military Property in Zone of Interior, Carbon, G–4 400.703 (Disposal Levels in Z/I).

35. Memo, WDGSP/Dl 10723, Ch., Sup. Control Br., SS&P, for Chfs. Tech. Servs., 13 Mar. 47, sub.: Return of Military Property from Overseas, hectograph copy, G–4 400.703.

36. Senate Report 110, Pt. 5, 79th Cong., 1st Sess., p. 22.

37. TM 38–420, Feb. 46, Cl, 7 Aug. 46, 7–9; WD Memo, 700–45, 9 May 45, par. 12–14; TM 38–420, Feb. 46, 39; Memo for Record, on DF WDGDS 2931, G–4 (Jewett to TAG), 13 Sept. 44, sub.: Disposition of Salvage, Excess, and Surplus Property Overseas, G–4 400.703 (1).

38. TM 38–420, Sept. 45, par. 48; and also TM 38–420, Feb. 46, par. 40.

39. Memo, WDSIG 333.1–ASF Depot (classification), TIG for ACofS, G–4, 25

July 45, sub.: Survey of Activities Engaged in Disposition of Material and Salvage Returned from Overseas, mimeographed copy, G–4 400.703 (3).

40. TM 38–420, Feb. 1946, Cl, 7 Aug. 46, 11.

41. Memo, CSCAP, Col. W. H. Heavy, Ch., Program Review and Analysis Div., G–4, for Dept. Counselor, 3 Oct. 50, sub.: Demobilization of Materiel after World War II. Copy. Supply Planning Br., G–4.

42. Rpt., Property Disposition (other than Real Property), prepared by Supply Planning Br., Log. Div., Z/I, Dec 1949, Oversea Cmds., Nov and Dec 1949, p. 4. Photostatic cpy, Supply Planning Br., G—4; *Annual Report of the Secretary of the Army*, (Washington, D.C. 1948), 222–23.

43. Memo, CSCAP, Col. W. H. Heavy, Ch., PR&A Div., G–4, for Dept. Counselor, 3 Oct. 50, sub.: Demobilization of Materiel after W.W. II; Department of State, OFLC, *Report to Congress on Foreign Surplus Disposal*, (Washington, D.C., Jan. 1947), 18; same rpt., July 1947, 10.

44. Department of State, OFLC, *Report to Congress on Foreign Surplus Disposal*, (Washington, D.C., Jan. 1947), 18.

45. (1) Correspondence of Secretary of State, SW, State-War-Navy Coordinating Committee, JCS, CG USFET, ACofS OPD (Aug. - Dec. 1945), filed in OPD 386. 3 (Sec. 3A) Case 78; Memo for Record, n.d., n.s., (About 4 Mar. 46), G–4 400.703 (5); Ltr., SPOPP, Col. John E. Metzler, to CG ASF, 18 Mar. 46, sub: Rpt. of Trip to ETO, carbon, G–4 400.703 (5).

46. Memo WDG SP/O 435, Brig. Gen. T. M. Osborne, Ch., Sup. Grp., SS&P, 20 Sept. 46, sub.: Unresolved Surplus Property Problems, carbon, CofS, 400.703.

47. Memo, WDG SP/B4, Ch., Plans and Policy Office, for Director, SS&P, 9 Sept. 46, sub.: French Rearmament Program, carbon, G–4 400.703.

48. *Surplus Property*, Occupation Forces in Europe Series, 1945–46, Office of Chief Historian, EUCOM, OCMH 804.29, 29; Senate Report 110, Pt. 5, 79th Cong., 1st sess., 23–30.

49. Informal Memo, U.S., for Gen. Lutes, 11 June 46, G–4 400.703; TWX 7256, USFET, from Magruder to AGWAR, for Lutes, 28 Oct. 46, sub.: Property Situation in Belgium, G–4 400.703; Interview, Carrol Meigs, Lend-Lease and Surplus Property Office, Department of State, 20 May 52; Ltr., Chester M. Carre, Monetary Consultant, OFLC, to Lt. Col. Charles I. Davis, Overseas sub-unit, SS&P, 3 Apr. 47, ms, G–4 400.703.

50. Department of State, OFLC, *Report to Congress on Foreign Surplus Disposal*, Oct. 1947, 13–15.

51. Memo, CSCAP, Col. W. H. Heavy, for Department Counselor, 3 Oct. 50, sub.: Demobilization of Matériel after World War II, copy in Supp. Planning Br., G–4.

52. Department of State, OFLC, Reports to Congress, Apr. 1947, 15; Oct. 1947, 16–17; July 1947, 13–14; Disposal of Surplus Property, 1 July 1946–30 June 1947, Occupation Forces in Europe Series, Hist. Div., EUCOM, Typescript, OCMH 8–3.1 CB8 Cl), 78.

53. Statement of Glenn Wolfe, Director of Administration, Office of High Commissioner for Germany, Hearings before a subcommittee of the Committee on Expenditures in the Executive Departments, H.R., 82d Cong., 1st sess. (Bonner Subcommittee), Pt. 1, March, April, July, August 1951, 466–67. See also Exhibit 59, Ltr. to Glenn G. Wolfe, 16 June 51, sub.: History and Developments of STEG, 467, 568–69.

54. Memo for Record, n.d., (around 30 Aug. 46), G–4 400.704; Memo, Brig. Gen. T. M. Osborne, Ch., Sup. Grp., for Asst. Secy. of War, 3 Oct. 46, sub.: Surplus Disposals in Germany.

55. Memo, Brig. Gen. T. M. Osborne, Ch., Sup. Grp., for Asst. Secy. of War, 3 Oct. 46, sub.: Surplus Disposals in Germany.
56. *Disposal of Surplus Property, 1 July 1946–30 June 1947*, Occupation Forces in Europe series, Hist. Div., EUCOM, 64.
57. Ibid.
58. Ibid.
59. *Annual Report of the Secretary of the Army*, 1948, 223.
60. Department of State, OFLC, *Report to Congress on Foreign Surplus Disposal*, Jan. 1947, p. 17.
61. Department of State, OFLC, *Report to Congress on Foreign Surplus Disposal*, Jan. 1948, 13–16; Apr. 1948, 11–12; Oct. 1948, 12; Apr. 1949, 11; Agreement (Contract) between U.S. and Bizonal Economic Council, Bulk Sale, 23 Jan. 48, reprinted, 582–84; Memorandum of Understanding, printed, 594–86; SOP 108, EUCOM, 5 Mar. 48, printed, 574–82; Hearings before Bonner Subcommittee, Pt. 1, 569–70.
62. Department of State, OFLC, *Report to Congress on Foreign Surplus Disposal*, Jan. 1948, 16; *Annual Report of the Secretary of the Army*, 1948, 223; Department of State, OFLC, Apr. 1949, 11.
63. (1) Msg, WAR 80924, Log. Div. (C. G. Jones) to Hq EUCOM, 1 May 48, sub.: Proposed Transfer of Excess Supplies and Equipment to the German Economy, (CM–OUT 80924); Msg, WARX 81611, Dir. Log. Div. (Jones) to CINCEUR, 11 May 48, sub.: Transfer of Supplies and Equipment to German Economy, (CM–OUT 81611).
64. Interview, Col. C. O. Frake, Chief Disposals Sec., G–4 19 May 52.
65. Interview, Carrol Meigs, Lend-Lease and Surplus Property Office, Department of State, 20 May 52.
66. Ltr, The President to Secretary of War, 17 Aug. 45. G–4 400.703 (3).
67. Memo, Lt. Col. Arno J. Jewett, no addressee, 28 Aug. 45, sub.: Meeting of Overseas Disposal Committee 24 Aug. 45, mimeographed, G–4 400.703 (3).
68. (1) George Woodbridge and staff, *UNRRA, The History of the United Nations Relief and Rehabilitation Administration*, 3 vols. (New York: 1950), 1: 389–92; Ltr, Robert P. Patterson, Actg. S/W to the President, 24 Aug. 45, copy., G–4 400.703; Memo, Lt. Col. W. B. Bennett, for ACofS, G–4, 28 Aug. 45, sub.: Meeting UNRRA Requirements out of Surplus Army Supplies, G–4 400.703 (3); Memo, Lt. Col. Arno J. Jewett, no addressee, 28 Aug. 45, sub.: Meeting of Overseas Disposal Committee, 24 Aug. 45, mimeographed, G–4 400.703. (3); Memo for Record, n.d. (approx. 6 Aug. 46), G–4 400.703; Dan Regan, "UNRRA: World Shipper." *Army Transportation Journal*, 2 (Aug 1946): 3.
69. Catlett, "Quartermaster Scrap Disposal in the European Command," *The Quartermaster Review*, 21, 94–96.
70. Msg, CM–OUT 82824, William H. Draper, US/A, to CINCEUR, 28 May 48.
71. Department of State, OFLC, Report to Congress, July 49, 11.
72. *Annual Report of the Secretary of the Army*, 1948, 68; Testimony of Brig. Gen. Morrill W. Marston, G–4 Army Forces Middle Pacific, 1 Jan. 46, Hearings before the Mead Committee, Pt. 36, 19655; Brig. Gen. Gerson K. Heiss, "Operation Roll-Up," *Ordnance* 36 (Sept.–Oct. 1951): 242; Col. E. B. Kearns, Jr., "QMC in the Far East," *The Quartermaster Review* 28 (May–June 1949): 10; TM 38–420, Feb. 1946, Cl 7 Aug. 46, 12.
73. Paraphrase of Rad. of AFWESPAC, sgd Christianson, 22 July 46, in WD Msg WDGSP/D OUT 93707, to CG's AFMIDPAC, 13 Aug. 46, sub.: Disposal of Surplus Property to China. G1–4 400.703; MRS, Brig. Gen. S. L. Scott, Ch. Plans and Policy Office, to Lt. Gen. Lutes, 24 July 46, sub.: Disposal of Surplus Property in Philippines to Chinese; Memo, SS&P 4628, Brig. Gen. T. M. Osborne, Ch. Sup. Grp., for US/W,

7 Oct. 46, sub.: Dollar-Wise Comparison of Values Between Mil Prop Listed 28 June 46 and that listed 30 Aug. 46. (Carbon) G–4 400.703.

74. Ltr. Col. H. E. Eastwood, G–4, USARPAC, to Lt. Gen. LeR. Lutes, 11 July 46, ms, G–4 400.703.

75. Ltr, Ch. Sup. Grp., SS&P, to Ben. G. Crosby, Spl. Asst. to FLC, 21 Apr. 47, (Carbon) G–4 400.703.

76. Ltr, Thomas B. McCabe, FLC, to Robt. P. Patterson, 29 May 46, ms, G–4 400.703.

77. Ltr, WDGSP/D5, 400.703, US/W, to Foreign Liquidation Comm., 24 June 46, (Carbon) G–4 400.703.

78. Interview, Carrol Meigs, Lend-Lease and Surplus Property Office, Department of State, 20 May 52; OFLC, *Report to Congress on Foreign Surplus Disposal*, Apr. 1947, 23; July 1949, 19.

79. OFLC, *Report to Congress on Foreign Surplus Disposal*, July 1949, 19.

80. Memo, n.s., n.d. copy., CG AAF, for US/W (approx. 18 Dec. 45), sub: Report of Investigation, Alleged Destruction of AAF Property at Karachi, G–4 400.703 (4).

81. Ltr, Chester M. Carre, Monetary Consultant, OFLC, to Lt. Col. Charles I. Davis, SS&P, 3 Apr. 47, ms, G–4 400.703; OFLC, *Report to Congress on Foreign Surplus Disposal*, Jan. 1947, 25–26.

82. Ltr, OAGG 400.703, Ch. Army Advisory Grp., to Dir. SS&P, 2 Jan. 47, sub.: Property Disposal in Overseas Commands, ms, G–4 400.703.

83. Ltr, Lt. Gen. W. D. Styer, CG USARWESPAC, to Kenneth C. Royall, US/W, 10 Apr. 46, copy, G–4 400.703. (5); Memo, n.s., n.d. (approx. 17 July 46), sub.: Comparison of Plans for Bulk Sale to China, G–4 400.703; Ltr, Thomas B. McCabe, FLC, to Kenneth C. Royall, 19 July 46, carbon, G–4 400.703; Draft Ltr, US/W to FLC, n.d. (approx. 19 July 46), G–4 400.703; WD Msg. OUT 96359, Lt. Gen. W. D. Styer, to CG USAFWESPAC, for Christiansen, 2 Aug. 46, carbon, G–4 400.703; WD Msg., WDGSP/D OUT 93707, to CG's AFMIDPAC, Eighth Army, China Serv. Comd. (pass to Howard Petersen) for info to CinC AFPAC, 13 Aug. 46, sub.: Disposal of Surplus Property to China, G–4 400.703.

84. Draft Cable, OFLC, to CG AFWESPAC, Manila, for FLC Vogelback, Action CG China Service Comd. for info. Office of Gen. Marshall, Nanking, 17 July 47, sub.: Bulk Sale to China, carbon, G–4 400.703.

85. Memo, n.s., n.d. (approximately 19 July 46); G–4 400.703.

86. OFLC, *Report to Congress on Foreign Surplus Disposal*, July 1949, 19.

87. Msg., CM–OUT 80314, SS&P (Col. Isbell) to CINCAFPAC, 13 Sept. 46, sub.: Administrative Aid to China in Taking Over Surplus Property from U.S.

88. Msg., CM–OUT 80441, SS&P, to CINCAFPAC, 16 Sept. 46.

89. Summary Sheet, WDGSP/D3 1533, Spl. Asst. to US/W to US/W, 17 Sept. 46, sub.: Return of Military Property from Overseas Commands, carbon, G–4 400.703.

90. FLC Regulation 8, 30 Oct. 46, Sec. 8508.15

91. OFLC, *Report to Congress on Foreign Surplus Disposal*, Apr. 1947, 22; Ibid., Jan. 1948, 25–26; Apr. 1948, 23–24.

92. OFLC, *Report to Congress on Foreign Surplus Disposal*, July 1949, 16.

93. P. L. 370, 70th Cong., Title 2, Sec. 201–206.

94. Memo, CSCAP, Col. W. H. Heavy, for Dept. Counselor, 3 Oct. 50, sub.: Demobilization of Materiel after WW II, copy. Supply Planning Br., G–4.

95. OFLC, *Report to Congress on Foreign Surplus Disposal*, Apr. 1948, 27.

96. OFLC, *Report to Congress on Foreign Surplus Disposal*, Oct. 1947, 24.

97. OFLC, *Report to Congress on Foreign Surplus Disposal*, Apr. 1948, 24–25; Oct. 1947, 19–20; Apr. 1949, 17.

In the Wake of World War II   51

98. Hearings before the Bonner Subcommittee, Disposition of Surplus Property, Mar. 15, 1951, 70.

99. Memo WDGDS 10103, Chas. M. Ankcorn, Proj. Br., Sup. Div., G–4 for ACofS, G–4, 6 Mar. 46, sub.: Formal Concurrence, ms. G–4 400.703 (5); Ltr., Kenneth C. Royall, US/W, to John W. Snyder, Dir., WMR, 17 June 46, carbon, G–4 400.703; Rad. WARX 90211, SS&P, to CinCFE, 21 Jan. 47, copy, G–4 400.703 (9); Memo for Record, Col. Davis, n.d. (approx 17 Jan. 46), carbon, G–4 400.703; Memo for Record, n.d. (approx 30 Aug. 46), carbon, G–4 400.703; OFLC, *Report to Congress on Foreign Surplus Disposal*, Apr. 1947, 23; Apr. 1948, 24; Hist. of Office of For. Liquidation Comm. Field Commissioner for Japan and Korea, Tokyo, prep. by Lt. Col. A. K. Akin, Field Commissioner for Japan and Korea, processed copy. OCMH, 9–13.

100. OFLC, *Rpt. to cong. on For. Surpl. Disposal*, Apr. 1947, 23; Oct. 1948, 21; Memo, Exec. US/W, for Dir. SS&P, 28 Feb. 47, sub.: Disposal of Surpl. in Hawaii, carbon, G–4 400.703; Hist. of Office of For. Liquidation Comm. Fld. Comm. for Japan and Korea, 8–9, 14–16.

101. Woodbridge and staff, *UNRRA, The History of the United Nations Relief and Rehabilitation Administration*, (New York, 1950) 1: 394.

102. OFLC, *Report to Congress on Foreign Surplus Disposal*, July 1949, 15.

103. DF ORD 452.1 (20 July 45), ACofS OPD, to ACofS, G–4, 20 July 45, sub.: Disposition of Surplus in Latin America, G–4 400.703 (3); ACC No. 17, Latin American Subcommittee, 1 May 45, Disposal of Surplus Aircraft, Latin American Subcommittee Recommendations as to Policy, mimeographed. G–4 400.703 (3); Ltr., Lt. Col. Wm. Barclay Harding, Dir. Avn. Div., to Avra M. Warren (State Dept.) mimeographed copy, 10 Apr. 1945, G–4 400.703 (3); Ltr., W. L. Clayton, Adm. SWPA, to S/W, mimeographed copy, G–4 400.703 (3); Aide Memoire, n.d., sub.: Surplus Aircraft, mimeographed copy, G–4 400.703 (3); Memo, Ch. Avn. Div., Dept. of State, for Interdepartmental Working Committee on Surplus Aircraft Disposal, mimeographed copy, G–4 400.703 (3); ACC 17/1, presented by Dept. of State, 28 June 45, mimeographed copy, G–4 400.703; Rad. WAR 70850, WARGFOUD Sqn. WARCOS to Military Attaché, Rio de Janeiro, 20 Sept 45, G–4 400.703; DF OPD 336.2, Brazil (20 June 45), OPD to G–4, for Info. to CG ASF for action, 27 July 45, sub.: Nonaddenda and Nonauthorized Items, G–4 400.703 (3).

104. Draft Memo, SDFCMP 400.3295, Field Commissioner for Mil. Programs for the For. Liq. Commissioner, 11 June 46, sub.: Dept. of State Memo of 23 May 46, Pricing Policy, Copy, included in Exhibit F, Hist. Rpt., Office, Field Commissioner for Mil. Prog., June 1946, mimeographed, G–4 400.703; Memo for Record SDFCMP, Maj. Gen. Ralph H. Wooten (Field Comm. for Mil. Programs), 24 June 46, sub.: Pricing Policy, Copy, included in Exhibit F, Hist. Rpt. Office of Field Comm. for Mil. Programs, mimeographed, G–4 400.703; Memo, Thomas B. Cabe (FLC), for Dean Acheson (U/S State), 14 May 46, n.s., incl. in Exhibit F, Hist. Rpt., Office of Field Comm. for Mil. Programs, June 1946, mimeographed, G–4 400.703.

105. Memo, Lt. Col. M. H. Clark, for ACofS, G–4, 6 Dec. 45, sub.: Conf with US/W, ms, G–4 400.703 (4).

106. Ltr., 400.703, CG Antilles Dept., to Dir. SS&P, through CG Carib. Def. Cmd., 25 July 46, sub.: Surplus Property Disposal, ms, G–4 400.703; Ltr., SPDDS 400.703 Serial No. 6499, CG ASF to CG, Antilles Dept., through CG Carib., Def. Cmd., 3 May 46, sub.: Surplus Property Disposal, copy, G–4 400.703; Ltr., F. W. Haeussler (H. V. Grosch Co., San Juan, P. R.) to U.S. Army Chem. Warfare Div., 1 Apr. 46, copy in G–4 400.703.

107. 160 U.S. Vs. Jones, 176 F 2d 278.

108. *New York Times*, (city ed.) 6 March 1952.

109. Memo, Lt. Col. M. H. Clark, Proj. Br. for ACofS, G–4, 27 Feb. 46, sub.: Meade Committee Trip, MS, G–4 400.703 (5).
110. Memo for Record, Lt. Col. C. A. Cozart, 24 Oct. 46, G–4 400.703; Memo, Exec US/W, for Gen. Parks, Dir. of Publ. Rel., 28 Oct. 46, sub.: Navy Surplus Disposal, G–4 400.703.
111. Memo for Record, Maj. Leffingwell, 13 Aug. 46, sub.: Cut-off Dates for Determination and Declaration of Surplus, G–4 400.703.
112. DF, W. M. Hines, Jr., to Dep. Ch., PRD, 1 Nov. 46, sub.: Program of Releases on Surplus Property Disposal, carbon, CofS 400.703.
113. Memo, P&O TS (22 Aug 46), Dir. Plans and Operations, for Dir. SS&P, 22 Aug. 46, sub.: Civilian Type Items, G– 400.703 (Disposals Levels in Z/I, MS).
114. Memo, WDGSP/D1 6182, Dir., SS&P, for CG AAF and Chiefs Tech. Servs., 21 Oct. 46, sub.: Disposal Levels in Z/I, G–4 400.703 (Disposal Levels in Z/I, hectographed).
115. ASF Manual M419, 1 Aug. 45, sub.: Disposition of Excess and Surplus Army Service Forces Military Property in Continental United States, Foreword.
116. Memo, WDGSP/E1, Brig. Gen. Orval R. Cook, Ch. Procurement Grp., for CG AAF (Attn. Col. W. D. Eckert, Ch. Readjustment Div.), 16 Aug. 46, sub.: Repurchase by AAF of Former Govt. Surplus Property, G–4 400.703.
117. Memo, WDGSP/E4, Brig. Gen. John K. Christmas, for Brig. Gen. O. R. Cook, 8 Aug. 46, sub.: Repurchase by AAF of Former Govt. Surplus Property, carbon, G–4 400.703.
118. Lt. Col. W. C. Strum, "Disposition of Surplus Property," *The Quartermaster Review* 26 (May–June 1947): 36; TM 38–419, July 1946 (supersedes M419).
119. TM 38–419, July 1946, par. 23–24; TM 38–419, Mar 1947, par. 25–26; WD Cir. 34, 5 Feb. 46, par. 19–20.
120. Notes, H S A, 30 Dec. 45, sub.: Surplus Property, CofS 400.703. See also, Memo, WDCSA 400.703 (3 Jan. 46), Hodes for ACofS, G–4, 3 Jan. 46, MS, forwarding copies of notes received by CofS, 30 Dec. 45.
121. Ltr., Nat'l. Committee for State Educational Agencies for Surplus Property, to Arthur L. Harris, Ch. Surp. Prop. Utilization Prgm., U.S. Office of Education, 19 Nov. 48, copy incl. with ltr., Arthur L. Harris, to Ch., Distr. Br., Logistics Div., 6 Dec. 48, G–4 400.703 (6 Dec. 48), G–14 Records Br.
122. Memo for Record, Maj. Leffingwell, 22 Aug. 46, sub.: Furniture and Equipment for a Community Center from Surplus, carbon, G–4 400.703; Misc. Ltrs. and Memos in G–4 400.703 (4) and (5).
123. Misc. ltrs. in OCS 400.703 (1946).
124. Ltr., Col. J. W. Bowen, Sec./Gen. Staff, to Clara Greenleaf Perry, Boston, 19 Feb. 46; A special committee of the House reported:

> Records show that only about 1 out of every 25 complaints submitted, with alleged facts, turns out to be anything other than a misunderstanding of circumstances or regulations regarding disposal. About 2,100 such investigations were started during the third quarter of this year. Those with criminal implications were referred to the Department of Justice for prosecution. By the end of September, 38 arrests had been made and 26 indictments secured.

(*Final Report, House Special Committee on Postwar Economic Policy and Planning*, 12 Dec. 1946, House Report 2729, 79th Cong., 2d sess., 40.)

125. RS WDGDS 9834, In G–4, 23 Feb. 46, G–4 400.703.
126. *G–4 Review of the Month*, 30 Apr. 47, 19.
127. Memo, WDGSP/D 435, Brig. Gen. T. M. Osborne, Ch. Sup. Grp., SSP, 20 Sept. 46, sub.: Unresolved Surplus Property Problems, carbon, G–4 400.703.

128. *G–4 Review of the Month*, 31 May 1947, 24.

129. Ibid., 7.

130. DF, W. M. Hines, Jr, to Deputy, Ch. PRD, 1 Nov. 46, sub.: Program of Releases on Surplus Property Disposal, carbon, CofS 400.703; WD Memo, 5–45, 27 Aug. 45, Excess Industrial Facilities.

131. Logistical Operations Summary, 1 June 50, 2; *G–4 Review of the Month*, Apr. 1948, 1, 8, 32; Annual Report of the Secretary of the Army, 1948; Memo, 602 (Gen) ENGLH, V. W. Saari, Ch., Realty Rqmts. Div. OCofEngrs, for Dir. SS&P, 21 Jan. 47, sub.: Monthly Report on Declarations to War Assets, ms, G–4 400.703 (9); *G–4 Review of the Month*, 1 Feb. 50, 3.

132. *G–4 Review of the Month*, 30 Apr. 47, 23.

133. *G–4 Review of the Month*, Dec. 1947, 30.

134. Interview, Col. C. O. Frake, Ch., Disposals Sec., G–4, 19 May 52; See also *Annual Report of the Secretary of the Army*, 1948, 101.

135. Interview, Col. Frake, 19 May 52; Interview, Carrol Meigs, Lend-Lease and Surplus Property, Dept. of State, 20 May 52.

136. Federal Property and Administrative Services Act of 1949, P L 152, 81st Cong., 1st Sess., Sec. 105, 203 (Effective July 1, 1949).

137. Ibid., Sec. 401.

138. Hearings before a subcommittee of the Committee on Expenditures in the Exec. Depts., H. R. (Bonner Committee), Mar., Apr., July, Aug. 1951, Disposition of War Surplus Property, 82d Cong., 1st Sess.

139. Hearings before the Bonner Subcommittee, Disposition of Surplus Property, 63; Memorandum for Asst. CofS, G–4, Report of Major Actions, G4/B1 4060 SF, 27 July 50, 2. (Hereinafter this report will be cited as G–4, Report of Major Actions.)

2
Cutting Off the Tap–Termination of Lend Lease

> Now, what I am trying to do is to eliminate the dollar sign . . . get rid of the silly, foolish old dollar sign. . . . Suppose my neighbor's home catches fire, and I have a length of garden hose. . . . Now, what do I do? I don't say to him, "Neighbor, my garden hose cost me $15; you have to pay me $15 for it." What is the transaction that goes on? I don't want $15—I want my garden hose back after the fire is over.
> —Franklin D. Roosevelt,
> Press Conference,
> 17 December 1940

The liquidation of Lend-Lease operations presented problems hardly less complex than the other major aspects of matériel demobilization. By 1945 lend-lease goods and services of all kinds being furnished to allies of the United States had reached an annual rate of $15 billion. Total lend-lease aid furnished from 11 March 1941 to 31 December 1946 amounted to more than $49 billion. This included aircraft and parts ($8.2 billion), tanks and other combat vehicles and parts ($3.9 billion), trucks and other vehicles and parts ($2.5 billion), weapons ($3 billion), ammunition ($1.5 billion), military clothing, signal equipment, chemical warfare equipment and other military equipment and supplies as well as ships, industrial equipment, raw materials, food, and various other goods and services.[1] Conceived as an instrument for providing effective matériel assistance in a common war effort without provoking the irritating consequences incident to equating a war measure to a commercial loan, such as troubled international relations after World War I, lend-lease aid went without any assumption of full repayment. The understanding was that the recipient governments would, at the end of the war emergency, return only such articles as had not been destroyed, lost, or consumed, and which the president should determine "to be useful in the defense of the United States of America or of the Western Hemisphere or to be otherwise of use to the United States of America."[2]

The original Lend-Lease Act provided that, unless sooner terminated by a concurrent resolution of Congress, the authority to enter into lend-lease arrangements would end on 30 June 1943, and the authority to carry out contracts or agreements made with foreign governments before that date would continue until 1 July 1946.[3] Congress then made one-year extensions of the act three times, so that the final date set for making lend-lease commitments was 30 June 1946, with authority to carry them out until 1 July 1949. In commenting on the third extension of the act in April 1945, President Truman promised that lend-lease aid would be carried on "until the unconditional surrender or complete defeat of Germany and Japan."[4] This seemed to be reassuring news to the allied nations depending upon that aid, for the assumption was that the war against Japan was likely to continue for eighteen months after the surrender of Germany. On the contrary, it should have been taken as a warning against the time when lend-lease would cease.

Cutbacks in lend-lease aid followed quickly after V–E Day, and doubts began to arise in many countries about what the policy was going to be. But the secretary of state announced, "Lend-Lease *has been* and *will be* supplied to our allies—be it the Soviet Union, the United Kingdom, France, the Netherlands or other countries—on the scale which is necessary to achieve final victory as speedily and effectively as possible and with the least cost in lives."[5] On 4 June President Truman asked Congress for an appropriation of $1,975,000,000, which, added to unused balances of the current year of $2,400,000,000, would provide a lend-lease program of $4,375,000,000 for the year beginning 1 July 1945.[6] But in a directive to the Joint Chiefs of Staff a month later the president made it clear that approval of the transfer of lend-lease military equipment would be limited to what could be used in the war against Japan, and it would not be issued for any other purposes.

As the end of hostilities appeared to be approaching, the early termination of lend-lease had been hinted at, but apparently the first positive statement to that effect occurred in the letters of 20 August 1945 that Leo Crowley, director of the Foreign Economic Administration, sent to the heads of all foreign purchasing commissions in Washington.[7] In ordering an abrupt end of all further lend-lease operations, President Truman directed that all outstanding contracts be cancelled, "except where Allied Governments agree to take them over, where it is in the interest of the United States to complete them."[8] Administration spokesmen hastened to explain that this did not mean the immediate cutting off of supplies; the only difference would be that after V–J Day recipient governments would have to pay cash or obtain credit for the goods and services they had been receiving. Furthermore, the allies were to be given an opportunity to buy the goods in the lend-lease "pipeline"—that which they had ordered and was in the process of manufacture—on the basis of an undertaking to pay for the goods in thirty annual installments with interest at 2 2/3 percent.[9] This was little comfort to governments, such as the British in particular, who were caught in the midst of a redeployment of forces to the Far East and who had been operating on the assumption that lend-lease would continue for another year and a half.

On the same day that the allied note had gone to the Japanese stating the conditions for their unconditional surrender (11 August), the Joint Chiefs of Staff had prepared a draft memorandum from the president to themselves for President Truman's signature to the effect that lend-lease aid should stop immediately after the surrender of Japan. In the event that the surrender should be announced before the president had had a chance to act upon the directive, the Joint Chiefs proposed to apply the policies outlined therein on an interim basis. The president approved the memorandum on 5 September, but it actually was effective as of 2 September, V–J Day. It stated that upon the surrender of Japan, the lend-lease procured and sponsored by the War and Navy Departments would stop except for aid to Chinese forces engaged in taking the surrender of the Japanese troops remaining in China. The only other exceptions would be "in certain unavoidable cases where the abrupt cessation of aid would cause undue hardships." But this aid was not to include arms or ammunition, and it was to stop as soon as other arrangements could be made. "In no case" was it to "extend beyond six months from the effective date" of the memorandum.[10]

Protests against such an abrupt cancellation of lend-lease were soon reaching Washington, but President Truman held firm to his announced policy. In a special message to Congress on 6 September the president reiterated that policy, but, referring to the consideration of the settlement of lend-lease accounts, he recognized that the allies could not be expected to pay dollars "for the overwhelming portion of lend-lease obligations."[11] Administration spokesmen expressed surprise that foreign governments had been surprised by the termination of lend-lease as of V–J Day. In November 1944 President Roosevelt had stated in a letter to Congress that lend-lease would end when the war ended; Leo Crowley had stated this in February 1945.[12] But while statements were being recalled to the effect that lend-lease was to end when the war ended, President Truman was urging Congress "not to end the war status hastily," and to continue selective service.[13] When the war was considered to have ended, of course, depended upon the purpose in question.

On the other hand, Congress had made its intention clear that lend-lease was to be used only for the prosecution of the war and not for postwar activities. When President Roosevelt returned to Washington from the Quebec Conference in September 1944, he was anxious to find a way to provide further assistance to Britain after the cessation of hostilities. It appeared briefly that he intended to use lend-lease for this purpose. Although a strong supporter of the lend-lease policy, and no less anxious to provide postwar reconstruction assistance, Secretary of War Henry L. Stimson thought that this would be a most unwise course. He thought that this, even if it were found to be technically legal, would be contrary to the intentions of Congress and would likely result in less cooperation from them for future appropriations. The secretary of war later concluded that it would have been much better, while the war was still on, to close out the lend-lease account, writing off much of the huge balances due the United States, and then to develop another program, on a similar basis, for postwar assistance.[14] In its third extension of the Lend-Lease Act, approved 16 April 1945, Congress inserted the proviso, "That nothing in section 3 (c) (granting authority until 1 July 1949 to carry out an agreement with a foreign government made before 1 July 1946) shall be construed to authorize the President to enter into or carry out any contract or agreement with a foreign government for post-war relief, post-war rehabilitation or post-war reconstruction."[15]

Apparently any assistance for the post-hostilities period was going to be strictly on a cash or loan basis. Secretary Stimson thought this policy also to be an unwise one. He could see no practical distinction between money used to fight war and that used to recover from its destruction, and he thought the attempt to make such a sharp distinction was "dangerous nonsense." The "war debts" repudiated amidst such ill feeling in the 1930s had been debts arising largely from postwar reconstruction after 1918.[16]

The "hardship cases" referred to in the presidential directive of the Joint Chiefs of Staff covered situations in which direct hardship would result to persons concerned by the immediate withdrawal of lend-lease aid, but it was not intended to cover those broader situations of economic distress resulting from a shortage of dollars.[17] This special aid could include rations, medical supplies and services, petroleum products, fuel, and transportation services where the foreign government concerned could not reasonably furnish them and where denial would work immediate hardship on allied or American forces who were dependent upon continued support by allied commands. Considered a liquidation measure, this type of aid was to be reduced and finally ended at the earliest possible date—and no later than six months after V–J Day. This meant that the army would have to wind up most of its lend-lease activities by 2 March 1946. Maintenance, repair, training, transportation and other services already begun could continue until the nearest practicable stopping point as determined by overseas theater commanders, and the secretary of war would determine the actual stopping date for all other lend-lease projects sponsored by the War Department.[18]

The abruptness of the lend-lease termination extended to the stopping of many shipments in transit to the ports. The International Division of Army Service Forces instructed the chief of transportation to stop the shipments and to return the supplies to the technical services for assimilation into U.S. army stocks.[19]

When it came to the consideration of the settlement of lend-lease accounts, the secretary of war indicated to the foreign economic administrator that the interest of the War Department in the matter was limited to the physical return of those lend-lease items that were needed for the army's own supply requirements; to be returned or destroyed for reasons of technical security; or needed for reasons of "strategic security"[20]—presumably to keep them from being used to build up potential enemies. Later surveys by the Intelligence Division of Army Service Forces, and by Army Air Forces, indicated that the recovery of lend-lease articles in the interests of technical security or national security would not be warranted.[21] Although the United States in the lend-lease master agreements with the various allied governments reserved the right of recapture of items not "destroyed, lost, or consumed," the American policy generally was not to exercise that right. Recipient governments paid only for nonmilitary lend-lease items that had value for peacetime purposes. Lend-lease military equipment generally was included in the agreements covering disposal of surplus property.[22]

After the technical services had completed supply control studies, the War Department concluded that it should not request "non-voluntary" recapture of lend-lease material. The only occasion for diverting from this policy would be in cases where a recipient government wanted to transfer lend-lease equipment to a third government. A War Department Committee on Recapture and Retransfer of Lend-Lease Equipment acted on such requests, on the basis of the need of the U.S. army for the items in question, and made its recommendation to the State Department.[23]

Whenever allied governments offered to return lend-lease equipment on their own initiative, the policy of the War Department was to accept only those serviceable items that were needed for military operations, requested for return to the United States by the Foreign Liquidation Commissioner, or needed by the navy. The War Department had advised allied governments in July 1945 that lend-lease articles in overseas theaters that were no longer needed for war purposes should be offered for return to theater commanders. Then commanders would accept, on behalf of the United States, lists—but not physical transfer—of all articles offered. After withdrawing from the lists articles needed for his own mission or by the navy or listed for return to the United States, the commander would declare the remainder surplus to the local field commissioner of the Office of the Liquidation Commissioner. The intention of the War Department was to avoid adding to the burdens of theater commanders and staffs by asking them to accept custody of unwanted lend-lease materiel that might be returned by foreign governments.[24]

Lend-lease settlements also involved, of course, the disposal of reverse lend-lease or reciprocal aid property that foreign governments had provided for the United States. Title to that property was assumed to remain with the supplying government and it was not to be disposed of without first obtaining the consent and the instructions of the supplying government. Overseas commanders had the authority to determine that any reverse lend-lease property in their commands would be surplus and to return it without any further approval to the supplying government. This included real estate and fixed installations, with the exception of airfields having an investment value of over $100,000 and radio facilities of the Army Command and Administrative Network. These were to be reported to the chief of engineers before disposal.[25] All reciprocal aid property in the United Kingdom, where the United States received nearly $5 billion worth of the total of $7.8 billion in reverse lend-lease goods and services worldwide, was returned to the British government by 1 February 1946.[26]

The sharpest reaction against the abrupt termination of lend-lease came from Britain. Prime Minister Clement Attlee said that this action had placed Britain "in a very serious financial position," and Winston Churchill called it "very grave and disquieting news."[27] They had believed that some new program would be forthcoming when lend-lease stopped. It still was expensive to bring troops home from worldwide deployments, and, from their point of view the costs of demobilization and reconversion were as much a part of the costs of war as was the actual fighting of it. A tentative agreement reached in the autumn of 1944 on the use of lend-lease during the expected eighteen months of war against Japan that would follow the defeat of Germany had given the British some hope that aid would be available during the period of reconversion to peacetime production. But after V–E Day difficulties were being anticipated.[28] Fleet Admiral William D. Leahy had reported that the British objective of obtaining lend-lease supplies for rehabilitation and reconstruction "produced the biggest controversy of the Potsdam military missions."[29]

The British argued that the sharing of the economic burdens of the war that lend-lease had accomplished should be continued to include the liquidation of the war effort, but leaders of the United States government considered this to be politically impracticable in light of the sentiments expressed in Congress.[30] Instead of developing a long-range, integrated program, domestic political considerations and the failure to recognize either the vastness or the integrity of the international economic problems led the United States to a policy of living from crisis to crisis. This led first to the extension of credit for the purchase of lend-lease pipeline materials, then to the granting of the large British loan, and eventually to a return to something of the lend-lease idea in the military aid to Greece and Turkey, then to the European Recovery Program, and finally to the Mutual Defense Assistance Program and the Mutual Security Program.

In October 1945 a delegation of high British officials headed by Lord John Maynard Keynes and Lord Halifax met with United States officials in Washington to negotiate for the dollar loan and for the settlement of lend-lease and surplus property accounts. Before going into the details of the loan, the American negotiators asked for a complete inventory of all lend-lease material held by the British forces at the time of the termination of lend-lease. This led to the complicated question of whether the British government should assume the responsibility for all lend-lease material in the Commonwealth countries and whether goods actually in the hands of troops should be counted. While the British held that it would not be practicable for them to account for equipment in the hands of Indian and Commonwealth forces, the American answer was that no accurate inventory could be made unless the British assumed administrative responsibility for it, because the items had been programmed and assigned to the United Kingdom in bulk, and the British then in many cases had allocated the goods to Commonwealth and Indian forces. The British view prevailed on this point, however, and the United States entered into separate settlement agreements with the governments of India, South Africa, Australia, and New Zealand. Even then it was not easy to distinguish between the items sent to India, for example, which were for the direct use of British forces and those that actually were transferred to the Indian government. Further compromise was necessary on the question of the physical inventory of lend-lease goods. The agreement was that all goods up to a certain point in the British supply system should be counted, and all beyond that point should be estimated.[31]

After allowing for offsetting arrangements by which reverse lend-lease accounts reduced the total amount due to the United States, the British agreed to pay an estimated $650,000,000 to cover that difference and the cost of surplus property being accepted in the bulk transfer. The United States granted credit to cover this sum, which was to be repaid in fifty annual installments beginning 31 December 1951 with interest at 2 percent. Final accounting reduced the amount due the United States for pipeline goods (i.e., the amount by which lend-lease pipeline goods exceeded reverse lend-lease pipeline goods) by $27,500,000 so that the final total due for lend-lease, surplus property, and fixed installations was $622,500,000. A supplementary agreement of 12 July 1948 set this figure as final.[32]

Agreements on similar terms followed with most other allied governments. The French entered into a preliminary agreement in February 1946 and a memorandum of understanding on 28 May 1946. They agreed to pay a total of $653,000,000 for goods for civilian use remaining in their hands, for pipeline goods and for surplus property. The Export-Import Bank granted credit to cover this sum on the basis of an obligation to pay interest at 2 percent beginning 1 July 1946, and to pay the principal in thirty annual installments beginning 1 July 1951.[33] Belgium enjoyed the unique position of having given more aid to the United States than it had received in lend-lease. The addition of charges for supplies that had been provided for the civilian population brought the lend-lease accounts into balance.[34] Canada, though using lend-lease machinery for obtaining some supplies in the United States, had paid for all goods procured in this country, and the Canadian lend-lease account was considered closed.[35]

The settlement of accounts with the Soviet Union presented more difficulties. Shipments of lend-lease equipment to European Russia ended, in the main, with the proclamaton of V–E Day.[36] It had been expected that this would be the policy, but the sudden manner in which this was carried out—including the unloading of ships about to sail for Russian ports with cargoes of lend-lease goods—piqued Marshall Stalin. He made his resentment clear to Harry Hopkins who went to Moscow for special conversations with the Soviet premier in May 1945. Hopkins's reply was that under the Lend-Lease Act the

United States could furnish goods only for the purpose of prosecuting the war, and since hostilities had ended in Europe and the Soviet Union had not at that time joined in the war against Japan, further lend-lease assistance could not be provided. Stalin understood that, but what he objected to was its abrupt cancellation without any warning; it appeared to him to be an effort to put pressure on the Soviet Union. He suggested that much could be done when the Russians were approached in a friendly manner, but reprisals in any form would have the opposite effect.[37] As a matter of fact, lend-lease aid did continue to go to the Soviet Far East after V–E Day under what Foreign Economic Administrator Crowley called "a program sponsored by our military," even though the Russians had not entered the war in that area. The purpose was to support the build-up of supplies in Siberia when the Russians did enter the war against Japan, as they had agreed to do.[38]

In the period between V–E Day and V–J Day the United States accepted commitments to send to Siberia lend-lease material amounting to $1,700,000,000. At the time of the Japanese surrender, $900,000,000 worth of this in airplanes, tanks, jeeps, ammunition and other matériel had been delivered.[39] Total wartime shipments of lend-lease goods to the Soviet Union amounted to $9.5 billion. Among other things this included military equipment such as the following: 14,795 airplanes; 7,056 tanks; 51,053 jeeps; 375,883 trucks; 35,170 motorcycles; 8,071 tractors; 8,218 antiaircraft guns; 131,633 submachine guns; 345,735 tons of explosives; 1,981 locomotives; 11,155 freight cars, and 15,417,000 Army boots.[40]

A credit agreement signed with the Soviet Union on 15 October 1945 covered the transfer of articles "that were in inventory or procurement in the United States for the purpose of providing war aid to USSR but were not transferred prior to the date of the agreement."[41] Terms called for repayment in twenty-two annual installments beginning 1 July 1954, with interest at 2 3/8 percent. This material, amounting to $250,000,000, consisted mainly of machine tools and other industrial and mechanical equipment. It did not include any munitions.[42]

Cancellation of lend-lease procurement contracts by the technical services dampened Soviet hopes of getting a number of locomotives and dump cars that were under construction, and the director of matériel, Army Service Forces, reaffirmed a policy against reinstating any contracts.[43] A lot of forty-six wide-gauge locomotives built for the Soviet Union in 1944 remained in storage at the Voorheesville area of the Schenectady general depot until they were offered for sale to the highest bidder—restricted to use in continental United States—in April 1952.[44] However, members of the USSR's purchasing commission pointed out that certain Treasury Department contracts, under the control of the State Department, had been continued after V–J Day in expectation of Soviet purchases, and they could not understand why the War Department took a different position when there had been no clear statement regarding the termination of War Department contracts in the credit agreement. Postponement of certain contract termination proceedings then made available to the Soviets at least some of the equipment they were trying to get. Since the War Department had no funds to cover the costs of inspection, packaging, and other handling incident to transferring supplies to the Soviet government under the credit agreement, it was necessary for the secretary of war to request a transfer of funds from the State Department.[45]

After a meeting with representatives of the International Branch, ASF, and of the Office of the Foreign Liquidation Commissioner, the Soviet purchasing commission in December 1945 presented a formal request for various types of heavy trucks and mobile construction and earth-moving equipment. Since this far exceeded anything remaining in the lend-lease pipeline, the Soviet agents were referred to the Foreign Liquidation Commission for possible purchases of surplus property remaining in Europe.[46]

The program envisaged under the Soviet credit agreement for lend-lease pipeline goods never was quite completed. Congress inserted a proviso in the Third Deficiency Appropriation Act, 1946, to the effect that no funds appropriated in that act should be used for any expenses of shipping abroad any commodities after 31 December 1946.[47] Even though, at the suggestion of the State Department, the foreign governments concerned had deposited $800,211.98 to a special account in the Treasury Department to cover the shipping expenses, the comptroller general ruled against using those funds unless Congress indicated that this would not violate the intent of the Third Deficiency Appropriation Act.[48] This put the United States in the position of backing down on international agreements freely entered into. After extensive hearings and a special message from the president in June 1947, Congress included in the Supplemental Appropriation Act for fiscal year 1948 a provision for $500,000 for liquidating the lend-lease pipeline activities. However, the act listed by name those countries to which deliveries could be made under this appropriation. The omission of the Soviet Union from the list meant that pipeline material in storage and on order for the USSR under the October agreement could not be transferred. Consequently this material had to be disposed of under the Surplus Property Act.[49] Negotiations for a final settlement of lend-lease affairs with the Soviet Union dragged on through 1951. The principal points at issue were the terms and amount of a satisfactory financial settlement for the civilian-type materials that the Soviet Union retained, the return of certain ships to the United States, and compensation to American companies for the use of their patented oil refinery processes, which had been furnished to the Soviet Union under lend-lease.[50]

China enjoyed a special, favored status as the only nation that continued to receive straight lend-lease aid after V–J Day. Indeed, transfers of goods and services under lend-lease to China between 2 September and 31 December 1945 totaled in value $517,410,354.59. (Only some $870,000,000 worth of lend-lease supplies had reached China during the whole time before V–J Day.) Nearly $300,000,000 of this represented the costs of transporting four Chinese armies in American aircraft to take over control of areas in northern China and Manchuria. Another $68,000,000 went for vehicles and $50,000,000 for ammunition out of U.S. army stocks in the Far East. The disarming and repatriation of more than a million Japanese troops remaining in China and Manchuria after the surrender made these steps necessary.[51]

As was the case with other post-hostilities policies—such as the occupation policies in Germany and Japan and in the Charter of the United Nations—American policy in China seemed to be based more on an assumption of danger from the continued resistance or a possible early return to power of the defeated enemy states than on any possible threat that might result from the defection of wartime allies or the appearance of new enemies. The army's mission in the China theater was to continue in support of Generalissimo Chiang Kai-shek in case Japanese forces there continued to resist, and American forces were to support the Chinese Nationalist government in reoccupying all areas previously held by the Japanese and in sending occupation forces to Japan, Formosa, and Korea. But the president's JCS memorandum of 5 September restated clearly, "the United States will not support the Central Government of China in a fratricidal war."

At the same time the Chinese agreed to accept nearly $50,000,000 worth of goods in the lend-lease pipeline on terms for repayment (under an agreement signed 14 June 1946) similar to those granted to other allied nations. But negotiations for a final settlement of the lend-lease accounts, as in the case of the Soviet Union, dragged on through 1951. By that time the weakened position of the Chinese Nationalist government on Formosa made it appear unlikely that any final settlement would be forthcoming soon.[52]

Transfers of surplus property and lend-lease goods made up but a part of the total United States aid to over fifty countries in the period between 1 July 1945 and 31 December 1946. That assistance—including cash loans, transfers of goods and services on terms of deferred payment, and grants in money and in kind—totaled $14.3 billion. Only $7.8 billion of that amount actually was spent in that time, but the commitment remained to be added to other assistance that would be granted in succeeding years.[53] Foreign military aid would continue to be a dominant consideration in the army's logistic policies, as it began reorganizing for the postwar period.

Notes

1. Brookings Institution, *Major Problems in U.S. Foreign Policy, 1947* (Washington, D.C., 1947), 162; Twenty-Second Report to Congress on Lend-Lease Operations, House Document 663, 79th Cong., 2d Sess., June 14, 1946, 17–18.
2. British Master Agreement, 23 Feb. 42, printed in Appendix 5, Twenty-First Report to Cong. on Lend-Lease Ops., House Doc. 432, 79th Cong., 2d Sess., 17 Nov. 1947.
3. P. L. 11, 77th Cong., 55 U.S. Stat. at Large, 32.

4. Statement of the President, released 17 Apr. 45, printed in *The Department of State Bulletin*.
5. Secretary of State Stettinius, 15 May 45. See Dept. of State Press Release No. 24, dated 15 May 45.
6. Ltr., President Truman to Speaker of House of Representatives, 4 June 45, printed in *The Department of State Bulletin*, 12 (10 June 1945): 1061.
7. Felix Belair, Jr., in *The New York Times* (late city ed.) 9 Sept. 1945.
8. The New York Times (late city ed.), 22 Aug. 1945.
9. *The New York Times* (late city ed.), 25 Aug. 1945. See also Twenty-First Report to Congress on Lend-Lease Ops., House Doc. 432, 79th Cong., 2d Sess., 31 Jan. 1946, 7–10; and First Supplement to vols. 1 and 2, *History of International Division, ASF, Lend-Lease as of 31 Dec. 1945*, 21–23.
10. Memo, President to JCS, 5 Sept. 45. Mimeographed copy in G–3 Records.
11. *The New York Times* (late city ed.), 7 Sept. 1945.
12. Statement by Asst. Secy. of State Joseph C. Grow, Dept. of State Press Release 433, dated 14 May 1945; Edwin L. James, *The New York Times*, 26 Aug. 1956.
13. *The New York Times* (late city ed.), 28 Aug. 1945.
14. Henry L. Stimson and McGeorge Bundy, *On Active Service in Peace and War*, (New York, 1947), 592–93.
15. Text of the Lend-Lease Act, as amended, Twentieth Report to Congress on Lend-Lease Operations, House Doc. 279, 79th Cong., 1st Sess., 5 Sept. 1945, 56–59.
16. Stimson and Bundy, *On Active Service in Peace and War*, 218–19.
17. Internat'l Div., ASF, Rpt. on Lend-Lease Ops., 1 Jan.–10 June 1946 (2d. Supplement to vols. 1 and 2), 10.
18. Memo, President to JCS, 5 Sept. 45.
19. Internat'l. Div., ASF, Report on Lend-Lease Ops., (2d. Supplement to vols. 1 and 2,) 11. See also Internat'l. Div., ASF, Lend-Lease Ops., 1 Oct.–31 Dec. 1945 (1st Supplement to vols. 1 and 2), 60, in OCMH.
20. Internat'l. Div., ASF, Lend-Lease, 1 Oct.–31 Dec. 1945, (1st Supplement to vols. 1 and 2), 63–64.
21. Ibid., 7.
22. Brookings Institution, *Major Problems in U.S. Foreign Policy, 1947*, (Washington, D.C., 1949), 163.
23. Memo, Col. L. E. Fellenz, Ch. Program Br., Sup. Div. G–4 for ACofS, G–4, 16 Oct. 45, sub.: Meeting of State-War-Navy Subcommittee on Rearmament, MS, G–4 400.703 (4); Memo, WDGSP/O 435, Brig. Gen. T. M. Osborne, Ch. Sup. Grp. SSp, 20 Sept. 46, sub.: Unresolved Surplus Property Problems, carbon, CofS 400.703.
24. WD Memo, 700–45, 18 July 45, sub.: Return of Lend-Lease Materials Overseas not Required by Foreign Governments; Internat'l Div., ASF, Rpt. on Lend-Lease Ops., 1 Jan.–10 June 1946, (2d. Supplement to vols 1 and 2), 74–75; TM 38–420, Sept. 1945, para. 68; TM 38–420, Feb. 1946, para 51.
25. TM 38–420, Sept. 1945, para 69; TM 38–420, Feb. 1946, para 52; WD Memo, 700–45, 20 July 45, Disposal of Property Overseas; Occupation Forces in Europe Series, 1945–46, Office, Chief Historian, EUCOM, 18.
26. Twenty-Third Report to Congress on Lend-Lease Ops, House Doc. 41, 80th Cong., 1st Sess., 3 Jan. 1974, 41.
27. *The New York Times*, (late city ed.), 25 Aug. 1945.
28. Brookings Institution, *Major Problems in the U.S. Foreign Policy, 1947*, 163; Statement by Asst. Secy. of State, Joseph C. Grew, Department of State Press Release 433, date 14 May 1945.
29. Fleet Admiral William D. Leahy, *I Was There*, (New York, 1950), 410.
30. Brookings Institution, *Major Problems in U.S. Foreign Policy, 1947*, 163.

31. Internat'l. Div., ASF, Lend-Lease Ops., 1 Oct.–31 Dec. 1945 (1st Sup. to vols. 1 and 2), 62–68; Twenty-first Report to Congress on Lend-Lease Operations, House Doc., 432, 79th Cong., 2d Sess., 31 Jan. 1946, 21–35.

32. Twenty-Second Report to Cong. on Lend-Lease Ops, House Doc. 663, 79th Cong., 2d sess., 14 June 1946; *Surplus Property, Occupation Forces in Europe Series, 1945–46*, 29; Brookings Institution, *Major Problems in U.S. For. Pol., 1947*, 163–64; Internat'l. Div., ASF, Rpt. on Lend-Lease Ops., 1 Jan.–10 June 1946 (2d sup. to vols. 1 and 2), 74–75; Internat'l. Div., ASF, Rpt. on Lend-Lease Ops., 1 Oct–31 Dec. 1945, (1st sup. to vols. 1 and 2), 66; Twenty-Seventh Rpt. of Operations Under Lend-Lease Act, House Doc. 75, 81st Cong., 1st sess., 14 Feb. 1949, vii-viii.

33. Internat'l. Div., ASF, Rpt. on Lend-Lease Ops., Jan.–June 1946 (2d Sup. to vols. 1 and 2), 78–80; *Surplus Property*, Occupation Forces in Europe Series, 1945–46, 47, 49; Twentieth Rpt. to Cong. on Lend-Lease Ops, House Doc. 279, 5 Sept. 1945, 33; Twenty-first Rpt. to Cong. on Lend-Lease Ops., House Doc. 432, 31 Jan. 1946, 27; Twenty-third Rpt. to Cong. on Lend-Lease Ops. House Doc. 41, 3 Jan. 1947, 8–11, 41–43; Twenty-eighth Rpt. to Cong. on Lend-Lease Ops., House Doc, 263, 18 July 1949, 1–2.

34. Twentieth Rpt. to Cong. on Lend-Lease Ops., House Doc. 279, 5 Sept. 1945, 35–36; Twenty-third Rpt. to Cong. on Lend-Lease Ops., House Doc. 41, 3 Jan. 1947, 14–15.

35. Twenty-third Rpt. to Congress on Lend-Lease Ops., House Doc. 41, 3 Jan. 1947, 8.

36. Twentieth Rpt. to Cong. on Lend-Lease Ops., House Doc. 279, 5 Sept. 1945, 23; Statement by Asst. Secy. of State, Joseph C. Grew, Dept. of State Press Release 433, dated 14 May 1946.

37. Robert E. Sherwood, *Roosevelt and Hopkins, An Intimate History*, (New York, 1948), 894–97; James F. Byrnes, *Speaking Frankly* (New York, 1947), 62.

38. *The New York Times*, (late city ed.), 11 Aug. 1946.

39. *The New York Times* (late city ed.), 11 Aug. 1946; Sen. Arthur H. Vandenberg, Statement to Senate, 18 Apr. 47, (prepared for the Senator by the State Dept. and given out in New Release 18 Apr. 47).

40. Twenty-First Rpt. to Cong. on Lend-Lease Ops., House Doc. 432, 31 Jan. 1946, 25.

41. Internat'l. Div., ASF, Lend-Lease, 1 Oct.–31 Dec. 1945 (1st Sup. to vols 1 and 2), 84.

42. Ibid., 85–88; Sen. Arthur H. Vandenberg, Statement before Senate, 18 Apr. 47.

43. Internat'l. Div., ASF, Rpt. on Lend-Lease Ops., 1 Jan.–10 June 1946 (2d Sup. to vols. 1 and 2), 90.

44. *The New York Times* (late city ed.), 27 Apr. 1952.

45. Internat'l. Div., ASF, Rpt. on Lend-Lease, 1 Jan.–10 June 1946 (2d sup. to vols 1 and 2), 93–94.

46. Ibid., 99–100

47. P. L. 521, 79th Cong.

48. Twenty-fourth Rpt. to Cong. on Lend-Lease Ops., House Doc. 437, 17 Nov. 1947, 11.

49. Supplemental Appropriation Act, 1948, P. L. 271, 80th Cong.; Twenty-Fourth Rpt. to Congress on Lend-Lease Ops., House Doc. 437, 17 Nov. 1947, 12.

50. Thirtieth Report to Congress on Lend-Lease Ops., House Doc. 576, 27 Apr. 1950, 1; Thirty-Second Rpt. to Cong. on Lend-Lease Ops., House Doc. 227, 3 Oct. 1951, 5–7.

51. Internat'l, Div., ASF, Rpt. on Lend-Lease Ops, 1 Jan.–10 June 1946 (2d Sup.

to vols 1 and 2), 13, 89–93; Twenty-Second Rpt. to Cong. on Lend-Lease Ops., House Doc. 663, 79th Cong., 2d Sess., 14 June 1946, 15–16.

52. Agreement between the U.S. and China for Disposition of Lend-Lease Supplies in the U.S., 14 June 1946, in Dept. of State Publ, Treaties and Other Internat'l. Acts Series, 1501–11565; Twenty-Third Rpt. to Cong. on Lend-Lease Ops., House Doc. 41, 3 Jan. 1947; Thirtieth Rpt. to Cong. on Lend-Lease Ops., House Doc. 576, 27 Apr. 1950, 1; Thirty-Second Rpt. on Cong. on Lend-Lease Ops., House Doc 227, 3 Oct. 1951, 4.

53. Brookings Institution, *Major Problems in U.S. Foreign Policy, 1947*, 165–66; *Annual Report of the Secretary of the Army, 1948*, (Washington, D.C., 1948), 126.

3
Housekeeping and Preparedness

After successful conclusion of the hostilities of World War II, Old Army men could permit themselves to look forward with nostalgic yearning to the early exchange of shelter tents and foxholes for brick barracks, jungles and hedgerows for trim lawns, endless mud for smooth pavement, beachheads for swimming pools, and night combat patrols for Saturday morning inspections. They could look forward to a return to the "normal peacetime functions" of housekeeping, paper work, the care and cleaning of equipment, guard duty, and when time permitted, some desultory training. Sentimental attachments to certain features of the Old Army persisted outside the army in such actions as that of Congress to prolong the quartermaster remount service for procuring horses, even though no horse cavalry saw action in World War II and that arm had become wholly obsolete.[1]

Housekeeping was, of course, no end in itself, but it consumed a great deal both in time and resources of the postwar military establishment. Rapid demobilization in itself created unprecedented problems in logistics, but while that went on, other activities relating more directly to the maintenance of an army on a permanent footing could not be ignored. The decline in activities for the logistic support of the army was not proportional to the decline in the troop strength of the army. It was true that the logistic services would have but a fraction of the troops to support that they had had during the war, but it also was clear that the peacetime army would be far larger than any the United States had previously maintained. This meant immediate demands for permanent quarters and facilities where temporary wartime structures were insufficient. At the same time, many logistic activities were not directly related to the troops strengths of the moment, but more to the potential forces that might be mobilized in the event of another emergency. Indeed, the problem of storing and caring for weapons and equipment was much greater, rather than less, than it had been during full mobilization. As the chief of ordnance put it, "If the Army was reduced to ten men and a boy, the same amount of work we are doing now would be necessary."[2] With an army of 10,000,000 men, most of the equipment would be in the hands of the troops, and it would be their job to take care of it; reduced to a million men, the army had to find ways of taking care of its equipment in huge lots.

Installations

During demobilization the emphasis was upon the deactivation of installations in order to avoid the continuing costs of maintaining them. Even then, however, the acquisition of new land and facilities was necessary from time to time. Expansion in one place in order to close out two others, changing needs, and the revision of programs made changes in installations continuous.[3]

The army's repair and maintenance job as of March 1949 included the upkeep of sixty-one active forts and camps in the United States, the largest of which were Fort Benning, Georgia; Fort Bragg, North Carolina; and Fort Lewis, Washington; twenty inactive forts and camps, of which the largest were Fort Leonard Wood, Missouri; Camp McCoy, Wisconsin; and Camp Polk, Louisiana; seventy-eight depots and arsenals; twenty-six standby industrial facilities such as Morgantown Ordnance Works, West Virginia; Wabash River Ordnance Works, Indiana; Twin City Arsenal, Minnesota; and Joliet Arsenal, Illinois; fourteen general hospitals, and eleven port facilities.[4]

At the end of the war an accumulation of repairs that had been put off in favor of more urgent demands during the war itself now awaited attention. Engineer officers in 1946 estimated that it would take some $214 million to get needed buildings back into good repair.[5] But that situation got worse before it got better. When demands for economy were pressing, the easiest places to put off expenditures for another year without having any immediately noticeable effect on army strength were in the areas of buildings and grounds maintenance. But those economies were also the kind that could be the most expensive in the long run. In March 1947 Lt. Gen. R. A. Wheeler, chief of engineers, appeared before the House Subcommittee on Military Appropriations to defend his request for $229 million for utilities and repairs and maintenance in the fiscal year 1948 budget. Explaining that the figure of $229 million was the result of careful study in which each item had been considered for possible reduction or elimination, he said that this was the minimum necessary for good management and sound business practice. He pointed out that this amount would provide only 90 percent of the fire protection and other essential services required, and would permit maintenance at only 40 percent of the low war time standard.[6] Yet Congress cut the barracks and quarters appropriation from $229 million to $191,353,000.[7] In January 1950 Maj. Gen. Lewis A. Pick, who had by then become chief of engineers, stated to the House subcommittee, "The reduced appropriations with which the maintenance work has been done for the past several years has resulted in inestimable loss of valuable Government real property through . . . deterioration and decay."[8]

An especially troublesome aspect of the whole installations problem was that of maintaining storage space for huge stocks of equipment and supplies at a time when the army was deactivating as many installations as possible and releasing as many service troops as it could. Maj. Gen. G. J. Richards of the Office of the Chief of Engineers estimated in May 1946 that it was costing $35 to $40 million to care for surplus property until the War Assets Administration could take it over.[9] In April 1950 unserviceable but repairable property occupied nearly two-thirds of the army's occupied storage space, and the stockpile of strategic and critical materials occupied another sixth of the space.[10] The storage system included approximately 160 million square feet of warehousing—equivalent to about twenty-six times the total floor space of the Pentagon Building, and open storage areas amounting to about 250 million square feet—about forty-five times the area of the mall between the Capitol and the Washington Monument. Army supplies and equipment in storage early in 1950 amounted to about forty million measurement tons (a measurement ton being forty cubic feet).[11]

Family Housing

Nothing probably discouraged the enthusiasm of young officers and noncommissioned officers from a career in the military services more than the absence of facilities for the housing of their families. An acute housing shortage was to be found after World War II in areas near permanent military posts as well as in most other parts of the country. The absence of housing construction during the war in many places, together with the rapid growth in population, had brought about this situation generally, but the expanded size of the peacetime army in comparison with its prewar strength made conditions near major military posts especially difficult. Army people had the further disadvantage of frequent changes of station, which denied to them the opportunity to build houses of their own and multiplied the problems of frequent adjustments to new communities, always with a quest for living space the major consideration of any move. The army's policy was to provide family quarters for married officers and noncommissioned officers of the first three grades, or, when unavailable, to grant them a monthly rental allowance. This meant that most of those eligible received the rental allowance, rather than quarters on a post, and their problem was to match that allowance with the scale of rent prevailing in local communities in times of scarcity and keen competition. Fortunately for them federal rent control kept the charges within certain ceilings, but that did little to improve the conditions under which they found themselves forced to live and rear their children. Most enlisted men who went into the army for a career could expect, sooner or later, to become a noncommissioned officer of the grade eligible to be furnished family quarters, so that the situation was a matter of deep interest for all who looked forward to a military career.

In an attempt to interest private enterprise in building housing projects near army posts, the assistant secretary of the army called a series of conferences with officials of large insurance companies to discuss the possibilities of investments in this kind of undertaking, and he directed army commanders to discuss these possibilities with local companies in their areas. The results of these efforts seemed to be encouraging, but it soon became clear that this approach was not going to fill the need. The principal difficulty was in persuading private interests to risk capital in housing developments that depended upon the uncertain continuation of current troop strengths at the adjacent military posts.[12]

Apart from whatever plans materialized to relieve the long-term housing shortage, something had to be done to meet the immediate situation. In September 1948 the chief of staff approved an emergency plan for providing trailer camp facilities for soldier families. These were to include individual lots and hard stands for the house trailers, individual electric and water connections, hard surface walkways, and community bath, toilet, laundry, and parking facilities. The plan was for service men to furnish their own trailers. They then would receive their regular rental allowances, and would pay only about $95 a year for the site rental and utilities.[13] As it worked out the uniform rental rate was $42 a year for the trailer parking sites, and the monthly utility bills varied from $5 to $15. (In May 1952 the annual rental was increased to $72.) In some areas where privately owned trailers were not available, the government furnished them, but that cost the inhabitants their monthly rental allowances.[14]

Mutual ownership projects, trailer parks, the conversion of temporary buildings, and the limited new construction that Congress was willing to approve could not begin to meet the needs. Clearly one of two courses had to be taken: either the construction of government-owned buildings on a large scale, or the inducement of private enterprise to undertake building projects near military posts. Reluctant to appropriate more funds, Congress turned to the second alternative with the passage of the Wherry Bill (approved 8 August 1949) to provide for mortage insurance to protect private investors. Patterned after the Defense Housing Insurance amendment to the National Housing Act passed in 1941, the Wherry Act—also an amendment to the National Housing Act—established a Military Housing Insurance Fund through which the Federal Housing Administration could insure mortgages for up to 90 percent of the project costs. Upon certification by the secretary of defense, or his designated representative, that the housing was necessary for military personnel and that the installation near where it was to be built was considered permanent and that the Defense Department had no plans to curtail activities there, application for insurance could be made. The insurance could cover mortgages of up to $5 million, but they could not be for more than 90 percent of the replacement cost of the project, not more than $8,100 per family unit in multiple-unit dwellings, or over $9,000 where single-family homes were required. The total amount of all mortgages insured could not be over $500 million, though the president could double that amount. Initially the authority to issue insurance was to continue to 1 July 1951. By

February 1950 the Department of the Army had approved projects comprising over 11,500 units of 15,000 planned for in the initial program.[15]

In practice, a number of shortcomings emerged from the Wherry Act. The difficulty in deciding which of several plans and specifications submitted for a particular project was the best, as well as which presented the best price, led to complaints of favoritism and discrimination on the part of unsuccessful bidders—and sometimes there were as many as twenty bidders for one project. After a schedule of rental rates for a project had been approved by the army, the Federal Housing Administration might require their revision (usually upward) as a condition for issuing mortgage insurance. This opened the way for charges that successful bidders had deliberately submitted more attractive rental scales than they knew the FHA would approve in the hope of being able to remain the chosen sponsors under whatever revisions the FHA might require. Moreover, sponsors' proposals in actual practice seemed to be based upon the assumption that the 90 percent of replacement value that mortgage insurance was permitted to cover under the law would cover all costs incident to complete construction.[16]

In effect the arrangements under the Wherry Act amounted to granting to the private sponsor, without any risk of capital on his part, a fixed income from the property and, after the expiration of the thirty-three-year, eight-month amortization period, clear title to the property. The source of revenue from such property was the monthly rental allowances that the government granted to eligible military personnel. If the government had owned the property, all rent, in the form of withholding the rental allowances, would have remained with it. Thus if Congress had been willing to appropriate the money outright, it would have cost no more over a period of thirty-three or probably fewer years than did the payment of individual rental allowances during that same period; and after that a considerable savings would have resulted, since the government would then have owned the property.[17]

An amendment to the act approved in May 1950 removed the most objectionable features. The new procedures called for competitive bidding against identical plans and specifications, and title to the properties could revert to the government after the period of amortization.[18]

Bomb Shelters

The effects of strategic bombing in World War II and the potentialities of the atomic bombs then being developed and their even more devastating results suggested the possible necessity of moving key industrial and storage facilities underground in the event of a future war. German achievements in that direction during the war suggested the possibilities. The Germans had adapted mines for the storage of ammunition, gasoline, clothing, and rubber, and for the manufacture of ammunition, aircraft engines, precision instruments, and ball bearings, and for the generation of electricity. They had converted railroad and highway tunnels to plants for manufacturing airplanes, ammunition, and electrical equipment. They had made beer cellars into plants for manufacturing chemicals, liquid oxygen, airplane parts, ball bearings, and for storage. In one cave they built a nine-story building, and in another a four-story building where they turned out radio tubes, gears, and ball bearings. In addition they had undertaken an ambitious program of new excavations, but most of those remained unfinished at the end of the war. Yet the Germans had completed at least 239 underground installations, including seventy-four new excavations. Their greatest failure had been in the execution of their program. Their experience suggested that the time to prepare underground sites was before the war in which they would have to be used.[19]

Army planners lost little time in beginning inquiries into the problem. Their investigations suggested that underground factories and depots were feasible without unreasonable costs in relation to the protection gained. One study involved the consideration of setting up an underground plant on the basis of the facilities of the division of the Frankford Arsenal, which made artillery fire control instruments. A precision manufacturing plant such as this one required close control of temperature and humidity. Estimated construction costs for installing this plant in a suitable existing mine were 19 percent greater than for a comparable above-ground factory. A second special study considered the construction of a chemical plant in a mine—a problem the Germans had found to be one of the most difficult. Based upon the model of the facilities of the Niagara Falls Chemical Plant, this construction would cost 34 percent more than the construction of the plant on the surface, but the operating costs would be only 4 percent more than that of a surface plant. An operational storage depot could be put in a mine at a cost 22 percent less than it could be built above ground, and its operating cost would be 1.7 percent less.[20]

The greatest weakness of underground installations was the transportation system that served them. In Germany the underground plants themselves had not been damaged seriously by bombing, but the interdiction of rail lines leading to them frequently hampered their production. Good highways and heavy vehicles with a certain amount of crosscountry mobility could relieve some of the dependence upon vulnerable rail lines, but in hilly regions, where many of the mines were located, automotive traffic would be as surely canalized as rail traffic. Yet a dense rail and highway net where labor and materials were available for rapid repair of damaged sections would not necessarily be unduly susceptible to crippling air attacks.[21]

Supply and Industrial Reserves

SUPPLY STOCKS

Determination of the kinds and quantities of supplies and equipment that should be stored in reserve was basic to the development of policies on disposal of surplus property in the years immediately following World War II and in developing requirements for new procurements later. Provision for establishing a War Department war reserve in 1945 followed the criterion generally governing that kind of stocks. The war reserve was to include those quantities of supplies and equipment necessary to outfit the mobilized army, i.e., the M-Day forces plus reserves, and to maintain it in active operations as well as in training for a period of eighteen months following a future M-Day—less the production available from the arsenal system and standby plants, and less the production that reasonably could be expected from commercial sources.[22] The special reserves were stocks set aside for special purposes, and they could not be touched without the approval of the chief of staff. Theater commanders were responsible for storage, inspection, and maintenance of special reserves stored overseas, and the chiefs of the technical services had that responsibility for those in the United States, but both remained directly under General Staff control.[23]

These reserves were in addition to stocks in the supply pipeline, in the hands of troops, and in the stocks of overseas theaters. Most overseas commands were authorized to maintain a minimum, or safety level of thirty days of supply plus an operating level of another thirty days, which made a total maximum level of sixty days of supply for most items other than ammunition, which came under separate tables.[24]

INDUSTRIAL FACILITIES RESERVES

The second line of reserves for matériel support in time of emergency was the factories and the tools that had been earmarked or set aside for a return to war production when necessary.

At its peak the war production program for World War II for all services was taking approximately 70 percent of the total industrial capacity of the United States. The army's policy was to continue to put its chief reliance for war goods on private industry, but consideration of the problems of conversion to war production and the long time required to start new production of weapons and military equipment led to the development of a policy late in 1944 that resulted in the retention in the army's own hands of enough industrial capacity to provide specialized military items for a force equal to about 40 percent of the World War II peak troop strength. The army's reserve industrial facilities, a part of the Industrial Plants Reserve of the National Military Establishment, as it was called in the 1947–1949 period, included the permanent arsenal system, the standby installations, and the National Industrial Plant Reserve.[25]

The facilities of the army's permanent arsenal system—including some seventeen installations—were army-owned and generally operated by civilian employees of the army. The standby installations, comprising over sixty plants, works, arsenals, and laboratories, were army-owned but generally were operated, when active, by private companies under contracts with the army. Thus the U.S. Rubber Company operated the Kankakee Ordnance Works at Joliet, Illinois, the Remington Arms Company operated the Lake City Arsenal at Independence, Missouri, the Chevrolet Division of General Motors Corporation operated the Chevrolet Shell Plant at St. Louis. One of the major problems in keeping those army-owned plants that were inactive available when needed was that of maintenance. The army's policy was to lease these facilities to private users whenever possible, with a proviso that the lessee accept responsibility for the maintenance of the facilities, and with the clear understanding that the plant should be returned to army use whenever needed. This was not practicable in many cases, however, because plants set aside as standby installations generally were those needed for wartime manufacture of munitions, and as such, they had no counterparts in civilian industry.[26]

Most of the facilities in the National Industrial Plant Reserve were factories the government had built during World War II for operation under contract or lease by private companies. After the war, the Reconstruction Finance Corporation, the War Assets Administration, or, later, the General Services Administration had sold or leased them after the responsible military department had declared them surplus. By selling or leasing these plants subject to the national security clause, the army (or other military service) kept a string tied to them so that they would be available for return to war production if needed. In general this clause guaranteed that the plant would be maintained in a condition to be reconverted to war on 120 days' notice, and this condition would continue for a period of twenty years, or for some other agreed time. Altogether the federal government had financed the construction of approximately 1,595 manufacturing plants during World War II at an estimated cost of $12.7 billion. As of 30 June 1950 the total reserve facilities included 260 in the Departmental Industrial Reserve (the permanent arsenal system plus the standby installations of the military departments) and 194 in the National Industrial Reserve reserved under the national security clause. Industrial plants under the army's control, supervision, or inspection totalled some 125.[27]

No less important than the retention of plants in reserve was the storing of a reserve of machine tools and other industrial equipment that would make possible the rapid conversion of other plants to war production. A nation's capacity to wage modern war could almost be gauged by its machine tool capacity. Shortages of machine tools was one of the most serious in industrial mobilization bottlenecks. The program of storing industrial equipment toward overcoming that danger began after World War II under the supervision of the Joint Army-Navy Machine Tool (JANMAT) Control Committee, and continued after unification under the auspices of the Munitions Board. The JANMAT program then became the Departmental Industrial Equipment

Reserve (DIER), and, in addition, the General Services Administration began storing other tools—approximately 10,000 of these ultimately were earmarked for the Department of Defense—in the National Industrial Equipment Reserve.[28] On 30 June 1950 the army's industrial equipment reserve included 38,195 items of machinery and equipment, including about 17,000 machine tools. Over 25,000 of these had been processed for long-term storage. The remainder were being used in army industrial installations or were on loan to private industry. The reserve was not well balanced, and it was far short of what staff planners considered to be necessary—the total machines in the Departmental Industrial Reserve represented less than 2 percent of the number used to support the wartime economy in 1945. Yet this reserve program did much to indicate the feasibility of long-term storage of machinery, and it made available a significant quantity of specialized machines that would be critically needed for rapid expansion of the munitions industry.[29]

STRATEGIC AND CRITICAL MATERIALS STOCKPILES

Industrial facilities were of no use without raw materials. Many items of military equipment and weapons required materials that were difficult to obtain in the qualities and quantities that would be needed for war production. The United States was wholly dependent upon overseas sources—sources that might be cut off in time of war—for a number of key materials. Many others, even though they were produced in the United States, would have to be supplemented by foreign supplies or by additional, and often costly, new facilities and methods. In the long run a stockpile of these materials could represent an important accumulation, not simply of minerals and products, but of savings of the manpower and expense involved in overcoming the obstacles of time and space that would become so great under wartime conditions. The billions of dollars in other materials and the months of effort that the United States had to expend in the midst of World War II in order to create a synthetic rubber industry and to bring in meager supplies of crude rubber after normal trade channels had been cut was testimony to that.[30]

The United States was in a fortunate position in its mineral resources. Its supply of the three basic minerals needed for industry—coal, iron, and petroleum—were among the richest known in the world. But in the metals essential for important steel alloys it was a different story. Over half the tungsten—an indispensable element for making highspeed steel, armor plate, and electronic equipment—had to be imported. Manganese—essential for purifying steel of sulphur content, and as an alloy for toughening steel—came from abroad to the extent of over 90 percent of all used. Domestic production of chromite—a basic ingredient of the heat-resisting brick used to line steel furnaces, and an important alloy for armor plate and armor-piercing projectiles—filled less than one half of one percent of U.S. needs. Other items, such as copper, lead, and zinc, in which the United States once had been more than self-sufficient—and which before 1940 never would have been included on any list of strategic and critical materials—now were becoming matters for serious concern. In the 1870s the United States had supplied most of the world with mercury; in 1950 its production of mercury was only 10 percent of that in 1877—and demands were much greater. If peace were assured indefinitely, then such dependence would be unimportant. In war it could be disastrous. One way to meet the problem was to lay in a stockpile of strategic and critical materials during times when they could be obtained in order that they would be at hand when sources of supply were cut off and their continuing availability had become matters of life and death.[31]

This had become apparent during the period of recurring crises on the eve of World War II when Congress passed the Strategic and Critical Materials Stock Piling Act of 1939 (approved 7 June) in order to begin the building up of a national stockpile. Little had been accomplished by this program before war itself was upon the nation and all efforts had to be turned toward getting materials for current production. The World War II production program did leave large quantities of critical and strategic materials under government control. These surpluses became the basis for the new national stockpile. The Surplus Property Act of 1944 permitted the transfer of strategic and critical materials to permanent defense stockpiles. Then the Strategic and Critical Materials Stock Piling Act of 1946—an amendment to the 1939 act—set in motion a positive long-range program for building and maintaining a stockpile.[32]

The nature of the stockpiling program perhaps made it inevitable that it should be subject to divided authority. The Munitions Board was the custodian for the stockpile. The Department of Commerce licensed exports of these types of materials and supervised the allocation of them. The Economic Cooperation Administration had the responsibility of obtaining strategic materials from abroad with the 5 percent of the Marshall Plan counterpart funds set aside for the purpose. The State Department supervised the purchasing activities of ECA and conducted negotiations in other countries seeking other materials. The Treasury Department's Federal Bureau of Supply at first made the actual purchases for most of the materials, and later the General Services Administration received the responsibility. But certain exceptional cases were dealt with separately, as in the case of tin, the Reconstruction Finance Corporation did all the buying.[33]

Economic and defense activities of the kind associated with national stockpiling patently invited other than economic and defense considerations in its execution. Exploitation of minerals always has been a fertile field for political activity aimed at encouraging policies by which special advantages would redound to the benefit of special interest groups. A protective tariff on manganese, for example, had cost the steel companies millions of dollars over a period of fourteen years in order to protect a submarginal domestic industry that was able to contribute only 5 percent of the nation's requirements of that important strategic material.³⁴ Now politics brought its influence to bear on the program of stockpiling for national defense. People interested in copper, zinc, lead, mercury, tungsten, and other materials produced in the United States tried to persuade the Munitions Board to go beyond its planned programs in order to absorb temporary surpluses—sometimes even at prices higher than the going market price. Other pressures sought aid for British and other foreign economies by heavy purchases of certain other materials. Officers concerned felt that secondary results of the stockpiling program should not supersede primary objectives. If it were desirable to subsidize domestic mining industries or to stimulate production for an ally abroad, that was a separate matter, which, in their view, should be acted upon apart from the national stockpiling program.³⁵

Another complication developed when the orientation of American policy against trading with the Soviet Union resulted in the cutting off, in 1949, of shipments of strategic materials from that country. Russian sources had been supplying 20 to 25 percent of American requirements for manganese, 50 percent of the chromite, and much of the platinum. This was a serious loss, but, though some further shipments from the Soviet Union on a smaller scale might be expected, perhaps some advantage resulted in requiring the development of other sources of supply that would be less likely to be cut off in time of war.³⁶ Similarly the loss of trade with China cut off important supplies of tungsten and silk.

Determination of which materials were to be listed as strategic and critical was the responsibility of the Munitions Board.³⁷ Technically there was a distinction between strategic materials and critical materials. "Strategic materials" were those materials vital to national security that had to be obtained entirely or to a substantial degree from outside the continental United States; "critical materials" were those whose main sources were within the continental United States but that might not be produced in quantities and quality sufficient to meet emergency needs.³⁸ The Munitions Board's list lumped them together as "strategic and critical materials," but the emphasis was upon those that would be most difficult to get in wartime—generally those that would come under the technical definition of "strategic." Of the sixty-nine materials listed in 1950, the United States produced only eight of them to the extent of half of peacetime requirements, and produced practically none of forty-two of the listed materials. These included such diverse items as beryl (important for atomic bomb production) from Brazil, hog bristles from China, industrial diamonds from the Belgian Congo, mica from India, quebracho from Argentina, and sperm oil from Norway. They were divided into categories according to which Group A—materials for which stockpiling was deemed the only satisfactory way of assuring adequate supplies for an emergency—was most important. Group B consisted of other materials that the Munitions Board considered could be stockpiled to advantage. These came only from surpluses of other government agencies. Group C was a relatively small list of strategic and critical materials not recommended currently for stockpiling because of the difficulties of storing them.[39]

In contrast to the stockpiling project set up in 1939 on the basis of a $100 million investment for a four-year program,[40] the program undertaken in the postwar period had for its goal, based on plans and prices of 30 June 1948, a stockpile of $3.403 billion worth of strategic and critical materials. Strategic and critical materials were stored in 155 locations—depots, tank farms, vaults, warehouses, government-owned and privately owned—in the continental United States and one in Alaska. These included seventy-six military depots. The army's share of the storage space amounted to about fifteen million gross square feet. Most of this was in reserved areas of the army's regular installations, though the Casad Engineer Depot at New Haven, Indiana, was being operated solely for stockpiling purposes.[41]

Support for Reserve Components

What, in a sense, amounted to another aspect of building up reserve supplies for emergency use was the logistic support for the National Guard, Organized Reserve Corps, and Reserve Officers' Training Corps. Equipment issued to National Guard and reserve units would be in responsible hands for care and storage, and to the extent that it would fill their mobilization needs it was the same as a part of the mobilization reserve stocks. All logistic support for the reserve program was, in effect, an accumulation of man-hours and materials in the same way that the stockpile of strategic materials was. If peacetime training would save wartime training to some degree for those units, the result was the same as the accumulation of reserves of the equipment that would be needed for the additional training time of raw troops and officer candidates upon emergency mobilization. The further that reduction in the standing army proceeded after World War II, the greater was the presumed reliance on reserve forces of the civilian components. For the National Guard and reserve units to be anything more than paper organizations meant that they had to have a complete and continuous training program—which meant that they had to have equipment for training. For them to have real significance for national defense, they had to have some degree of mobilization readiness—which meant that certain equipment for rapid expansion and for emergency missions had to be on hand.

According to policies approved by the secretary of war in October 1945, the Department of the Army was to have responsibility for arming, equipping, and clothing the National Guard in the same manner as the regular army. This did not mean, however, that the technical services were to budget for National Guard items as for others. Supplies and equipment would be furnished to the National Guard from army stocks, without reimbursement except for overhaul and rebuilding, whenever those stocks were excess to the needs of the active army and could be made available without new procurements. It was up to the heads of the technical services to determine when supplies were available for the National Guard on the basis of supply control studies and Department of the Army priorities. The cost of new procurements, on the other hand, came out of National Guard appropriations.[42]

In each state and territory an officer known as the United States property and disturbing officer (USP&DO) handled all the administrative details in connection with the supply of National Guard units. According to the legal procedure this officer was a civilian appointee of the state or territorial governor, but according to a practice that had developed during World War II and then continued thereafter, these positions in all the states were filled by "acting United States property and disbursing officers" who were National Guard, reserve, or sometimes army of the United States officers on extended active duty. They were appointed by the chief of the National Guard Bureau with the concurrence of the governors, and they were assigned to the National Guard Bureau. But their assignment was a permanent one, and they had no part in the general army practice of rotating officers from one station to another. This system had the approval of the assistant chief of staff, G–4, as well as of the National Guard Bureau and the state governors, but G–1 objected to a system that contrary to the general policy of rotating assignments, gave a permanent assignment to an officer on extended active duty.[43]

The USP&DO was the accountable officer for all federal property issued to the National Guard of his state. He was responsible for the operation of the state distributing point (the state warehouse), for making property settlements and inventories, for editing requests for supplies from units and preparing consolidated requisitions, and for keeping complete property records.[44] In addition he was the National Guard Bureau contracting officer appointed by the chief of the National Guard Bureau under the authority of the Armed Services Procurement Regulation. As such, he was responsible for all National Guard procurements with federal funds within his state.[45]

The thing that complicated National Guard logistics was the fact that National Guard units were under state control. In theory the state governors requisitioned the supplies for their troops, and the Department of the Army had the responsibility for procuring and issuing supplies for federally recognized units. This control over supply naturally gave the army a strong position in effecting standards of training as well as uniformity in equipment. Loss or damage to federal property through carelessness or neglect was to be paid for out of state funds.[46]

With neither the weaknesses nor the advantages of the state control that characterized the National Guard, the Organized Reserve Corps was made up of units and individuals under purely federal authority. Its units were supposed to be of such types and numbers as taken together with the regular army and the National Guard would constitute balanced forces of the army of the United States. The program for its logistical support was similar to that of the National Guard. The active army furnished most of that logistical support, but it was paid for through Organized Reserve Corps appropriations. Supplies and equipment would be furnished on a free-issue basis whenever stocks in excess of higher priority activities were available. Cost of rehabilitation of unserviceable items had to be borne by ORC funds. Issues from stocks held for other programs could be made if they could be replaced, with ORC funds, in time to meet the other demands.[47]

In each state, usually, a state ORC property officer held accountability for supplies and equipment issued to senior instructors and ORC units in much the same way that the USP&DO held accountability for equipment issued to the National Guard. The state ORC property officer, however, was responsible neither to the state governor nor to the executive for reserve and ROTC affairs in Washington. He was responsible to the continental army commander who appointed him. Neither were his duties as extensive as those of his National Guard counterpart, for he did not have the responsibilities for local procurement and for construction that the USP&DO did.[48]

Reserve Officers' Training Corps units at schools and colleges throughout the country continued adding second lieutenants to the pool of reserve officers, and training other men to carry noncommissioned officer responsibilities when called upon. Logistical support by the active army, with special appropriations of funds to cover certain special items and maintenance work, applied to the ROTC in much the same way as to the Organized Reserve Corps.[49]

A military property custodian in each educational institution performed the kind of supply functions that the USP&DO did for the National Guard and the state ORC property officer for the Organized Reserve Corps. But he was appointed by the head of the institution, and could not be an officer or enlisted man on active duty. He was the agent of the school for requisitioning, storing, issuing, and accounting for property furnished by the army. All supplies except uniforms and expendables had to be covered by bond. The military property custodian submitted his requisitions directly to the depot. The institution was responsible for organizational maintenance.[50]

The *raison d'être* of the reserve components, like that of the army itself, was the likelihood of emergency. The logistic accumulations that they represented, not only in terms of the matériel that they happened to have on hand, but as well in the stores of time and space their training, and indeed their very organization, comprised, added indisputably to the capabilities of the army in maintaining the national security. It is not unlikely, moreover, that Congress and the public would have been much less disposed to the laying aside of stocks of supplies equivalent to those issued to the reserve components had there been no reserve forces whose physical, current requirements could be more obviously justified than could requirements for some vaguely defined stockpile. Indirectly as well as directly, therefore, the reserve components had a significant effect upon matériel reserves. The moot question was whether their contribution should have been greater.

Armed Forces Procurement

An important corollary of armed forces unification was the adoption of generally uniform procurement policies for the military services that would allow considerably greater flexibility to them. While few exceptions had been permitted in peacetime to the rule of competitive bidding for military contracts, the Armed Forces Procurement Act of 1947 (actually approved in February 1948) permitted the services, at their discretion, to place contracts by negotiation rather than by advertising and competitive bids if any of a number of stated conditions prevailed. Procedures of negotiation might be used if:

(1) determined to be necessary in the public interest during the period of a national emergency declared by the president or by the Congress;

(2) the public exigency will not permit of the delay incident to advertising;

(3) the aggregate amount involved does not exceed $1,000;

(4) for personal or professional services;

(5) for any service to be rendered by any university, college, or other educational institution;

(6) the supplies or services are to be procured and used outside the limits of the United States and its possessions;

(7) for medicines or medical supplies;

(8) for supplies purchased for authorized resale;

(9) for perishable subsistence supplies;

(10) for supplies or services for which it is impracticable to secure competition;

(11) the agency head determines that the purchase or contract is for experimental, developmental, or research work, or for the manufacture or furnishing of supplies for experimentation, development, research, or test . . . ;

(12) for supplies or services as to which the agency head determines that the character, ingredients, or components thereof are such that the purchase or contract should not be publicly disclosed;

(13) for equipment which the agency head determines to be technical equipment, and as to which he determines that the procurement thereof without advertising is necessary in order to assure standardization of equipment and interchangeability of parts and that such standardization and interchangeability is necessary in the public interest;

(14) for supplies of a technical or specialized nature requiring a substantial initial investment or an extended period of preparation for manufacture, as determined by the agency head, when he determines that advertising and competitive bidding may require duplication of investment

or preparation already made, or will unduly delay procurement of such supplies;

(15) for supplies or services as to which the agency head determines that the bid prices after advertising therefore are not reasonable or have not been independently arrived at in open competition: *Provided,* That no negotiated purchase or contract may be entered into under this paragraph after the rejection of all bids received unless (A) notification of the intention to negotiate and reasonable opportunity to negotiate shall have been given by the agency head to each responsible bidder, (B) the negotiated price is lower than the lowest rejected bid price of a responsible bidder, as determined by the agency head, and (C) such negotiated price is the lowest negotiated price offered by any responsible supplier;

(16) the agency head determines that it is in the interest of the national defense that any plant, mine, or facility or any producer, manufacturer, or other supplier be made or or kept available for furnishing supplies or services in the event of a national emergency, or that the interest either of industrial mobilization in case of such an emergency, or of the national defense in maintaining active engineering, research and development, are otherwise subserved.[51]

The act further authorized any type of contract considered in the best interests of the government to be used in a negotiated procurement, except that the cost-plus-a-percentage-of-cost still was expressly forbidden. The fee permitted under a cost-plus-a-fixed-fee contract was limited to 6 percent, 15 percent, or 10 percent of the estimated cost according to whether it was for architectural or engineering services, research and development, or for other procurement. Advance payments on negotiated contracts were permitted, and a provision was included requiring that a "fair share" of contracts be placed with small business. The procurement act gave effect to principles and procedures resulting from the war experience, and in doing so it cleared the way for a rapid expansion of procurement to meet a future emergency without the need for drastic changes in procedures.[52]

The likelihood of an emergency against which the army had to maintain preparedness even as it went about its tasks of reorganization and retrenchment was rising in 1947 and 1948. A background of recurring international tension overshadowed continuing efforts at peacetime economy.

American reaction to threats of further expansion of Soviet areas of domination was swift, but in some ways it also was fickle. At times it seemed a part of the American character to rise to heights of miraculous achievement in meeting a crisis, and then to relax to the wishful complacency that would require new miracles to meet the next crisis. Demands for economy and sharp cuts in appropriations for current military functions after V–J Day made it necessary to keep all logistic activities not relating directly to the liquidation of the war effort to a bare minimum. During this period of postwar economy, budgetary figures arrived at after long hours of consideration and revision in the offices of the chiefs of the technical services and in the office of G–4 bore little resemblance to the congressional appropriations with which the army's logistic agencies had to work. Often estimates compiled after thousands of man-hours of calculations and deliberations fared little better than might have some figure plucked from the air without any thought at all. For the fiscal year 1948 budget the Ordnance Department estimated that, to cover procurement of essential ammunition and equipment, storage and distribution of ordnance matériel, maintenance of standby plants and arsenals, industrial mobilization planning, training, and research and development activities, it would need $750,000,000. The Bureau of the Budget cut this figure to $275,000,000.[53] Congress reduced the appropriation to $245,532,800 together with authorization to enter into contracts to the extent of another $2,000,000.[54]

For the same budget the quartermaster general's original estimate was $1,177,353,089. The Budget Advisory Committee of the War Department cut this to $908,418,100. The Bureau of the Budget reduced it to $727,901,000 before approving its submission to Congress. The House of Representatives then cut this to $685,000,000. The Quartermaster General, General Larkin, went before the House Appropriations Committee to urge the restoration of $26,997,991 to the appropriation as absolutely essential. He pointed out that prices had risen 35 percent to 150 percent above the average used in computing the previous year's budget.[55] The House restored something less than half the amount asked.[56]

By the spring of 1948 critical international developments had impressed upon military and political leaders the importance of looking again to military preparedness.[57]

Notes

1. Gen. Dwight D. Eisenhower, testimony before Senate Subcomm. on Appropriations, 24 June 46, 79th Cong., 2d Sess., 17.
2. Maj. Gen. E. S. Hughes, CofOrd, testimony before the Hearings of the House Subcomm. on Appropriations, 14 Mar. 47, 80th Cong., 1st Sess., 963.
3. Lt. Gen. R. A. Wheeler, CofEngrs, 24 May 46, Statement before House Subcomm. on Appropriations, 79th Cong., 2d Sess., 24 May 46, 796.
4. Maj. Gen. R. C. Crawford, Hearings before House Subcomm. on Armed Services Appropriations, 81st Cong., 1st Sess., 15 Mar. 49, Pt. 4, 532–42.
5. Maj. Gen. R. A. Wheeler and Brig. Gen. J. S. Bragdon, Hearings before House Subcomm. on Appropriations, 79th Cong., 2d Sess., 24 May 46, 780.
6. Lt. Gen. Wheeler, Hearings before House Subcomm. on Appropriations, 12 Mar. 47, 858–59.
7. Military Establishment Appropriation Act for FY 1948, P L 267, 80th Cong., 1st Sess., (approved 30 July 47), 61 U.S. Stat. 561.
8. Maj. Gen. Lewis A. Pick, CofEngrs, Hearings before House Subcomm. on Dept. of Defense Appropriations, 81st Cong., 2d Sess., 26 Jan. 50, Part 2, 695.
9. Lt. Gen. R. A. Wheeler, Maj. Gen. G. J. Richards, and Brig. Gen. J. S.

Bragdon, Hearings before House Subcomm. on Appropriations, 24 May 46, 776.

10. *G-4 Review of the Month,* 1 Apr. 50.

11. Tansey, "Activities of the Supply Group," *The Quartermaster Review* vol. no. (Mar-Apr 1950): 26.

12. *Annual Report of the Secretary of the Army,* 1948, 106.

13. *G-4 Review of the Month,* 30 Sept. 48, 3.

14. Interview with Lt. Col. R. F. Toomey, Chief, Family Housing Sec., G-4, 21 Aug. 52.

15. Amendment to the National Housing Act, P L 211, 81st Cong., approved Aug. 8, 1949, 63 U.S. Stat 571; *G-4 Review of the Month,* 1 Aug. 49, 1, 1 Sept. 49, 1, 1 Feb. 50, 1; Bradshaw, "Functions of the Service Group," 11-12; *Annual Report of the Secretary of the Army,* 1949, 159.

16. Final Report and Recommendations, D/D Housing Comm, 15 Jan. 51, 14-16, 30-33.

17. Ibid.

18. Ibid., 15, 32; P L 498, 81st Cong.; Memo, Louis Johnson, for Chairman, D/D Housing Comm, 13 Oct. 49, sub.: Mission, copy in Appendix 2, Table 1 of Final Rpt. and Recommendations, D/D Housing Comm.; Summary of verbatim Rpt. of Meeting of D/D Housing commission and Representatives of the Services, 26 Oct. 50, mimeographed copy in Appendix 1, Table 1, Final Rpt. and Recommendations, D/D Housing Comm.; *G-4 Review of the Month,* 1 Dec. 49, 1; *G-4 Report of Major Actions,* G-4/Bl 45384, 31 Aug. 50, 1.

19. "German Underground Installations," from Rpt. prepared for the Secy. of the Army, "Foreign Logistical Organizations and Methods," in *Military Review* 28 (June 1948): 56-62; Lt. Col. J. A. Goshorn, QMG, "Should We Go Underground?" *Military Review* 29 (May 1949): 33-43.

20. Progress Report 8, Underground Installations Program, 31 Dec. 48, prep. by the Office of the Chief of Engineers, 10, copy in OCMH; Progress Report 10, Underground Installations Program, 30 June 49, 7; *G-4 Review of the Month,* 31 Aug. 48, A and 1; *G-4 Review of the Month,* 31 Dec. 48, 9.

21. "German Underground Installations," *Militay Review* vol. 28 (June 1948): 62; Progress Report 10, Underground Installations Program, 30 June 49, 8-9.

22. Supply Supplement, Pt. 2 of The Troop Program and Troop List, 1 Aug. 50, 2 copy in OCMH.

23. Supply Supplement, Pt. 2, of the Troop Program and Troop List, 1 Aug. 50, 49; Msg, WAR 88539, G-4 to CINCEUR, 11 Aug. 50; Memo for Record, Lt. Col. Delaney, 10 Aug. 50, sub.: Supplies and Equipment for EUCOM Special Theater Reserve, copy in G-4 Special Files; Ltr, AGAO-S 400 TS (8 Aug. 49), CSGLD/D5, TAG to CinC EUCOM, 9 Aug. 49, sub.: Establishment of a Special Theater Reserve, copy in G-4 Special Files; Interview with John M. Ritchie, Stock Management Sec., G-4, 25 Aug. 52; Msg, WARX 93480, Dir. Log. Div. to COMGENUSFA, 26 Aug. 49; Change 2, 20 May 49, to the Supply Supplement, Pt 3 of the Troop Program, 1 Feb. 49, 49; DF G4/D5-2794 (SF), G-4, to CofEngrs, CofT, CofCmlC, CSigO, CofOrd, TQMG, TSG, Ch, Oversea Supply Div., Army Base, Brooklyn, N Y, sub.: Emergency Requisitions for EUCOM, Hectographed copy in G-4 Special Files.

24. Supply Supplement to U.S. Army Troop Program, Appendix (C 1, 26 Sept. 49) and also 1 Aug. 50, 85.

25. *Annual Report of the Under Secretary of War,* FY 1946, 1, 27-28; G-4 Historical Summary G4/B1 11218 (SF), 13 Dec. 51, Procurement Div., Industrial Facilities, copy in OCMH.

26. *Annual Report of the Secretary of the Army,* 1948, 200-01; *First Report of the Secretary of Defense,* 1948, Appendix B. Rpt. of Munitions Bd., 99; *Semiannual Re-*

port of the Secretary of Defense, Jan–Jun 1950, 41; *Second Annual Report to the Congress on the National Industrial Reserve, Munitions Board,* 1 Apr. 50, 1–10, copy in OCMH; D/A Industrial Facilities Including Permanent Arsenal System, Standby Installations, National Industrial Plant Reserve (NSC), as of 30 June 52, copy in OCMH; Status of Industrial Facilities (DIPR, NIPR and Privately Owned), Activation, Construction, and Conversion Status Accomplished with Expediting Funds, 30 Apr. 52, copy in Production Control Sec., G–4; Interview with David Christy, Production Br., G–4, 25 Aug. 52.

27. *Second Report of the Secretary of Defense,* 1949, 74; *Annual Report of the Secretary of the Army,* 1948, 201; *Second Annual Report to the Congress on the National Industrial Reserve, Munitions Board,* 1 Apr. 50, 137–44; *Semiannual Report of the Secretary of Defense,* Jan–Jun 1950, 41.

28. G–4 Historical Summary G4/B1 11218–SF, 13 Dec. 51, Procurement Div., Industrial Equipment, in OCMH; *Annual Report of the Secretary of the Army,* 1948, 204; *First Report of the Secretary of Defense,* 1948, 100; *Second Annual Report to the Congress on the National Industrial Reserve, Munitions Board,* 1 Apr. 50, 11–16.

29. *Annual Report of the Secretary of the Army,* FY 1949, 168; Interview with C. A. Rockwood, Industrial Facilities Sec., G–4, 25 Aug. 52; *Annual Report of the Secretary of the Army,* 1948, 204; *Semiannual Report of the Secretary of Defense,* Jan–Jun 1950, 41; *Logistical Operations Summary,* 1 June 50, 22; *Logistical Operations Summary,* 1 July 50, 24; G–4 Historical Summary G4/B1 11218–SF, 13 Dec. 51, Procurement Div., Industrial Equipment, 2.

30. A. B. Quinton, "Stockpiling for National Preparedness," *The Military Engineer* 11 (May–Jun 1950): 173–75.

31. Elmer Pehrson, Chief of Econ. and Stat. Div., Bureau of Mines, lecture before ICAF, 15 Sept. 49, sub.: "Mineral Resources of the World," ECAF pub L50–15, copy in OCMH; Elmer Pehrson, "Problems of US Mineral Supply," *Annals of the American Academy of Political and Social Science,* 278 (Nov 1951): 169–71; Richard H. Hippelheuser, "Our Phantom War Stockpiles," *Nation's Business,* 36 (Dec 1948): 42.

32. Strategic and Critical materials Storage Manual, The Munitions Board, May 1948, 1; *Strategic and Critical Materials Stock Piling Act,* (approved 23 July 46), P L 520, 79th Cong., 2d Sess.

33. Hippelheuser, "Our Phantom War Stockpiles," *Nation's Business,* 42; Readiness for Mobilization, NSRB, 127–133.

34. Elmer Pehrson, "Mineral Resources of the World," Transcript of lecture, 16.

35. Maj. Gen. A. B. Quinton, "Stockpiling—It May Save Our Skins," *Armed Forces Chemical Journal,* 3 (Jan 1950): 20.

36. Pehrson, "Mineral Resources of the World," Transcript of lecture, 12.

37. P L 520, 79th Cong.

38. SR 320–5–1, Dictionary of US Army Terms, Aug. 1950, 64, 226.

39. Quinton, "Stockpiling—It May Save Our Skins!" *Armed Forces Chemical Journal,* 20–22; *Stockpile Report to the Congress, the Munitions Board,* 23 Jan. 51, 34; Maj. Gen. Sidney P. Spalding, "Stockpiling: A National Defense Assurance," *Armored Cavalry Journal,* 56 (Sept–Oct 1947): 3.

40. Pehrson, "Mineral Resources of the World," Transcript of lecture, 8.

41. *Stockpile Report to the Congress, The Munitions Board,* 23 Jan. 51, 30; *Annual Report of the Secretary of the Army,* 1948, 100.

42. *Annual Report of the Chief, National Guard Bureau, Fiscal Year ending 30 Jun 49,* 37; SR 130–400–1, 17 May 49, par 7–8.

43. SR 130–420–1, Supply and Accounting Procedures for the National Guard, 21 Nov. 49, par 6; Interview with Col. Dean E. Coonley, Adjutant General of District of Columbia, (formerly Chief, Reserve Components Br., G–4), 3 Sept. 52; Interview

with Col. R. W. Meals, Chief, Logistics Branch, National Guard Bureau, 4 Sept. 52.

44. SR 130–400–1, Logistical Support Policies for the National Guard, 19 May 49, par 6.

45. SR 130–420–1, 21 Nov. 49, par 39.

46. SR 130–420–1, Supply and Accounting Procedures for the National Guard, 21 Nov. 49, par 4.

47. Change 2, 20 May 49, to Supply Supplement, Pt. 3 of The Troop Program, 1 Feb. 49, par 40–42.

48. SR 140–420–1, 18 May 1949, par 2; Interview with Col. Dean E. Coonley, 3 Sept. 52.

49. Change 2, 20 May 49, to Supply Supplement, Part 3 of The Troop Program, 1 Feb. 49, pp 35–36.

50. AR 145–20, 11 Oct. 48, Reserve Officers' Training Corps Supply and Equipment, par 1–9; SR 145–420–10, 13 May 49, ROTC, Requisitioning and Distribution of Quartermaster Items for ROTC Institutions; SR 145–425–5, 20 July 50, Civilian Components Droppage of Allowances for Items of Non-Expendable Property Issued to ROTC, par 1.

51. P L 413, 80th Cong., 2d Sess., sec. 2c, quoted in John Perry Miller, *Pricing of Military Procurements* (New Heaven, 1949), 227–28.

52. Miller, *Pricing of Military Procurements*, 228–29.

53. Statement of Gen. E. S. Hughes, 14 Mar. 47, Hearings before House Subcommittee on Appropriations, 80th Cong., 1st Sess., 941, 967.

54. P L 267, 80th Cong., 1st Sess. (61 U.S. Stat.), 562.

55. Statement of Maj. Gen. T. B. Larkin, QMG, 26 June 47, Hearings before Senate Subcommittee on Appropriations, H R 3678, 80th Cong., 1st Sess., 160–64.

56. P L 267, 80th Cong., 1st Sess., 30 July 47 (61 U.S. Stat.), 558.

57. Testimony of Gen. Omar N. Bradley, CofS, 29 Mar. 48, Hearings before the House Subcommittee on Appropriations on the Military Functions, National Mil. Est. Appropriation Bill for 1949, 80th Cong., 2d sess., 12.

4

Rebuilding Forces in Europe and North Africa

The maintenance of relatively large forces overseas on a more of less permanent basis was a new role for the U.S. army after World War II. Overseas garrisons had been growing in importance for the United States since the turn of the century, but until World War II they had been confined generally to possessions of the United States in the Pacific, Alaska, and the Canal Zone, and to a few countries where the United States had special interests— and to the short-lived occupation of the Rhineland after World War I. What had begun primarily as occupation missions in the Far East and Europe gave way to a concern for security against communist aggression. This concern led to the extension of alliances, the material build-up of friendly powers, and the maintenance of American military advisory groups or missions in many of the countries of the noncommunist world. In 1948 about half the army was overseas, but the earlier cutbacks in military strength left even that force hard put to carry out necessary duties of occupation in maintaining law and order and making military government effective, much less to gird itself fof defense against possible aggression from outside the occupied countries. Moreover, the support and maintenance of those forces abroad consumed a large part of the energies of troops remaining within the continental United States.[1]

The Berlin Blockade

On 5 March 1948 General Lucius D. Clay, commander in chief of the European Command and military governor of Germany, cabled a message to Lt. Gen. Stephen J. Chamberlin, Director of Intelligence (G–2), Army General Staff:

> For many months, based on logical analysis, I have felt and held that war was unlikely for at least ten years. Within the last few weeks, I have felt a subtle change in Soviet attitude which I cannot define but which now gives me a feeling that it may come with dramatic suddenness. I cannot support this change in my own thinking with any data or outward evidence in relationships other than to describe it as a feeling of a new tenseness in every Soviet individual with whom we have official relations. I am unable to sub-

mit any official report in the absence of supporting data but my feeling is real.[2]

The shock waves that this message sent through the Pentagon, the State Department, and the White House received further impetus by Soviet actions later that month. On 20 March the Soviet delegation walked out of the Allied Control Council meeting in Berlin. On 31 March the Soviet Deputy Military Governor for Germany notified Clay's headquarters that beginning 1 April new and more stringent regulations, including on-board inspection by Russian soldiers, would be applied to traffic between Western and Soviet zones of occupation. When Clay sent railway trains into the Soviet zone to test their resolve, the Soviets, in control of the signals and switching, turned the trains aside. Then, with the support of his political adviser, Robert Murphy, Clay proposed to send a truck convoy with armored escort down the autobahn. But leaders in Washington, perhaps overly influenced by Clay's message of 5 March, had cold feet on this one.

At the same time they raised the question of the evacuation of the one thousand dependents of American servicemen from Berlin. Even though this might ease the logistic problem of supplying American forces in Berlin, Clay resisted on the ground that evacuation might cause war hysteria in Berlin and Western Europe. He said that the forces and their families could be supplied indefinitely with a small airlift. While no written agreements guaranteed access by surface transit, though such had been given orally and surely were implied by the occupation itself, there was a precise written agreement on the air corridor.

Clay began a small-scale airlift on 2 April. Almost immediately the Soviets began to ease their restrictions. After eleven days of this airlift the Soviet authorities rescinded their inspection order, and military supply by rail, subject only to the normal inspection of shipping documents, could be resumed.[3]

But this was only the prelude. During the next several weeks Soviet officials renewed and extended various kinds of interference. On 23 June the Western powers announced plans for currency reform in their zones. On 24 June the Russians stopped all rail shipments—civilian as well as military—to Berlin. On 25 June the Western Powers began issuing their new currency and the Russians announced that they would not supply food to the German population of the western sectors of Berlin. Extended to autobahn and canals as well as railways, the blockade was complete. A logistic problem of major proportions loomed.

Already the president had made it clear to Secretary of Defense Forrestal that the policy would remain fixed: to stay in Berlin. A meeting of State Department and military officials at the Pentagon on Sunday afternoon, 27 June, upheld this view. On the same day Lt. Gen. Curtis E. LeMay, commander of the United States Air Forces in Europe, was meeting with General Clay in Berlin to discuss plans for an extended airlift. At first a number of advisers and the Joint Chiefs of Staff, including the Air Force Chief of Staff, were cool toward the idea of a major airlift—an idea first proposed by Lt. Gen. Albert Wedemeyer, veteran of the China Theater in World War II. They feared putting too many air transport eggs in one basket. But General LeMay saw it as a personal challenge. The day after his conference with General Clay, and with the approval of Washington, LeMay announced that he was going to send air freight to Berlin at maximum capacity, twenty-four hours a day, seven days a week, on a wartime basis, with no holidays. Four squadrons of C–54 transport planes were on the way to Germany and were due to arrive about 5 July.[4] Meanwhile, the debate over Clay's proposal to send an armed convoy down the autobahn continued until 20 July. Then President Truman bowed to the opposition of the Joint Chiefs of Staff and decided against it.[5]

Already the airlift for the supply of military forces in Berlin had begun on 21 June. The experience of the airlift in April had permitted planning for rapid action. Tonnage jumped from 5.88 tons, in three C–47 planes, on 21 June, to 156.42 tons in sixty-four planes on 24 June. But the supply of the civilian population of western Berlin was something else. Headquarters of the European Command first learned of such a project on 26 June, and the first civilian supplies went into Tempelhof Airfield, Berlin, on 28 June. This called for hasty planning and improvisation.[6]

The maximum air effort needed to carry out these missions of civilian as well as military supply called for essential support from army logistic agencies of the European Command. It was up to them to furnish necessary trucks and to keep them in repair, to provide quarters for the air crews, to expand the air terminal facilities, to provide communications, to bring in gasoline. They had to deliver to the airports the supplies destined for the military forces in Berlin, to receive them at the Berlin end, and to distribute them to the Berlin garrisons. In the beginning of the civil supply program—which became known as "Operation VITTLES"—the army forces had the responsibility for finding the supplies and getting them to and from the airplanes. Later (28 July) the Bipartite Control Office took over responsibility for getting the German food to the airports. Then civilian agencies of military government and of the German local governments handled the procurement, storage, financing, and movement to the airfields of the civilian supplies. But the army had to continue important logistical activities in order to keep the airlift going.[7]

The EUCOM Transportation Division set up and maintained traffic control points at the two air bases in the U.S. zone, Rhein-Main and Weisbaden. The post transportation officer in Berlin set up a transportation corps airhead at Tempelhof to exercise traffic control there. By the end of 1948 six heavy truck companies of the transportation corps were assigned to Operation VITTLES. Army engineers went to work to expand the airfield facilities at Berlin, to improve those at Rhein-Main and Weisbaden, and to construct quarters for the additional air crews being brought into the Frankfurt area. Expansion of airfield facilities at Berlin included the building of two new runways at Tempelhof and the construction of the Tegel Air Base in the French sector. These projects themselves required air shipments (by December 1948) of 5,562 tons of asphalt, 3,300 tons of pierced plank, 671 tons of heavy construction equipment, and 505 tons of general engineer supplies and spare parts. Ordnance support for the airlift involved special problems of vehicle maintenance both in Berlin and in the U.S. zone. As of November 1948 the 1,182 ordnance vehicles being used for Operation VITTLES were requiring 118 rebuilt vehicles, 732 rebuilt tires, and 659 tons of spare parts and supplies a month above what had been normal. Signal corps troops had to expand communications facilities and maintain the signal corps equipment used by the air force. Quartermaster units provided subsistence and individual clothing and equipment for the men assigned to the airlift, and the gasoline and oil for the airplanes as well as for the trucks.[8] In April 1949 aviation gasoline requirements reached a peak of 15,604,800 gallons for the month. It took three ocean-going tankers and 1,500 rail tank cars a month to get the gasoline to the air bases.[9]

Through the winter the Berlin airlift continued—carrying food, clothing, coal, raw materials, and medicines to the two and a half million people of the western sectors of Berlin. By the spring of 1949 the American and British allies had reached an average daily air delivery rate of eight thousand tons. On the record day (16 April 1949) they delivered nearly thirteen thousand tons—more than was being brought into Berlin by rail and water before the imposition of the blockade. The results suggested that the air supply operation might go on indefinitely, and American leaders seemed determined to do just that if it were necessary. At last on 4 May 1949 the western allies arrived at an agreement with the Russians for lifting the blockade, and on 12 May all transport, trade, and communication services between the eastern and western zones of Germany were restored. Nevertheless the airlift continued in operation in order to build up a reserve against a possible renewal of restrictions. It was gradually reduced in scope until the last load was flown from Rhein-Main to Tempelhof on 30 September 1949.[10]

From a logistic standpoint the airlift was a resounding and spectacular success. But while American leaders in Washington were congratulating themselves on this demonstration of American resourcefulness and determination, others harbored doubts. The United States, instead of meeting the Soviet challenge head on, had chosen to jump over it. After contemplating on the matter for sixteen years, Robert Murphy still thought that was a mistake. In fact, at the time he even considered resigning from his post in order to dramatize his dissent from a decision that he thought betrayed a weakness. Indeed, he gave it as his opinion that the American failure to take a firmer stand on Berlin probably contributed to the willingness of the North Koreans to invade South Korea in 1950.[11]

Ironically, General Clay may have contributed to his own undoing on the proposal by his alarming message of 5 March 1948. It turned out that this message was the result neither of the General's prescience nor of a critical analysis of the situation, but was more than anything else simply a contribution to the army's efforts for increased congressional appropriations and support for universal military training. It stood in sharp contrast to Clay's earlier and later estimates of the Soviets' unlikely resort to war.[12]

European Lines of Communication

Forces stationed in Europe, whatever their size and purpose, had to be assured supply lines that would provide them with the food, clothing, and equipment necessary for their existence and for the performance of their mission. That mission in the beginning, of course, was conceived to be one of occupation and military government in Germany. In those circumstances the setting up of a line of communications was principally a problem of administration to be worked out in the way that would be most economical and efficient. Little thought, supposedly, had to be given to tactical considerations in the disposition of troops and the facilities of the supply line serving them. But as soon as the military problem in Europe was seen more as one of meeting threats of new aggression from the east than one of controlling the Germans, it was necessary to revise thinking on matters of delivering supplies. Now thought had to be given to the continuation of effective supply in the event of a renewal of war in Europe.

In order to provide port facilities for civil and military needs in the American occupation zone of Germany after the conclusion of World War II hostilities, the United States arranged for an enclave including Bremen and Bremerhaven to be set aside under American control, and for goods to move from those ports southward across the British Zone to Hesse. Bremerhaven became the military port serving American occupation forces. The line of communications connecting Bremerhaven with American installations in southwest Germany ran through Bremen-Hanover-Kassel to Frankfurt. From Frankfurt one line branched southwestward to Wurzburg and Nuremberg, while another continued southward through Mannheim to Karlsruhe and then turned to the southwest to Stuttgart, Augsburg, and Munich. Running generally north and south as it did, this line of communications was parallel to the boundary of the Soviet zone, and thus it lay athwart the route of advance of any major attack from East Germany. At Kassel this line of communications was within twenty miles of Soviet-occupied Thuringia. No defensible barrier protected it against possible attack from the east.[13]

For purposes of the occupation this seemed a logical and satisfactory arrangement. The United States did not have to depend upon the port and transportation facilities of any other country, and the costs involved were borne by German mark funds provided under the occupation statutes. Then the coup in Czechoslovakia and the Russian blockade of Berlin in 1948 opened the eyes of everyone concerned to the reality of the danger of a communist attack. If this needed further emphasis, the communist attack in Korea provided it. With complete dependence on the Bremerhaven line of communications—schedules in 1951 called for the unloading of an average of 79,000 long tons a month, and a peak of 100,000 long tons a month by the Bremerhaven Port of Embarkation—commanders had visions of the whole American army in Germany being imperiled by a sudden thrust of communist forces across their supply route. Now security had to supersede economy and convenience in logistic thinking, and friends had to be called upon to make other facilities available.[14]

Under the stimulus of the Berlin blockade, the Logistics Division of the European Command in 1948 and early in 1949 set about investigating the possible establishment of a line of communications across France. In November 1949 the Joint Chiefs of Staff approved such a move, and straightaway the European Command appointed a team to survey the proposed route and to meet with French military representatives to determine what installations, facilities, and services would be required.[15]

There remained the matter of concluding an agreement with the French government. This introduced a situation almost without precedent in recent international military affairs: negotiations for the army of one nation to set up a complete line of communications across the territory of another fully sovereign, friendly state in peacetime. It was to be expected that the strong communist elements in France would exploit the novelty fully in order to show that the United States was establishing military bases in France in preparation for war and in violation of French sovereignty. For this reason it was essential that the negotiations proceed most carefully and diplomatically. Both sides were anxious to avoid political repercussions in France, to limit the inflationary pressures resulting from large-scale local spending that might dislocate elements of the French economy, and to discourage situations that might lead to ill feeling and clashes between the local civilian population and the troops that soon would be arriving. In addition the U.S. army was anxious for the French to assume a major share of the costs of the line of communications.[16]

Eleven months after the first military discussions on the subject, and five months after the opening of diplomatic negotiations, Ambassador David Bruce of the United States and Alexandre Parodi, secretary-general of the French Ministry of Foreign Affairs, on 6 November 1950 signed the agreement on the line of communications. The basic agreement provided very simply that a line of communications would be established from the La Pallice-Bordeaux area to the German frontier over which the principal means of movement would be by railways. Procedures for the establishment and operation of the line of communications were to be worked out by the military authorities of the two countries. The agreement was to remain in effect for five years, and then would be renewed automatically unless terminated by six months advance notice by one of the parties.[17]

Rebuilding Forces in Europe and North Africa

The increase in American logistic activities in France after 1949 made necessary some revisions in the army's own administrative organization in that area. While carrying out its mission since the end of World War II, the American Graves Registration Command, European Area (AGRC–EA), with headquarters in Paris, had served as the agent of the European Command in France in carrying out various administrative and logistical functions not related to its primary mission. With the practical completion of its mission by late 1949, and the turnover of cemeteries in France to the American Battle Monuments Commission, the American Graves Registration Command prepared for phase-out and deactivation. But some organization would be needed to fill the void thus created at the time when plans were going forward for activating installations for a line of communications across France. In December 1950 Headquarters 7966 EUCOM Detachment moved from the Astoria Hotel in Paris to the Caserne Coligny in Orleans where it would be in a better position to control activities along the line of communications. Meanwhile two area commands, one designed to act as a base section headquarters and the other as an advance section headquarters, had been organized under the detachment headquarters in Paris. Now the 7964 Area Command moved to La Rochelle to control American military port activities in the Bordeaux-La Rochelle area, and the 7965 Area Command moved its headquarters to

U.S. Communication Zone headquarters, Orleans, France.

Verdun to exercise control over the forward storage area. Special detachments remained at Paris, Fontainebleau, and Cherbourg to carry out specific missions of the 7966 EUCOM Detachment.[18]

With the setting up of the two area commands, the reorganization of its staff, and the expansion of its mission, the 7966 EUCOM Detachment clearly was assuming the form of a communications zone organization. But fearful of the local political reaction on the part of extreme nationalists and communists to anything that could be interpreted as the setting up of a territorial military administration that might impinge on French sovereignty, American military leaders avoided the term "communications zone" until the agreement for establishing the line of communications had been signed by the French government. On 15 July 1951 the European Command Communications Zone became operative. The headquarters of the 7966 EUCOM Detachment became the headquarters of the communications zone, still at Orleans; the 7964 Area Command became the base section, EUCOM COMZ, with headquarters remaining at La Rochelle, and the 7965 Area Command became advance section, with headquarters still at Verdun.[19]

By a somewhat peculiar arrangement, depots and certain other installations in the communications zone passed from the control of the commanding general, communications zone, to the heads of the European Command Technical Services, and then back again to communications zone according to their state of readiness under a phased program of development.[20] By the end of 1951 thirty depots and subdepots had been transferred to the command of European Command technical service chiefs. Seventeen of these, including three quartermaster depots, two subdepots, and twelve POL subdepots (nine of which were in French Army installations), came under the chief quartermaster. In addition seven ordnance depots, including the 34,000-acre ammunition depot at Captieux,[21] and the engineer rebuild plant at Bordeaux, two signal depots, two chemical depots, one medical depot, and one transportation depot became temporary class 2 installations about the same time. By early 1953 depots in France, for most purposes, had reverted to class 1 status.[22]

In line with the thinking that underlay the establishment of communications across France, it was necessary to reorient logistic support facilities in Germany. Now that tactical considerations had superseded the occupation mission in Germany, and dependence upon the Bremerhaven line of communications was being minimized, it seemed prudent to move all these installations west of the Rhine where they could be disposed to receive supplies being shipped across France, and where they might find a measure of protection against attack from the east. But all German territory west of the Rhine was in the French zone of occupation (except for the North Rhineland, which was in the British zone). At the same time allied planners considered that it would be well to assign to the French responsibility for defending a portion of the battle line if and when an attack should come. This led to the consideration of an exchange of territory by redrawing the boundaries of the occupation zones. But French Foreign Minister Robert Schuman suggested that the objective might be achieved more simply by agreeing to exchange certain facilities and to permit troops to be located without regard to zonal boundaries, while retaining those boundaries for the purpose of administrative responsibilities. This was agreeable to both the British and the Americans. Specific arrangements depended upon further agreements that had to be worked out to cover questions of jurisdiction of forces, a revision of budgetary procedures so that one nation could account for the costs of its forces in more than one zone, the acquisition of real estate in various zones, procedures for hiring local labor, local procurement for the forces of one nation in the zone of another, improvement of uniform transportation regulations, and responsibilities for occupation damages. American and French high commissioners and military commanders on 2 March 1951 signed an agreement on an exchange of facilities and a transfer of troops between the two zones of occupation. The relocation program called for the complete phase-out of engineers, medical, and signal, most ordnance, and a major part of quartermaster depot activities in the area over the next two years.

The peace treaty with Italy that became effective 15 September 1947 provided that all occupation forces should be withdrawn from that country within ninety days. The last ship carrying American troops sailed from Leghorn on 14 December.[23] In Italy therefore no American troops remained who could accept logistic missions for forces now being disposed to meet the threat of attack. As in France, it was necessary to make new agreements so that troops could return and installations be set up to carry out a decision for establishing a line of communications. In this case it would be for the purpose of supplying current needs for U.S. forces in Austria, and emergency stockpiles for the support of war plans of forces in Trieste as well as those in Austria. The whole operation came under the control of U.S. forces in Austria. The line of communications would extend from the port of Leghorn on the Liqurian Sea northeastward some three hundred miles through Verona to the Austrian border, and thence to the Camp Drum Storage Depot at Innsbruck in the French zone of Austria.[24]

This program was but a fraction of the size of the one being undertaken in the establishment of the line of communications across France, but the diplomatic negotiations were even more drawn out. Communist agitators were, if anything, more active in Italy than in France, and the government had to move slowly in accepting new foreign commitments. The American Embassy in Rome began negotiations with the Italian government on 25 September 1950; arrangements were not concluded until nine months later, 29 June 1951. A leak to the press—one that had signs of being a trial balloon to test political opposition to the agreement—late in June created some last-minute problems and further delays when members of the Italian parliament demanded a full discussion of the negotiations, but at last an acceptable arrangement in the form of an exchange of notes between the Italian foreign minister and the American ambassador was concluded.[25]

The arrangement represented a concrete expression of Italian participation in mutual defense, and the Italian government justified it as a measure in fulfillment of general obligations under the North Atlantic Treaty. The arrangement was to continue in effect as long as the North Atlantic Treaty remained in force unless terminated sooner by mutual consent.

Flexibility was the rule for working out the technical details necessary to making the line of communications effective. Negotiators found it advisable to accept simple and informal Italian forms and procedures where possible instead of urging the acceptance of American or other foreign procedures. The voluminous and detailed railway contract reported by an American officer to have been acceptable to the French railway system, for example, was completely unnecessary with the Italian Railway Administration.[26] Once the line of communications was in operation most of the details appeared to work our smoothly.[27]

U.S. Forces in Europe

COMMAND STRUCTURE

Although success in carrying out missions depended as much on logistics as upon anything else, it was in this realm that the authority of the American commander in chief was most restricted. He had responsibility for coordinating the logistic support for the elements of his command, but he lacked command authority over the logistic elements of the services under his command. He could invite air force and army units to negotiate on the joint use of facilities, but he could not, without appealing to the U.S. Joint Chiefs of Staff, order such joint use. He was expected to make comments and recommendations on all phases of logistics affecting his command, but these had to be approved by the Joint Chiefs of Staff before they could be put into effect. Respective service commanders in a unified command were supposed to operate under the broad policy direction of the commander in chief of the command, but they also were to retain operating details of any logistic support system in accordance with instructions of their respective military departments in Washington.

The vagueness in logistic authority and responsibility in U.S. unified commands overseas reflected a certain vagueness in the Department of Defense and among the service chiefs arising from an inability to resolve differences sufficiently to present clear-cut decisions. As a result diplomacy often had to replace military direction, and *ad hoc* arrangements to meet each difficulty in turn as it arose had to replace reliance on firm policies for logistic control.

If the test of war could not be met, then the whole program of building up American forces in Europe as well as military assistance to European allies could be of little use. A military build-up of any magnitude less than one capable of some significant military contribution in the event of war in the area concerned was worse, because of the false appearances and expense involved, than no military build-up at all. A military force half strong enough to achieve the minimum essential military objective could hardly be of greater value than no military force at all. The value of such a force would be only in in supporting diplomacy to the extent that potential enemies could be led to overrate its real strength. Actually effective forces on the ground, measured against potential build-up, undoubtedly could deter aggression on the part of a power unwilling to take the risk clearly implied.

Nowhere, outside of the United States itself, was the maze of military organization more perplexing than in the European area. Although unified command had become a basic principle with the Joint Chiefs of Staff for overseas areas, that principle had not become sufficiently well established in Europe to bear smoothly the expansion of military forces there under the stimulus of the communist attack in Korea and the accompanying deterioration in international relations generally. Anxious to maintain the independence of their particular forces, some leaders eschewed unity of control and direction in favor of coordination and persuasion. For a time they fought the windmills of separation of powers, but at last gave way to obvious necessity in accepting a concrete reaffirmation of the principle of war to which all gave lip service in the abstract: unity of command.

Succeeding U.S. forces, European theater, which in 1945 had replaced the wartime European theater of operations, the European Command on 15 March 1947 was activated as the unified command over American forces assigned to the occupation of Germany. The staff of European Command, as had been the case in the Far East Command until 1952, was essentially an army staff. U.S. army, Europe, was established on paper, but in the beginning it was not an operating headquarters. Army technical services, ports, and area commands were directly under the commander in chief with no intervening headquarters. The other major commands of European Command were U.S. Air Forces, Europe, U.S. Naval Forces in Germany, and, until 23 May 1949, U.S. Forces in Austria.[28]

With the separation of U.S. Forces in Austria from the European Command in 1949, the latter had become, for all practical purposes, a unified command for western Germany only. This fact became more firmly established when U.S. Air Forces in Europe was established in January 1951 as a separate Joint Chiefs of Staff command on a par with the European Command itself. The twelfth air force replaced the former U.S. Air Forces in Europe as the major air component of European Command.[29] Now no less than six independent commands were operating directly under the Joint Chiefs of Staff in the European area: European Command; U.S. Air Forces in Europe; Naval Forces, Eastern Atlantic and Mediterranean; U.S. Forces in Austria; Trieste U.S. Troops, and the Strategic Air Command. This situation permitted the development of problems of logistics that became intolerable with the expansion of military activities brought about by the build-up to meet what appeared to be growing threats of war after the Korean attack. The tactical structure of the Supreme Headquarters, Allied Powers, Europe, set up under the North Atlantic Treaty Organization was superimposed on this for emergency war plans. This tended to give some unity to tactical planning, but it was of no assistance in solving immediate logistic problems.

As long as the activities of the European Command were restricted to Germany, and as long as support of the occupation remained paramount, the organizational structure worked reasonably well. But when the build-up of military forces and facilities extended to France, serious problems of coordination between European Command and U.S. Air Forces in Europe arose. Problems had to be settled by negotiation between the two commands, referred to Washington, or left unsettled. In the Far East the commander in chief, Far East Command, always had been recognized as the supreme military authority in Japan, and when the Korean conflict broke out, his authority immediately had been extended to Korea. Thus problems of the nature of those appearing in Europe had not been permitted to arise, and experience in the Far East offered little precedent for settling such problems. Little contact was maintained, apparently, between European Command headquarters in Heidelberg and Air Forces headquarters in Weisbaden. If a problem arose upon which the two commands did not immediately agree, the procedure was for each to submit the matter to its respective department in Washington. In the Pentagon an "action officer" of the army general staff and his counterpart on the air force staff would attempt to arrive at a solution that seemed satisfactory to them. Obtaining the approval of their respective chiefs, they would then dispatch similar messages, one from the army chief of staff to the commander in chief, European Command, and another from the air force chief of staff to the commanding general, U.S. Air Forces in Europe. Such a procedure was slow, cumbersome, and given to misunderstandings at a time when close coordination was essential. Some problems remained in stalemate for months or even years. In war this would have been unthinkable.

One pressing problem was the matter of coordinating negotiations, particularly with the French, for rights and facilities. In open competition with each other, and following different standards of value, European Command and Air Force agencies bid for facilities, already scarce, in a way that made for neither economy nor efficiency. In response to State Department appeals for some kind of coordination for all these negotiations, the secretary of defense set up another agency—the Military Facilities negotiating Group—in Paris. This was made up of civilian representatives of the secretaries of each of the military departments with the secretary of the air force designated as executive agent for the secretary of defense. This group provided a single point of contact with the American Embassy in Paris, but it did not resolve the major points of difference between the army and the air force.[30] As a further step the president in January 1952 designated William H. Draper as U.S. special representative in Europe to act for the secretary of defense as well as the secretary of state, the secretary of the treasury, and the director for mutual security in international security matters in that area.[31] Still there was no central military authority for American forces in Europe.

A second major problem was the coordination of construction. On a field inspection trip to Europe in September 1951 the chief of engineers found that the total army and air force construction programs being planned in France for the next three years were considerably greater than the capabilities of the entire French construction industry to handle, but the French opposed the bringing in of American contractors and laborers to do the work. It was evident that some instrument was needed to eliminate duplication and competition for labor and materials in the Army and Air Force programs. Since there was no such authority in Europe, and the respective service views could not be reconciled by negotiation, this problem too had to be referred to the Pentagon, where it lay unsettled in staff plans offices.[32]

A third problem was that of offshore procurement. Each service was charged legally with its own offshore procurement, and as long as no superior coordinating agency was to be found in Europe, the same competition in bidding and duplication of effort noticeable in other fields continued to prevail in that area.

Yet another unsolved problem was that of the air forces supply system. Until 1951 the army had been providing logistic support in common supply items and services for the air forces in Europe, but air force leaders had indicated a desire to set up their own supply system independent of the army. After the establishment of the U.S. Air Forces in Europe as an independent command this trend became more pronounced. For its part, the army had no objection to being rid of what had come to be a thankless task, and in June 1951 the Department of the Army agreed to an arrangement whereby each service in Europe would be responsible for its own logistic support, except that the army would continue to make bulk distribution of subsistence and gasoline and to operate seaports and land transportation, and local agreements still could be made for one service to provide specifically defined support for the other. This meant that the air force would store in its own depots all items for its own individual and organizational equipment, construction materials and equipment, and ammunition; the air force would perform all levels of maintenance on all of its own equipment, and the air force would provide its own medical service in its own hospitals. This was all right with the army, but not with a Congress which had been sold on unification as a means of eliminating duplication and waste in the military supply systems. In the next year the air force actually was able to accomplish little in acquiring the necessary facilities to put the new system into effect. Meanwhile concern in Congress was growing. Seeing the handwriting on the wall, the secretary of defense in March 1952 suspended the arrangement.[33] In April the House of

Representatives clarified its position by inserting in the Defense Appropriation Bill for 1953 this statement: "No part of the funds herein appropriated shall be used to expand the personnel, facilities or activities of the Department of the Air Force to establish or maintain a separate system for providing such supplies and services as were furnished to the Department of the Air Force by the Department of the Army prior to August 1, 1951."[34]

After the secretary of the army presented the problem again to the secretary of defense, the latter requested the Joint Chiefs of Staff to review the policy. The Joint Chiefs concluded that the legislative restriction would not prevent carrying out the program in Europe as previously agreed upon, and they recommended that this be done. But in September 1952 the secretary of defense issued a directive stating, "No additional independent or expanded supply facilities for common-use standard stock items of supply shall be created without the prior approval of the Secretary of Defense."[35] Plans for the continuation of army support of the air force in Central Europe still met with the disapproval of U.S. Air Forces in Europe.

Attempts to deal with the various unsolved problems in logistic coordination for the European area were bound to lead sooner or later to a realization of the need for a supreme military authority in Europe. At last in July 1952 the Joint Chiefs of Staff took the inevitable step of setting up a true unified command in Europe. Actually the Joint Chiefs of Staff had continued to hold to their original unified command directive of 1947 as an objective, but they had agreed to certain modifications for delaying the carrying out of that objective as noted above. Throughout much of 1949 and 1950 staff studies and planning went on both in the European Command and in the Joint Chiefs of Staff for making the unified command completely operational, but the lack of personnel to form a joint staff, and persisting difference among the services in Europe on certain aspects of the organization prevented the fulfillment of the original plan. Now the problem had grown beyond what originally had been restricted to Germany. Now the major problems of coordination were to be found in France, since the Joint Chiefs of Staff had established U.S. Air Forces in Europe as an independent command. While serving as Supreme Allied Commander in Europe, General Eisenhower in March 1952 had replied to a query from the Joint Chiefs of Staff with a recommendation for a central authority over American military activities in Europe, but he did not go so far as to recommend an over-all unified command. Both the army and the air force had favored a Joint Chiefs of Staff unified command for the whole area of Europe that would coincide with the area of responsibility of the supreme allied commander. The navy, on the other hand, had recommended the retention of the existing Joint Chiefs of Staff commands in Europe, and in the addition of another as a logistic coordinating agency—without the power of decision.[36]

Following the army and air force view, the Joint Chiefs of Staff agreed at the end of June that a unified command should be set up in Europe with

General Ridgway, previously designated as supreme allied commander to replace General Eisenhower, as commander in chief. Some semantic gymnastics were necessary in order to distinguish the new command from the old European Command. The new organization was designated the U.S. European Command, and subordinate to it were the three former Joint Chiefs of Staff "unified" or "specified" commands—European Command, now redesignated as U.S. Army, Europe, with headquarters remaining at Heidelberg; U.S. Air Forces in Europe, with headquarters at Wiesbaden; and U.S. Naval Forces, Eastern Atlantic and Mediterranean, with headquarters in London. Headquarters for U.S. European Command would be at Frankfort, initially, and later would be moved to the Paris area. General Thomas T. Handy, previously commander in chief, European Command, was named deputy commander in chief of the new U.S. European Command with broad authority to exercise actual command on behalf of General Ridgway who still would have to give much of his attention to the allied organization in Europe for which he also was responsible. Insofar as General Ridgway now "wore two hats," as allied commander and as United States commander in Europe, the situation was similar to that in the Far East. But General Ridgway had two distinct staffs, and two separate headquarters to carry out his functions, while the headquarters organization for the United Nations Command in Tokyo was practically identical with that of the Far East Command. In Europe the participation of allied forces of the European powers formed a major part of the total strength allocated to the supreme allied commander. A further difference in the American military organization in Europe was that there the commander in chief was not also the commander, in his own name, of the army forces, as was the commander in chief, Far East. The commander of U.S. Army, Europe (CINCUSAREUR) under the new set-up was Lt. Gen. Manton S. Eddy who previously had been commander of the Seventh Army. General Ridgway notified the Joint Chiefs of Staff that he would be prepared to assume command of the new organization on 1 August 1952. The Joint Chiefs instructed the commanders of the old European Command, U.S. Air Forces in Europe, and U.S. Naval Forces, Eastern Atlantic and Mediterranean, to report to him on that date.[37]

The principal mission of the U.S. European Command was to support the supreme allied commander and to coordinate planning for the participation of American forces in emergency actions; to coordinate United States military matters of a logistic or administrative nature of joint interest, including construction, negotiations for base rights, and offshore and local procurement, and to administer the military aspects of the Mutual Security Program. Where appropriate, these activities were to be coordinated with the U.S. special representative in Europe. The U.S. commander in chief, Europe, had command over American commands and military agencies within the area of the supreme allied commander's responsibility, including Continental Europe, the British Isles, North Africa, and Turkey, but excepting, at first, American forces in Berlin, Austria, Trieste, and Yugoslavia. Thus General Ridgway's territorial jurisdiction as an allied and as a United States commander practically were coextensive. The three former unified commands continued as Joint Chiefs of Staff specified commands for activities outside the area of U.S. European Command. This included U.S. Army, Europe, as a specified command charged with the mission in Berlin. Modifications in the original instructions in December 1952 extended the authority of the U.S. commander in chief, Europe, to include American forces in Berlin, Austria, and Trieste. Previously U.S. Forces in Austria, after the separation from the old European Command in 1949, and Trieste, U.S. Troops had been reporting directly to the chief of staff of the army. Those headquarters continued to report directly to Washington on matters of occupation policy, but their forces now were a part of the overall U.S. European Command. Thus at the end of 1952 the area of responsibility of the U.S. commander in chief, Europe, included Norway, Denmark, Western Germany, Berlin, Belgium, Luxembourg, the Netherlands, France, the French departments of Algeria, Italy, Austria, Trieste, Greece, Turkey, the United Kingdom, the territorial waters adjacent to all those countries, the Mediterranean Sea, and the Mediterranean islands (excepting the Balearics). In addition USCINCEUR had responsibility for the military aspects of negotiations for base rights and for joint planning in French Morocco, Algeria, Tunisia, and Libya.[38]

What amounted to an "Achilles heel" of unified command in certain situations was the limitation retained on the commander's authority over logistics. All of the strategic and tactical skill in the world could not overcome fundamental failures in logistic coordination. The problems that had induced the Joint Chiefs of Staff to set up an overall European Command were primarily logistical. But General Ridgway soon found that reorganization itself was not enough to resolve those problems unless authority went along with it. In October 1952 he wrote to the Joint Chiefs of Staff that the authority delegated to USCINCEUR was "inadequate to his logistical responsibilities." The European commander said further:

> In short, his (USCINCEUR's) authority in the logistical field does not provide "command authority" but merely authority to "coordinate." In JAAF (Joint Action Armed Forces) it is precisely stated what is meant by "coordination," which is essentially persuasion. If persuasion fails to produce agreement between the services, then by JAAF the matter must be referred to Washington for decision. I feel that this procedure is inefficient and that power of decision must rest with CINCEUR.[39]

The result was a far-reaching decision on the part of the Joint Chiefs of Staff to grant to the commander in chief in Europe directive authority in the field of logistics. This did not mean that logistic activities in Europe would thereby be consolidated. Individual service responsibilities would remain much the same as before, but in the event of disagreement between the services on matters of joint interest, the commander in chief could settle the matter without having to refer it to Washington. At the same time the Joint Chiefs of Staff, again following Ridgway's recommendations, instructed the commander in chief in Europe that headquarters of U.S. European Command would perform directly the functions of a joint communication zone headquarters without setting up any intervening headquarters for those functions. One special joint agency would be established—a joint construction agency. In adopting these measures for strengthening the position of the commander in chief, Europe, in logistics, the Joint Chiefs of Staff made it clear that their recommendations were not necessarily applicable to unified commands in general. Similar problems in other areas would have to be handled specifically as they arose.[40]

At the time of this Joint Chiefs of Staff decision, the question of providing logistic support for the air force in Europe still was hanging fire. Earlier in the year, the secretary of defense had suspended plans for setting up a separate air force supply system in Europe. In November 1952 Ridgway proposed to the Joint Chiefs of Staff that U.S. European Command arrange for providing common use supplies and maintenance in the areas of France, Germany, and the BENELUX (Belgium, Netherlands, Luxembourg) countries. The army would continue to be responsible for all such supplies except for quartermaster items already stocked by the air force, ammunition, and certain signal corps items. U.S. Air Forces in Europe did not agree to that arrangement. But now the Joint Chiefs of Staff could advise Ridgway that he had directive authority to settle this problem. Here the matter would rest until the secretary of defense should rule otherwise.[41]

On matters of construction the commander in chief, Europe, reported to the secretary of the army for the secretary of defense, rather than to the chief of staff of the army for the Joint Chiefs of Staff. Initially set up for practical reasons under U.S. Army, Europe, the Joint Construction Agency as soon as it was feasible was brought directly under U.S. European Command.

Early in 1953 the location of the headquarters of the U.S. European Command was shifted from Frankfurt to the Paris area, a few miles from General Ridgway's other headquarters, Supreme Headquarters, Allied Powers, Europe.[42]

BUILD-UP

Although army commanders had indicated concern about the position of their forces in Germany, apparently the Berlin blockade of 1948–1949 had made no really lasting impression on logistics planners. By the end of 1949 the EUCOM Logistics Division had concluded that current troop strengths in Europe would have to be maintained for another four years. But this was attributable to the fact that the Russians were reported to have exploded an atomic bomb, and to the expectation that it would be January 1954 before other states of the North Atlantic Treaty Organization could approach military self-sufficiency. Demands in Congress for economy were expected to result in some reduction in the overall strength of the armed forces, but it could be assumed that international political and military considerations would require that forces in Europe be maintained at their current strength until 1954. But the EUCOM Logistics Division also accepted a planning assumption that a treaty would be signed with Austria by 1 July 1950, and that U.S. Forces in Austria would be phased out by the following October. The logistics staff in Europe further assumed at this time that U.S. forces in Germany would be reduced after mid-1954 to a strength of about fifty thousand men by 1 July 1956. The communist attack in Korea in June 1950 radically changed those planning assumptions.[43]

Since 1945 most planning for American forces in Europe had emphasized troop reductions and retrenchment. Now the Korean attack at last convinced everyone that forces in Germany no longer were there primarily for occupation purposes, but for the defense of Western Germany and the countries of Western Europe. Germany, like Korea, was a divided country, and what had happened in East Asia also could happen in Central Europe. This was the first indication that communists were willing to resort to force of arms openly in order to gain their objectives. With or without the instigation of their Soviet patrons, forces from East Germany might at any time undertake the violent reunification of the country. Or Soviet leaders leaders might decide that this was the time to bid for domination of Western Europe, and red divisions might strike from Germany. In these circumstances it appeared that the major trend affecting American logistics in Europe during the coming five years would be the strengthening of forces both in terms of manpower and fighting potential, and the relocation of facilities and lines of communication in order to be prepared to stand and fight in a defensive war.[44]

Thus, in the last half of 1950, EUCOM Logistics Division based its plans on an assumption that there would be a gradual increase in strength from the 100,885 (including 17,800 air force and 485 navy) of 1 July 1950 to a total of 105,562 during the next year, and ultimately to 140,962 by July 1955.[45] Actually the Department of Defense soon determined to build up the strength of forces in Europe far beyond this modest increase. Indeed in January 1950, when EUCOM was assuming only the maintenance of current strength, and six months before the Korean attack, the Department of the Army was already making plans for sending another division to Europe before the end of that year.[46] Even as operations in Korea were generating increasing demands for men and matériel, Department of the Army in September 1950 was expanding its plans for reinforcing the European Command by adding the activation of a regimental combat team in Berlin to the division already planned for shipment from the United States. Personnel for the new combat team would come from units already present, but expedited supply action was necessary to obtain from the United States the additional equipment that would be authorized under the table of organization and equipment. The sixth Infantry Regiment was activated in Berlin on 16 October 1950.[47]

By early 1951, when the situation in the Far East was most critical, plans for reinforcement of the European Command involved sending four divisions. But now a certain amount of opposition to these plans arose in Congress. Objections centered mainly on the right of the president to send forces overseas without consulting Congress. Some congressmen expressed a fear that such action might establish a precedent that would lead to a usurpation on the part of the president of the power of Congress to declare war. For all practical purposes the president, in his conduct of the nation's foreign policy, could involve the country in war anyway. Moreover the precedent of sending units of the armed forces abroad by executive authority had been well established for at least 146 years, since a marine detachment participated in the march on Derne—"on the shores of Tripoli"—in 1804, and it was a policy that had frequently been followed since that time on such occasions as the sending of marines to Sumatra and the Fiji Islands, to Formosa in 1867 to 1870, to Korea in 1871 and 1903, and to several of the republics in the Caribbean area at various times; it involved sending the China Relief Expedition to Tientsen and Peking at the time of the Boxer Rebellion in 1900; Pershing's expedition into Mexico in 1916; the expedition to Siberia in 1918; the sending of marines to Nicaraqua and to Shanghai and Tientsen in 1927; and the action in Korea in 1950. But the Senate Committee on Foreign Relations and the Committee on Armed Services jointly conducted lengthy hearings on the subject throughout the month of February 1951.[48] At the conclusion the committees recommended, and the Senate adopted, a resolution stating:

> The Senate hereby approves the present plans of the President and the Joint Chiefs of Staff to send four additional divisions of ground forces to Western Europe, but it is the sense of the Senate that no ground troops in addition to such four divisions should be sent to Western Europe in implementation of article 3 of the North Atlantic Treaty without further congressional approval.[49]

The Fourth Infantry Division arrived in Germany 27 May 1951, the Second Armored Division arrived 14 July, the Forty-third Infantry Division on 21 October, and the Twenty-eighth Division on 21 November.[50] Together with the First Division, the Sixth Infantry Regiment, three armored cavalry regiments and three armored infantry battalions previously assigned to the constabulary, this brought U.S. combat troop strength in Germany up to the equivalent of over six divisions. This was comparable to the Eighth Army in Korea, which also had six U.S. army divisions and one independent regiment assigned to it. Senate Resolution Ninety-nine of course did not have the force of law, but to an army anxious to maintain amiable relations with Congress, the resolution practically amounted to such. In testimony before the Senate Foreign Relations and Armed Services Committees on 31 July 1951, General J. Lawton Collins, chief of staff, gave the total strength of the army in the European area (including the divisions scheduled to arrive in the fall) as approximately 284,000 men. For all practical purposes this figure then became the troop ceiling for that area, and the army contemplated no further increases without first obtaining congressional approval. Two years later the strength of the army in Europe remained about the same.[51]

The build-up of troop strength in Europe indicated that Europe still was receiving consideration as the area of prime importance in worldwide strategy. Specific reasons underlying the decision to send additional divisions to Europe at that time appeared to be these: (1) By their presence to deter an attack against Western Europe: (2) to defend key areas if attacked; (3) by their presence to encourage resistance on the part of allies.

More than tripling the troop strength of the European Command had important implications for logistics. Not only did it involve equipping the units being sent, but also making available supplies to maintain them and to build up theater stocks for their support.[52] In terms of days of supply, theater stocks were of course automatically reduced by more than two thirds upon the arrival of the reinforcements. And these additional supplies had to be found for Europe when more and more supplies were being required for operations in the Far East. It will be recalled that before the outbreak of hostilities in Korea, the European Command had enjoyed top priority for the supply of troops. By 1 August 1950 Far East Command had been put in a priority classification equal to that of the European Command,[53] and in September forces in Europe had been dropped to a classification below that of the Far East Command.[54]

As in the Far East, one of the principal sources of supply in Europe was the rebuilding of World War II equipment and of equipment currently being turned in as unserviceable. The use of German automobile factories permitted the occupation forces in Germany—which in 1945 had not been able to retain even enough serviceable vehicles to fill table of organization and equipment authorizations—not only to maintain themselves for the next four years without the shipment of any new vehicles from the United States, but to improve the condition of those in use, and to add considerably to the proportion of combat serviceable vehicles in theater reserve. At the same time the rebuilding program gave an important impetus to the German economy by getting idle factories into operation. At first this had to be done with some care in order not to interfere with current plans for dismantling certain German industrial facilities. All were operated by German managers and workers under the supervision of U.S. army technical staffs.[55]

Factories used in the ordnance rebuilding program included the Opel plant at Russelsheim, near Frankfurt, the Mercedes-Benz plant at Stuttgart, the Bayerne Motor Werke near Munich, and smaller plants and shops at Ober

Ursel, Ober Ramstadt, Esslingen, Boeblingen, Kassel, Schwaebish Gmuend, and Butzbach. In the two years between 1 April 1947 and 1 April 1949 these plants turned out nearly thirty-eight thousand rebuilt army vehicles of all types. The vehicles, engines, tools, tires, and parts reclaimed during this period had an estimated original cost of over $110,000,000, and the replacement cost probably would have been twice that. The total cost of rebuilding them was about $5,250,000 for American materials, and the equivalent of about $29,750,000 in German marks for German materials and labor. In addition to thirty-eight thousand vehicles, this included three hundred thousand tires and ninety-three thousand tubes reclaimed in the shop at Ober Ramstadt. A total of fifteen thousand Germans were working in the plants in 1949. The biggest of the rebuilding operations was at the Bayerne Motor Werke, which had become the Karlsfeld Ordnance Center—the largest tank-automotive rebuild shop in the world. Here two-and-a-half-ton trucks as well as engines and transmission assemblies were rebuilt. Built in 1938, the factory had ben turning out six hundred aircraft engines a month for the German air force until it was captured in April 1945. By June 1951 over one hundred thirty-five thousand automobile and truck engines—including forty thousand jeep engines and sixty thousand General Motors truck engines—had come off its production lines for the U.S. army. The plant itself included 273 acres within its grounds, and 243 acres of this space were being used in 1952 for industrial operations and supply storage. Shop space covered 917,225 square feet, and the Germans had provided protection against air attack by building within the plant a huge bunker with roof and walls of reinforced concrete eleven and one-half feet thick. Under the supervision of twenty-five officers and nineteen enlisted men of headquarters and headquarters detachment, Eighty-fourth Ordnance Battalion, and the 7840th Ordnance Depot Detachment, and twenty-six civilians from the Department of the Army, over six thousand Germans and displaced persons were working in the plant in mid-1952.[56]

The Maintenance Division of the Hanau Engineer Depot set up a similar program for the reclamation of engineering equipment. After the rapid return of troops from Europe to the United States in 1945, tons upon tons of engineering equipment that had been left behind began arriving by barge, truck, and rail at the Hanau depot—formerly a German engineer depot—on the Main river. It was more than the 485th Engineer Heavy Shop Company (later the 507th Heavy Shop Company) could cope with. The only thing to do was to try to put Germans to work in German shops to reclaim the unserviceable equipment and junk. The first plant began operating in the fall of 1947, and by the spring of 1949, six were operating. The Daimler-Benz plant near Stuttgart worked on truck-mounted cranes and similar equipment. Tractors were rebuilt in the Maschinenfabrik-Augsburg-Nurnberg plant at Nurnberg—ultimately at the rate of one a day. In Fulda the shop of Karl Schmidt rebuilt about seventy-five generators a month. The Kaeble factory at Backnang, near

Stuttgart, reclaimed road construction machinery. Friescke and Hoepfner in Erlangen-Bruck rebuilt such equipment as engineer trailers and shop equipment. The Henschel and Sohn locomotive factory in Kassel handled large cranes, pumps, and various other items. In mid-1950 these plants each month were rebuilding equipment valued at approximately $1,340,000 for a cost of about $400,000.[57]

With the expansion of forces in Europe, and the increasing anxiety to bring matériel reserves up to authorized levels at the same time that the Far East Command was demanding greater shares of equipment from the United States, it was important to find new sources of supply. By this time most of the surplus property left over from World War II had been disposed of. But it still might be possible to get some of it back. On 21 August 1950 the European Command requested of the Department of the Army authority to reacquire some of the billion dollars' worth of property that had been transferred to the German public corporation organized for the purpose, Staatliche Erfassungsgesellshaft fur offentliches Gut m. b. H. (STEG). This property now was out of the control of the United States after its transfer to the Germans, and the only way any of it could be recaptured legally was by making an arrangement with the German government. The U.S. high commissioner to Germany, at the request of European Command, did make an arrangement for all property remaining in the hands of STEG to be frozen effective 15 September. This was to give representatives of the technical services in Germany an opportunity to survey the fourteen STEG depots to determine what equipment might be available to fulfill needs of the army in Europe. Five weeks later European Command received permission from Department of the Army to reacquire property from STEG with the concurrence of the high commissioner. Under this arrangement the army got back property valued at about $75,000,000, based on original cost to the Army (about $15,000,000 based on cost to STEG).[58]

Meanwhile some things had been happening that officers disposing of surplus property back in 1946–1948 had dreaded most—the resale of disposed property to the army by private dealers. The most serious aspect of this was that some of this property was being reimported into the United States for resale to the army there. In seeking scarce parts and vehicles needed to build up support for the Korean operations, the army had awarded contracts to some low bidders who had obtained these items from STEG. The difficulty was that these specialized military items were not then in production, and it was hard to get them quickly at a reasonable price. Ordnance procurement officers might have come out all right if they could have found the needed equipment locally at even twice the price, but when they sought to save some money by repurchasing equipment that the army had disposed of overseas as surplus, that brought down the wrath of congressional investigators on their heads. On the other hand the army might have saved itself some grief by being more alert to the possibilities of reacquiring matériel directly from

STEG, so that contributions to the profits of third party speculators would not have seemed so necessary. But the timing of the Korean attack was the thing that saved the speculators and cost the army.

The most notorious of these profiteers was one George Dawson, a London used car and junk dealer who previously had been in difficulty because of alleged black market operations during the war and illegal financial transactions before that. In February 1950 Dawson had made a contract with STEG for all of its remaining trucks, cars, half-tracks, and parts. By this time there was little demand for American trucks in Europe, because smaller, more economical European models were again becoming available, and when STEG had a chance to get rid of its remaining stocks, it took it. Dawson organized a company known as Trucks and Spares, and set up offices in the same building with STEG to handle the 18,500 pieces of automotive equipment and miscellaneous spare parts he had acquired. Dawson was acting as the agent of Continental Motors Trust, a company also under his control organized in Lichtenstein, which deposited a $250,000 performance bond on the $3,200,000 purchase price in March and April. In September a new contract assigned to Trucks and Spares, Inc., the rights in the original contract. But then the stock of Trucks and Spares was sold to Continental Motors. Whether or not Dawson's deals would have paid off had there been no Korean War remains problematical. There were indications that he was sending vehicles to Hungary and other countries behind the iron curtain. Then the Korean conflict, with the new demands that created for vehicles in the U.S. army, assured at least some measure of success for his enterprise. The freeze order in October 1950 interfered with Dawson's operations. It made possible the reacquisition of property, including that transferred to Dawson but still physically in STEG depots, by the army, but it invited claims against the army for expropriation of property the title to which had been transferred by STEG to other parties.[59]

Upon completion of the army's survey, the freeze order was lifted. After the European Command had reacquired the property it then needed, approximately $100,000,000 worth at the original cost still remained in STEG depots. Under pressure from Representative Herbert C. Bonner, chairman of a subcommittee of the House Committee on Expenditures in the Executive Departments, Secretary of the Army Pace on 16 March 1951 requested a second freeze on STEG property. Again the high commissioner for Germany relayed the request to the Federal Republic of Germany, and the freeze was made effective the very next day. Certain financial complications resulted, but the army was able to recover another $26,500,000 worth (at original cost, or $5,800,000 at current estimated value) of property. This time the Department of the Army sent technical service survey teams from the United States to see what property might be reacquired for the worldwide needs of the army. About half of the reacquired signal equipment was marked for return to the United States, but the remainder went into European Command stocks—either directly or through the rebuild programs.[60]

The Korean conflict at the same time made the shipment of additional supplies to Europe more urgent but more difficult. The "pull to the Pacific" was especially noticeable in new and special weapons and equipment and in ammunition. While Far East Command in 1950 was receiving what M–46 Patton tanks were available, European Command had to be content with M–26 Pershings. Only after Far East requirements had been met could newer models be shipped to Europe. Since war actually did not come to Europe during the period, this procedure worked out satisfactorily. By September 1952 it could be reported that all armored units of the Seventh Army had been equipped with M–47 tanks. During the same time 90 percent of the Seventh Army's trucks and jeeps had been replaced with new models, and nearly all of its communications and electronic equipment had been replaced. Army aircraft, helicopters and fixed-wing planes as well similarly had to await the fulfillment of requirements in the Far East before units in Europe could obtain them.[61]

Even before reports had been received on the performance of new 3.5-inch rockets in Korea, the European Command on 17 July 1950 put in a request for 2,000 rocket launchers and 480,000 rockets, and asked that 650 of the launchers and 9,100 rounds of ammunition be shipped by air. But all current production then was going to the Far East, and the best that the Department of the Army could do was to send an instruction team to Europe with a few samples to show the troops there how to work the things when they did become available. The first sizeable shipment of rockets for the European Command came in October when 13,100 of the new models went by sea.[62]

A request for an additional 254,000 rounds of ninety-milimeter tank ammunition in November 1950 could be approved because it did not interfere with planned shipments to the Far East. In March 1951 the commander in chief, Europe, requested authority to issue 10,416 rounds of 4.2-inch mortar ammunition from the special reserve in Europe to the units in order to increase their basic loads in this ammunition from 20 rounds to 144 rounds. In this case the Department of the Army approved the request and then moved to divert an equal amount from Far East requirements to make a special issue to EUCOM from current production, so that the reserves could be replenished within a period of sixty to ninety days.

Noting that allowances in antiaircraft and tank and field artillery ammunition were on the whole somewhat less for the European Command than for the Far East Command, while the potential for air and tank operations in Europe appeared to be much greater than in Korea, CINCEUR in March 1952 asked for a substantial increase in the authorized ground ammunition day of supply, which formed the basis for the computation of supply levels and reserve stocks. After Department of the Army G–4 had made a study of the question, General Maxwell Taylor, deputy chief of staff for operations and administration, in October disapproved the request mainly for the simple reason that the ammunition was not available. Still U.S. Army, Europe, insisted that ammunition consumption in the first months of a war would be considerably greater than the rates given in the ground ammunition day of supply. In the spring of 1953 the Department of the Army made allowance for this, not by increasing the ammunition day of supply, but by increasing the authorized level of supply from 60 days to 105 days.[63]

Approved supply levels for the European Command (later U.S. Army, Europe) were virtually the same in days of supply as those for agencies of the Far East Command before the increase in Far East levels authorized in mid-1952—thirty days safety level and thirty days operating level, making a stockage objective of sixty days of supply for most classes of supply. The authorized supply level for bulk petroleum products in Europe was thirty days safety level and fifteen days operating level. Order and shipping time was the same as that allowed for the Far East, 120 days. But there was an important difference in the actual quantities of supplies authorized for Europe and for the Far East. Supply levels in the Far East Command had to be figured on the basis of operational rates. Supplies to support emergency operations in the European theater had to be provided for in special reserves built up as special projects approved by the Department of the Army.[64]

As negotiations proceeded in the summer of 1950 for the establishment of a line of communications across France, G-4 in Washington was making studies relative to the establishment of reserve stockpiles in France and for equipping the combat and service units that would be sent to France immediately after a D-Day in Europe.[65]

Plans for increased stockpiles grew more rapidly than did the storage facilities in France. A phased program that EUCOM Logistics Division issued in February 1951 called for the storage in the first phase of forty-five days of reserve supplies in France for the emergency support of one hundred thousand troops, and of fifteen days of reserve supplies in the French northern zone of Germany for the same force. During the second phase these emergency levels would be increased to sixty days for 259,000 troops—thirty days to be located in the advance section and thirty days in the base section of the communications zone. At the same time thirty days of EUCOM's normal sixty-day stockage objective would be stored in the French northern zone of Germany (the Rhine military post) and the other thirty days would be stored in the base section area in France. Combat serviceable reserves in Germany in excess of those indicated, as well as Mutual Defense Assistance Program supplies, would be moved to France to the extent that space was available. Within two months this program had become obsolete, though it hardly had begun to be fulfilled. The new plans retained the same general objectives without dividing them into phases, and added somewhat to the total amounts of supplies to be stored. These tonnages too were in turn superseded by more ambitious figures. By October 1952 the total operating and reserve stock requirements amounted to more than 1,700,000 tons.[66]

During the first six months of 1951 an average of more than sixty cars of ammunition were unloaded daily at the Captieux depot.[67] Other supplies and equipment of all classes arrived in France both at the ports and by rail from Germany. But the supplies were arriving more quickly than they could be absorbed in the new storage system. A year later depots still were makeshift installations where supplies were being put under cover as much as possible, but where much would have to be restored before it could be issued in an effective way to support an emergency. Roads and shipping facilities as well as storage space still were lacking. This was especially serious at ammunition depots. By the summer of 1952 approximately 40 percent of the required tonnage of supplies had been received in France, but less than 10 percent of the necessary construction had been completed. Shortages of food supplies and gasoline and oil particularly were attributable to the shortage of storage facilities. Lack of storage facilities was perhaps the major reason for shortages in European Command supply reserves in the summer of 1952, but it was not the only reason. Particular shortages also were to be noted in bridging and certain other engineer equipment, in certain types of ammunition (critical shortages of some ammunition would have appeared even more serious if the requested revisions in the ground ammunition day of supply had been granted), and in some medical and chemical supplies. Some of this was due to shortages in the United States and to delays in filling requisitions.[68]

Rapid replenishment of items taken from the special reserves was difficult because of the failure of agencies in the United States to fill requisitions, especially for ordnance and engineer spare parts, within the 120-day order and shipping time. Even before the Korean attack seldom more than 75 percent of ordnance requisition line items, and seldom more than 50 percent of engineer requisition line items were being received within the 120 days order and shipping time. Of 688 engineer line items ordered in December 1949, only about 26 percent had been received within 120 days, and 23 percent still had not been received after nine months. About 75 percent of the quartermaster requisition line items, and nearly all signal items, were being received within 120 days. After the Korean attack, the filling of requisitions for Europe immediately dropped off sharply. Only 41 percent of the 5,742 ordnance requisition line items ordered in May 1950 were received within 120 days.[69]

Shortages in special reserves still were being reported in the spring of 1953, but when the situation was brought to the attention of the G–4 Supply Division in Washington, action followed to get most of the needed items on the way, though certain special types of ammunition were not expected to be available before September and November 1953. Some items included in lists of critical shortages had not been requisitioned—presumably because of the lack of storage facilities for them in France. The situation improved considerably during 1953, but it was still doubtful whether stocks on hand were adequate to fully support American forces should they become involved in hostilities. The lack of facilities in the communications zone still was given as the most critical aspect of the reserve supply problem in Europe. But shortages at home also continued to have some effect.[70]

In May 1951 G–4 undertook a study to determine a way to equip divisions that might be sent to Europe immediately after D-Day. One plan was to wait and ship the units with complete equipment and thirty days maintenance, convoy loaded. The alternative was to prestore equipment and thirty days maintenance along the line of communications in France, and then if hostilities should break out, to send only the personnel, minimum essential equipment (MEE), and individual weapons of the reinforcing divisions. Clearly the second alternative would have great advantages in saving time when that would be most essential. But the whole question turned out to be academic at that time, because no division slice sets of equipment could as yet be made available for storing in France. In September 1952 the chief of staff decided that this plan would have to be put aside as currently infeasible.[71]

Nevertheless the logistic build-up that had already been accomplished in Europe during the Korean conflict indicated the importance the United States attached to the defense of that area. Few things could have been better calculated to attract the support of friends or to discourage the ambitions of foes. The question was whether the build-up could continue at a sufficiently rapid pace to ensure the effectiveness of defense as well as to indicate the determination to attempt it.

U.S. Forces in Austria

After the separation of U.S. Forces in Austria from the European Command in May 1949, European Command continued to be responsible for the logistic support of those forces. Since the American zone of Austria was adjacent to the American zone of Germany it seemed reasonable for logistics facilities in southern Germany to continue to serve the forces in Austria. At meetings in June and July representatives of the two headquarters worked out administrative details of the continuing logistics support. In general these provided for the maintenance of normal stock levels in Austria, for base maintenance support by European Command, and for various equipment status reports, forecasts, or requirements, and approved tables of allowances to be routed through European Command. U.S. Forces in Europe would submit to the Department of the Army directly requests for approval of additional strategic reserves. Strategic reserves then on hand in Austria would be retained in addition to normal stock levels of supplies. There would be no change in the handling of surplus or excess property through European Command.[72]

Early in 1951 U.S. Forces in Austria was able to establish its own line of communications across Italy from Leghorn. When that line of communications became operative, the Department of the Army designated U.S. Forces in Austria as a separate requisitioning agency for submitting requisitions for army supplies direct to the New Orleans Port of Embarkation. This relieved

European Command of its responsibilities for requisitioning, processing, and transshipping these supplies. The European Command continued to be responsible for base maintenance and for hospitalization above station hospital level.[73]

Operations at the Leghorn end of the line of communications came under a logistical command, at first a provisional unit, and then a standard type B organization, the Fourth Logistical Command. After visiting congressmen had suggested that men and money might be saved by eliminating the logistical command as an intermediate headquarters, and then some local difficulties developed, U.S. Forces in Austria G–4 in November 1952 recommended that the logistical command be phased out of operations. Thereafter the Fourth Logistical Command ceased to function as such. It remained as a paper designation, but it was reduced to one officer who was charged with coordinating military sea transportation service shipments. Now the local commands in Leghorn—the Leghorn military post, the USFA general depot, and the ninth medium port reported directly to the technical service chiefs at headquarters in Salzburg.[74] This system apparently worked well enough for the peacetime activities being supported, but it seemed unlikely that that organizational set-up would bear the strain of emergency operations. On the assumption that peacetime should be regarded as normal for the army even in such an exposed position as Austria, economy of operations for the moment had been permitted to take precedence over effective organization for possible emergencies in the future. Presumably one of the reasons that a separate line of communications for forces in Austria had been established was to ensure the continuation of logistic support in the event of an emergency. Now if that line of communications itself was not being prepared to meet such an emergency, there was little reason for its existence. If it could have been assumed that there would be no European war, then it would have been as well to continue the support of forces in Austria through Germany. Indeed, if it could be assumed that there would be no war, there was little reason for keeping any forces in Austria at all.

Extension of communications zone activities in Italy included the opening of a storage point at Verona about midway on the rail line between Leghorn and Innsbruck in the French zone of Austria. In Austria itself the administrative organization comprised three commands—the Tactical Command with headquarters at Salzburg, the Troop Command with headquarters at Hoersching, and the Vienna Command. Local administration was coordinated in the Salzburg, Linz, and Vienna military posts. The depot system as of November 1951 included a storage depot at Innsbruck, a medical depot at Salzburg, signal, quartermaster, and special service depots at Wels, and an engineer depot and an ordnance-chemical depot at Hoersching.[75]

In December 1952 U.S. Forces in Austria came under the operational control of U.S. European Command, but the former continued to operate its own logistics system. At the end of the year U.S. Forces in Austria was making plans for further expanding logistic activities in Italy for the support of a marine air group scheduled for deployment to that area. The logistic support was governed by an agreement worked out by Department of the Army and Department of the Navy and the Marine Corps.[76]

North African Air Bases

At the time of the Berlin blockade in 1948 the Strategic Air Command considered for a time the advisability of returning American air units to bases in Morocco. But fields abandoned in 1945 had deteriorated, and new heavy bombers would require extensive construction before any bases in that area could be made operational for their use. However, this was the period when a new economy drive quickly superseded the modest plans for military expansion that had grown on the series of international crises culminating in the Berlin blockade. Then, after lying dormant for two years, plans for establishing air bases in North Africa quickly leaped to life after the outbreak of hostilities in Korea. The 1950 decision to build air bases in North Africa was a part of the overall program being developed by the Joint Chiefs of Staff for the worldwide security of the United States and as a part of the policy of containing possible Soviet aggression. French Morocco lay within 2,800 miles of the rich Donetz-Dnieper industrial region of the Soviet Union, and its separation from Europe by the Mediterranean Sea made it especially useful for air attacks against an invasion of Europe.[77]

Soon after Congress made available some $22,000,000 for the purpose, a group of air force officers, accompanied by Colonel George T. Derby representing the Corps of Engineers, in October 1950 set out (in civilian clothing) to make a preliminary survey in Morocco. On its return to Washington a few weeks later, the survey mission recommended the expansion of four existing French air force bases (at Meknes, Sale, Khouribga, and Marrakech) and the construction of a new base and depot at Nouasseur, near Casablanca.

Negotiations already proceeding in Paris led to a basic agreement on 22 December under which the United States received permission to go into Morocco to undertake the base development. An American firm was to be the principal contractor, but it was understood that subcontractors in Morocco would be used whenever possible, and materials and services to the extent practicable would be obtained through local procurement. The United States would retain complete control of the base construction, and would assume the entire financial burden, but at the conclusion of the current international emergency, the whole development would be turned over to the French. A French liaison mission would coordinate matters of subcontracting and local procurement. Like the agreement that had been concluded six weeks earlier for establishing a line of communications across France, this one provided for technical details to be worked out in "service-to-service" negotiations. In this case the technical agreements would require the approval of the French resident general in Morocco, General Alphonse Juin.

Anticipating the conclusion of diplomatic negotiations, the North Atlantic division of the Corps of Engineers meanwhile was going ahead with preliminary planning and contract negotiations in New York. On 29 November 1950 the chief of engineers received the first allotment of funds—$11,400,000—and a directive from the air force to go ahead. Speed was a keynote of the directive. "In view of the immediate need for a beneficial occupancy of the facilities, planning and construction will proceed concurrently and cost-plus-fixed-fee contracts are authorized when required in your judgement," the directive said. It stated further:

It is definitely recognized that the work is to be prosecuted at a faster-than-normal rate requiring the mobilization of more than the usual amount of equipment for a job of the magnitude. It is desired that sufficient equipment be mobilized to insure the completion of the 6-month phase of the program within 6 months of the date when clearance to enter the country where the sites are to be located is obtained. The work should be prosecuted in such a manner as to produce the maximum of operational facilities within a minimum of time.[78]

This was to be a "crash" operation. This was at the time when the Chinese had just intervened in force in Korea, and apparently high military and government leaders were expecting full-scale war by the next summer. The president himself noted on 9 December, "I have worked for peace for five years and six months and it looks like World War III is near."[79]

On 22 December 1950 a cost-plus-a-fixed-fee letter contract was let to the firm of Porter-Urquhart, Associated, of Newark, New Jersey, for the architect-engineering work at a fee of $657,000. A joint venture known as Atlas Constructors received the construction contract. Participants in this enterprise were the Morrison-Knudsen Company of Boise, Idaho; the Nello L. Teer Company of Durham, North Carolina; the Ralph E. Mills Company of Salem, Virginia; the Blythe Brothers Company of Charlotte, North Carolina, and the Bates and Rogers Construction Corporation of Chicago. After prolonged nogotiations the fee was set at $5,350,710. At a conference with the Atlas partners in the offices of the North Atlantic division on 3 January 1951, when the preliminary letter contract was signed, Colonel Derby, designated to be district engineer of a new East Atlantic district soon to be organized to have immediate supervision over the project, directed that procurement of equipment, wherever it could be found at a reasonable price, begin at once. Colonel Derby's instructions were to go out and corner the market on equipment. It would be obtained without regard to the conventional procedures of going through the Chicago procurement office or formal advertising. The East Atlantic district became operational on 9 January with the stated mission of carrying out construction required to support operations of the Strategic Air Command in Morocco.

Rebuilding Forces in Europe and North Africa

With activities well underway in the United States, Colonel Derby joined an air force mission headed by Brig. Gen. P. M. Hamilton, which hurried to Rabat, Morocco, to begin negotiations with General Juin on the technical agreements that would have to be completed before work could begin. There two major points of controversy arose immediately—the location of the bases and the size of the American forces to be stationed in Morocco. Highly sensitive to the ticklish Arab political problems in Morocco, the resident general insisted that the air bases be located away from centers of population and that the number of airmen to be stationed there be limited to two thousand—about one-tenth of what the air force was planning. In a compromise the American officers agreed to accept new sites away from the cities and Juin agreed that seven thousand five hundred airmen might be brought in. Accordingly sites at Ben Guerir, Sidi Slimane, and Mechra bel Ksiri were substituted for Marrakech, Meknes, and Sale. At the same time Khouribga was dropped for operational reasons. The fifth site would be chosen later. Other points to be settled touched rentals, leases, procurement, banking and currency, the hire of local workers, and off-base construction.

By the middle of February 1951 the Atlas constructors had the advance shipments of $25,000,000 worth of construction equipment on the high seas—equipment that included 1,450 heavy trucks and other vehicles, 550 electric power plants, 200 earthmovers and compactors, 200 welding machines, 175 compressors and pumps, 125 tractors, 60 concrete mixers, 50 cranes and power shovels, and 35 rockcrushers and asphalt plants. But technical negotiations were still going on when the men and materials began arriving at Casablanca. French authorities did permit the equipment to be landed, but instead of going directly to job sites, it had to be stored in a nearby dispersal area where it was subject to deterioration and pilferage. Architect-engineering employees and Corps of Engineers employees were permitted to enter without limit, but only one hundred of the contractor's employees were permitted entrance. Expensive machinery and highly paid labor thus remained tied up until mid-April. By an exchange of notes between the U.S. Embassy in Paris and the French Foreign Office on 13 April authority was granted to begin work, and two days later two technical agreements were signed. In these agreements the French reserved the right to build all facilities not directly on the bases—including the all-important fuel pipelines, to approve and purchase the land for the bases, to control all local purchases of more than $3,000, to supervise local hiring and the letting of subcontracts, and to station a French resident commander at each base.

Since the sites were at some distance from sizeable towns, it first was necessary to build camps for the workers. Erection of a construction camp at Nouasseur (about twenty miles southeast of Casablanca) began on 12 March, and one at Sidi Slimane (about sixty miles northeast of Rabat) began on 9 April. Work on the base itself began at Nouasseur on 19 April and at Sidi Slimane on 3 May 1951. For the next three months work went forward at a feverish pitch to get minimum operational facilities in at the two bases by July. As Dallas and Quonset huts were being set up at construction camps, crews went to work drilling wells, building roads, putting up asphalt plants, blasting quarries, moving earth, and then at laying the runways and taxiways. With the benefit of searchlights for night work, men worked sixty to seventy hours a week—and skilled hands drew $1,200 to $1,500 a month.

On 13 July Maj. Gen. Archie Old, commanding general of the Fifth Air Division, which had operational jurisdiction over the bases, Colonel Derby, and the French air force commander made landings at both fields. On Bastille Day nine B-29 and B-50 bombers and six jet fighters landed at the two bases. At that time there was a nine-thousand-foot paved runway, two hundred feet wide; parallel and connecting taxiways; two bulk storage tanks of fifty-five-thousand-barrel and ten-thousand-barrel capacity, and rudimentary camp facilities at each place. The first stage of construction had been finished in whirlwind style. But from this point things began to bog down.

For operational reasons the air force had decided to renegotiate the other three sites. On 10 April a start had been made on a construction camp at Ben Guerir, but nine days later local air force officers ordered the suspension of base construction there, and about 10 May the site was abandoned and the whole camp moved to Mechra bel Ksiri, about two hundred miles away. The French released this site for construction on 25 May. Then after less than a month's work, the air force decided that this site would not do either. Now construction crews were shifted temporarily to Sidi Slimane. In September the air force decided to try Ben Guerir again, and the camp at Mechra bel Ksiri was dismantled and brought all the way back, and crews returned to their jobs. Estimates of the financial loss resulting from this moving back and forth varied from $143,000 to $300,000. It was beginning to appear that the only way to ensure the permanency of a site selection was to do a rush job on it, as had been done at Nouasseur and Sidi Slimane, before anyone had a chance to change it. Air force and engineer officers examined seventy-one potential sites before agreeing, tentatively, upon returning to Ben Guerir and upon two new sites at Boulhait (between Casablanca and Rabat) and El Djema Sahim (northeast of Safi).

In the fall of 1951 criticism began to arise not only of the delays and frustrations in getting work started on the remaining bases, but of the inefficiencies found in connection with the work that had been done at the first two bases. Reports by research engineer consultants, by the executive officer of the East Atlantic district, and by various inspectors indicated the use of faulty materials in runway construction, a lack of proper administrative procedures on the part of the contractor, and a lack of sufficient supervision on the part of the Corps of Engineers. In December Lt. Col. W. L. Beadle, air force liaison officer in Morocco, stated in a memorandum to General Old that there had been continuous violations of sound engineering practices, and that airfield paving had gone "through the entire gamut of poor aggregates, no sizing or grading, failure to use screens, use of reject materials, inadequate compaction, clay and inorganic materials in aggregates, lack of prime and tack coats, low density and excessive use of asphalt mix to level the north section of the Nouasseur runway."[80] Pavement failures predicted in October by John M. Griffith, research engineer for the Asphalt Institute who was acting as a consultant for the Corps of Engineers, came to pass in November and December after the heavy rains at both Nouasseur and Sidi Slimane. Army spokesmen generally attributed these failures to the rush in which the job had been undertaken.

Inquiries into the affair in January 1951 by the Preparedness Investigating Subcommittee of the Senate Committee on Armed Services, under the chairmanship of Senator Lyndon Johnson of Texas, and by a subcommittee of the House Committee on Expenditures in the Executive Departments, under the chairmanship of Representative Porter Hardy of Virginia, touched off a flurry of criticisms in Congress and the press.[81] Members of the Senate committee were highly critical of the chief of engineers for what they considered to be his evasive testimony, and for his failure to exercise closer supervision, and they were critical of his subordinates on the spot. These considerations appeared to carry more weight in their conclusions than did the demands for haste during what had been considered a most critical time for national security or the difficulties involved in local negotiations and the frequent changes in air force plans.

In addition to unsound construction practices and maladministration, the committees found some indications of fraud and theft at local levels. A resident auditor for the Army Audit Agency in North Africa told the House committee of over-charges ranging from 25 to 110 percent resulting from collusion between people in the contractors' office and local sellers, "kickbacks" on the purchases of supplies, a conspiracy to raise prices, a lack of control over Arab workers who had been charged a thousand francs for their jobs, and excessive drinking, loafing, and sleeping by workers on the job, which had resulted in the firing of a thousand of them on a single day. The auditor estimated that waste, "kickbacks," and price-boosting had added $50,000,000 to the cost of the construction project.[82]

The Senate committee uncovered what was perhaps an even uglier situation at the Claremont terminal, in Jersey City. In January 1951 the Atlas Constructors, with the approval of the Corps of Engineers, had issued a purchase order to Dade Bros., Inc. to handle and process construction equipment for overseas shipment from Jersey City. The purchase order amounted to a time and materials contract—a type discouraged by Armed Services Procurement Regulations—under which Dade Bros. would receive payment upon a stipulated hourly wage rate for all men directly engaged, plus handling and the renting of equipment at specified rates, plus materials at cost, and compensation for Dade's overhead and profit. All this, of course, would be marked as cost under the Atlas cost-plus-a-fixed-fee contract. The original purchase order called for Dade to process some twelve hundred pieces of equipment at an estimated cost of $150,000. A series of changes spiraled the contract to an estimated $9,000,000 by December 1951. The most unsavory part of the affair emerged from the waterfront labor situation. Committee investigators uncovered evidence of extensive payroll padding on the part of union leaders, of loafing, gambling, drinking, and narcotics traffic on the job, of breakage, pilferage, and waste of materials, and of the mishandling of rented materials handling equipment. Given the type of contract under which it was operating, the company prospered as it had not done in the past three or four years, but the cost to the government was about three times the cost per ton that a commercial company in another part of the New York area was showing for comparable tonnage during the same period.

> The committee heard several witnesses, including representatives of the police force of Jersey City. Also, it examined certain documentary evidence, which tended to establish that, at least until the arrival of the committee's investigators, Claremont Terminal was used as a dumping ground for exconvicts, idlers, petty criminals, and other hangerson, who were friends of, or had influence wih, racketeers and their political friends.[83]

The committee concluded bitterly:

> The conditions which we found to exist at Claremont Terminal unquestionably had a direct effect on the cost of overseas shipment of materiel necessary to the adequate defense of our country. These conditions appear to constitute the general pattern in the port of New York. That port is one of the principal avenues through which military equipment and supplies are shipped to our forces overseas and to our allies. The plain fact appears to be that the cost of those shipments is continuing to be materially increased by these malpractices. At a time when the resources of our country are being so heavily taxed to provide the necessary defenses for ourselves and our friends in the free world against a ruthless aggressor, it is an effrontery to the American people that a small group of racketeers and hoodlums should be permitted to levy tribute on the shipment of military supplies and materiel necessary to that task.
> Consequently, the committee demands that all Federal agencies having appropriate jurisdiction and authority immediately take action in the national interest to insure the free and unfettered flow of materiel to the armed services overseas through the port of New York, or any other American port, at a fair cost and without undue interference by any group. The committee also recommends to the Department of Defense and other interested executive agencies that if additional legislation is needed to achieve these ends that the appropriate committee of Congress be so advised.[84]

As for the situation in Morocco itself, Secretary of the Army Pace at first seemed disposed to discount somewhat the reports of unsatisfactory supervision and results, and he suggested that the critics tended to forget the speed element that had been uppermost at the time in getting the job done. But then he moved swiftly to take corrective action. On 21 March 1952 he announced that the chief of engineers had established a new division, the Mediterranean division, under Brig. Gen. Orville E. Walsh, with headquarters at Rabat, to supervise the project. Colonel Jack P. Campbell, formerly district engineer at Chicago, and Lt. Col. R. P. Davidson had been ordered to Morocco to replace Colonel Derby and Lt. Col. Leonard Haseman as district engineer and deputy engineer respectively of the East Atlantic district, and six additional officers had been assigned to that headquarters as area engineers. On 15 January 1952 the air force announced that the emergency phase of the program was over. Thereupon the army got away from its "crash" operation procedures and it was possible to set up regular work schedules to include the reduction of the work week to a maximum of sixty hours and the elimination of excessive overtime pay. The audit team from the Army Audit Agency was increased in order to make the final audit of reimbursement vouchers, and two additional auditors were assigned to the project on a permanent basis. At the insistence of the army, a vice president of Morrison-Knudsen Company went to Morocco to serve as resident manager. The heads of the companies participating in the Atlas venture met twice with Under Secretary of the Army Alexander in Washington. Alexander told them frankly of the unsatisfactory features of the work thus far, and that the situation would have to be remedied if the contract were not to be suspended or terminated. The contractors promised full cooperation. Secretary Pace appointed a survey group of well-known construction men headed by Glen Maxon to evaluate the whole project in the summer of 1952. The conclusion of this group was that by that time the program was in good hands in generally was being carried out in an effective manner.

When the Moroccan air base construction program was being planned in 1950, the total cost had been estimated at $300,000,000. But the project grew in the doing. Revised plans added nearly one-third to the size of the bases. Moreover the original estimate had been based upon the construction of only one new base and the expansion of four existing bases; now five completely new ones were to be constructed. In the spring of 1952, with some work still remaining to be done at Nouasseur and Sidi Slimane, the base at Ben Guerir half finished, and the other two not even begun, at least $200,000,000 of the $250,000,000 so far appropriated already had been spent. It seemed unlikely that the whole project would be completed for less than $600,000,000.

After additional tests and studies of the pavement at Nouasseur and Sidi Slimane, General Pick concluded that repairs on the runways, taxiways, and aprons at the two bases could be effected by rolling with a two-hundred-ton pneumatic tired super compactor and by replacing unsatisfactory materials at a relatively low cost—perhaps a total of $1,160,640 for both bases.

In August 1952 General Pick wrote to the secretary of the army:

I am pleased with the current operations and the high quality of the paving now being placed. Throughout my inspection I sought the views of General Old and Air Force base commanders, and they invariably expressed satisfaction with our present work and planned operations. Other operations of the contractor are being carried on in an efficient, business-like manner. There is still too much lag in financing this large undertaking, and as a result, procurement and planning cannot be performed to effect the greatest economy obtainable. Also, the fact that the remaining two sites have not been started and are still under discussion with the French, as to the respective shares of responsibilities of France and the United States, and the provision of additional real estate for the El Djema Sahim site, if not soon resolved will result in restricted operations and will cause demobilization of the contractor's forces beyond the point considered desirable for the effective execution of the remaining work.[85]

After receiving the report of the special survey team and other reports, Secretary of the Army Pace explained further actions he had taken and his conclusions regarding the Moroccan effort in a letter to Senator Johnson, saying, in part:

Before determining if disciplinary action was warranted against any of the Army officers concerned, I have waited to receive and carefully to consider the Maxon report, supplemental reports from the Inspector General, and the full recommendations of the staff. As a matter of principle, I have always insisted that all officers and civilians of the Army Establishment make every effort affirmatively to bring before committees of the Congress all data relevent to the particular inquiry and actively to cooperate with those committees to the end that confusion and misunderstanding may be avoided. In the light of all the evidence now available to me and in view of the recommendations made by the Inspector General and the Chief of Staff of the Army upon the matter, I have admonished Lt. Gen. Lewis A. Pick, Chief of Engineers, for not testifying in a clear and complete manner before your committee and for not causing the Moroccan bases to be adequately inspected by representatives of his office during the critical stages in 1951. Some of the difficulties which existed during the crash phase of the construction program might have been earlier corrected had their existence been made fully known to me and to others in the Department of the Army here in Washington. I have also admonished Col. F. F. French, then division engineer in New York, for not having representatives of his office inspect the bases during the same period. In addition I have admonished Col. Geroge T. Derby, the district engineer in Morocco at the time, for failing fully to inform his superiors of the magnitude of the construction difficulties he was encountering and of the short cuts, however necessary under the circumstances, which he was taking in construction methods.

When the Army undertook to go into French Morocco and build bases for the Air Force, we engaged a group of most highly qualified construction firms who were assisted by architect engineers of acknowledged reputation. We had available the top talent in the field. However, when the magnitude of the Moroccan construction is considered, particularly in the light of the equally tremendous project which we had undertaken for the Air Force at Thule simultaneously and our much expanded domestic construction responsibilities, it is apparent that the talent we had available, both civilian and military, was of necessity thinly spread.

I do wish to emphasize the great sense of urgency which characterized the defense thinking of all Americans back in the days of November 1950 when the Moroccan bases were being planned—a time when our forces were being pushed back in Korea by the Chinese Communists and when grave concern existed for the future of western democracies. Any consideration of what we accomplished in Morocco in 1951 should, I feel, be set in a frame of reference applicable to the times.

Having in mind the paramount requirement imposed upon us to complete the maximum construction in the minimum period, we were able to complete two 9,000-foot runways, with accompanying facilities, within 3 months time and ground which was not broken until April 22, 1951, had been converted into operational airfields by July 14 of the same year. . . . I am satisfied that the construction work in Morocco, insofar as it is within the area of responsibility of the Army, is proceeding on a sound and efficient basis. You may be assured that if any further deficiencies develop in the future, I shall take aggressive steps to correct them forthwith.[86]

For its part, Senator Johnson's Committee concluded in its report of 19 February 1953:

On the basis of the Maxon report and the considered judgment of the Secretary, the committee concludes that the deficiencies and shortcomings of the construction effort in Morocco have been or are being corrected and the work is currently proceeding on a sound basis. Consequently, it is our view that no useful purpose will now be served by additional investigation of the errors of the past in Morocco. Disclosure of past mistakes is useful only to the extent that it serves as a guidepost pointing toward a proper course in the future.[87]

In the Morocco air base project the Corps of Engineers was handling its biggest single contract overseas since the digging of the Panama Canal—and it was possible that the strategic significance would be as great.

Notes

1. *Annual Report of the Secretary of the Army*, 1948, 73.
2. Quoted in Walter Millis, ed., *The Forrestal Diaries* (New York, 1951), 387.
3. Ibid., 407; Lucius D. Clay, *Decision in Germany* (New York, 1950), 358–61; Avi Shlaim, *The United States and the Berlin Blockade* (Berkeley, 1983), 106–35; Jean Edward Smith, "The View from USFET: General Clay's and Washington's Interpretation of Soviet Intentions in Germany, 1945–1948," in Hans A. Schmitt, ed., *U.S. Occupation in Europe after World War II* (Lawrence, KS, 1978), 75–76; Douglas Botting, *From the Ruins of the Reich* (New York, 1985), 304–6; Robert Murphy, *Diplomat Among Warriors* (New York, 1965), 350–52.

4. *Annual Report of the Secretary of the Army*, 1948, 53–55; Elizabeth S. Lay, "Berlin Air Lift," 1 January–30 September 1949 (Occupation Forces in Europe Series, European Command, Hqrs., Hist. Div.), Pt. 1, 9–11; Millis, *The Forrestal Diaries*, 451–54; Botting, *From the Ruins of the Reich*, 307–9.

5. Murphy, *Diplomat among Warriors*, 353–54.

6. Lay, "The Berlin Airlift," Pt. 1, 7, 10–12.

7. Lay, "The Berlin Airlift," Pt. 1, 12–13, 129.

8. Ibid., 28–48.

9. Ibid., Pt, 2, 105–106.

10. Clay, *Decision in Germany*, 381; Lay, "The Berlin Airlift," Pt, 2, 3, 78, 107–108; Campbell, *The U.S. in World Affairs 1948–1949*, 133–49; Germany 1947–1949; The Story in Documents, Dept. of State Publ. 3556, Mar. 1950; *Annual Report of the Secretary of the Army*, 1948, 147–50; Monthly Report, Military Government of Germany, Millis, *The Forrestal Diaries*, 469–70.

11. Murphy, *Diplomat among Warriors*, 353–54.

12. Smith, "Soviet Intentions in Germany," in Schmitt, *U.S. Occupation in Europe*, 75–76; Shlaim, *The U.S. and the Berlin Blockade*, 106–9.

13. Mil. Govt. of Germany, Monthly Rpt. of Mil. Governor, U.S. Zone, No. 5, 20 Dec. 45, copy in Army Library, 3–4; Mil Govt. of Germany, Monthly Rpt. of the Mill. Governor, No. 19, 1–31, Jan. 47, 6–7; Monograph, Establishment of Communications through France, 1950–1951, Hist. Div., USAREUR, 1952, 1, and Map 1.

14. DA G–4 Hist. Summary, 1951–1952, Tab. B, Plans Off, Europe, 12; Establishment of Communications Through France, 1950–1951, 122–24.

15. Establishment of Communications Through France, 1950–1951, 1–2; 5–10; EUCOM Briefing for Mr Pace and General Collins, 19 Dec. 1950, Line of Communication Across France, Transcript in G–4 Plans Off, Theaters Br., French Line of Communications; Brig. Gen. Mason J. Young, CG EUCOM COMZ, "Our New European Supply Line," *Army Information Digest*, 6 (Oct 1951): 56; EUCOM Annual Narrative Rpt. 1950, 22–25, 115; EUCOM Cmd. Rpt. 1951, 210–12.

16. Establishment of Communications through France, 1950–1951, 2–3; James P. O'Donnell, "We're All Fouled Up in France," *The Saturday Evening Post*, 11 April 1953, pp. 40–41.

17. Agreement between the United States of America and the Republic of France Regarding the Establishment and Operation of a Line of Communication Across France, copy in Establishment of Communications Across France, 1950–1951, Annex 3; See also Basic Policies of the Dept. of the Army (DA–PB–50A), copy in OCMH, Change No. 8, May 1952, 29.

18. EUCOM Annual Narrative Rpt., 1949, 123–26; EUCOM Annual Narrative Rpt., 1950, 63; EUCOM Annual Narrative Rpt., 1951, 70–71; Monograph, Establishment of Communications through France, 1950–1951, Hist. Div., USAREUR, 1952, 21–23.

19. Establishment of Communications through France, 1950–1951, 25–30; USAREUR Annual Narrative Rpt., 1950, 62–63; EUCOM Cmd. Rpt., 1951, 71–73; Rpt. of Army Field Forces Inspection of European Cmd, Oct. 1951, Tab. D, Sec. 2.

20. Establishment of Communications through France, 57–61, and Appendix C, 130–31; EUCOM Cmd. Rpt., 1951, 211–12.

21. O'Donnell, "We're All Fouled Up in France," *The Saturday Evening Post*, 11 April 1953.

22. Establishment of Communications through France, 60–61, 130–31; Interview with Colonel Zimmerman, 3 June 53.

23. *Annual Report of the Secretary of the Army*, 1948.

24. G–4 Memo of Important Actions, 15 Mar. 51, 1.

25. Foreign Service Despatch No. 8, American Embassy Rome to Dept. of State, 2 July 51, sub.: Arrangement for Lines of Communication in Italy concluded 29 June 1951; *Semiannual Rpt. of the Secretary of Defense*, 1 Jan.–30 June 1951, 63.
26. Foreign Service Despatch No. 8, American Embassy Rome to Dept. of State, 2 July 51.
27. Edmund Stevens, *Christian Science Monitor*, 12 Aug. 52.
28. Hq. USAREUR Annual Narrative Rpt., 1 Jan.–31 Dec. 1950, (attached to EUCOM Annual Narrative Rpt.), 4–8; *Annual Report of the Secretary of the Army*, 1948, 52.
29. EUCOM Cmd. Rpt., 1951, 28–65.
30. Establishment of Communications through France, 1950–51, 38–40; Interview with Lt. Col. Larry J. O'Neil, Eur. Med. ME. Sec., Theaters Br., Plans Office, G–4, 26 May 53.
31. Second Report to Congress on the Mutual Security Program, 30 June 52, 5–6.
32. DA G–4 Historical Summary 1951–1952, Plans Office, Europe, 1–2.
33. Rpt., COA, sub.: Measures and Recommendations of Major Importance to the Improvement of the Army, 1 July 50 to 30 Dec. 52, prep. in response to instructions from outgoing S/A, Frank Pace, mimeo copy, Pt. 3, 10; Interview with Archibald S. Alexander, US/A, 17 Apr. 52; Memo of Important Actions, G4/B1, 10 Apr. 51, 1; DA G–4 Hist. Summary 1951–1952, Tab. D, Supply Div., Distr. Br., Army Support of AF, for Common Use Standard Stock Items at Depot Level.
34. Quoted in Rpt., COA, Measures and Recommendations of Major Importance to the Improvement of the Army, 1 July 50 to 30 Dec. 52, Pt. 3, 10.
35. Quoted in Rpt. of Critical Problems, G–4, 61, 22 Jan. 53; See also D/D Dir 4000.8, 17 Nov. 52, sub.: Basic Regulations for Military Supply System.
36. EUCOM Annual Narrative Rpt., 1949, 134–44; Memo, ACofS, G–3 for CofS USA, 26 Apr. 52, sub.: U.S. Command Structure in Europe.
37. Msg. ALO 1374, Gen. Ridgway to JCS, 21 July 52; Draft memo, JCS for Sec. Def., 28 July 52, sub.: U.S. Military Structure in Europe; Lecture, Maj. Gen. C. D. Eddleman, Army War College, 4 Feb. 53, Joint Action Armed Forces.
38. Draft Msg., JCS personal for Ridgway, USLO Paris, as revised 9 July 52; Questions and Answers from Address by Maj. Gen. C. D. Eddleman, Army War College, 4 Feb. 53, 11–12; DA G–3 Hist. Summary 1951–52, Europe and Middle East Br. 1–3; Chart, Army and AF Logistic Relationship in European Area, 13 Oct. 52; Interview with Lt. Col. Frank Meszar, Europe—Middle East Br. Ops. Div., G–3, 29 May 53.
39. Ltr. Gen. M. B. Ridgway to CofS USA for JCS, 18 Oct. 52, sub.: Establishment of a Joint Logistical Command in Europe.
40. Memo, JCS for Sec. Def., 21 Nov. 52, sub.: Functions and Organization of Hq. EUCOM; Msg., JCS to CINCEUR, 21 Nov. 52.
41. DA G–4 Hist. Summary 1951–52, Tab. D, Supply Div., Distr Br., Army Support of AF for Common Use Standard Stock Items at Depot Level.
42. *The New York Times*, 24 Feb. 1953.
43. EUCOM Logistic Planning Forecast, 1 Jan. 50, copy in OCMH, 1.
44. EUCOM Logistic Planning Forecast, 1 July 50, 1; EUCOM Annual Narrative Report, 1950, 1–5.
45. EUCOM Logistics Planning Forecast, 1 July 50, 10–11.
46. G–4 Memo of Important Actions, G4/B1 5209 (SF), 5 Jan. 50, 2.
47. G–4 Memo of Important Actions, G4/51203, 2 Oct. 50, 3; Tp. Conv., AG Orgn. and Director Sec., 18 June 53.
48. Hearings, Senate Comm. on For Rel. and Comm. on Armed Forces, Assignment of Ground Forces of U.S. to European Area, 82d Cong., 1st Sess., 1–28 Feb. 1951; Senate Rpt. 175, 14 Mar. 1951, Assignment of Ground Forces of the U.S. to Duty in the European Area.

49. Congressional Record, 82d. Cong., 1st Sess., Vol. 97, Pt. 3, 4 April 1951, 3282–83.

50. Tp. Conv., AG Orgn. and Directory Sec., 18 June 53.

51. Testimony of General J. Lawton Collins, CofS, 31 July 1951, Hearings before Comm. on For. Rel. and Comm. on Armed Services, U.S. Senate, 82d Cong., 1st Sess., on S. 1762, Mutual Security Act of 1951, 166–67; DA G–3 Hist. Summary, 1951–1952, Europe Middle East Br., 10–11; Directory and Station List of the U.S. Army, 15 Apr. 53, 496–500.

52. See Statement of General J. Lawton Collins, CofS, 18 June 1952, Senate Hearings, Dept. of Def. Appropriations for 1953, 1212.

53. Supply Supplement, Pt. 2 of Troop Program and Troop List, 1 Aug. 50, 15.

54. Supply Supplement, Pt. 2 of Troop Program and Troop List, 15 Sept. 50, 13.

55. Comments of Maj. Gen. Carter B. Magruder, Dep. CofS, G–4, on DF, to OCMH, 19 Nov. 51, sub.: Hist. Outline.

56. "Ordnance Rebuilds and Saves," *Ordnance* 34 (Sep–Oct 1949): 109–11; Major Fred P. Dyhrmann, "'Detroit on the Isar,'" *Ordnance* 37 (July–Aug 1952): 5–7.

57. Alex G. Sutton, Jr, "The Engineer Rebuild Program in Germany" *The Military Engineer* 62 (Nov–Dec 1950): 456–58.

58. Statement of Frank Pace, Sec/Army, 15 Mar. 51, Hearings before the Bonner Subcommittee, Disposition of Surplus Property, 58–60.

59. Hearings before a Subcommittee of the Committee on Expenditures in the Executive Departments, House of Representatives, 82d Cong., 1st Sess.; Ltr., John J. McCloy, U.S. High Commissioner for Germany, to Rep. Herbert C. Bonner, 29 Mar. 51, printed in Hearings before the Bonner Committee, 669–70; Interview with Carrol Meigs, Lend-Lease and Surplus Property Off, Dept. of State, 20 May 52; Michael Stern, "How Back-Door Dawson got $100,000,000" *True*, May 1952.

60. EUCOM Comd. Rpt., 1951, 299–300; Statement of Sec/Army Frank Pace before Bonner Subcommittee, 15 Mar. 51; *The Washington Post*, 3 Apr. 1952.

61. Memo of Important Actions, G4/B1 51798, 4 Oct. 50, 2; Drew Middletown, "7th Army's Power Shows Sharp Gain," *The New York Times*, 8 Sept. 1952.

62. Memo of Important Actions, G4/B1 36009, 17 July 50; Memo of Important Actions, G4/B1 6407 (SF), 9 Oct. 50, 3.

63. Da G–4, Hist. Summary, 1951–1952, Tab. F, Rqmts. Div., No 2; Logistics Policies and Priorities, 1 Nov. 52, 95–96.

64. Supply Supplement of the Troop Program and Troop List, 1 Aug. 50, 85; Logistics Policies and Priorities, 1 Nov. 52, 93.

65. Memo of Important Actions, G–4/B1 5166 (SF), 1 Sept. 50.

66. Establishment of Communications through France, 1950–1951, 53–68; Chart, France-Germany Depot Support Load, 24 Oct. 52.

67. O'Donnell, "We're All Fouled Up in France," *The Saturday Evening Post*, 11 April 1953, p. 41.

68. USAREUR Report of Critical Logistics Deficiencies, as of 30 June 52; Memo for Record, 2 Sept. 52, Rpt. of Trip to Europe of Secy. Pace and Party, 3; DA G–4 Hist. Summary, 1951–1952, Tab. B, Plans Off, Matters of Worldwide Interest, 14.

69. USAREUR Report of Critical Logistics Deficiencies, CSGLD–524, as of 30 June 52; EUCOM Logistics Division Monthly Review, Sept. 1950, 8–13.

70. DF G4/D1 Chief Supply Div., to Chief Plans Off, 28 May 53, sub.: Hq. USAREUR's Rpt. of Critical Logistics Deficiencies; USAREUR Rpt. of Critical Logistics Deficiencies, as of 31 Mar. 53.

71. DA G–4 Hist. Summary, 1951–1952, Tab. B, Plans off, Europe, 9.

72. EUCOM Annual Narrative Rpt., 1949, Occupation Forces Series, 150–52, 500–508.

73. EUCOM Cmd. Rpt., 1951, 314–15.

74. Directory and Station List of the U.S. Army, 1 Nov. 51, 502; Interview with Colonel Chalmers H. Armstrong, Jr. European and Middle East Br., Ops. Div., G–3, 27 May 53; Interview with Major Walter E. Conway, Orgn. Br., G–3, 27 May 53.

75. Directory and Station List of the U.S. Army, 1 Nov. 51, 473–75; Directory and Station List of the U.S. Army, 15 Apr. 53, 512–20.

76. DA G–4 Hist. Summary, 1951–1952, Tab. D, Supply Div., Supply Planning Br., 8.

77. Unless otherwise noted, this section is based upon the following: Hist. of Corps of Engrs. Activities in French Morocco, prep. by Colonel George T. Derby, Distr. Engineer, in Corps. of Engrs. Hist. Summary, 30 Oct. 51, covering pd. 25 June 50–8 Sep 51, Pt. 2 B: Corps of Engrs. Field Agencies: Div. Engrs., East Atlantic Div; Forty-Second Rpt. of Preparedness Investigating Subcomm. of Comm. on Armed Services, U.S. Senate, 82 Cong., 2d Sess., Interim Rpt. on Moroccan Air Base Construction; Forty-fourth Rpt. of Preparedness Investigating Subcomm. of Comm. on Armed Serv., U.S. Sen, 83d. Cong., 1st Sess., 19 Feb. 53, Second Rpt. on Moroccan Air Base Construction; James P. O'Donnell, "What's Behind the Air-Base Scandals?" *The Saturday Evening Post*, 28 June 1952; Memo, Lt. Gen. Lewis A. Pick, CofEngrs, for Secy/Army, 20 Aug. 52, sub.: Moroccan Air Base.

78. Quoted in 42d. Rpt. of Preparedness Investigating Subcomm, Interim Rpt. on Moroccan Air Base Construction, 3.

79. Quoted in William Hillman, *Mr. President*, (New York, 1952), 143.

80. Quoted in 42d. Rpt. of the Preparedness Investigating Subcomm., Interim Rpt. on Moroccan Air Base Construction, 8.

81. See, for example: "Overseas Job Cost Put at $178 a Man," *The New York Times*, 12 Jan. 52; John G. Norris, *The Washington Post*, 2 Feb. 52; *The New York Post*, 6 Feb. 52; *The Washington Post*, 28 Feb. 52; *The Washington Post*, 19 Mar. 52; Clyde Farnsworth, *The Washington Daily News*, 17 Mar. 52; Clyde Farnsworth, *The Washington Daily News*, 18 Mar, 52; Editorial, *The Philadelphia Inquirer*, 24 Mar. 52; C. B. Allen in *The New York Herald Tribune*, 25 Aug. 52; *The New York Times*, 27 Aug. 52; *The Washington Post*, 25 Aug. 52; Editorial, *The Washington Daily News*, 26 Aug. 52; "African Air Bases Defended by Pick," *The New York Times*, 26 Aug. 52; Victor Riesel, in *The New York Mirror*, 27 Aug. 52; C. B. Allen, in *The New York Herald Tribune*, 27 Aug. 52; Editorial, *The Washington Times-Herald*, 28 Aug. 52; Editorial, *New Orleans Times-Picayune*, 8 Sept. 52; George E. Sokolsky, *Philadelphia Inquirer*, 16 Jan. 52.

82. *The Washington Post*, 28 Feb. 1952.

83. 44th. Rpt. of Preparedness Investigating Subcomm, Second Rpt. on Moroccan Air Base Construction, 12.

84. Ibid., 19.

85. Memo, General Pick for Sec/Army, 20 Aug. 52.

86. Ltr., Sec/Army Frank Pace, Jr to Sen. Lyndon B. Johnson, 4 Nov. 52, printed in 44th. Rpt. of Preparedness Investigating Subcomm, Exhibit B, 33–36.

87. 44th Rpt. Preparedness Investigating Subcomm., Second Rpt. on Moroccan Air Base Construction, 4.

5
Foreign Military Aid

> In the meantime our own preparations may be going forward; we may seek for allies wherever we can find them.
> —Thucydides, *History of the Peloponnesian War*

> Dealing with the enemy is a simple and straightforward matter when contrasted with securing close cooperation with an ally.
> —Maj. Gen. Fox Conner

One of the most far-reaching developments in American military affairs during the first half of the twentieth century was the evolution of a policy for furnishing military equipment to allies. This development reached its climax in the undertaking of the logistic build-up of allies in peacetime as a measure of security in the "Cold War."

Until World War I international finance generally had been the preserve of "international bankers," and governments for the most part limited themselves to the encouragement or discouragement of private foreign loans as they might affect national policy. When the government of Mexico sought to refund its national debt, it looked not to the government of the United States, but to J. P. Morgan and Company of New York. In the same way governments generally refrained from direct participation either in the financing or the sale of munitions of war to foreign governments. To act otherwise in favor of a belligerent power would immediately bring protests against a violation of neutrality obligations.

On occasion the United States government had been involved in transfer of arms to foreign governments. After the Civil War the sale of surplus munitions went on for several years. Turkey obtained some 350,000 pieces, and Russia purchased similar large quantities. After the outbreak of the Franco-Prussian War in 1870, War Department sales of arms and ammunition continued to the extent of some 425,000 pieces and 54,000,000 cartridges. Many of these were sold to Remington and Company, who in turn sold them to the French. After protests by the Prussian minister in Washington that this amounted to a violation of neutral obligations, and objections on the part of some leaders of the Senate and by the secretary of state, this practice was stopped in January 1871—about the time that the war ended.[1]

The same kind of situation arose again at the outbreak of World War I in 1914. At that time the U.S. army had on hand sizeable quantities of Krag-Jorgensen rifles, which had become obsolete. When it became known that the War Department was considering the sale of these surplus weapons, persons purporting to be agents of various Latin American governments quickly appeared to arrange purchases. Again there were strong indications that the rifles were going to the French. The German minister in Washington insisted that the French were attempting to buy 300,000 to 400,000 of the rifles through indirect means. In November President Wilson expressed the belief that the rifles should not be sold to anyone as long as the war continued, and all sales stopped. But this policy applied only to government-owned munitions. Nothing in the laws of neutrality prevented the private traffic in arms to belligerents, and for finance as well as manufacturing, the allied governments of Europe turned to American private enterprise.[2]

In June 1915 New York banking firms handled a loan of over $44 million for Rothschild Frères of Paris. In October 1915 a banking syndicate headed by J. P. Morgan and Company entered into an agreement with the British and French government for a loan of half-a-billion dollars. Other loans followed to the British, French, Canadian, Russian, Italian, and Chinese governments and agencies, until by the time the United States entered the war the total funds advanced had reached more than two-and-one-half-billion dollars. With financial difficulties overcome for the time being, the allied governments in the fall of 1915 began to place large orders for munitions in the United States. J. P. Morgan and Company became the purchasing agent for the British government in this country. Total exports of munitions from the United States to the allied powers from August 1914 to March 1917 amounted to over $2,187,000,000.[3]

By late 1916 the allies again found themselves in serious financial difficulties. Much to their relief, one of the first acts of Congress after the declaration of war in April 1917 was to authorize governmental loans to the allies. Under this and succeeding acts the United States advanced to the allied governments nearly $9,600,000,000 in return for notes bearing interest at 5 percent. Most of this went for the purchase of war materials in the United States. The addition of credits after the armistice for the purchase of surplus military goods and for relief (largely in the new states of Eastern Europe) brought the total of loans granted to approximately $10,338,000,000 by 30 June 1919. After funding at considerably reduced rates of interest, the total of principal and interest that the debtor nations agreed to pay to the United States over a period of sixty-two years was approximately $22,000,000,000.[4]

On the eve of World War II Great Britain and France again turned to the United States as a source for arms as they hastened their rearmament programs against the growing peril of Nazi Germany. Because of the fact that the Johnson Act of 1934 prohibited the sale of new securities of any foreign government in default on its existing obligations to the United States, all these purchases had to be handled strictly on a cash basis. Those governments were able to place a number of orders with American private industry in 1938, but shipments stopped when they declared war on Germany in September 1939. Convinced that traffic in arms and international loans had been instrumental in drawing the United States into World War I, Congress had passed neutrality legislation in the late 1930s calculated to keep the United States out of future wars by prohibiting such transactions with belligerent powers. President Roosevelt called Congress into special session soon after the outbreak of war to ask for a revision of the Neutrality Act. The result was the "Cash and Carry" law of 4 November 1939, which permitted belligerent governments to purchase munitions from American firms so long as they were paid for with cash in advance and were carried away in foreign vessels. Government-to-government transactions still were prohibited. The Anglo-French Purchasing Board, and its successor, the British Purchasing Commission, coordinated procurement activities in the United States.

On 29 May 1940, as survivors of the British Expeditionary Force began arriving in England from Dunkirk without their weapons, Prime Minister Winston Churchill sent an urgent message to President Roosevelt asking assistance. The response was prompt. By 3 June U.S. army depots and arsenals were packing surplus rifles, artillery pieces, ammunition, and explosives to be sent to the allies. Now, in sharp contrast to its position in 1870 and 1914, the government openly participated in the subterfuge to get around the neutrality laws. From army reserve stocks the government sold a half million 1917–1918 Enfield rifles, with 130,000,000 rounds of ammunition, nine hundred 75-mm field artillery pieces, with 1,000,000 rounds of ammunition, eight thousand machine guns, and small quantities of bombs and explosives to the United States Steel Export Corporation as a trade-in on new contracts for armor plate and new guns. The company immediately resold the arms and ammunition to the British and French governments at the same price. Another 250,000 rifles and some aircraft were shipped later under the same arrangement. The first shipment was about halfway across the Atlantic when France capitulated, so that the whole lot had to go to Britain.[5]

Hoping to keep the war away from "this hemisphere," Congress about the same time (June 1940) authorized the secretary of war and the secretary of the navy to manufacture in government arsenals, or to purchase in the open market, munitions for direct sale to the government of any American republic. This was a first step toward bringing the army's procurement machinery directly into action for the assistance of foreign powers. Already in 1938 the administration had granted a loan of $25,000,000 to China through the extension of a loan by the Export-Import Bank to a Chinese trading company incorporated under the laws of New York. These funds were not to be used for war matériel, but the loan brought criticism from Tokyo. In this case the procurement staff of the Treasury Department assisted the Chinese in making their purchases. In September Congress increased the lending authority of the

Export-Import Bank by $500,000,000 for the purpose of financing arms procurement for the Latin American republics. Thus the government itself was willing to extend loans to Latin America and even to warring China, while citizens were forbidden even privately to provide similar assistance to France and Great Britian.[6]

From September 1939 through December 1940, British gold and dollar resources dwindled by more than $2.3 billion. During fiscal years 1940 and 1941 the sale of gold by the allies exceeded $5 billion. In addition a large part of British investments in the United States had been pledged to obtain dollar funds. By late 1940 it seemed evident that if Britain were to remain in the fight against Germany some way would have to be found to finance further purchases of war materials. Abandoning all pretense of any fine impartiality between aggressors and their victims, and giving up the appearances of a "proper neutrality" that so far had restricted its activities, the United States now moved swiftly toward open support of the anti-Axis cause. On 3 September 1940 President Roosevelt announced the trade of fifty overage destroyers to Britain in exchange for ninety-nine-year leases on a series of base locations off the American continents. At a press conference on 17 December Roosevelt announced his far-reaching plan for matériel support, which soon came to be known as "lend-lease." He presented his proposals to Congress in his State of the Union message on 6 January 1941. The Lend-Lease Act became effective on 11 March, and the same day the first shipment, to Greece, was on its way. After the Pearl Harbor attack and American entry into the war, control of international transactions passed almost completely to government agencies and corporations. Lend-lease became the vehicle for furnishing military equipment to allied nations throughout the war. In the fiscal years 1940–1945, Lend-lease comprised 95 percent of all foreign aid provided by the United States. The total value of supplies and equipment transferred to other governments under the lend-lease program amounted to approximately $49.1 billion—28.6 for Britain and the dependencies, 10.8 billion for the Soviet Union, 2.6 billion for France, and 5.1 billion for all other recipients. In addition lend-lease procurement channels were used for nearly a billion dollars worth of matériel purchased by foreign governments for cash. Goods and services furnished to the United States by foreign governments as "reverse lend-lease" amounted to about $7.8 billion. Lend-lease completed the process of evolution from private loans to government loans to government grants. The next step was to carry this principle over to peacetime defense preparations.[7]

It will be recalled that after the Japanese surrender President Truman promptly announced that lend-lease would be terminated effective V–J Day. The only major exception was the extension of further lend-lease assistance to China—to the extent of about $700,000,000—for the purpose of reoccupying North China and accepting the surrender of Japanese troops remaining in that area. Otherwise the policy of the United States was to return foreign assistance to a cash or loan basis. The sale of surplus property provided some further military assistance, though military equipment often was sought more for the economic benefit of reselling it than for its utility in defense establishments.[8]

The Truman Doctrine

In March 1945—before the United States had yet had a chance to begin its precipitous demobilization—the Soviet Union began to apply pressure on Turkey with an announcement that the Soviet-Turkish treaty of neutrality and friendship of 1925 would not be renewed. Reviving an expansionist policy that the Russians had pursed off and on for over a century and a half, the Soviet Union now sought joint control of the Turkish straits—the Bosporus and the Dardanelles—and the annexation of Turkey's northeastern provinces of Kars and Ardahan. In November 1945 the United States suggested that the international convention governing the straits be revised. While willing to accept the Soviet proposals on navigation through the straits, the United States resisted any arrangement for joint Soviet-Turkish defense of that area. This, in the view of American officials, would lead inevitably to Soviet domination of Turkey and would create a serious threat to the strategically important Near East. The differences led to a diplomatic impasse, but Turkey remained in control of the straits as well as of the northeastern provinces.[9]

Now the U.S.S.R. turned its attention to Iran and Greece, where internal weaknesses might permit relatively easy domination. This would isolate Turkey as well as give command of the important strategic positions and resources of these two countries themselves. In November 1945 the pro-Soviet Tudeh Party merged with the Democratic Party to stage a revolt in Iran's northern province of Azerbaijan, and Soviet troops there refused to permit the entry of Iranian forces to put down the revolt. The Soviet troops were there as a result of joint occupation with the British in August 1941 aimed at protecting the Baku oil fields of the Soviet Union and the holdings of the Anglo-Iranian Oil Company in southern Iran. By a treaty of January 1942 those powers had agreed to withdraw their troops within six months after the termination of hostilities. When Soviet troops failed to depart during the next few weeks, Iran lodged a complaint with the United Nations Security Council on 19 January 1946. In March Iran brought a further complaint that the Soviet Union still was maintaining troops in Iran in violation of the treaty. Then, strangely enough, while the Security Council was debating the question, Iran suddenly withdrew the complaint. At the insistence of the United States, however, the Security Council kept the Iranian question on its agenda. In May the Iranian government reported that Soviet troops apparently had withdrawn, but it was not until December that Iranian troops were able to enter Azerbaijan and reestablish control of that province. Before the withdrawal of their troops, the Soviet Union had negotiated an oil agreement with Iran by which a joint Soviet-Iranian oil company was to be formed on the basis of 51 percent Soviet control for a period of twenty-five years—and then the Iranian parliament refused to approve the agreement.[10]

Just two days after Iran brought its complaint to the Security Council, the Soviet delegation—doubtless with a view to attracting attention away from Iran—charged that the presence of British troops in Greece constituted interference in the internal affairs of that country. On a proposal of the United States, the Council rejected that contention. Then in August 1946 the Ukrainian S.S.R. brought a further complaint before the Security Council regarding affairs in Greece. The complaint was that Greek armed forces were provoking incidents along the Greek-Albanian border. On the very face of it this was a situation fraught with danger. Yet when the United States proposed that the Security Council establish a commission to investigate the facts of the matter, with authority to call upon Albania, Bulgaria, Greece, and Yugoslavia for information, the Soviet Union vetoed the resolution![11]

Troubles in Greece continued unabated. In December 1946 the matter of guerrilla warfare along the northern border of Greece again came before the United Nations Security Council—this time at the instance of the Greek government itself. Contending that the neighboring states to the north—Albania, Yugoslavia, and Bulgaria—were lending support to the violent guerrilla warfare being waged in northern Greece, the Greek government asked the Security Council to make an on-the-spot investigation. This time the Soviet Union acceded, and an investigating commission made up of representatives of all the members of the Security Council went to Greece. Early in the summer of 1947 a majority of the commission reported that the disturbances were in fact being caused primarily by illegal assistance being furnished to the Greek guerrilla bands from Albania, Yugoslavia, and Bulgaria. But now the U.S.S.R. vetoed all proposed action. Meanwhile other events had overtaken United Nations procedures.[12]

Previously the United States had shown a lively interest in the fate of Greece, though by tacit agreement the British had been conceded the leading role in that country. In January 1946 the Export-Import Bank had extended a loan of $25,000,000 to Greece, and in September 1946 a display of American naval power off the Greek coast had attested further to this interest. American military leaders had agreed with the British that Greece should be kept outside the Soviet orbit because of its strategic importance. Now it was for the Americans to decide how far to go to maintain that position.[13]

British military and economic advisers had remained in Greece, and in Turkey as well, after World War II, and British support was helping to reorganize the armies of those countries. British troops in Greece, moreover, offered some measure of security against the menace developing along the northern border. Then on 24 February 1947 the British ambassador in Washington notified the secretary of state that, because of serious financial difficulties at home, the British government would have to discontinue assistance to both

Greece and Turkey at the end of March. At the same time one-half of the British troops in Greece would be withdrawn, and the remainder would be withdrawn later in the year. A note from the Greek government asking aid from the United States arrived about a week later. This was short notice and it called for swift action. The United States had three clear-cut choices: (1) to let events run their course without taking any positive action—which President Truman and Secretary of State Marshall regarded as a disastrous abdication to the Soviet; (2) to take the matter to the United Nations—where the Soviet Union already had hamstrung effective action on the Greek question; (3) boldly to take over the primary responsibility for holding Greece and Turkey against Soviet penetration—a course fitting the temperaments as well as the judgment of the president and the secretary of state. After a series of hastily arranged conferences among military and political leaders, the president decided to meet the problem head-on. Fundamentally the decision was based on considerations of military strategy. It led to the first major action of the United States in what was coming to be known as "the Cold War."[14]

Appearing before a joint session of Congress on 12 March 1947, President Truman asked for $300 million for assistance to Greece and $100 million for Turkey. Half of the funds for Greece and all of those for Turkey were to go for military assistance. This was a case where military necessity took precedence over economic assistance, for no economic aid could be made effective until military stability had been established. To back up this request the president said, in part:

> The gravity of the situation which confronts the world today necessitates my appearance before a joint session of the Congress.
>
> The foreign policy and the national security of this country are involved.
>
> One aspect of the present situation, which I wish to present to you at this time for your consideration and your decision, concerns Greece and Turkey. . . .
>
> The very existence of the Greek state is today threatened by the terrorist activities of several thousand armed men, led by Communists, who defy the Government's authority at a number of points, particularly along the northern boundaries. A commission appointed by the United Nations Security Council is at present investigating disturbed conditions in northern Greece and alleged border violations along the frontier between Greece on the one hand and Albania, Bulgaria, and Yugoslavia on the other.
>
> Meanwhile the Greek Government is unable to cope with the situation. The Greek Army is small and poorly equipped. It needs supplies and equipment if it is to restore authority to the Government throughout Greek territory.
>
> Greece must have assistance if it is to become a self-supporting and self-respecting democracy.
>
> The United States must supply that assistance. We have already extended to Greece certain types of relief and economic aid, but these are inadequate.

There is no other country to which democratic Greece can turn.

The future of Turkey as an independent and economically sound state is clearly no less important to the freedom-loving peoples of the world than the future of Greece. The circumstances in which Turkey finds itself today are considerably different from those of Greece. Turkey has been spared the disasters that have beset Greece. And during the war the United States and Great Britain furnished Turkey with material aid.

Nevertheless, Turkey now needs our support.

Since the war Turkey has sought additional financial assistance from Great Britain and the United States for the purpose of effecting that modernization necessary for the maintenance of its national integrity.

That integrity is essential to the preservation of the Middle East. . . .

As in the case of Greece, if Turkey is to have the assistance it needs, the United States must supply it. We are the only country able to provide that help. . . .

One of the primary objectives of the foreign policy of the United States is the creation of conditions in which we and other nations will be able to work out a way of life free from coercion. . . . We shall not realize our objectives, however, unless we are willing to help free peoples to maintain their free institutions and their national integrity against aggressive movements that seek to impose upon them totalitarian regimes. This is no more than a frank recognition that totalitarian regimes imposed upon free peoples, by direct or indirect aggression, undermine the foundations of international peace and hence the security of the United States.[15]

Essentially the president's address was a plea for logistic support. It called for military supplies and equipment to be supplied to these threatened countries, and it called for military, as well as economic, advisers to be sent to supervise the positive application of this assistance program.

The clear implication of what journalists quickly termed the "Truman Doctrine" was this: Wherever Soviet expansion threatened to swallow up independent nations, that threat would have to be met by the use of American matériel resources to strengthen those nations. The doctrine could be summed up in one sentence from the president's message: "I believe that it must be the policy of the United States to support free peoples who are resisting attempted subjugation by armed minorities or by outside pressures."

To what extent Congress would be sympathetic to this policy was uncertain. Senator Robert A. Taft of Ohio expressed fears that approval of the proposed program of logistic assistance to Greece and Turkey might lead to a Soviet declaration of war. Others felt that the lack of such a firm policy was more likely to lead to war. After Senator Arthur H. Vandenberg of Michigan, a leader of bipartisan foreign policy, accepted the basic features of the program, approval seemed likely. Several weeks of sharp debate followed, but finally both houses of Congress passed the Greek-Turkish Aid Bill by more than two-to-one majorities. The president approved the act 22 May 1947.[16]

In the support of United Nations and other relief programs and in foreign loans the United States granted during late 1945 and 1946, the emphasis was upon economic rehabilitation. But by the end of 1946 it was becoming clear that military assistance was necessary for some countries in order for them to be able to develop the internal stability needed as a basis for economic recovery. In particular this was the case in Greece. When the British gave notice that they would be unable to continue full responsibility for military aid to Greece and Turkey, the United States stepped in. Truman's appeal on 12 March 1947 to Congress for approval of a program of military and economic assistance to Greece and Turkey came just six years after the shipment of a cargo of military equipment to Greece had marked the beginning of the lend-lease program. The Truman Doctrine of assistance to the victims of aggression indicated that the United States would not return to its traditional policy of neutrality, and the Greek-Turkish Aid Program that went with it indicated a revival of the principles of lend-lease. In the next year China received further military assistance, and other programs were developed for Latin America and the Philippines. In the period from the termination of lend-lease to 30 November 1948, the value of military equipment furnished to foreign governments amounted to $923 million—$280 million for China, $202 million for Greece, $90 million for Turkey, $174 million for Latin American republics, and $177 million for the Philippines.[17]

Mutual Defense Assistance Program

Even as the North Atlantic Treaty was being discussed (see pp. 161–62), the implication was clear that American matériel assistance to the participating countries would be necessary if the new organization were to have any real effectiveness as a deterrent to aggression.[18] But President Truman waited until the day after he signed the instrument of ratification to follow it up with a formal request for military assistance. Calling for $1,450,000,000, this proposal would consolidate in one act the existing programs for Greece and Turkey, Iran, Korea, the Philippines, and the Western Hemisphere, with a new program for North Atlantic Treaty countries. It envisaged three types of assistance: (1) direct transfer of American military equipment; (2) expert guidance in using the equipment and in production of equipment; (3) dollar aid to increase direct military production in Europe. Ten weeks later Congress approved the program in the Mutual Defense Assistance Act.[19]

Initially, the assistance was to go to eight signatories of the North Atlantic Treaty, Greece, Turkey, Iran, Korea, and the Philippines, and for assistance "in the general region of China." Congress made the availability of $900,000,000 for the North Atlantic Treaty countries contingent upon the formation of an integrated defense plan by the North Atlantic Treaty Organization. Economic recovery in Europe still was to have priority over rearmament.[20]

In general the Mutual Defense Assistance Program got off to a slow start.

Most foreign aid actually delivered during fiscal year 1950 was what already had been scheduled under previous programs. It was obvious from the beginning that a large part of the funds appropriated for fiscal year 1951 could not be committed for specific programs before the end of that fiscal year. The original act itself had not been approved until 6 October 1949, the appropriation act was approved three weeks later, and the required bilateral agreements were not completed with the European countries until 27 January 1951.[21] The fiscal year 1951 was half gone, and supply action had not even commenced. Foreign requirements brough back by preliminary survey teams could not be reprogrammed until the State and Defense Departments agreed upon criteria. The military assistance advisory groups would be able to contribute little to reprogramming for fiscal year 1950 in the time left to them after their arrival in foreign countries. Procedures still had to be worked out for meeting all the administrative problems involved in such a complex undertaking. Considering all these circumstances General Larkin recommended that fiscal year 1950 funds be carried over to the next fiscal year. The 1951 MDAP should be limited, in his view, to providing necessary training, the replacement of training ammunition and other consumed items, spare parts, and administrative expenses; new funds requested for the next fiscal year he thought should not exceed $100,000,000. Any further substantial program of reequipping selected foreign armies should be deferred to fiscal year 1952.[22] Actually the General Appropriations Act passed in September 1950 contained $1.223 billion for MDAP (for all services), and already, a month after the commitment of ground forces to action in Korea, President Truman had asked Congress for additional funds for military aid. Here was clear testimony of the stimulus to foreign aid the Korean attack had provided. The Supplemental Appropriations Act, passed less than three weeks after the General Appropriations Act, included an additional $4 billion for the Mutual Defense Assistance Program—nearly a billion more than that provided in the act for the expansion of the army itself and for its conduct of operations in Korea. In addition nearly $300,000,000 (for all services) remained unobligated from the 1950 appropriation. At the end of June 1950 the army had obligated $470 million, and spent only $25.6 million of the $524.8 million in MDAP funds that had been allocated to it.[23]

The Mutual Defense Assistance Act of 1951 carried the proviso that economic recovery was to have priority over programs of military assistance. By 1951 the economic recovery of the European nations with the benefit of the Marshall Plan had progressed notably, but external threats to security seemed as dangerous as ever. The Marshall Plan came to an end officially with the enactment of the Mutual Security Act, approved 10 October 1951, which brought economic and technical assistance as well as military assistance programs under the general supervision of a single director for mutual security. From this time the emphasis was upon military assistance. Even the economic programs frequently had to be justified as contributing toward the effective military defense of the countries concerned. Military aid under the Mutual Security Program continued to be known as the Mutual Defense Assistance Program. The new act continued the general title designations of countries with some modifications. Now Title 1 provided for programs—economic, technical assistance, and military aid—for Europe, Title 2 for the Near East and Africa, Title 3 for Asia and the Pacific, and countries of the Western Hemisphere got into the act under Title 4. The program was to end 30 June 1954.[24] The Mutual Security Act of 1952, approved 20 June, made a number of additions and amendments to the original law, but retained its principal provisions.[25] The president signed the appropriation bill on 15 July 1952. Carrying a total of $4.22 billion for foreign military aid, the appropriation act represented a reduction of nearly 8 percent from the amount that Congress had authorized just a month before. It was a cut of 22 percent from the amount the president had requested. The total appropriation, for economic and technical assistance as well as for military aid, was $5.995 billion.[26]

Actual shipments under the Mutual Defense Assistance Program did not begin until March 1950. By the time of the Korean attack the army had programmed $1.0326 billion worth of equipment for MDAP, had initiated supply action on $155.1 million of this, and had shipped $19.2 million worth—of which $2 million worth was from excess stocks not charged against the MDAP appropriation. Total tonnage shipped by all services up to that time was about 139,000 measurement tons.[27]

The total of MDAP funds made available to the army through 31 December 1952 amounted to $8.3 billion. Disbursements up to that time totalled but $2.89 billion, and unpaid obligations totalled $4.14 billion.[28] Total army shipments through 30 April 1953 included supplies and equipment valued at $3.66 billion (including surplus property not chargeable to MDAP funds). By this time these shipments included 25,810 tanks and combat vehicles, 77,515 pieces of electronics and signal equipment, 136,114 motor transport vehicles, 24,397 artillery pieces, 1,459,228 small arms and machine guns, 725,729,000 rounds of small arms ammunition, and 18,279,000 rounds of artillery ammunition. Army shipments of approximately five million measurement tons comprised about 75 percent of all MDAP shipments. All this was in addition to the 25 million tons of supplies and equipment that had been shipped by this time to Korea.[29]

By early 1953 it was clear that fulfillment of mutual defense assistance programs was running at least eighteen months behind—about the lead time required for initial procurement of the items most difficult to manufacture.

Some idea of the progress being made could be found in the status of particular items being shipped, including those obtained both in the continental United States and those obtained through offshore procurement (see table 1).

Delays in completing mutual defense assistance programs could be attributed to the fact that current military production in the United States had not yet reached the point where it could provide all the equipment needed both

Table 1. Status of Selected Items Under MDAP

	Programmed FY 1950–1953	Total Shipped to 30 June 1952	Shipped 1 July 52–31 May 53	TOTAL
Radios, SCR 300	23,537	3,154	12,132	15,286
Medium tanks	7,383	1,883	3,565	5,448
Trucks, $2\frac{1}{2}$-ton	49,793	16,597	22,519	39,116
Howitzers, 105-mm.	2,803	1,371	207	1,578
Ammunition, 105-mm. HE	13,177M	1,783M	1,737M	3,530M

SOURCE: Army Foreign Military Aid, 1 June 53, 33.

for foreign aid and for operations in Korea at the same time. Closely related to this were the increasing worldwide matériel requirements for the army's own forces in these critical times, and the relative priority that had to be assigned to MDAP.

In addition to these grants of military equipment, other equipment was going to foreign governments during this period on a cash purchase basis under the provision (Section 408 (e)) of the Mutual Defense Assistance Act, which in effect put the procurement machinery of the army and the other military services at the disposal of allied governments for their purchases in this country. Over 1,000 requests, from forty-nine foreign countries for reimbursable assistance of this kind had been received through the end of June 1952. By 30 April 1953 arrangements had been completed with forty-five countries for the purchase of $654 million worth of equipment, including $224 million in army equipment. This called for no financial outlay on the part of the United States, but it was an additional claim on matériel resources of this country.[30]

Another objective of the Mutual Security Program was to stimulate the build-up of local defense industries in participating countries. One of the aspects of the original Mutual Defense Assistance Program had been the provision for furnishing tools and materials to foreign countries under what was referred to as "additional military production" projects. MDAP appropriations for fiscal years 1950 and 1951 each contained about $500 million for these projects. The hope was that by a small American contribution aimed at eliminating bottlenecks such as shortages of materials and machine tools European production facilities that otherwise would be idle might add many times the value of that contribution in finished military goods. Each project went through a long process of screening for military suitability, technical feasibility, availability of licenses and patents, availability of labor and technical skills, production resources, and other factors. Indeed the screening was so fine that little got through it. Only about $26 million of assistance for this purpose had been granted by 31 May 1951. While the value of the final production expected from the projects approved was about $321 million, this clearly was not putting much of the European industrial capacity into military production. By the end of 1951 "additional military production" practically was defunct. Results had failed to meet the hopes.[31]

But there were other ways of achieving the same end. One of these was through "offshore procurement." This was a part of the regular end-item grant program, but the procurement orders were placed in foreign countries instead of in the United States. It thus was possible to kill two or three birds with one stone. The finished equipment being furnished a foreign government would be the same type and quality as it would have been had it been manufactured in the United States. But since it was being produced in foreign countries, military production in those countries would be stimulated. Moreover, the drain on American resources and the demands on American industrial facilities at a time when so many demands had to be met would be relieved. By 31 December 1951 the three services had programmed over $500 million for the offshore procurement of ammunition, spare parts, and auxiliary vessels. Over half of this amount was for army procurement, and the Department of the Army was designated executive agency for the coordination of offshore procurement activities among the three services. The commander in chief, Europe, in turn became the executive agent for the European area.[32]

A detailed study of the fiscal year 1953 mutual defense assistance program by the U.S. special representative in Europe submitted in September 1952 carried with it recommendations for a far-reaching offshore procurement program in Europe. The army's share of this procurement for the fiscal year would have been $731.8 million. But now the pendulum began to swing the other way. Now army planners pointed to the necessity of retaining sufficiently large orders in the United States to maintain the production base here. Offshore procurement contracts actually placed under the fiscal years 1952 and 1953 mutual defense assistance programs totalled $1.757 billion for all services on 31 May 1953; the army had placed $993 million of these contracts. Nearly half of the contracts, in value, had been placed in France. Great Britain and Italy were the next most important sources. Only $34 million of the amount so far contracted had been placed in the Far East—$28.6 million (including $4.7 million by the air force) in Japan, and $5.8 million in Formosa.[33]

Yet another approach to encouraging the development of local military production in friendly foreign countries was the broad program of economic assistance known as "defense support" administered by the Mutual Security Agency. In effect this was a successor on a much broader basis to the additional military production projects. Virtually all economic aid now had to be justified as contributing to defense support. It was administered in much the same way as had been the previous economic assistance given under the Economic Cooperation Administration, but the emphasis had been shifted away from economic recovery per se to the building of production for military support. This made the objective of the former additional military production program—the providing of scarce materials and tools—the major objective, while avoiding the tangle of screening for individual projects that had contributed to the suffocation of the earlier effort.

Offshore procurement was the responsibility of the military. Defense support was the responsibility principally of the Mutual Security Agency. Secretary of Defense Robert Lovett explained the difference between these two approaches as follows:

> Offshore procurement, as used by the military departments, refers to the purchase outside of the continental limits of end items which we are permitted to deliver to the NATO groups or to other friendly countries around the world.
>
> Military support, or defense support, or economic aid, as you choose in this matter, applies to that form of procurement which deals mainly with raw materials or similar items which, when delivered to an ally, permits that ally to do the work himself on the manufacture of certain forms of end items needed.
>
> The difference, therefore, is essentially between the procurement by this country of the completed end item abroad, which is offshore procurement, whereas defense support, as used in this act, applies to the provision of raw materials, by which the foreign ally uses his own labor, carries his own overhead and produces an end item for his particular use.[34]

Programs of offshore procurement and "defense support" were not without their objectionable features. It was possible that the emphasis being placed upon military production instead of upon general economic improvement might have unfortunate long-term consequences in which apparent economic health would be found to be without solid foundations. Under certain circumstances, where idle industrial plants and manpower were to be found and a country was unable to expand its own military budget, there was an opportunity for American military buyers to place dollar contracts and thus to stimulate the use of idle resources, increase employment, and provide much needed dollar exchange while obtaining the required military equipment. But often the economic and political objectives of improved conditions and higher morale were in conflict with the military procurement objective of obtaining certain needed equipment of good quality at reasonable prices. In a situation such as that found in England, where the economy already was working at near capacity and the local military budget already was at a satisfactory level, the effect of American offshore procurement was to divert industrial capacity and raw materials away from production for civilian consumption or for long-range, dollar-earning export markets. In those circumstances the result was likely to be a net lowering of the standard of living, and to that extent, a nullification of the effects of the earlier Marshall Plan. One leading British industrialist told a member of a Mutual Security Program survey team: "We're converting some of our very scarce capital structure to get your OSP dollars. We are willing to do it, if your people feel it essential, but we're worried. We know that as soon as your own munitions production lines catch up on their contracts and need more to keep them going, neither your Congress nor your military will want to justify placing contracts here for goods you can make in the United States.[35]

Some observers saw in the growing offshore procurement program a danger of the too prominent participation of military officers in foreign economic policies. Clearly procurement implied certain controls. It was more than a matter of going out to buy something on the open market. Specifications had to be met, delivery schedules set up, inspections entertained. American military advisers were appearing in most of the countries of the free world; military procurement officers were dealing with foreign industrialists; military officers and government officials might, unless handled with skillful restraint, contribute to a certain measure of popular acceptance of the communist propaganda that American intentions were purely imperialistic. Some Europeans thought that Americans still had their eyes too close to the present, and were seeking quick results at the expense of more fundamental long-range objectives.[36] Whether such interpretations were valid or not, they had to be taken into account in developing an effective American policy. Subsidies granted with conditions implying ulterior motives could defeat their own higher purposes. Even gifts freely given, if too obviously granted as alms from the powerful to the weak, might injure national pride more than they helped national defense. Only a mutuality of purpose and effort, based upon national self-respect, could be expected to turn the resources of the free world to common defense.

The Mutual Defense Assistance Program was not adapted to furnishing military equipment to allies under wartime conditions. War could not wait for the months of programming, reprogramming, revision, coordination, and multilateral approval. It was ironic that when the Korean War came, the far-reaching program of foreign military aid that was just beginning to become effective offered no help in supplying allies willing to participate in the collective action in Korea. Plans and programs aimed solely at building strength for war left void the area of serious consideration of what actions should be taken in case the war against which all this preparation was being taken should in fact break out. A year after the Korean attack had pointed so forcibly to the need for such plans, none had yet been drawn up. In March 1951 G–4 had stated, "Up-to-date guidance for war-time aid to allies is required at earliest practicable date by G–4 and Technical Services."[37] At last by October 1951 the Joint Chiefs of Staff had approved guidance that the Joint Logistics Plans Committee and the Joint Strategic Plans Committee had prepared to govern such assistance.[38]

Carrying a total of $4.22 billion for foreign military aid, the appropriation act of 15 July 1952 represented a reduction of nearly 8 percent from the amount that Congress had authorized just a month before. It was a cut of 22 percent from the amount the president had requested. The total appropriation, for economic and technical assistance as well as for military aid, was $5.995.[39]

In January 1953 President Truman asked for a total of $7.6 billion for the fiscal year 1945 Mutual Security Program. After reconsideration, the new Eisenhower administration trimmed this to $5.8 billion, and Congress finally appropriated $4.532 billion, of which $3.165 billion was for million aid and another $874 million for defense support and the financing of multilateral projects. The act also extended $2.121 billion of unobligated balances so that total mutual security funds available for the fiscal year amounted to $6.652 billion.[40]

As of 31 May 1953, a total of $15.5 billion of fiscal year 1950, 1951, 1952, and 1953 funds had been authorized for financing military assistance activities of the Department of Defense. In the overall obligation of funds, now amounting to approximately $13 billion, the Department of the Army's share represented some 56 percent.[41]

Organization for Foreign Military Aid

Reserving certain authority on technical points to himself, the president designated the secretary of state as the agent responsible for general direction and control of the Mutual Defense Assistance Program. While policy direction thus was in the hands of the State Department, most of the execution of what was essentially a military program fell to the Department of Defense. The Economic Cooperation Administration entered the picture, particularly in coordinating the programs for economic recovery with those aimed at stepping up the production of military equipment in other countries. The heads of those three agencies (State, Defense, and ECA) constituted the Foreign Military Assistance Steering Committee. The working committee under that group was the Foreign Military Assistance Coordinating Committee, an outgrowth of the original Foreign Assistance Correlation Committee, made up of the director for MDAP in the State Department, the director of the Office of Military Assistance representing the secretary of defense, and a top official of the Economic Cooperation Administration. The group met regularly and frequently to consider problems of policy and operation.[42]

In December 1950 the Foreign Military Assistance Coordinating Committee gave way to the International Security Affairs Committee, which was made up of the director of International Security Affairs of the State Department and advisory representatives from the Office of the Special Assistant to the President (Averill Harriman), the Office of Defense Mobilization, and the Treasury Department as well as the regular members from the Department of Defense and the Economic Cooperation Administration. Working subcommittees included the Foreign Aid Committee, which was responsible for questions relating to direct military assistance; the Political-Military Group, to handle international security matters such as those of the North Atlantic Treaty Organization; the Defense Production Group, for assistance in European military production; the Financial and Economic Group, and the Public Information Committee. A year later the International Security Affairs Committee became the Mutual Assistance Advisory Committee. The new committee had essentially the same membership as the old except that now the Mutual Security Agency replaced the Economic Cooperation Administration, and the director for Mutual Security or his representative became the chairman. This was in keeping with the new arrangement under the Mutual Security Program by which the director for mutual security became the overall director on behalf of the president in place of the secretary of state as had been the case earlier. Effective August 1953 the Foreign Operations Administration succeeded the Mutual Security Agency.[43]

Within the Department of Defense the secretary appointed an assistant to the secretary of defense (Foreign Military Affairs and Military Assistance), later redesignated assistant secretary of defense (International Security Affairs). Under the assistant to the secretary, the director of military assistance was the coordinator of military aspects of the assistance programs and the point of contact between the director of the Mutual Defense Assistance Program (State Department) and later the director for Mutual Security, and agencies of the Defense Department and the military departments. The Joint Chiefs of Staff had responsibility for establishing the military objectives of programs, requirements level, pricing policies, priorities among recipient countries, the apportionment of funds among recipient countries, and among the three services, the consideration of joint strategic and logistic matters and the designation and support of agencies overseas for the execution of the programs (except that the U.S. military representative for military assistance in Europe was responsible directly to the secretary of defense). The Joint Chiefs of Staff designated the chief of staff of the army as executive agent for all matters pertaining to their responsibilities under the Mutual Defense Assistance Program.

The Munitions Board had to take into consideration the possible impact of foreign military aid on American mobilization requirements, industrial potential, and economic stability. The Research and Development Board correlated research and development aspects of the military assistance programs and evaluated requests for military assistance involving the release of classified technical information.

Beneath all these coordinating superstructures, the three military departments were responsible for developing final programs for approval and for their execution. It was up to them to procure and ship the needed equipment and to provide the personnel to handle it. Special responsibilities fell upon the army since it was the executive agency for the Joint Chiefs of Staff, and since more than half the matériel to be sent abroad would be army equipment. The army G–3 had important functions in supervising organization, in carrying out the army's functions as executive agency for the Joint Chiefs of Staff, and in training assistance, but military assistance in the main was matériel assistance, and that came under the assistant chief of staff, G–4. This office had inherited the International Division of Army Service Forces at the end of World War II, a part of which now had become the Foreign Military Assistance Division.

In Europe additional complex organizational structures sought regional coordination of assistance programs.[44] As the staff agency for the U.S. senior military representative, the Joint American Military Advisory Group (JAMAG) was set up in London. In particular it coordinated the activities of the military assistance advisory groups in the various countries belonging to the North Atlantic Treaty Organization. After the activation of the new U.S. European Command in August 1952, the Military Assistance Division of that headquarters absorbed the functions and personnel of the Military Assistance Planning Group of JAMAG. Europe was the only area where organizations were interposed for the purpose of coordinating integrated regional programs. Elsewhere the Caribbean Command had some ill-defined functions in coordinating assistance programs for Latin American countries, and the U.S. Military Advisory Group to the Republic of Korea (KMAG) after the 25 June 1950 attack came directly under the commander in chief, Far East; otherwise the military assistance advisory groups in the various recipient countries reported directly to the Department of the Army.

The sending of American assistance groups to the countries designated to receive aid was one of the distinctive features of the Mutual Defense Assistance Program. Under lend-lease and other programs the United States had depended originally upon the foreign governments themselves to compute their requirements, and for representatives of those governments in Washington to make their presentations. The lend-lease missions sent overseas after late 1941 were the forerunners of the MAAG's that appeared upon the scene nearly a decade later. Now from the outset of the new military assistance program, the impetus was to be in the other direction, and at the same time supervision on the part of the United States would be much closer.

In general the military assistance advisory groups (MAAG's) consisted of army, navy, and air force sections each headed by the senior officer of the respective service, except that the chief of the MAAG might designate the next senior member of his section as section chief. The senior officer, whatever his service, was chief of the MAAG. His responsibility on general policy matters was to the American ambassador or minister in the country where located, but on questions of military programming, supply, and related questions, he reported, in Europe to JAMAG (later Military Assistance Division of U.S. European Command) and in other areas directly to the Department of the Army as executive agency for the Joint Chiefs of Staff. Section chiefs were authorized direct communications with their ambassadors, with their respective military departments in Washington, and with corresponding components of the recipient countries' armed forces on questions affecting their service alone. The strength of the sections of the MAAG was a matter for determination by agreement betweent the Departments of State and Defense. Individual assignments were as directed by the service concerned.[45]

It was the duty of the military assistance advisory group to advise and assist the recipient government in the preparation of general requests for aid and to forward recommended country aid programs. It assisted in arriving at matériel requirements on the basis of approved plans and policies and submitted itemized lists of equipment and desired delivery schedules under the general programs after they had been approved. It was up to the MAAG to recommend priorities of equipment in approved programs, to help in the preparation of requisitions, to receive the matériel and transfer title to the foreign country when required, to assist in the identification, storage, and maintenance of the supplies received, and to advise in the local production of military equipment. In addition to these purely logistical functions, the military assistance advisory group also had certain training functions— often closely related to the proper use of the equipment being furnished.[46] By the end of 1950 military assistance advisory groups had been established in the United Kingdom, France, Belgium (serving also Luxembourg), Denmark, Norway, the Netherlands, Italy, and Portugal. These were in addition to the groups already established with similar functions in Greece, Turkey, the Philippines, and Korea. During the first half of 1951 MAAGs were sent to Iran, Thailand, Indochina, Indonesia, and Formosa.[47] Military missions in most of the Latin American republics and a joint commission in Brazil exercised somewhat similar functions in addition to their training and defense coordination duties. Later MAAGs also were established in Chile, Colombia, Cuba, Ecuador, Peru, and Uruguay.[48] In the spring of 1952 approximately 3,200 officers and men were assigned to military assistance advisory groups overseas.[49]

The military assistance advisory group, together with the economic or technical assistance mission under the ambassador or minister were referred to as the "country team." The chief of diplomatic mission was charged with overall coordination within the country of the activities of American representatives providing all types of assistance under the Mutual Security Program.[50] In countries receiving aid under the Act for International Development (popularly known as the Point Four Program by reason of its origin as the fourth major recommendation in President Truman's inaugural address of 1949), a Technical Cooperation Administration (Department of State) mission from the Mutual Security Agency (formerly Economic Cooperation Administration) participated. If a country was receiving both types of assistance, the general rule was that a single mission from the agency having the major interest would perform the functions for both. In any case, the military assistance programs were not to be isolated from other forms of assistance intended to contribute to the strength, stability, and well-being of the countries concerned.

Procedures

Planning for annual mutual defense assistance programs began ten to twelve months before the beginning of the fiscal year in which the particular program was to be put into effect. The Joint Chiefs of Staff, acting on the recommendation of the military assistance advisory groups in each country, was the agency responsible for determining the forces to be equipped and for setting up the criteria to govern the supply programs. From the total forces approved for a country by the Joint Chiefs of Staff, the government concerned and the military assistance advisory group assigned would develop a list of overall requirements. Matériel already in the hands of that government, goods that it would be able to purchase economically, and ones that would be in the process of manufacture during the time being considered would then be subtracted from the overall requirements. The resulting net deficiency represented that part that the United States would undertake to provide under the grant assistance programs, insofar as it was practicable in relating to other commitments and available resources.

For the fiscal year 1953 program, for example, the Joint Chiefs of Staff in July 1951 developed a time schedule for foreign nations and the respective military assistance advisory groups to present their requests and recommendations. At the same time the Joint Chiefs issued the criteria according to which they would determine the types and number of forces that they would consider eligible for military aid and the types of equipment which could or could not be included. In general the criteria required that: (1) Equipment for members of the North Atlantic Treaty Organization would be provided only for the forces called for by that organization's defense plan and accepted by each country as a definite commitment to that plan; (2) equipment for other countries would be furnished only for forces in being, or those capable of immediate mobilization; (3) the programs would be "on the most austere basis, and limited to items of highest priority"; (4) equipment of questionable value for military operations would not be included; (5) equipment that could be produced in the country, or in the case of Europe, by other members of the North Atlantic Treaty Organization, would not be furnished by the United States.[51]

The director for mutual security (after 1 November 1951) acting for the president set the tentative dollar ceilings for both economic and military assistance programs after consultation with the Bureau of the Budget and with administration leaders. After receiving the recommendation of the MAAGs, the Joint Chiefs of Staff arrived at an agreed force basis to be supported under the program and drew up tentative budgetary ceilings for each of the four major areas of the world—Western Europe, the Near East, the Far East, and Latin America, for each country and for each service supplying equipment. On the basis of known country deficiencies and the force goals set by the Joint Chiefs of Staff, the Departments of the Army, Navy, and Air

Force developed a budgetary basis for the equipment for which each respectively was responsible. The Joint Chiefs of Staff forwarded their criteria for screening country deficiencies through the Department of the Army as executive agent to the Military Assistance Division, U.S. European Command (formerly Joint American Military Advisory Group) and to all the MAAGs. Each military assistance advisory group asked representatives from the local government to submit requirements for the support of forces approved by the Joint Chiefs of Staff. On receiving the list of deficiencies with supporting data, the MAAG reviewed it on the basis of the JCS criteria, eliminated questionable items, and forwarded it to the Department of the Army (or of the Navy or Air Force for equipment provided by those services). Lists submitted from countries of Western Europe went through a further screening at Military Assistance Division, U.S. European Command, for the purpose of determining whether deficiencies in one country might be made up by a surplus of items or extra raw materials or productive capacity in neighboring countries.

Then the military departments would examine the lists critically and draw up their tentative programs. The Office of Military Assistance, Department of Defense, reviewed and consolidated the tentative programs submitted by the three military departments and forwarded them to the director for mutual security. Putting the military programs together with the economic and technical assistance programs, the director for mutual security submitted the whole thing to the Bureau of the Budget. This bureau, with the approval of the president, then fixed budget limitations for each agency and submitted the figures to the director for mutual security. Now in effect the process had to begin all over again.

On the basis of the limitations set by the Bureau of the Budget, the director for mutual security would direct each agency to prepare new tentative programs. Within these ceilings the Joint Chiefs of Staff again set dollar limits for the military assistance program by region, country, and military department. With this guidance, the secretary of defense (Office of Military Assistance) directed the military departments to prepare their revised tentative programs for presentation to Congress. This revision was likely to involve further consultation with the military assistance advisory group and between representatives of these groups and representatives of the governments concerned. It was safe to assume that revisions would be downward. How small a proposed program would have to be in order to escape cutting somewhere along the line was difficult to say. But trimming of a well-worked-out program was more than the mere elimination of so many trucks or so many guns. Every change in the items to be furnished meant changes also in spare parts to go with it, in the transportation that had to be arranged for it, in the storage facilities to be provided, in the training programs to be planned, and in the defense missions that could be supported.

As with the initial programs, the Office of Military Assistance reviewed and consolidated the revised tentative programs and again passed them on to the director for mutual security. With his approval they became a part of the Mutual Security Program for presentation to Congress.

Proposed legislation to authorize the program in the House of Representatives was referred to the Committee on Foreign Affairs and in the Senate sometimes jointly to the Committees on Armed Services and Foreign Relations, and at other times to the Committee on Foreign Relations alone. In any case representatives from the Department of Defense and the military services were called upon to explain and defend the proposed programs. It was common for hearings to go on before the committees of both houses simultaneously. At times an individual would testify before both on the same day. After all this testimony had been completed, and the legislation, changed in varying degrees, finally had been approved by both houses of Congress and by the president, the end was not yet.

Evidence again had to be marshalled to convince members of the two appropriations committees that the funds authorized in the previous legislation really ought to be appropriated. The appropriation bill was likely to embrace another round of cutting, and usually some delays in making the funds available. For the fiscal year 1953 program Truman requested $7.9 billion for military assistance. In the Mutual Security Act of 1952, approved by the president on 20 June 1952, Congress authorized $6.431 billion. The Mutual Security Appropriation Act, 1953 (Title 3 of the Supplemental Appropriation Act, 1953) passed by Congress on 7 July and approved by the president on 15 July 1952, reduced the amount to $5.995 billion—a reduction of 22 percent from the president's request.

Now, about the same time that initial planning for the 1954 tentative program had to begin, the cycle had to begin again for approving a 1953 program before supply action on it could commence. With the approval of the secretary of defense, the Joint Chiefs of Staff had to establish new regional, country, and military department ceilings on the basis of the funds actually available. Here some measure of flexibility could be introduced by the president's authority to transfer up to 10 percent of the funds appropriated for programs under one title of the Mutual Security Act to those under another title in order to reduce the amount of assistance provided in one area and increase it in another area.[52]

In the case of the fiscal year 1953 program, the Joint Chiefs of Staff were unable to reach agreement on the apportionment of the funds that Congress had appropriated and the director for mutual security had allocated. The secretary of defense had to resolve the impasse by recommending apportionment of the full appropriation on a percentage basis without approving specifically the programs of any of the services. This was done in mid-August 1952. The army's share was to be $1.918 billion. After all the months of close figuring, screening, and revising, programs now had to be based on an arbitrary division of available funds.[53]

After approval of the adjusted ceilings was obtained, the secretary of defense (Office of Military Assistance) would issue directives to the military departments to prepare refined country programs. Again further consultation with Military Assistance Division of U.S. European Command and with the MAAGs would be necessary. After approval by the foreign governments at last the refined programs—the fourth round of programming—would be forwarded by the military departments to the Office of Military Assistance for review and consolidation and submission to the director of mutual security. Still the programs could not be finally set until funds became available. After approval of the programs, the director for mutual security allocated the funds for military assistance to the Department of Defense, which in turn allocated them to the military departments. The Department of the Army suballocated the funds to the technical services.

Again in the case of the fiscal year 1953 program, the army proceeded with reprogramming on the basis of the funds it expected to receive. Country programs had been completed and approved by the various chiefs of military assistance advisory groups by 12 September, and then they were ready for processing again to the secretary of defense and to the director for mutual security. Meanwhile, the army had to begin supply action if it were to come near fulfilling even the reduced programs.

The ordinary difficulties in obligating funds now were compounded by the release to the army of available funds piecemeal, as increments of the program were approved. Increments submitted included only items of the highest priority that reasonably could be expected to remain whatever program should be finally approved. On 28 August the Department of the Army submitted a request for a first increment of $164 million to cover the foreign procurement in Great Britain of Centurian tanks. On 12 September a second increment called for $209 million for procurement in the United States. A third request submitted on 30 October asked for another $140 million for offshore procurement. The Office of the Secretary of Defense approved all three increments and released the necessary funds on 16 September, 18 September, and 6 November respectively. On 12 September the Department of the Army submitted its revised overall 1953 program to the office of the secretary of defense. This was approved on 22 October, but a number of reservations were attached that prevented immediate execution of it. Of the $1.918 billion originally apportioned to the army, the secretary of defense released $1.551 billion by 28 November. Various changes and adjustments reduced the total figure of apportioned funds to $1.789 billion by 20 January 1953.[54]

Foreign Military Aid Branch of G–4 Supply Division sent copies of approved country matériel programs to the Procurement Division of G–4, the procurement and supply divisions of each of the technical services, the overseas supply division at each primary port of embarkation, and to each military assistance advisory group. On receiving the approved programs, the technical services would transfer listed items available in stock to an MDAP property account. After physically verifying the major items to be furnished from army stocks, the technical service would issue a freeze order on them and then submit to G–4 a list of major items in the MDAP property account and the deficiencies requiring new procurement. In addition the head of the technical service was to prepare a statement of the funds needed for replacement procurement and he would submit a complete procurement program to G–4. Lists of major items already available would be furnished to the chiefs of the MAAGs to serve as a basis for requisitioning.

The allocation of available equipment and priorities for its distribution had yet to be taken into consideration. The Joint Chiefs of Staff delegated to the Joint Munitions Allocations Committee (JMAC) this responsibility. Under the authority and direction of this joint committee the allocations committee (army) had the function of recommending the distribution of army-procured matériel among: (1) United States forces as required under approved strategic plans, and (2) nations participating in the Mutual Defense Assistance Program. This army committee met usually once a month. The Foreign Military Aid Branch, G–4, prepared the agenda for the meetings according to the equipment anticipated to become available during a given period. Minutes of the meeting went out to the technical services and to the overseas supply divisions of the ports of embarkation.

On receiving the minutes of the allocations committee, the Industrial Division of the Office of the Chief of Ordnance, for example, indicated whether the equipment would be furnished from stocks or from new procurement. In the cases where items on hand were to be furnished for military assistance programs to be replaced from new procurement as a step toward modernization of the army's own equipment, the determination to furnish items form stocks did not necessarily coincide with the sources of acquisitions shown on the original approved programs.[55]

Requisitioning procedures underwent a number of changes in the course of the first four years of the Mutual Defense Assistance Program. At first the military assistance advisory groups themselves prepared and submitted the requisitions. Then the foreign governments were given the responsibility of preparing the requisitions and submitting them through the military assistance advisory groups directly to the heads of the technical services. Later requisitions were prepared in the Office of the Assistant Chief of Staff, G–4; then by G–4 in collaboration with the oversea supply divisions of the primary ports of embarkation (New York and San Francisco). Finally by late 1952 and early 1953 the practice had grown up informally of having the oversea supply divisions prepare all requisitions of programmed end-items on the basis of approved programs and the minutes of the allocations committee (army). Requisitions for spare parts continued to be submitted by the foreign governments through the military assistance advisory groups, but these requisitions too went to the oversea supply divisions at the ports rather than directly to the technical services. Regularized by a revision in the regulations in August

1953, this procedure simplified foreign military aid requisitioning and within the United States brought it more into line with the army's normal procedures. Ports of embarkation called forward portions of shipments as necessary to facilitate loading, and notified the respective MAAGs of the shipment so that arrangements could be completed for receiving the goods.[56]

Revisions in programs and plans did not cease with formal approval. Four or five cycles of programming and screening through half a dozen or more headquarters and staff agencies often was not enough. At times the compulsion to revise followed country programs to the very ships carrying the matériel away. The Oversea Supply Division at the New York port of embarkation reported that between 7 January and 31 March 1953 it received eighty-seven telephone calls relating to hold orders, change orders, or the remarking of MDAP cargo.

After 1951 the director for mutual security in effect held a position analogous to that of the lend-lease administrator after establishment of the Office of Lend-Lease Administration in October 1941. But the newer effort at foreign military aid was more closely coordinated and its execution was more closely bound with the army's regular procurement and supply procedures. Appropriations still were separate, but in effect MDAP amounted to a separate bank account against which the procurement agencies could draw checks in financing an integrated overall procurement program. The fact that procurement assistance also was provided for countries seeking equipment on a cash basis served further to coordinate the total procurement program. During World War II manufacturers at times would have to satisfy foreign purchasing agencies that had placed contracts directly with them and the lend-lease administrator or the president for lend-lease commitments, as well as the various army agencies having procurement responsibilities. Now all procurement for given items went through the same people, whether the eventual purpose was for the army's own use or for foreign military aid.

Difficulties did arise in keeping the records straight on the use of MDAP funds. One complication resulted from the army's modernization program under which matériel on hand would be supplied to the foreign country and the funds would be used to finance the procurement of new equipment to replace that in the army's stocks. Such procedures would make available equipment to foreign countries in the shortest possible time, American units would receive more modern equipment, while stock levels in general could be maintained. After the outbreak of hostilities in Korea, however, it was not possible to make such transfers from stocks immediately. Indeed the supply of many items dwindled toward depletion. Moreover, much of the equipment that was on hand could not be shipped without extensive repair or renovation. It seemed prudent to withhold the transfer of matériel to foreign countries at least until replacement equipment was in sight. But the Department of Defense authorized the military departments to "obligate" MDAP funds on the basis of issuing supply directives for amounts estimated to cover the items to be furnished from service stocks when they did become available for shipment. The result was to show the obligation of funds for equipment that in fact was not yet available in stocks. At the same time the bookkeeping procedures tended to show duplicate obligations in the transfer of equipment under the modernization program. When reports of obligations of MDAP funds for June 1952 showed a big jump over preceding months (as often was the case for the last month of the fiscal year), Clarence Cannon, chairman of the House Appropriations Committee asked the comptroller general to look into the matter of unliquidated obligations to see if they were being recorded and reported properly.[57] The resulting General Accounting Office survey indicated that there was an overstatement of obligations in reports as of 30 June 1952 "in excess of $1 billion."[58]

On the other hand a comptroller general's decision of 13 January 1949 remained in effect, which provided that the issuance of a procurement authorization by the mutual security constituted an obligation of mutual security appropriated funds. This meant that the placement of an order by the army under a specific Mutual Security Agency authorization in effect amounted to a subobligation of the particular MSA appropriation. But this had to do specifically with the status of appropriated funds. It meant that the army could continue to obligate funds appropriated for fiscal year 1953 after 30 June 1953 without further action by Congress to the extent that they were covered by MSA procurement authorizations. Thus whether or not particular funds had been "obligated" technically depended upon the reference and the point of view.[59]

Whenever equipment that had been procured with MDAP funds was diverted to other uses, it seemed reasonable that agencies actually receiving it immediately should reimburse MDAP. This the Department of Defense proposed to establish as regular procedure in mid-1953. But G–4 recommended that this be done only when it clearly was to the advantage of the army and of the Mutual Defense Assistance Program to do so.

The Strategic Logistics Branch of G–4 Plans Office developed a study, based on the Joint Mobilization Plan and Joint Chiefs of Staff criteria, to show the army mobilization requirements to give aid to allies after a future D-Day. This was submitted to the Munitions Board in early 1952. But when these foreign military aid requirements were added to those that had already been established for U.S. forces, the total mobilization requirement as computed was found to be industrially infeasible. Clearly additional guidance, based upon revisions in strategic assumptions and capabilities, would have to be provided in the new mid-range plan then being prepared. In April 1953 G–4 completed the preparation of draft directives in coordination with U.S. European Command and Far East Command, calling for studies to develop a tentative scale of army wartime aid to bring mobilization requirements within capabilities.[60]

Munitions Allocations and Priorities

Whenever demand exceeds supply in military equipment troublesome questions of priority arise. Foreign assistance programs introduced important new considerations to be taken into account. In 1948 the Joint Chiefs of Staff established the framework for a Joint Munitions Allocation Committee, but no problems arose that year requiring committee action.[61] Presumably World War II stocks still were sufficient to meet most demands. Then in the planning for the Mutual Defense Assistance Program in 1949, the Joint Chiefs analyzed the impact of that program on other matériel requirements and they outlined priorities for the allocation of equipment among the active armed forces, reserve components, matériel reserves, and approved foreign aid programs. At first the foreign aid programs were not included in the army's chart of priorities, which governed the allocation of equipment to other claimants, but with the shortages that began to develop with the coming of the Korean conflict, some method of relating mutual defense assistance requirements to the army's own needs clearly was necessary. In August 1950 Secretary of Defense Johnson directed that a general supply priority be established for MDAP. While the Joint Munitions Allocations Committee appointed a special committee to recommend what machinery ought to be set up for the purpose of allocating critical items in short supply and to recommend what priorities should be approved for foreign aid programs, the Requirements Division of G-4 made a study of army priorities with a view to putting the Department of Defense directive into effect. The vice chief of staff approved a revised chart of priorities on 4 September, which now listed MDAP in priority group I-T, i.e., the lowest sub-group in priority group 1, the active army. Although this placed foreign aid ahead of the reserve components, as well as ahead of certain parts of the mobilization reserve and miscellaneous army programs, minimum training requirements of the reserve components would not be reduced to supply the mutual defense assistance program.[62]

Made up of three members from G-4 (deputy assistant chief of staff, G-4, Foreign Military Aid, chief of the Supply division, and chief of the Requirements Branch) and two officers from G-3, the allocations committee (army) began functioning early in 1951 to decide upon the distribution of assets between the army and mutual defense assistance. The committee held the first meeting on 9 March 1951.[63] Once the procedure became established that requisitions for mutual defense assistance equipment should be based upon the minutes of the allocations committee, the listing of foreign military aid in the regular chart of priorities lost its significance. The availability of items requisitioned already had been established before the formal requisitions were issued, and then it was up to the technical services simply to ship the goods in time to meet the time indicator. In February 1952 foreign aid was deleted from the army's chart of priorities given in the supply supplement.[64]

As on other aspects of logistics, the Korean conflict had both a primary and a secondary effect on foreign military aid programs. The first was to reduce the matériel immediately available for those programs. But the second was to add new impetus to these programs in the long run. If the communists would attack in Korea, they might attack anywhere. So mutual defense assistance acquired greater significance than ever before in the quest for security. It was difficult to determine specifically just what items had been diverted from foreign aid to the support of operations in Korea. In response to a congressional inquiry, G-4 attempted to make a listing of items, but found it impossible because items were being replaced continuously. Only in a few cases, such as the transfer of 167 Bailey bridges from MDAP to meet shortages in Korea in 1950, could diverted equipment be itemized. Diverted equipment was replaced as soon as possible—sometimes within a month, sometimes not for three years. The only effective gauge of diversions from foreign aid programs was in terms of monetary value. The total for such diversions still outstanding in May 1953 G-4 estimated to amount to about $450 million. Early in the Korean conflict it seemed clear to high officials that the mutual defense assistance program had been set back by at least a year. Yet it was possible that three or four years hence the foreign aid program, because of the added impetus now given it, would in fact be considerably beyond the point where it would have been had there not been any Korean or similar conflict.[65]

Priorities and allocations for foreign aid involved not only a division of equipment between the foreign aid programs and the army's own needs, but also the apportionment of that part made available for foreign aid among the various countries participating. This too had to be closely related to worldwide concepts of American security requirements. In general, top priorities for equipment at the end of 1951 were in this order: (1) Korea; (2) Indochina; (3) Continental United States; (4) Western Europe.[66] In January 1952 President Truman directed that "a policy of allocating military equipment be established which will assure that U.S. forces in Europe and NATO forces, as well as other forces of certain foreign countries, which in case of war are most likely to be first engaged with the enemy, are adequately equipped."[67] During the first six months of 1952, the army allocated 1,400,000 measurement tons of military equipment to MDAP. Army allocations to foreign aid during the month of June 1952, 414,000 tons, were more than twice as great as the total allocated during the last four months of 1951. Allocations were not shipments, but they were an important prior step.[68] As of January 1953, it could be said that foreign aid priorities encompassed a wide range. Foreign aid to Indochina was immediately below the top priority, supplies for Far East Command; military assistance for NATO countries had an equal priority with supplying the U.S. Forces in Europe; and aid for South American countries was a lower priority than supplying the National Guard and Reserve in the United States.[69] In the spring of 1953, the National Security Council determined that chief attention should be given in Western Europe to France because of its key position in Europe and because of its heavy commitments in Indochina, and to Germany to help equip its military units when they would be approved and to bring its large capabilities into the common defense effort; in the Far East, to Indochina as the vulnerable point of further communist advances, and to Japan for equipping its military units when they would be approved and for bringing its economic strength into common efforts in that area; in South Asia, to India and Pakistan with moderate annual aid; in the Near East, moderate aid to Egypt to encourage a regional defense organization. In carrying out the Mutual Security Program the United States would concentrate on vital free countries to help the weak gain economic strength and to encourage the strong to greater efforts in sharing the overall defense burdens. Emphasis would be upon new and modern weapons for allies, and on an increase in the competence but an eventual decrease in the numbers of American forces overseas.[70]

Notes

1. Charles Callan Tansill, *America Goes To War*, (Boston, 1938), 33; Allan Nevins, *Hamilton Fish*; *Inner Story of the Grant Administration*, (New York, 1936), 403–4.
2. Tansill, *America Goes To War*, 34.
3. Ibid., 53, 79–131, 660–61.
4. Arnold J. Toynbee, *Survey of International Affairs, 1926*, (London, 1928), 100–105; F. Lee Benns, *Europe Since 1914*, (New York, 1943), 259–60; John Maurice Clark, *The Costs of the World War to the American People Economic and Social History of the World War*, James T. Shotwell, general editor (New Haven, 1931).
5. Office of Business Economics, U.S. Dept. of Commerce, *Foreign Aid by the United States Government 1940–1951*, A Supplement to the Survey of Current Business, Nov. 1952, 2, 33–34; Progress Rpt. Statistics Foreign Military Aid, Statistics Div., Munitions Bd., 19 Jan. 49, Appendix A.
6. Whitney H. Shepardson, *The United States in World Affairs, 1938*, Council of Foreign Relations, (New York, 1939), 166.
7. *Foreign Aid by the U.S. Govt. 1940–1951*, 2, 35–38; Shepardson, *United States in World Affairs, 1938*, 270; *Annual Rpt. of the Army Service Forces for the Fiscal Year 1945*, prep. by the Office, CG, Army Serv. Forces, 63–74.
8. *Foreign Aid by the United States Govt., 1940–1951*, v, vi.
9. Brookings Institution, *Major Problems of United States Foreign Policy 1948–1949*, 70; Harry N. Howard, "Some Recent Developments in the Problem of the Turkish Straits, 1945–1946," *The Department of State Bulletin*, 16 (Jan. 1946), 143–51, 167; Campbell, *United States in World Affairs, 1945–1947*, 149 ff.
10. Brookings Institution, *Major Problems in U.S. Foreign Policy 1948–49*, 71–72; *United States and the United Nations; Report Series No. 7, Report by the President to Congress for the Year 1946* (Dept. of State Publication 2735), 33–34.
11. *The United States and the United Nations*, Report Series No. 7..., 35–36; Campbell, *United States in World Affairs, 1947–1948*, 30.
12. *The United States and the United Nations, 1946*, 36; The Brookings Institution, *Major Problems of the United States Foreign Policy, 1947*, 64–65.
13. Campbell, *United States in World Affairs 1945–47*, 147–48, 474–80.
14. Campbell, *U.S. in World Affairs 1947–48*, 30–32; *Aid to Greece and Turkey*: A

Collection of State Papers Supplement to The Department of State Bulletin, 16, 409A (May 1947).

15. Text given in Message of the President to the Congress, Recommendations on Greece and Turkey, *Department of State Bulletin*, Supplement, *Aid to Greece and Turkey*, 829–32.

16. Campbell, *The U.S. in World Affairs 1947–48*, 34–38.

17. The Brookings Institution, *Major Problems of U.S. Foreign Policy, 1948–1949*, 72–74; Millis, *The Forrestal Diaries*, 370–87, 411, 451–54; *Annual Report of the Secretary of the Army*, 1948, 15, 53–55.

18. See Millis, *Forrestal Diaries*, 425 (23 Apr. 48) and 500 (10 Oct. 48).

19. Stebbins, *The U.S. in World Affairs 1949*, 79–84.

20. The Brookings Institution, *Major Problems of U.S. Foreign Policy, 1950–1951*, 3, 132.

21. Dept. of Defense Ops. Under MDAP, June 1952, v.

22. DF, Lt. Gen. T. B. Larkin, Dir. Log., to Dir. Plans and Ops., 22 Dec. 49, sub.: Continuation of MAP, and incl. Staff Study.

23. Dept. of Defense Ops. Under MDAP, June 1952, v.

24. P L 165, 10 Oct. 51.

25. P L 400, 20 June 52.

26. Dept. of Defense Ops. Under MDAP, June 1952, vii.

27. *Semiannual Report of the Secretary of Defense*, 1 Jan.–30 June 1950, 11; G–4 Memo of Important Actions, 3 Aug. 50, 1; Rpt. on Opns., MDAP, prep. by Progress Rpts. and Statistics Off., Secy. of Def., 28 Aug. 50, 28, 34, 42.

28. Army Progress Rpt. 16–A, Financial Statement, D/A, Dec. 1952, 9, 33, 57.

29. Dept. of Defense Ops. Under MDAP, May 1953, ix, 33; Statement of General J. Lawton Collins, CofS, quoted in *U.S. Army Combat Forces Jnl.* 3 (July 1953): 41.

30. *The Mutual Security Program*, Second Rpt. of Pres. to Cong. for the six months ending 30 June 1952, 48; *The Mutual Security Program*, Third Rpt. of Pres. to Cong. for the six months ended 31 Dec. 1952, 14; Dept. of Defense Ops. Under MDAP, May 1953, xi.

31. Stanley L. Scott, "The Military Aid Program," *The Annals of the American Academy of Political and Social Science* (Nov 1951): 50; *Semiannual Report of the Secretary of Defense*, 1 Jan.–30 June 1951, 66; Seminar, ICAF, 17 Dec. 51; G–4 Hist Surmmary, 13 Dec. 51, Procurement Div.: Foreign Procurement. DA G–4 Hist. Summary 1951–1952, Purchases Br., Procurement Div., 3–11; Dept. of Defense Ops. Under MDAP, Dec. 1951, viii–ix.

32. Army Foreign Military Aid, 1 June 53, 9; Dept. of Defense Ops. Under MDAP, May 1953, x, 35.

33. DA G–4 Hist. Summary 1951–1952, Tab. G, Purchases Br., Procurement Div., 3–11.

34. Statement before House Comm. on For. Affairs, 21 Mar. 52, *Mutual Security Act Extension*, 180.

35. Herman Miles Somers, "Civil-Military Relations in Mutual Security," *Annals of the American Academy of Political and Social Science* 288 (July 1953): 29–30.

36. Ibid., 27–34; See also Richard M. Bissell, "Foreign Aid. What Sort? How Much? How Long?" *Foreign Affairs* 31 (Oct. 1952): 15–38.

37. G–4 Critical Problems Report, 9 Mar. 51.

38. Rpt. of Critical Problems, 25 June 53, Guidance for Mil. Aid to Allies.

39. Department of Defense, Ops under MDAP, June 1952, vii.

40. *New York Times*, 8 Aug 1953.

41. Department of Defense, Ops under MDAP, May 1953, v–vi; President's Letter of Transmittal, 16 Jan. 53, *Third Rpt. to Cong. on the Mutual Security Program*, v–xiii;

Semiannual Rpt. of the Secy. of Defense, 1 Jan. to 30 June 1951; Major Gen. George H. Olmsted (Dir., Off. of Mil. Assist.), *Armor* vol. no. (May–June 1952): 20–23; *The Military Assistance Program*, Dept. of State Publ. 3563, Gen. For. Pol. Series 13, released July 1949, 41 pages.

42. Unless otherwise indicated this section is based upon the following sources: Directive, Sec. Def., 25 No. 49, Functions and Respesibilities within the Dept. of Def. for Military Assistance, Appendix "A" to Enclosure, JCS Info. Memo 697, 1 Dec. 49; Scott, "The Military Aid Program," *The Annals of the American Academy of Political and Social Science* 278 (Nov 1951): 52–53; Presentation by Colonel Mayo, Conf. Brief, 15 Sept. 49; Operation M-Dap, Fiscal Year 1953, Orientation Course for Officers en route to MAAG's, prep. by DACofS FMA, revised Feb. 1953, Orgn. for Mutual Security; *First Rpt. to Congress on the Mutual Security Program*, 31 Dec. 51, 44–48; History of the Joint American Military Advisory Group, typescript, vol 1, Background Information, 222–37; OSD Organization Manual, 19 Nov. 52, 7.01–7.14; *Semiannual Rpt. of the Secy. of Defense*, 1 Jan. to 30 June 1951; Robert H. Connery and Paul T. David, "The Mutual Defense Assistance Program," *American Political Science Review* 45, 2 (June 1951): 321–47; Maj. Gen. George H. Olmsted, "Security for the Free World," *Armor* 41 (May–June 1952): 20–23; Dept. of Defense Ops. under the Mutual Security Program, 6 May 53, 7; Seminar, ICAF, 10 Dec. 51; Tp. Conv. with Charlie A. Baker, OSD, 27 July 53; Organization and Functions of MAAG's Appendix to Enclosure "A", Rpt. by JSPC to JCS, 25 Jan. 50, Planned Orgn. within the Dept. of Def. for Handling the Mil. Assist. Program.

43. *The New York Times*, 1 Aug. 1953.

44. Report of U.S. Special Representative in Europe, 22 Aug. 52, 3–5.

45. Orgn. and Functions of Military Assistance Advisory Groups (MAAG's) in U.S. Embassies of Title 1 Countries; Msg. 939118, G–3 to USCINCEUR and Chiefs MAAGs, 16 May 53.

46. Ibid.

47. *Semiannual Rpt. of the Secy. of the Army*, 1 Jan.–30 June 1951, (included with *Semiannual Rpt. of Secy. of Def.*)

48. Operation M–DAP, FY 1953, Lists, 1.

49. Statement of Maj. Gen. George H. Olmsted, 26 Mar. 52, *Hearings before Senate Committee on For. Rel., Mutual Security Act of 1952*, 82d Cong., 2d Sess., 323.

50. Executive Order 10338, 4 Apr. 52.

51. Unless otherwise indicated, this section is based upon the following: Statement of General of the Army Omar N. Bradley, Chairman, JCS, 13 Mar. 52, *Hearings before House Comm. on For. Affairs*, Mutual Security Act Extension, 82d Cong., 2d Sess., 24–25; Statement of Maj. Gen. George H. Olmsted, Dir., Off., of Mil. Assists., OSD, 26 Mar. 52, *Hearings before Sen. Comm. on For. Rel., Mutual Security Act of 1952*, 82d Cong., 2d Sess., 324–26; Operation M–DAP, FY 1953, FMA Br. 1–7; SR 795–200–1, *General Procedure for Furnishing Mil. Assists. to For. Govts.*, 9 Jan. 50, and Change 1, 7 Feb. 50; Change 2, 27 Mar. 50; Change 3, 14 Apr. 50; Change 4, 31 July 50; Change 5, 1 Feb. 51, and Change 6, 15 Feb. 51, and other Special Regulations in the SR 795–200 series relating to specific countries; ICAF lecture, John O. Bell, Asst. Dir., MDA, 13 Feb. 50, L50–91, 7–9; Dept. of Def. Opsn. Under the Mutual Security Program, 6 May 1953, 13; Testimony of General J. Lawton Collins, CofS, 31 July 51, *Hearings before Comm. on For. Rel. and Comm. on Armed Services, U.S. Senate, Mutual Security Act of 1951*, 82d Cong., 1st Sess., on S. 1762, 199–200, 270–74.

52. Mutual Security Act of 1951, as amended, Sec. 513, 22 U.S.C. 1664.

53. Draft Memo G–4/D3–1360, Sec/Army for Sec/Def, n.d. 19 Jan. 53, sub.: Obligation of FY 1953 MDAP Funds, obligations of MDAP Funds, Tab. 2.

54. Ibid.

55. Preliminary Rpt. by GAO Survey Team, 16 Jan. 53, Synopsis of System of Obligations of MSAP Funds in Army Ordnance, Obligations of MDAP funds.

56. SR 795-200-1; Tp. conv. with Lt. Col. Robert H. Oppelt, Foreign Military Aid Br., G-4, 28 July 53.

57. Preliminary Rpt. by GAO Survey Team, 16 Jan. 53, Synopsis of Systems of Obligation of MSAP funds in Army Ordnance; Memo G4/D3-37067, DACofS G-4 FMA for Dir. OMA, OSD, 27 June 53, sub.: GAO Survey of MSP Obligations, Obligations, Tab. 6; Dept. of Def. Opns. Under MDAP, May 1953, vii-viii.

58. Ltr., Comptroller General to Sec/Def., 7 Apr. 53, quoted in Dept. of Defense Opns. Under the Mutual Security Program, May 1953, vii.

59. Memo for Record, G4/D3, Lt. Col. R. H. Oppelt, 25 June 53, sub.: Procedure for Requisitioning Items to be Supplied from Overseas Command Stocks, Procedures, Tab. 2; Ltr., Controller, MSA to Deputy Chief, Budget Div., OCA, 14 May 53, Obligations of Funds, Tab. 8.

60. Rpt. of Critical Problems, 25 June 53, Guidance for Mil. Aid to Allies.

61. First Report of the Secretary of Defense, 1948, Append A, Rpt. of JCS to SD, 85.

62. Supply Supplement, Pt. 2 of Troop Program and Troop List, 1 Aug. 50, 11; *Second Report of the Secretary of Defense*, 1949, 41; G-4 Memo Of Important Action, 25 Aug. 50, 3; G-4 Hist. Summary, 13 Dec. 51, Rqmts. Div., Tab. 27b; Summary Sheet, ACofS G4 to CofS, 31 Aug. 50, sub.: Supply Priorities; Supply Supplement, Pt. 2 of The Troop Program and Troop List, 15 Sept. 50, 11-15.

63. *Semiannual Rpt. of the Secy. of the Army*, 1 Jan.-30 June 1951, 130; Tp. Conv. with Lt. Col. Robert J. Low, FMA Div., G-4, 31 July 53.

64. Supply Supplement, Pt. 2 of The Troop Program and Troop List, 1 Mar. 52, 13; Logistics Policies and Priorities, 1 November 52, 15.

65. DF, ACofS G-4, to Heads of Tech. Servs., 29 Aug. 52, sub.: Effects of Korean Ops. on U.S. Army World-Wide Commitments; Memo, Brig. Gen. Sam C. Russell, DACofS G-4 for FMA, to Maj. Gen. G. C. Stewart, Dir. OMA, OSD, 14 May 53, sub.: Congressional Inquiry "List of Items Diverted from MDAP"; Interview with General Reeder, DACofS, G-4, Oct. 1950; Corps of Engrs. Hist. Summary, 30 Oct. 51, Pt. 1, Off. of Chief of Engrs., 46.

66. Seminar, ICAF, 10 Dec. 51.

67. Quoted in Department of Defense Ops. Under MDAP, June 1952, xi.

68. Ibid.

69. Brief, incl. with DF, Brig. Gen. G. C. Stewart, DACofS G-4 FMA, for Chief Control Off., 2 Jan. 53, sub.: G-4 Problems of Major Importance, Obligations of MDAP Funds.

70. Basic Policies of the Dept. of the Army (DA-PB-50), Change No. 11, May 1953, 26b-27; Cf. DA G-4 Hist. Summary, 1951-1952, Tab. B, Plans Off., Matters of World-Wide Interest, 40.

6
North Atlantic Treaty Organization and Aid to Western Europe

> Above all, our enemies are your enemies, which is the best guarantee of fidelity in an ally.
> —Thucydides,
> *History of the Peloponnesian War*

As an integrated program of military aid, mutual defense assistance developed mainly from the alarming necessity of doing something about building up the defenses of Western Europe. There had been earlier assistance programs—for the Philippines, for Greece and Turkey, for China. But as a coordinated, long-term proposition, the Mutual Defense Assistance Program had as its first objective supplying the matériel support to European allies that would make the North Atlantic Treaty really effective.

The forerunner of the North Atlantic Treaty Organization was the Western Union Defense Organization, which developed under the Treaty of Economic, Social, and Cultural Collaboration and Collective Self-Defence, signed at Brussels on 17 March 1948 by Belgium, France, Luxembourg, the Netherlands, and the United Kingdom—states thereafter referred to collectively as the "five powers." Like the Treaty of Alliance and Mutual Assistance that the French and British had signed at Dunkirk a year earlier, the Brussels Pact was intended to remain in force for fifty years. The pact declared that in the event of an armed attack in Europe against one party, all the others would give all military and other assistance in their power in accordance with the provisions for collective self-defense of Article 51 of the United Nations Charter. To carry out the aims of the Brussels treaty, the five powers established elaborate machinery for consultation and coordination.

The central organ was the Consultative Council, made up of the five foreign ministers, which met at the various capitals in turn. A permanent commission was composed of the ambassadors of the four continental members in London together with a special British representative. A secretariat and a security committee (concerned with safeguarding classified information) in London served the permanent commission and other organs. Defense ministers of the five states formed a Defense Committee. In addition there was a Permanent

Military Committee made up of an officer from each member state (except for Luxembourg, which was represented by the Belgian representative), a Western Union Chiefs of Staff Committee, a Miltary Supply Board with a subordinate supply executive, a Finance and Economic Committee, which operated under the informal control of the finance ministers, and a Principal Administrative and Planning Committee. Later a Commander in Chief Committee, including a land commander in chief, air commander in chief, and naval adviser, was formed. This grew into a combined military headquarters, which was set up under the direction of Field Marshal Bernard L. Montgomery at Fontainebleu.[1]

A Summary of Inventories of Military Forces and Resources submitted to the Western Union Military Committee in August 1948 revealed pathetic weaknesses. All the ground forces that these once mighty powers could now raise among themselves for 1949 were ten divisions and thirteen brigades "in being," and a hope that another twelve divisions and nine brigades could be mobilized within three months time. Americans had been used to practically abolishing their ground forces in time of peace, but not the French, who had boasted the greatest army in the world in the 1930s. Worse of all was the equipment situation. Lists showed serious deficiencies in tanks, antiaircraft artillery, engineer equipment, and most types of guns, and little or no equipment was available for equipping additional forces on mobilization. Much of the World War II equipment was not serviceable, and it could not be rehabilitated soon because of shortages of spare arts and of technicians. Most of the difficulties in the way of complete mobilization of trained reserves could be boiled down to the shortage of matériel.[2]

The North Atlantic Treaty, signed on 4 April and coming into force on 24 August 1949, brought the United States into active participation with the Western European nations in developing plans and programs for defense. In addition to the five powers of the Brussels Pact, Norway, Denmark, Iceland, Portugal, and Italy associated themselves with these activities under the North Atlantic Treaty.[3] Most significantly the United States, together with those European states and Canada, had committed itself not only to come to the assistance of any member attacked in the North Atlantic area, but to contribute to a program of mutual matériel assistance.[4] "For the first time," said the secretary of defense in his annual report, "we have to face the security problems of our allies, in peace time, and to accept responsibility in quarters where in the past we gave only advice." [5]

The treaty itself provided for consultation among the parties, but it had not envisaged an active military organization. Probably it took the communist coup d'etat in Czechoslovakia and the Berlin blockade to bring the North Atlantic Treaty Organization into being. Two further events changed its character—the announcement in September 1949 of an atomic explosion in the Soviet Union, and the communist attack in Korea on 25 June 1950. The immediate fear of Europeans was that they might be next. The French inquired in August if the United States were prepared to contribute ground forces for the defense of Western Europe and whether forces of the allies should be integrated under a supreme commander. The American reply was an unprecedented affirmative on both counts. In Europe the Joint American Military Advisory Group (JAMAG) had prepared a study recommeding the organization of the European area as a single combined theater, with certain subordinate commands, and the appointment immediately of a theater commander designate.

At the meeting of the North Atlantic Council in September 1950—before the Inchon landing had yet restored confidence to the Korean situation—Secretary of State Dean Acheson presented the American proposal for an integrated command in Europe under a supreme commander. After a recess for consultation with their home governments on this and related matters, the representatives approved the plan on 26 September. General Eisenhower, then president of Columbia University, learned in October that he might be recalled to active duty to take over the Allied Command in Europe. Meeting again in Brussels in December, the North Atlantic Council approved a recommendation of the Defense Committee for the establishment of Supreme Headquarters, Allied Powers, Europe (SHAPE) and to ask General Eisenhower to take the Supreme Command. In February 1951—as the United States Senate debated the president's plans for sending four additional divisions to Europe—SHAPE was established physically in temporary facilities at the Astoria Hotel in Paris. On 2 April the new command became operational. On 27 May the Fourth Division arrived in Germany. Clearly one of the most significant consequences of the Korean attack was the reinforcement of Europe. What the condition of European defenses would have been without the stimulus of the Korean War is difficulat to say. It did seem clear that if the communists contemplated forceful expansion in Western Europe, they had made it infinitely more difficult for themselves by their attempts at expansion in far-off Korea. Here Stalin had his answer to the question which had kept the Kaiser and Hitler guessing. Even if two wars too late, the United States and the powers of Western Europe together had made their position clear. How effective these revitalized steps for mutual defense would be depended very largely on the matériel that could be found for the forces concerned.

The North Atlantic Treaty was open by unanimous invitation to the accession of other European states. The first extension of membership was to Greece and Turkey, effective 18 February 1952.[7] For some, this strained a bit the designation "North Atlantic," but British and French leaders long had regarded the eastern Mediterranean as a critical area for their own security, and Greece and Turkey had been the first recipients of the kind of aid from the United States that had developed into the Mutual Defense Assistance Program. The forces of the two countries, being built up with the assistance of American matériel and advisers, were welcome additions to the strength of the Western European powers.

It was not long until experience in NATO showed a need for some kind of central body, to be set up on a permanent basis, to coordinate the various agencies and to follow up agreed upon plans. The first step in this direction was the establishment of the council deputies in May 1950. Acting as representatives of the foreign ministers, the council deputies after July 1950 met in continuous session in London. As activities became more complex, organization needed to be simplified. The need was for fewer committees and more full-time operating agencies with clear-cut lines of authority. In May 1951 the North Atlantic Council was broadened to include the Defense Committee (defence ministers) as well as the foreign ministers. Further reorganization in April 1952 provided that the council should function in permanent session through the appointment of permanent representatives, and that a single integrated and strengthened international staff should be organized under a permanent secretary-general. Under this arrangement the council assumed responsibility for tasks previously performed by the Council Deputies, the Defense Production Board, the Financial and Economic Board, and by two special committees—the Temporary Council Committee and the North Atlantic Community Committee. Ministerial meetings of the council would continue to be held about three times a year, but the council would be able to function continuously through the permanent representatives.

Certain other specialized agencies continued to function. The Petroleum Planning Committee, organized by the council deputies in January 1952, retained its responsibilities for assessing the total wartime military and petroleum requirements of member countries in relation to availabilities, and for recommending what measures should be taken in peacetime and what plans should be adopted to meet wartime requirements. Two other groups were responsible for planning for wartime transportation coordination—the Planning Board for European Inland Surface Transport, and the Planning Board for Ocean Shipping. The Allied Maritime Transport Council had been one of the most effective instruments of allied cooperation in World War I, and as such it was an important precedent for later wartime coordination. Control of transportation in effect meant control of logistics, and this meant control of strategy. It was not suprising that allies in the "Cold War" should concern themselves with this area of coordinated effort as they planned for the defense of the West.

Major military commands of NATO were Allied Command Europe, with headquarters in Paris, where General Eisenhower first served as supreme allied commander and was succeeded by General Ridgway on 30 May 1952; the Allied Command Atlantic, with headquarters at Norfolk, for which Admiral Lynde D. McCormick was appointed supreme commander in February 1952, and the Channel Committee, composed of chiefs of staff of states bordering the English Channel and southern North Sea, with an operational allied commander in chief channel, also organized in February 1952.[8]

An inevitable weakness of the international military structure was to be found in provisions for logistic support. Initial emphasis on the creation of combat units resulted in serious shortages of service troops and of certain critical equipment necessary for the support of combat units. Each nation retained responsibility for the logistic support of its forces, and the result was a lack of flexibility in the supply system. In October 1952 SHAPE offered recommendations for an approved overall supply organization, but no organization could overcome the current lack of operational reserve stocks. Truly a coordinated international military command structure in peacetime was in itself no mean achievement. Already, with the appointment of a supreme commander for Europe, the allies had accomplished even before the outbreak of a possible European war what had taken three-and-one-half years to bring about in World War I, and, so far as the United States was concerned, had taken two years (although an embryonic headquarters had been established eight months earlier) in World War II. Shortcomings of Western European defense were chiefly logistical. Success or failure of the North Atlantic Treaty hinged immediately on the effectiveness of American matériel assistance.[9]

Where necessary coordination of efforts left off and layering of red tape began was not easy to say, though the structure of NATO in 1952 and 1953 presented a considerably improved organization over the disconnected committees and working groups of one and two years earlier. But it must be remembered that American logistics in Europe was tied to the far from simple American organizational structure that had developed from the coordination and control of U.S. forces and their supplies in Europe, and for the planning and execution of military assistance programs for European recipients. By the time a project had gone through all these national, international, interservice, service, and area agencies at various levels of authority, the wonder was that any substance remained.

Consideration of furnishing arms for Western European nations had begun as soon as had consideration of a North Atlantic pact.[10] Development of requirements for military assistance under the supply plan would be similar to that for economic assistance under the Marshall Plan. First of all Western Union would have to plan a coordinated defense with the means presently available. Then it would have to determine how measures undertaken by the five powers and mutual assistance among themselves could improve their collective military potential. This would include coordinated production and supply and standardization of equipment. Then the United States would consider and screen Western Union (i.e. the signatories to the Brussels pact) requests for supplemental assistance. In return the United States would expect reciprocal assistance to the extent practicable.

After some drastic revisions, the Joint Chiefs of Staff in February 1949 approved a general program of assistance based on a Western Union interim supply plan. If assistance were requested formally, and if agreements could be reached with the Western Union countries, the president was prepared to present to Congress a program of assistance for the fiscal year ending 30 June 1950.

Lists of minimum deficiencies had to be prepared by country, by service, and by dollar value for each priority, and then reviewed by the U.S. delegation in its role as forerunner of the Joint American Military Advisory Group.

The fiscal year 1950 program included $1.159 billion for the Western European countries, of which $859.7 million was for army equipment. By far the largest beneficiary was France, for whom well over half of the total was programmed. The objective of the army program for this year was to make up deficiencies in equipment for the equivalent of twenty-nine divisions. The regular program for army equipment for fiscal year 1951 was intended to provide 23 percent of the essential equipment needed for the equivalent of thirty-five divisions. Army equipment was put in second priority for the supplemental 1951 program, but $1.415 billion of the total of $3.085 billion programmed was to be for army equipment. A part of this was to go for equipment needed for forces in being, to be budgeted for by the various nations in calendar year 1951. The remainder was to be for long lead-time items for forces expected to be activated by 1 January 1953. The army earmarked about 40 percent of this total for tank procurement—for 1,535 medium tanks and eight hundred light tanks. Over 80 percent of the total army funds were to be committed for long lead-time equipment, including in addition to tanks other combat vehicles, heavy trucks, field artillery and antiaircraft guns, radar, and heavy engineer equipment. The troop basis that supposedly formed the basis for supply calculations contemplated an increase of eight-and-one-half divisions in 1953.[11]

Equipment approved for the fiscal years 1950–1952 programs were sufficient to make up most of the deficiencies in American-type items for ground forces to be in being and those scheduled for mobilization by D plus ninety. But with deliveries at least eighteen months behind the programs, it still would be some time before the naked defenses of Western Europe could be covered.

Before the North Atlantic Treaty Organization had yet begun to assume form, the five Brussels treaty powers already had begun work on an integrated program of military construction that they referred to generally as "infrastructure." That original program called for the completion of thirty-five airfields by the end of 1951 at a cost of approximately $92.7 million. With the development of the North Atlantic Treaty Organization, the infrastructure program was expanded to include the participation of the broader membership and the requirements of the combined European command. Thereafter the original program was referred to as the "first slice," and the various projects approved for subsequent years became parts of second, third, and fourth "slices." In May 1951 SHAPE submitted a survey of initial minimum requirements for additional airfields and communication facilities in the cen-

At work on a NATO pipeline in Europe.

tral European area. At the Ottawa meeting of the North Atlantic Council in September, the governments reached agreement on the division of costs for the resulting $233 million "second slice." The "third slice," approved at the Lisbon meeting of the North Atlantic Council in February 1952, provided for additional facilities to cost about $425.6 million (later increased to about $478 million because of rising prices) for 1952. The "fourth slice" comprised two parts, the first for $219 million approved at a ministerial meeting of the North Atlantic Council at Paris in December 1952, and the second for $187 million approved at a ministerial meeting, also at Paris, in April 1953. Construction projects financed in the fourth slice were to provide the infrastructure needed for the support of forces expected to be in being through December 1954. The April meeting then looked beyond the annual slice program to a long-term three-year program that would provide commanders and staffs with a firmer basis for planning. The agreement on the long-term program provided that projects should be approved for construction by the North Atlantic Council not later than 30 June 1955. The hope was that the funds to be made available under the three-year program would be enough to provide basic military installations needed for common defense through December 1956. Types of facilities programmed as common infrastructure included air bases, communications facilities, gasoline and oil storage facilities and pipe lines, headquarters, radar warning installations, navigational aids, naval bases, and training facilities. All this was in addition to facilities that member nations provided individually, such as the American lines of communications across France and across Italy.[12]

The estimated total cost and proportionate shares of each country for the four infrastructure slices were as shown in table 2. These figures represent the gross contributions, including taxes. But the Mutual Security Act of 1951 forbade the use of mutual security funds for the payment of taxes. Tax allowances actually would make the net cost to the United States some $64 million less than the figure shown in the table.

The basis for logistic planning and for the build-up and equipping of NATO forces had to be the strategic plans. International strategic plans for the defense of Western Europe had to be based upon logistical feasibility in the same way as joint war plans for the United States. Shortly after NATO came into being, the Military Committee and its standing group developed a strategic plan for the defense of Western Europe against aggression from the east. This plan was referred to as the midterm defense plan. Its whole tenor was defensive. On the basis of this strategic plan the Military Committee then developed a requirements study to translate the strategic concept into specific numbers of divisions, aircraft, ships, and supporting forces. After the organization of SHAPE in the spring of 1951, planning staffs of that headquarters studied further what would be needed in the way of forces to stop aggression, and General Eisenhower submitted an estimate of requirements in October 1951. Meanwhile air force chiefs agreed upon the so-called "Paris plan" for

Table 2. Country Participation in Infrastructure Program

(In millions of dollars and percent participation)

	First Slice Cost	%	Second Slice Cost	%	Third Slice Cost	%	Fourth Slice Cost	%	Total Cost	%
Belgium-Luxembourg	13	14	17	5	31	7	21	5	82	6
Canada	-	-	14	4	25	5	27	7	66	5
Denmark	-	-	-	-	19	4	13	3	32	2
France	42	45	70	22	63	13	56	14	321	18
Italy	-	-	-	-	38	8	27	7	65	5
Netherlands	13	14	10	3	20	4	17	4	60	5
Norway	-	-	-	-	15	3	12	3	27	2
Portugal	-	-	-	-	-	-	1	-	1	-
Greece	-	-	-	-	-	-	7	2	7	1
Turkey	-	-	-	-	-	-	13	3	13	1
United Kingdom	25	27	58	18	63	13	41	10	187	14
United States	-	-	157	48	205	43	172	42	534	41

SOURCE: U.S. Dept. of Defense, Operations under MDAP, May 1953, xiv–xv.

the build-up of air forces, and the five regional planning groups then operating developed further requirements. The standing group and the full Military Committee analyzed and reviewed all these studies and on that basis approved in November 1951 a comprehensive statement of requirements. Before plans could be accepted as realistic it still was necessary to investigate the industrial feasibility of the logistics involved.[13]

A function comparable to that of the Munitions Board in testing the industrial feasibility of strategic plans in the United States had to be carried out. For this purpose the North Atlantic Council at its Ottawa meeting in September 1951 established the Temporary Council Committee. The full committee actually included representatives from all twelve NATO powers, but its detailed work was charged to an executive bureau of three leaders—Averell Harriman of the United States (chairman of the committee), Jean Monnet of France, and R. A. Butler (or his deputy, Sir Edwin Plowden) of Great Britain—a group that came to be known as the "three wise men." The committee's job was to study the economic and political capabilities of the NATO countries to determine how much of the military requirements could be met, and what portion each state could bear. In setting up the committee the council "noted the danger of inflation, the burdens which increased defense efforts place on the balance of payments, and the obstacles to an adequate defense arising from price and allocations pressures on raw material supplies."[14]

The "three wise men" and their staff studied economic statistics, analyzed production potential, and listened to the testimony of defense officials and economics experts of the various countries. On the basis of the gross national product of each of the NATO countries, they determined what they considered to be the maximum defense effort that each country could make without overburdening its economy. In December 1951 the Temporary Council Committee submitted its report for consideration to member governments in preparation for the meeting of the council scheduled to be held in Lisbon in February 1952. The report indicated what should and could be done to give effect to the requirements study that the council would also be considering at the Lisbon meeting. The committee recommended specific actions for effective arrangements for operational logistical support, improved machinery for supply and production planning, and NATO machinery for determining priorities in training, equipment, and military construction for forces under NATO commands, as well as specific actions on standards of readiness of forces, better training and organization, and improved command arrangements.

At Lisbon the North Atlantic Treaty powers adopted with certain modifications the Temporary Council Committee recommendation. Of particular significance were the force goals the nations accepted. Going far beyond the scope of their previous commitments, the NATO powers agreed upon a program of fifty divisions (exclusive of Greek and Turkish units) for 1952. These fifty divisions—the so-called "firm force goals"—were to include twenty-five active divisions that could become operational immediately in an emergency, and twenty-five reserve divisions. Some of the reserve divisions were to be ready within twenty-four hours, some within seventy-two hours, some within ten days, and all were to be capable of mobilization within thirty days after a future D-Day. Previous force goals for western union as well as for NATO had listed reserve divisions capable of mobilization with ninety days. The shortening of that time to thirty days in the 1952 goals was hardly less significant than the increase in the total number accepted as provisional goals for 1953, and planning goals for long-lead-time matériel. Whether or not the goals set at Lisbon were too ambitious to be reached was yet another matter. A press dispatch of 27 February said that "Sources at General Eisenhower's headquarters" had made it clear that talk of a combat-ready fifty-division Atlantic pact army by the end of 1952 "smacks more of fancy than fact," and argued that the publication of such a figure was "both misleading and unfortunate."[15]

Even before acceptance of the ambitious Lisbon goals for expansion of NATO military forces, indications had appeared that some previous goals, set too high, had been the cause of tensions among the allies.[16] Some observers considered the Lisbon goals—in particular the land forces goal of fifty divisions to be capable of mobilization within thirty days of a D-Day—to be completely out of reason. In the months that followed, press reports varied widely on how nearly those goals were being attained; some suggested that the plans had completely collapsed; others stated that progress was satisfactory.[17] Without the final test of war itself, success or failure in such a thing as a defense program depends upon points of view and standards of judgment. High goals had some advantage in presenting a real challenge and in offering immediate hopes of significant achievement. They had the disadvantages of becoming reference points for "failure" when not met completely and then of giving rise to the friction resulting from attempts to place blame for the "failure."

Actually the Lisbon goals were in large part met in terms of numbers of aircraft, naval vessels, and army divisions by the end of 1952, though the combat effectiveness of the units fell considerably short of the planned achievement. The goal of twenty-five active divisions was reached by early 1953, but it took a few months more for all the twenty-five reserve divisions—those to be available within thirty days after D-Day—to be organized. Units themselves had been strengthened, and additional items of major equipment had been provided. But serious deficiencies remained in service units, in logistical establishments, and in stocks of ammunition and other supplies. Now the emphasis would be upon overcoming these deficiencies and upon improving the combat effectiveness of the units rather than on the creation of additional units. General Ridgway was not satisfied to have twenty-five reserve divisions "on paper." By personal inspection and evaluation he listed separately those units that by reason of shortages of equipment or of not having completed a satisfactory training program could not be considered as in fact available for combat on thirty days notice or less.[18]

Other European countries, though less remotely situated than some of the NATO members, presented more perlexing problems for military coordination. In particular, Yugoslavia and Spain fell into this category. Yugoslavia was frankly communist, but Tito's break with the Kremlin in 1948 opened the way for collaboration with the West against further Soviet aspirations in the Balkans. Prudence required the exploitation of every sign of weakness in the communist bloc. As for Spain, Franco, like Hitler, was an enemy of communism, and for many persons that was all that mattered. Just as common antifascism had been sufficient reason for an alliance with communist Russia during World War II, once communism had succeeded fascism as the chief threat to security in the world, it seemed no less reasonable to seek an alliance with Franco's Spain.

With an army of some thirty-two divisions and a total strength given variously at from 300,000 to 500,000 men, Yugoslavia offered an attractive area for the extension of military assistance. In 1949 and 1950 the Export-Import Bank extended three loans amounting to a total of $55 million to Yugoslavia, but the United States made no direct grant assistance available until the latter half of 1950. This took the form of economic assistance to relieve the stresses arising from a serious drought that year, mounting Yugoslav indebtedness, and economic pressures being applied by the Soviet bloc. Then followed an allocation of $29 million in MDAP funds for raw materials for the needs of the armed forces. At the same time the governments of the United States, the

United Kingdom, and France agreed upon a tripartite program of economic assistance in which the American military mission held informal exploratory discussions with Yugoslav military leaders to determine the nature and extent of military assistance that would be needed to keep the Yugoslav armed forces effective during the next several years. Under a bilateral agreement signed 14 November 1951, Yugoslavia became a recipient of regular mutual defense assistance. The mission established in Belgrade to supervise the program was known as the American Military Assistance Staff, Yugoslavia, though its functions were similar to those of military assistance advisory groups in other countries.[19]

Anxious to temper the misgivings of European allies, the American administration moved slowly in the direction of military assistance to Spain. Less sensitive to the attitudes of allies, Congress took matters into its own hands to appropriate funds for Spanish assistance. The first step in the fall of 1950 was the authorization of loans of up to $62.5 million for economic assistance. Slightly more than $52.8 million of this was approved for loans by the Economic Cooperation Administration (and the Mutual Security Agency), and loan agreements covering $35 million had been signed up to April 1952. Then in the Mutual Security Appropriations Act approved in October 1951 Congress provided: "for economic, technical and military assistance, in the discretion of the President under the general objectives set forth in the declaration of policy contained in the titles of the Economic Cooperation Act of 1948 and the Mutual Security act of 1951, for Spain, $100,000,000."

But conditions were not yet ripe for military assistance to Spain, and the president allocated none of these funds for expenditure. In July 1951 Admiral Forest Sherman entered into exploratory discussions with General Franco in order to determine the possible basis for mutual defense assistance. A month later a joint military survey team headed by Maj. Gen. James W. Spry, USAF, arrived in Spain to continue the discussions. Congress carried over the unspent $100 million in mutual security appropriations to the next fiscal year (1953), and authorized an additional $25 million for that fiscal year. By June 1952 the U.S. government was contemplating a program to include the use of the $125 million already authorized for grants of military equipment and for consumer goods and for developing Spanish industry, and the expenditure over a three-year period of $390 million for the construction of air and naval bases and of $15 million for the rehabilitation of railroads. Also in June 1952 the Joint Chiefs of Staff reconsidered an earlier action designating the army as executive agency for the Joint U.S. Military Group, Spain, and redesignated the chief of staff of the air force as executive agent in the negotiations on mutual aid and base rights then being conducted. The negotiations dragged on for months. Spanish estimates on needs for their air force and navy were not far from the assistance being planned, but their requests for modernization of the army went far beyond anything American planners had in mind. Franco, it appeared, was willing to grant base rights, but at a price that at that point was completely out of the question. The director for mutual security, on the recommendation of the State Department, withheld approval of the Spanish program until the conclusion of three agreements—(1) base rights, (2) military assistance, (3) economic aid—already being negotiated. This related in particular to the $125 million that Congress already had voted. The Spanish wished to divide this as $50 million for military aid and $75 million for economic aid. The proposed army program was $37 million.[20]

Even more puzzling than the Yugoslav and Spanish questions in the buildup of defenses for Western Europe was the position and contribution of Germany. Here was a question that lay beyond the scope of American iniative in a bilateral arrangement. The whole North Atlantic alliance was concerned. Plans for rearming the enemy, only five years after "unconditional surrender," lent an ironic twist to history and gave substance to inescapable doubts that surrender on some basis other than "unconditional" would have been less satisfactory. On the other hand, the gravest misgivings of the French would be reserved for any action tending toward the restoration of military power in Germany. That was the problem—how to bring German economic and military potential into the defense of Western Europe without reconstituting a new threat to the security of Western Europe.

At the same time that he proposed the organization of a supreme headquarters for allied forces in Europe at the meeting of the North Atlantic Council in September 1950, Dean Acheson also presented a proposal for seeking units from the Federal Republic of Germany for NATO forces. The immediate French reaction was one of reluctance to see Germany rearmed in any way before the French were able to rebuild their own strength. At a meeting of the North Atlantic Defense Committee in Washington in October, Jules Moch, the French defense minister, proposed a far-reaching innovation. The French could entertain no suggestions for reconstituting German divisions or a German general staff, but, said he, why not bring the Germans in as part of a unified European army? After a year's preliminary work, the six nations developed a comprehensive plan for a European Defense Force within the framework of the European Defense Community under which forces would be integrated for the common defense of Western Eruope. Once formed, the European Defense Force would come under SHAPE in the same way as the forces of the United States and those of Canada and the United Kingdom that had been allocated to that command. The effect would be to make Germany an "associate member" of NATO. All the North Atlantic Treaty powers approved the European Defense Community plan at the Lisbon meeting of the North Atlantic Council in February 1952. But early promises of success began to give way to doubts as delays developed on the ratification of the pact.[21]

Having proposed it, the French proceeded to kill the project when their parliament refused to ratify the agreement. Though Secretary of State John Foster Dulles warned that there was no alternative, Foreign Minister

Anthony Eden of Great Britain immediately set out to find one. He found it in a revitalization of Western European Union to which both Germany and Italy then were admitted, but it was not until 1955 that the Federal Republic became a member of NATO and German units were added to the NATO forces. This paved the way for American military assistance to the former enemy.[22]

The rebuilding of Western European defenses was not a story of unmixed progress. Political instability in France not only delayed effective French action but also discouraged action in neighboring countries. Nationalist agitation in Morocco further weakened the French position in Europe, not to mention the steady drain in men and resources that the continuing war in Indochina was taking. Italy was in an awkward position because of the limitations on armed forces imposed by the peace treaty, until the western powers agreed to revise those provisions. The touchy question of Trieste remained an unsolved problem that posed a dilemma for outside powers seeking the assistance of both Yugoslavia and Italy. Communist parties in Western Europe had opposed the North Atlantic Treaty from the beginning. So far direct political action on their part and propaganda aimed at promoting anti-American sentiment and at promoting neutralist feelings had failed as means of undermining NATO. But the danger of communist exploitation of labor grievances remained very much alive. A further financial crisis in the latter half of 1951 threatened to cut industrial production seriously in both France and Great Britian. This crisis was attributable in part to the loss of Iranian oil, which made it necessary to purchase oil for dollars, and to increasing dollar purchases of coal and raw materials needed for the higher industrial production.[23]

The American election in 1952 appeared to be a further deterrent to defense progress in European countries. The results of the election only made it clear that there would be a change in the political complexion of both the presidency and the Congress on the next 20 January, but European leaders were not sure what changes in policy would be introduced at that time—and to what extent American military aid would be cut for the next and succeeding years. On the financial side it might have been helpful for the United States to have put its aid programs on a two-year budget. Repeatedly American representatives were put in the position of urging European governments to undertake expenditures running beyond a one-year period, while the U.S. government could not be committed to undertaking such expenditures itself.[24]

Results of the program of assistance to Western Europe and of the efforts to build an integrated defense system under the North Atlantic Treaty Organization generally were encouraging. If, in terms of some of the goals set at Lisbon, the results were disappointing, and if the stretch-out of rearmament programs had been disturbing, in comparison with the situation four years earlier, the peacetime progress of the allies was little short of remakable. Now divisions in being could nearly match those of the Soviet Union in Germany, though it could not be overlooked that Soviet and satellite strength also had been increasing during this period. General Ridgway still had to conclude in the spring of 1953 that a full-scale Soviet attack would find his command critically weak to meet it. Much conjecture on possible changes in Soviet policy followed the death of Stalin in March 1953, but the North Atlantic Council at its April meeting "found that there had not yet in fact been any change in the fundamental threat to the security of free peoples."[25] Again it appeared that if time would permit, the job could be done. If Western Europe could be defended successfully, then of course NATO and the programs of military assistance to the NATO countries would have to be termed a complete success. It also would be a success if attacks against Western Europe were avoided.

After the communist attack in Korea on 25 June 1950 the problems of logistic support for forces in other parts of the world became more difficult. Interpreting the threat of communism to be worldwide, the president and this military advisers were anxious to build up American strength in other strategic areas even while building up combat forces in Korea.[26] In 1951 the garrison in Alaska was stengthened, ground forces were dispatched to Iceland, construction of new air bases was rushed in Greenland and North Africa, and four additional divisions were sent to Europe. In the worldwide game of chess, the king had to be kept covered, even as the knights were advanced to meet attacks on other parts of the board.

In actuality the Far East was the primary theater during the period from 1950 to 1953, for that was where active combat operations were going on. But potentially Europe was the decisive theater, and as such it had to be an area of major concern, even while active operations were being supported on the other side of the globe. With a population of over 230,000,000 and an industrial plant second only to that of the United States, Western Europe was critical for the security of the United Staes. With Western Europe the free world was able to outproduce the Soviet bloc by nearly four to one. Joined to the Soviet bloc, Western Europe might offset completely that industrial advantage of the free world over the communist countries. Should Soviet forces overrun Europe, the United States would find itself in the awful dilemma of having to resort to the pitiless bombing of friendly nations or of seeing the great industrial resources of those countries combined against it.[27]

Notes

1. Dept. of Defense, History of the Joint American Military Advisory Group, mimeo, 3 vols., 1, 1–54; *NATO Facts And Figures* (Brussels, 1969), 20–21.
2. Walter Millis, ed., *The Forrestal Diaries,* (New York, 1951), 500.
3. Text in *NATO Facts and Figures,* 238–41.
4. See Bernard Brodie, "Strategic Implications of the North Atlantic Pact," *Yale Review* 39 (Winter 1950): 193–208; and Royal Institute of International Affairs, *Defense in the Cold War: The Task for the Free World* (London, 1950).

5. *Second Report of the Secretary of Defense,* 1949, 24.
6. History of JAMAG, vol 1, 358–60, vol 2, 72–82, 398–417; *First Annual Report, Supreme Allied Commander Europe,* 2 Apr. 1952, 8–9; James Reston, The New York Times, 2 Mar. 1952.
7. Protocol to the North Atlantic Treaty on the Accession of Greece and Turkey, signed 17 Oct. 1951, printed in SRE special publication, North Atlantic Treaty and Related Docs.
8. *NATO Facts and Figures,* 165–71, 196–200.
9. Second Annual Report, SACEUR, 30 May 53, 16–18.
10. Millis, *The Forrestal Diaries,* 500.
11. History of JAMAG, vol 2, 276b–283, 462; Kreiling. The European Command and the Mutual Defense Assistance Program, 1 Jan 49–30 June 50, vol 1, 78–80; Report on Operation, MDAP, OSD, 28 Aug. 50, 33–34.
12. NATO Notebook Series, D–12, 8 Apr. 52, NATO Infrastructure, and D–2, 17 Sept. 49, Summary of Meetings of the North Atlantic Council; Dept/Def Opns. under MDAP, Dec. 1952, xi–xii; Dept/Def Opns. under MDAP, May 1953, xii–xvii; Fact Sht., Dept/Def OPI No 243–52, 29 Dec. 52, NATO Infrastructure; Second Annual Report, SACEUR, 30 May 53, 17; DA G–3 Hist. Summary, 1951–1952, Joint War Plans Br., 8–13.
13. This and succeedings paragraphs of this section are based upon the following: Statement of Frank C. Nash, Asst. Secy. Def., 19 Mar. 53, *Hearings before House Committee on Foreign Affairs, Mutual Security Act Extension,* 23–28; Statement of Robert A. Lovett, Secy. Def., 21 Mar. 52, *Mutual Security Act Extension, Hearings before House Comm. on Foreign Affairs,* 82d Cong., 2d Sess., 188–89; statement of Robert A. Lovett, Secy. Def., 13 Mar. 53, *Mutual Security Act Extension, Hearings before House Comm. on Foreign Affairs,* 82d Cong., 2d Sess., 16–21; *The NATO Handbook,* (1952) 20; Statement by W. Averell Harriman, Chairman TCC, 18 Dec. 51, in *The NATO Handbook,* 1 Jan. 52, Appendix 7, 67–69; Rpt. to the President by William H. Draper, Jr, 22 Aug. 1952, 7–8; NATO Notebook Series, D–2, Summary of Ministerial Meetings of the Council, 10 Mar. 52; Statement of General Alfred M. Gruenther, CofS SHAPE, 25 Mar. 52, *Mutual Sec. Ext., Hearings before House Comm. on Foreign Affairs,* 82d Cong., 2d Sess., 235–67; C. L. Sulzberger, *The New York Times,* 24 February 1952.
14. Communiqué, Seventh Session North Atlantic Council, 20 Sept. 51, Ottawa, reprinted in *NATO Handbook* (1952), 61.
15. *The Washington Post,* 27 Feb. 1952.
16. See "NATO Problem: Aims Too High, Tensions Grow," *Newsweek,* 19 Nov. 1951, 25–27.
17. See, for example: Homar Bigart, *The New York Herald Tribune,* 1 Aug. 1952; R. Brines, *The Washington Star,* 4 Aug. 1952; Kingsbury Smith, "NATO Lags," *The New York Journal American,* 10 Aug. 1952; C. L. Sulzberger, "NATO Goals in Sight Despite Some Setbacks," *The New York Times,* 10 Aug. 1952; Walter Kerr, *The New York Herald Tribune,* 11 Aug. 1952; Drew Middleton, "Soviet Army Loses Big Lead in Europe," *The New York Times,* 4 Sept. 1952; Benjamin Welles, "Ridgway Sees Progress in a Vast Defense Job," *The New York Times,* 16 Nov. 1952; Harold Callender, "Slight Arms Rise Seen in '53 in NATO," *The New York Times,* 26 Nov. 1952; Hanson W. Baldwin, "North Atlantic Treaty Powers Face A Crisis in European Defenses," *The New York Times,* 14 Dec. 1952.
18. Statement of Frank C. Nash, 19 Mar. 53, House Hearings, *Mutual Security Act Extension,* 28–30; Statement of General Mattew B. Ridgway, SACEUR, 18 May 53, *Hearings before House Comm. on For Affairs, Mutual Security Act Extension,* 83d Cong., 1st Sess., 392; Second Annual Report, SACEUR, 30 May 53, 14.
19. Rpt. of the Special Study Mission to Germany and Certain other Countries;

Supplemental Rpt. on Austria, Yugoslavia, Italy, Spain, by special subcomm, of House Comm. on Foreign Affairs, 7 Apr. 1952, 82d Cong., 2d Sess., 39–47; *Semiannual Rpt. of the Secretary of Defense,* 1 Jan.–30 June 1951, 64; NATO Notebook Series, D–4, 10 Mar. 52, Chronology of Events, 27.

20. Rpt. of the Special Study Mission to Germany and Certain other Countries, Supplemental Rpt., House Comm. on Foreign Affairs, 82d Cong., 2d Sess., 85–87; *Semiannual Rpt. of the Secretary of Defense,* 1 Jan.–30 June 1951, 64; Dept. of Defense Ops. Under MDAP, June 1952, xii–xiv; Memo, Dir. OMA, OSD for DACofS G–4 FMA, Dir. international Affairs, Dept, of Navy, Asst. for Mutual Security DCofS Materiel USAF, 22 June 53, sub.: Submission of MDA Materiel Programs for Spain and copy of undated memo, Actg. Spec. Asst. to Secy. of State for Mutual Security Affairs for John H. Ohly, Off. Dir. for Mutual Security, same subj. inclosed, in G–4 FMA hist. files, no 59, Programs proposed for approval; Lawrence Fernsworth, "Spain in Western Defense," *Foreign Affairs* 31 (July 1953): 648–62; Same Pope Brewer, "Spain: How Good an Ally?" *Yale Review* 41, 3 (Mar. 1952): 348–50.

21. *First Annual Report, Supreme Allied Commander Europe,* 2 Apr. 52, 21–26; History of JAMAG, 2:402–17; NATO Notebook Series, D–17/1, 27 May 52, Protocol to North Atlantic Treaty and Tripartite Declaration Regarding the European Defense Community, NATO Notebook No. 2; See also DA G–4 Hist. Summary 1951–1952, Tab. B, Plans Office, Europe, 3; Hist. Summary, Office of the Comptroller of the Army, 1951–1952, "U.S. Will Help Arm Bonn After Europe Implements Pace," *The New York Times,* 10 Apr. 1953; "Germans Go Ahead on Army Planning," *The New York Times,* 19 Apr. 1953.

22. *NATO Facts and figures,* 34–37, 198–201.

23. DA G–4 Hist. Summary, 1951–1952, Tab. B, Plans Off., Europe, 7–8; Hanson W. Baldwin, "French Defenses Thin," *The New York Times,* 22 Nov. 1952.

24. Harold Callender, *The New York Times,* 9 Nov. 1952; Michael L. Hoffman, "2-Year U.S. Budget on Arms Aid Urged," *The New York Times,* 30 Nov. 1952.

25. Second Annual Report, SACEUR, 30 May 53, 21–22.

26. *Semiannual Report of the Secretary of the Army,* 1 Jan. 1951 to 30 Jane 1951 (included with Semiannual Rpt. of the Secy. of Def.), 79.

27. Statement of General J. Lawton Collins, CofS USA, 18 June 1952, Senate Hearings, Dept. of Def. Appropriations for 1953, 1212–13; Chester Wilmot, "If NATO Had to Fight," *Foreign Affairs,* 31 (Jan. 1953): 201–3.

7
U.S. Military Aid in the Near East

> England...sees that her interests are inseparably connected with the independence of those nations who have shown themselves worthy of emancipation, and such is the case of Greece.
> —Lord Byron

> These newly emancipated races want to breathe free air and not through Russian nostrils.
> —Sir William White (1885)

The Near East

The opening rounds of the "Cold War" were laid in the intercontinental crossroads of the Near East. Only here did Russian efforts fail to consolidate a system of "friendly" buffer states along the Soviet borders. On the long frontier extending from Finland to Manchuria and Korea, Turkey, Iran, and Afghanistan remained as the only missing links in the continuous chain of Soviet-dominated buffer states. Even before World War II had ended in Europe, the Soviet Union had begun to apply pressure on Turkey for a share in the control of the straits, and then for the transfer of bits of Turkish territory. The refusal of the Soveit Union to withdraw its troops from the Azerbaijan province of Iran had created a situation that had given the United Nations Security Council its first case regarding the preservation of peace in the postwar world. Communist guerrillas in Greece had threatened to extend communist influence further in the Balkans, and to deliver to the Soviets another strategic area for possible domination of the eastern Mediterranean. That those countries had held firm undoubtedly was due in large part to the bold policy of the United States expressed in the Truman Doctrine, and to the effective military and economic assistance delivered to Greece and Turkey to back up that policy.[1]

What had brought matters to a head so far as American policy was concerned was not a new and sudden communist attack, but the announcement by the British (in February 1947) that they no longer would be able to continue the assistance they had been giving to Greece and Turkey. This might have opened the door to communist penetration. Actually it set the stage for the whole policy of military aid that came to be known as mutual defense assistance.

When Greece and Turkey became parties to the North Atlantic Treaty in February 1952 they brought to the organization for European defense some thirty relatively well-trained and well-equipped army divisions.[2] The performance of the Greek and Turkish battalions in Korea had already justified high confidence in their battle competence. Admittedly the position of these two allies added a measure of vulnerability to the NATO powers, but the growing effectiveness of their own armies, and their position as a barrier to Russian domination of the eastern Mediterranean and of the Middle East oil fields made of Greece and Turkey valuable assets to European defense.

Greece

The communist guerrilla warfare that became the object of immediate concern to the United States in 1947 was but a continuation of the raids, acts of sabotage, and civil strife that had been going on for some time. Ever since the departure of the German troops in November 1944, small but well-armed bands of communist guerrillas had been conducting a reign of terror in various parts of Greece. Indeed clashes between communist and royalist elements of the Greek resistance had broken out in the fall of 1943, even as they both fought against the nazi occupation. Then within a few weeks after the arrival of British forces and the German withdrawal, civil war broke out in December 1944. This continued until February 1945 when leaders of the warring factions signed an agreement at Varkiza. The uneasy truce that resulted lasted until the autumn of 1946 when communists resumed their attacks on a bigger scale than ever. The situation was becoming more serious when the British announced that they were unable to continue their assistance to the Greek government.[3]

Shortly after the passage of the Greek-Turkish aid bill, the Greek government in June 1947 requested the United States to furnish advice and guidance in administering the program. Already a small party of American army and navy officers had arrived in Greece on 24 May for the purpose of determining Greek military requirements and of establishing liaison with Greek staffs in preparing plans for receiving and distributing the supplies and for training Greek soldiers in the use of the equipment. On 2 August 1947 the first ship with American military supplies for aid to Greece arrived at Piraeus, the port of Athens with a cargo of vehicles, rations, and general supplies.[4]

The army and navy detachments that went to Greece to help get the aid program started became parts of the broader American Mission for Aid to Greece headed by Dwight P. Griswold, formerly governor of Nebraska. Originally the War Department had been reluctant to send a military mission as such to Greece because of fears that the United States might be accused of conducting military operations there. The hope was that while a special mission would be necessary to administer the economic aid contemplated, the military part of the program might be supervised through the office of the military attaché in Athens. A liaison section might be established, it was assumed, with the British Military Mission in Greece. Then the idea of a single mission, including both a civilian and a military branch for the two parts of the program, appeared to be more satisfactory. Actually the U.S. Army Group, Greece, had been organized in Washington under the command of Colonel Charles R. Lehner in April—before the Greek-Turkish aid bill had even been passed. The civil branch of the American Mission for Aid to Greece included divisions for civil government, public finance, commerce and supply, industry, agriculture, labor, public health, reconstruction, and relief and welfare. The chief of the mission was responsible to the secretary of state, though on military matters the heads of the military groups might communicate directly with their own departments. Here was the beginning of what later evolved into the "country teams" that administered the Mutual Security Program in many countries throughout the free world. Griswold arrived in Athens with a small staff on 15 July 1947. By 30 September the mission altogether included 206 American workers. Seventy-eight of these were military—forty-three army (including the air forces) and thirty-five navy. Commander of the army group now was Maj. Gen. William G. Livesay.[5]

Although the basic law authorizing the Greek-Turkish aid program permitted broad advisory functions, the War Department restricted the authority of the U.S. Army Group, Greece, to matters of supply. As had been the case in earlier emergencies and would be again in others yet to arise, the hope at first was that simply the furnishing of equipment and supplies would be enough to permit Greek forces to turn the tide against their adversaries. No observers were to be stationed with combat units in the field. The group's mission was to see that Greek forces got the supplies they needed to restore the order and security necessary for enabling the essential work of reconstruction in this war-ravaged country to proceed unhampered. The immediate job was to revise the initial lists of matériel requirements, to survey Greek supply facilities before supplies began to arrive, and to coordinate organization and functions with the British Military Mission and with the Greek military supply system.[6]

Hopes of confining military activities strictly to supply matters soon faded. Within a few months it became evident that if supply support were to be made really effective, more attention would have to be given to operations and training. In December 1947 the Joint Chiefs of Staff established the Joint U.S. Military Advisory and Planning Group (JUSMAPG) to give active assistance in operational and logistical advice to the Greek armed forces. General Livesay, in addition to his duties as commander of the U.S. Army Group, Greece, became Director of JUSMAPG. The new group included army, navy, and air force sections. Brig. Gen. Truman C. Thorson became head of the army section and assistant director of JUSMAPG. The director continued to work under the general supervision of the chief of the American Mission for Aid to Greece, but he had direct communication with the Joint Chiefs of Staff (through the chief of staff of the army) on military matters. The Athens headquarters of the Joint U.S. Military Advisory and Planning Group was divided into four advisory groups to assist the respective sections of the Greek general staff on problems of personnel, intelligence, plans and operations, and logistics. In the field, JUSMAPG advisory teams were attached to First Army, A, B, and C Corps, and to each of the seven combat divisions. Their job was to cooperate with members of the British mission in giving operational and logistical advice to the commanders and staffs of the units to which they were attached; to report on the status of administration, supply, services, and operations within the Greek forces, and to recommend to the director general changes in organization and training of the Greek forces. The U.S. Army Group, Greece, was concerned in getting needed supplies made available under the American aid program into the hands of the Greek forces. JUSMAPG was interested mainly in advising the Greeks on the proper use of that equipment, on their own logistical system, and on tactical operations. By an informal understanding with the British, members of JUSMAPG teams concerned themselves primarily with matters of logistics and operations, while members of the British Mission advised mainly on questions of organization and training. Later (July 1948) American teams assumed responsibility for infantry training while the British continued to have charge of other training.[7]

In February 1948 Lt. Gen. James A. Van Fleet replaced General Livesay as director of JUSMAPG and commander of the U.S. Army Group, Greece. A month later General Thorson had to be relieved as assistant director because of illness, and Brig. Gen. Reuben E. Jenkins arrived in April as his replacement. Now the U.S. army authorized strength in Greece was 366 officers and men. No American combat units were there, and American soldiers did not command Greek troops, but they did accompany Greek units in military operations. Here General Van Fleet won his spurs in mountain fighting against communist mountain strongholds. Upon the resignation of Griswold as chief of the American Mission for Aid to Greece, Henry F. Grady, already the U.S. ambassador at Athens, became the chief. This represented one more step in the general pattern established for the Mutual Security Program in which it was the rule for the ambassador to head the "country team." At the same time most of the economic sections of the mission were transferred to a separate Economic Cooperation Administration mission.[8]

A peculiarity of the Greek military supply situation was that the Greek forces had been equipped largely with British equipment. In the interest of preserving operational continuity, it seemed essential that replacement items and spare parts should be furnished from British sources, at least for the time being. In order to arrange for the procurement of these necessary British items, and to serve as financial agency in making payments to the British government for supplies obtained from its stocks, the General Staff Liaison

Group was established in London in May 1947—a week after the president approved the Greek-Turkish aid bill. The Liaison Group was an agency of the Logistics Division (later G–4), Army General Staff, and of the Materials, Supply, and Procurement Division of the air staff in coordinating, supervising, controlling, and making payments for supplies obtained from British depots for Greece and Turkey under the American aid program. For their part the British continued to maintain a relatively large mission and several thousand British troops in Greece at the expense of the British government.[9]

On arriving in Greece in the summer of 1947 the American mission found seriously deteriorating economic conditions. Some reconstruction had been accomplished by the United Nations Relief and Rehabilitation Administration and by the British government, but a great deal remained to be done. The Corinth Canal had to be cleared of landslides where the Germans had blasted; bridges and tunnels had to be reopened for the railways; destroyed piers and quays and loading equipment at Piraeus, Salonika, Volos and other ports had to be restored; many of the roads had deteriorated to the point where they were impassable, telephone and telegraph lines had to be restored to prewar status. In civil reconstruction work as well as in the programs of military aid, the army had an important role to play. Under the provisions of a State-War Department agreement concluded on 28 July 1947, the Corps of Engineers established a district office in Athens to furnish technical engineering and contracting services. The district engineer proceeded to let management-construction contracts with combines of private firms for railroad and road construction and for the restoration of the ports and the Corinth Canal. These firms in turn contracted for specific projects with individual Greek engineering companies. But little could be accomplished toward economic rehabilitation until the military situation could be resolved.[10]

Guerrilla forces in Greece were only about twenty thousand strong, but that number of armed bandits loosed on the country could create a remarkable amount of havoc. Under a hard core of communist leaders, people who found a life of brigandage satisfying or profitable and numbers of fugitives from justice made up much of the following. Many of the guerrillas were men who had been conscripted forcibly in raids on villages and then had been held obedient through terror. Although sporadic guerrilla activities had broken out in many parts of Greece, the attacks had been most numerous and successful throughout the rural sections of mountainous northern Greece—in Epirus, Macedonia, and Thrace. Attacks had driven local inhabitants from their farms and villages, until by the end of 1947 an estimated 420,000 were seeking refuge in the northern cities. With the benefit of training camps and administrative installations in Albania, Yugoslavia, and Bulgaria, the communist bands were able to establish strongholds along the border at Mourgana, Grammos, Vitsi, Kaimaktchalen, Beles, Boz Dag, Khaidou, and Evros. In addition they had won control of mountain areas in eastern and central Greece, on the island of Euboea, and in Peloponnesus. On the other hand the

Greek National Army, numbering some 120,000 men, had permitted itself to become paralyzed in dispersing detachments of one or two companies each to guard widely separated towns and installations. On 24 December 1947 a clandestine radio station, supposedly operated by Greek guerrillas, announced the establishement of a "Government of Free Greece" under the leadership of the communist General "Markos," but so far the rebel "government" had not been able to capture a populous city to serve as its capital. It was important to keep the guerrillas from doing so. This was about the time that JUSMAPG was organized. The time had come for a consolidation of forces and for revitalized action.[11]

First it was necessary to get supplies and equipment, to reorganize and expand somewhat the Greek armed forces, and to train units for large-scale tactical operations. Convinced of the primacy of the military effort to economic recovery, the Greek government requested modification of the original aid program to allot a greater portion of the available funds to military aid. The result was an increase in the military program from 50 percent ($149 million) of the total to 57.5 percent ($172 million).[12] By the end of December 1947, supply actions had been taken to obtain nearly $62 million worth of supplies and equipment from the United States, and another $12 million worth of food and maintenance items had been obtained from Great Britain between 22 May and 1 September. In contrast to military aid programs that would develop later, the largest category of supplies obtained from the United States at this time was not ordnance, but quartermaster supplies, to the extent of over half of the total value. Surplus property made up much of the early shipments to Greece, and a number of items came from surplus stocks still to be found in the European and Mediterranean areas. Additional equipment was obtained at no further cost to the United States by the recovery of lend-lease matériel from the British. Total shipments of military supplies from all sources reached 147,000 long tons, with an estimated transfer value of $40 million by the end of 1947.[13]

During the first weeks of supply operations under the aid program stocks of supplies and equipment were built up in the Greek military depots. Beginning in September the distribution of supplies to the troops proceeded rapidly. Within a few weeks the delivery of hundreds of motor vehicles increased the mobility of Greek units immeasurably. Principal logistic deficiencies were in the supply of automatic weapons, mountain artillery, mortars, ammunition for the light antiaircraft guns on hand, and motor vehicles, and in the organization and functioning of effective supply services, the maintenance system, and medical services. In consultation with American and British advisers, the Greek government increased the troop strength of the National Army from 120,000 to 132,000 and in October 1947 organized the National Defense Corps (a National Guard type of organization). First put at twenty battalions of five hundred men each, the strength of the National Defense Corps later was raised to one hundred battalions with a total of fifty thousand men. A further temporary increase in the authorized strength of the National Army to 147,000 men permitted the organization of the mountain artillery, signal, and engineering units necessary for a balanced force.

During the spring and summer of 1948 the U.S. Army Group, Greece, helped in locating and building up supply installations for the support of military operations getting underway. Perhaps General Van Fleet had developed the enthusiasm for artillery fire for which he was to become noted in Korea. Unexpectedly heavy expenditures of artillery ammunition during the early phase of operations in the Grammos area of northwestern Greece immediately made necessary a strict rationing system until further supplies could be built up. By 30 June 1948 sixty-nine ships had brought into Greece cargoes of military supplies totalling 382,000 measurement tons of trucks, weapons ammunition, communications and fire control equipment, engineer equipment, rations and supplies. Tactical operations being undertaken were not held back by shortages of supplies.[14]

In a ten-day battle at Konitsa near the Albanian border of northwestern Greece in late December 1947, Greek forces were able to give the communist-led outlaws their first serious setback. In another winter action early in 1948 army forces wiped out a pocket of some two thousand guerrillas in the Mount Olympus area. In April 1948 three Greek army divisions together with commando units and supporting artillery launched a "spring offensive" with an operation aimed at surrounding and destroying a band of twenty-five hundred guerrillas in the Roumeli area west of Athens. Within a few weeks 641 guerrillas had been reported killed and another 1,368 captured.

National Defense Corps battalions and gendarme units occupied the cleared area while the army divisions and supporting troops regrouped for a bigger action in June. This was Operation CROWN in which six divisions and supporting troops joined in an effort to isolate a guerrilla force estimated at seven thousand men in the Grammos Mountain area (near the Albanian border), and then to destory it. Here difficult mountain fighting dragged on for weeks. After a month of it the guerrillas brought up reinforcements from other parts of Greece to increase their strength here to about twelve thousand men. At the same time they intensified their local attacks, sabotage, and forced recruiting over a widespread area in an attempt to divert government forces from the Grammos area. Army divisions held firm and maintained their integrity for the major task. At last in August the guerrillas had to give up this area. An estimated three thousand to five thousand of them escaped across the border into Albania.

This asylum and the logistic support given the Greek rebels on foreign territory was the most vexing aspect of the whole situation. In a remarkably short time guerrilla forces began building up a new concentration in the Vitsi Mountain area—a short distance to the north and east of the area from which they had just been expelled. Joined by men released from hospitals and by others from "replacement training camps," guerrillas who had escaped previous capture now came down out of Albania and Yugoslavia, until by 30 September they numbered about six thousand in the Vitsi area. While smaller bands of guerrillas continued their harrassing attacks in other areas, those in the Vitsi area stood fast.

Sometimes it seemed that all the supply efforts and the tactical operations of the Greek force were going to be of no avail. The army would train men, distribute equipment, make a successful attack, and then a few weeks later would find themselves facing as many guerrillas as before. In 1948 Greek forces reported that a total of 15,727 guerrillas had been killed, 8,915 had been captured, and 8,256 had surrendered. Yet, after these more than 32,000 casualties—even without taking into account the probably much larger number of wounded—guerrilla forces had an estimated strength of 23,000—larger by two to three thousand than they had seen at the beginning of the year. Neither had there been appreciable relief from the raiding of farms and villages. By December 1948 the number of refugees who had fled to cities had swollen to more than 600,000.[15] President Truman shared the general disappointment with these results. He reported in December 1948: "The encouraging prospect for substantial elimination of the Greek guerrilla forces which existed at the time of the victory of the Greek National Army in the Grammos Mountains...has unfortunately not materialized. A military stalemate has ensued which has prolonged the struggle."[16]

But during this time there had been important developments outside of Greece that promised higher hopes for the success of the greater efforts to be undertaken in the ensuing months. Tito's break with Moscow in June 1948 and the subsequent closing of the Yugoslav-Greek frontier closed to the rebels their most important base of supply and sanctuary for refuge.

Meanwhile, the flow of supplies and programs for training and revitalizing the Greek armed forces had continued. One special measure was the arming of civilian groups so that they could have some means of protecting themselves against guerrilla raids. This went a long way toward persuading many of the refugees to return to their homes where they could resume their much-needed agricultural production, and it also involved bringing irregular military units under centralized control. Although the Greek government had decreed the disbanding of irregular units upon the formation of the National Defense Corps, most of these units, armed with German and Italian weapons, and subject to no higher military control, continued to exist. In August 1948 JUSMAPG authorized the arming of a limited number of new civilian home guard units on condition that they would be under proper military control. Late in the year fourteen thousand British rifles were issued to these men. In February and March 1949 the American Mission approved an issue of an additional fifteen thousand British rifles for the arming of refugees who were to return to their villages. This had important results in relieving demands for government doles and in relieving the congestion in the cities, while adding to farm productivity. During July and August over 256,000 refugees returned to their villages. Additional allotments of arms to civilians brought the total number issued to home guard units up to fifty-one thousand by the end of August.[17]

A change in supply procedures effective in August 1948 made the U.S. Army Group, Greece, responsible for deciding whether any given supplies should be requisitioned from the United States or from the United Kingdom. Previously this had been the duty of the director of logistics (later G-4) in Washington, but the advisers in Greece were in a better position to place requisitions according to the types of equipment that required British or American parts, the extent of replacemet of certain British equipment with American models, time factors, and other considerations upon which these decisions had to be based. On the average in 1949 it was taking six to eight months after the request for supplies to be delivered in Greece from the United States. It took four to six months for them to arrive from the United Kingdom. Requisitions now went from USAGG direct to the chiefs of the technical services (or to the London Logistics Group) rather than through the director of logistics as had been the practice formerly. In November 1948 a U.S. air force group, separate from the army group, was organized, but the U.S. army group continued to handle the procurement of air force supplies until 1 February 1949. After that date the air force group assumed responsibility for air force equipment, although the army group continued to procure fuel and other quartermaster supplies for the Royal Hellenic Air Force. In March 1950 the various American military groups became sections of the new Joint U.S. Military Advisory Group, Greece (JUSMAGG).[18]

Throughout 1948 and 1949 logistic support generally appeared to be sufficient for Greek military needs. At the end of June 1949, after two years of the aid program, 396 ships had delivered to Greece a total of 520,500 long tons of military supplies and equipment, and 131 ships had brought in another 55,450 long tons from Great Britain and the Middle East. All this represented a value in goods and services given at $296,462,000. By this time the military situation was looking much brighter.[19]

In December 1948 the Greek army with air force support began operations to clear guerrillas from the Peloponnesus. Here one advantage was that the bandits could not easily escape into Albania, nor could they depend upon foreign supplies and services. By the end of March 1949 guerrilla activity had been virtually eliminated from this area. The Peloponnesus, inhabited by nearly a million people, had been made safe for travel, commerce, and renewed reconstruction. In the meantime some important changes of command had come about. In January General Alexander Papagos, the man who had given Mussolini's legions such a rough time when they invaded Greece in 1940, accepted appointment as commander in chief of the Greek armed forces. Holding himself independent of political influence, the World War II hero enforced strict discipline in the senior ranks of the army, adopted many of the reforms that JUSMAPG had been recommending, and breathed new vigor into the whole Greek military effort. On the other side, General Markos fell from communist grace about this time and lost the leadership of the guerrillas.

The next step in the offensive against the guerrillas was a coordinated operation that began in May in the Roumeli and Agrafa-Tzoumerka areas of central Greece. This area had been cleared of most hostile groups by mid-July, though others, fleeing from pursuit in the north, came in later and had to be routed out in August and September.

The biggest strikes of all were against the communist strongholds that remained in the Vitsi Mountain area and against other groups that had reestablished themselves in the Grammos Mountains in order to control well-protected supply routes from Albania. Another important factor now was Yugoslavia's defection from the Communist bloc. While still claiming to be a communist state, Tito, the Yugoslav ruler, had broken with Moscow in 1948, and Yugoslavia had been expelled from the Cominform. Then in July 1949 Yugoslavia closed its border to Greece and thus denied the Greek guerillas their Yugoslav sanctuary. The "big push," called Operation TORCH, began against the rebels in those areas on 10 August. In the Vitsi area, wher stalemate had prevailed for a year, four Greek National Army divisions and five commando groups with air force support won a smashing victory. Within three days they had completely overrun what had been called "impregnable" defenses. Again many of the guerrillas withdrew into Albania, but this time their retreat was so disorderly that they abandoned most of their supplies and equipment. Leaving two divisions to hold this area, the other two Greek army divisions and the commandos immediately moved to the Grammos area to join two other divisions in the last big roundup. On 27 August the guerrilla defenses collapsed, and two days later government forces controlled the whole area. By 31 August the total guerrilla forces had been reduced to an estimated 3,580 men and women. Six months after what had seemed almost hopeless stalemate, victory had come swiftly and, except for islolated outbreaks, completely.[20]

While pleased with the rapid conclusion of offensive operations, General Van Fleet insisted that the Greeks make more complete their control of mountainous border areas. It was a disgrace, he said, that bandits should continue to move almost at will back and forth across the Albanian border. The problem could not be permanently settled until diplomats and the United Nations could do something about the use of neighboring territory for bases of operations against Greece. But in September plans went forward for the gradual demobilization of Greek forces to a size that could be maintained as a permanent peacetime establishment without overburdening the economy. The American Mission would continue its assistance in training and supplying, but the emphasis would be on fewer numbers and higher quality.[21]

By 31 December 1949 total supplies and equipment shipped by the army for

Greek aid amounted to more than 1,100,000 measurement tons—about 92 percent of the total authorized up to that time.[22] Orders and deliveries of some of the major items provided through the U.S. Army Group, Greece, included those shown in table 3.

Table 3. U.S. Army Matériel Sent to Greece, 1947–1949

	Total ordered as of 31 December 1949	Total delivered as of 31 December 1949
Motor vehicles	10,639	9,953
Tires	56,642	51,744
Automotive batteries	18,662	9,682
Motor vehicle and aviation fuel	52,861,890 gal. (subject to withdrawals from Greek petroleum pool)	
Mules	11,907	11,907
Radio sets	7,063	7,063
Small arms	159,922	153,152
Mortars and artillery pieces	4,130	4,080
Small arms ammunition	455,342,694 rds.	445,042,694 rds.
Mortar and artillery ammunition (rounds)	7,737,029	7,370,329
Bombs and rockets	89,438	89,438
Pierced steel planking	2,324,875 sq. ft.	2,324,875 sq. ft.
Major clothing items	7,770,453	6,488,568
Rations (to 31 Aug. 49)	240,569,900	225,625,284
Hospitals, personnel	6	6
Hospitals, animal	4	4

SOURCE: Hist of JUSMAGG, 25 Mar. 49 to 30 June 50, 58; Brief Hist of USAGG Procurement, 24 May 47 to 31 Aug. 49, 36.

In late 1949 the Greek army continued to be equipped mainly with British weapons. Three national army divisions and three light infantry regiments were equipped completely with American weapons. These included 1903 rifles, Browning automatic rifles, Browning light machine guns, submachine guns, 60-mm and 81-mm mortars, 75-mm pack howitzers, 2.36-inch bazookas, grenades, and Very pistols and signal flares. All the other Greek infantry units also had American mortars, pack howitzers, and some submachine guns and bazookas. Most of the weapons gave quite satisfactory performance. The Browning automatic rifle gave considerable trouble until Greek soldiers could be trained to use it. Those well trained in its use then preferred the BAR to the British Bren gun, but most Greeks preferred the Bren because of its simpler mechanism. It took time to teach the Greeks to use the mortars, but then they used them with great skill. The 81-mm mortar was somewhat too heavy for rapid movement in the mountain country; lightness was one of the big advantages of the 60-mm. The Greeks were enthusiastic about the 75-mm pack howitzer, but General Jenkins reported that as far as he was concerned, "they can have it." The weapon had good range and was adaptable to mountain warfare, but the light shell it fired had little effect against well-dug-in positions. American advisers generally preferred additional 81-mm mortars in place of the pack howitzers.[23]

In June 1950 Ambassador Grady reported:

> Three years ago Congress passed the first Greek Aid Bill. In that year, 1947, many people were doubtful about the advisability and efficacy of this aid. By 1948, we had made some progress but there had been discouraging turns of events in both the military and economic fields; there was talk in some quarters about "operation rathole."
>
> The next year, 1949, when the Executive Branch again requested Congress for substantial aid for Greece, we could point to a period of relative economic stability and to a trained and partially equipped Greek armed service. We were hopeful.
>
> This year, 1950, we can point to a continuation of the economic stability and to a completely victorious Greek military force. With the help of American arms, the communist guerrilla forces have been reduced to a few hundred ineffective men. The remainder of the 20,000 who were in Greece a year ago have been killed, repatriated, or have withdrawn into the "curtain countries," and the guerrilla recruiting and supply facilities within Greece have been broken up. By some time this summer the remainder of the 700,000 refugees from war areas will have returned to their homes. . . .
>
> We have met the emergency problem; our problem is now aimed at placing the country upon a firm basis which will enable it to stand on its own.[24]

Under the Mutual Defense Assistance Program, military aid continued to Greece for modernizing and furthering the training and effectiveness of the Greek armed forces. The aggregate cost of military goods authorized for shipment to Greece up to June 1949 amounted to $345,335,000, including costs of transportation and other services, of which $309,684,000 was for army-procured supplies and equipment.[25] Army shipments were at a somewhat lower rate under the Mutual Defense Assistance Program, though the total did not fall off sharply. The total approved programs for four years, fiscal years 1950 to 1953 inclusive, amounted to $522,100,000, including $42,700,000 worth of surplus property not chargeable to MDAP appropriations. The army's part of this total was $281,200,000.[26]

Success seemed to come slowly in Greece. In December 1948 the only reward for a year-and-a-half of effort in supplying, training, and advising the Greek armed forces seemed to be endless stalemate. An army that had thrilled the world as it drove invading Italians from its soil in 1940 stood impotent before twenty thousand bandits in 1948. Then success came. By the end of August 1949 the guerrillas had been eliminated as effective fighting forces. Perhaps the effectiveness of American assistance had not been unduly slow after all. Perhaps any such military venture should have been expected to take eighteen months to two years before any notable success could be achieved. It

Continuing coordination in Greece: Maj. Gen. R. E. Jenkins, chief, Joint U.S. Military Assistance Group, Greece, greets Admiral R. D. Carney, commander-in-chief, East Atlantic and Mediterranean, on his arrival at Athens, January 1951.

seemed to take about that long for programs to be approved, equipment to be obtained, and for the recipient forces to be trained and for them to absorb the equipment provided. Even in regard to its own forces, the United States seemed to need eighteen months to two years to be able to take the offensive with any descisive results. In World War I it was a year after the declaration of war before the First Division could launch the first local attack of American forces at Cantigny, and it was seventeen months before the American First Army could mount its first offensive against the St. Mihiel salient. It was nearly two years after the beginning of American mobilization, with the passage of legislation for activating the National Guard and for selective service in August and September, respectively, in 1940, that American ground forces could launch their first offensive action of World War II at Guadalcanal, and it was three months later befor army forces landed in North Africa—and it took six months in each case to bring those offensives to a successful conclusion. With American lend–lease assistance and their own efforts, the Russians were able to launch their counteroffensive at Stalingrad only after the passing of seventeen months from the German invasion in June 1941, and twenty months had passed before the decisive victory at Stalingrad had been completed. Surely the most outstanding exception to this pattern was in Korea, where General MacArthur had been able to mount the Inchon landing within two-and-one-half months after the initial surprise attack. But in other activities, the pattern of disappointingly slow beginnings, followed by great accomplishments, reappeared—in housing construction in Alaska, in air base construction in Alaska, in air base construction in North Africa, in setting up the line of communications across France, in developing the North Atlantic Treaty Organization, in making effective the whole program of mutual defense assistance.

The "end of the Greek case" in the United Nations came when the U.N. Special Committee on the Balkans held its final public session at Athens on 2 February 1952 and terminated its work three days later. Special committee observers had witnessed the use of the territory of Greece's northern neighbors as sanctuaries for guerrillas. But now that had ended. However, the United Nations did not ignore the possibility of future violations. The permanent Peace Observation Commission, organized under the "Uniting for Peace" Resolution adopted by the U.N. General Assembly on 3 November 1950 established a Balkan subcommission to succeed the special committee as "watchdog" in that troubled area.[27]

Turkey

Greece and Turkey, neighbors in the strategic Near East, both received military assistance from the United States under the same legislation, but conditions in the two countries differed greatly. Turkey had been spared the devastation of World War II and it was not the impoverished country that Greece was. Guerrilla bands and domestic violence did not dominate large areas of Tukish territory, as was the case in Greece. Here the threat was clear and direct. The Soviet Union coveted control of the Dardanelles and Bosporus and the annexation of provinces in northeastern Anatolia. As early as March 1945 the Soviet Union had given some indication of its intent by renouncing the 1925 treaty of friendship with Turkey. From that time the Soviet press and radio carried on an almost uninterrupted campaign of intimidation against Turkey. The Turkish answer was to maintain armed forces at their World War II mobilization strength and to hold firm.[28]

The same act of Congress that authorized the original $200,000,000 program of economic and military assistance for Greece also authorized a $100,000,000 program of military aid to Turkey. At the time Turkey had

Maj. Gen. William H. Arnold, chief of the American military mission in Turkey, examines a Turkish gun.

under arms a force of half a million men, though the army was, as Secretary of War Patterson put it, "What you might call a 1910 army."[29] The withdrawal of British aid affected Turkey as it did Greece. In May 1947 Turkey had been maintaining its armed forces at a strength of half-a-million men for six years, and it was spending more than 50 percent of its annual revenues on national defense. In other aid programs economic assistance would be offered as a means of strengthening military defenses. Here the tables were turned. Here military aid was seen as a method of relieving some of the economic burden. The aim was to increase Turkish military effectiveness by modernizing the weapons and equipment of the armed forces without adding appreciably to the national budget, and to permit the release of men from the armed forces so that they could return to productive civilian occupations. This was a case where the immediate objective was not to build up the troop strength of the armed forces, but to reduce it.

As with Greece, a preliminary survey team went to Turkey soon after passage of the assistance bill to analyze requirements.[30] After inspection of Turkish military installations, schools, factories, arsenals, roads, ports, and railways, and after conferences with Turkish military officers, and officials in the ministries of Communications, Public Works, National Economy, Agriculture, and Industry, members of the survey team recommended the apportionment of the $100,000,000 authorized for Turkish aid as follows:

Ground forces	$48,500,000
Air forces	26,750,000
Naval forces	14,750,000
Arsenal improvement	5,000,000
Highway improvement	5,000,000

The program as later approved retained this allocation.

The American Mission for Aid to Turkey was organized from the outset as a "country team" with the ambassador, Edwin C. Wilson, as chief. George Wadsworth became ambassador and chief of the aid mission 1 October 1948. By agreement between the army and the State Department in October 1947 the U.S. Public Roads Administration (Federal Works Agency) was given responsibility for the highway improvement program in Turkey. Thereafter the American Mission for Aid to Turkey was made up of the army group, air force group, navy group, and public roads group. Later the military sections were brought together in the Joint American Military Mission for Aid to Turkey (JAMMAT).

Machinery for cargo handling and road building made up the first shipments under the Turkish aid program. Early difficulties in handling, transporting, and storing equipment when it arrived brought increases in authorized numbers of officers, enlisted men, and civilians in the army and air force groups. The total approved strength (March 1948) was 126 for the army group, 100 for the air force, and 40 for the navy group, though the number actually assigned was considerably less than that until the summer of 1948.

It took two years to get the amount of equipment delivered to Turkey that had been authorized for the first year's program. The second year's program was cut back to $52,545,000 in new authorizations for procurement. All together the program for the two years, amounting to $152,545,000, included $81,000,000 for ground forces, and an additional $20,500,000 of army procurement for the air force. Shipments from ports through 31 December 1949 totalled 386,000 measurement tons for Turkey, representing about 87 percent of the total thus far authorized.[31] By 30 June 1950 the Turkish program, now superseded by aid continuing under MDAP, was practically complete; about $12,600,000 worth of authorized materials had not yet been shipped.[32] By this time members of the American Mission considered that the combat capabilities of the Turkish armed forces were greater than when the forces were double their current size.[33]

In addition to continuing the programs of modernization of equipment, improvement of facilities, and training of personnel that had already begun, the Mutual Defense Assistance program for Turkey also included an expanded program of air base construction. In May 1950 the chief of engineers established the U.S. Engineer Group, Ankara, to supervise this and other construction projects. The original assumptions had been that Turkish operators and mechanics would be trained to use the engineering equipment and then would do the work of airfield rehabilitation and construction themselves. But the Turks lacked the technical and mechanical experience necessary to take over the job completely. With the approval of the Foreign Aid Coordinating Committee, the ambassador in Turkey entered into an agreement with the Turkish government that provided that the American Mission would arrange for American contractors to do the work and would furnish the necessary construction engineers, technicians, and all supplies, equipment, and funds, other than those included in the Turkish contribution. The Turkish government agreed to furnish the real estate, all rail transportation within Turkey, construction equipment and materials previously received under the aid program, and would make available Turkish aviation engineer units. A joint venture formed by the Metcalfe Construction Company, Gordon Hamilton Contracting Company, and Grove, Shepherd, Wilson, and Kruge, Inc., received the contract to do the work on a cost-plus-a-fixed-fee basis. The construction work was to be done at Diyarbakir, Eskisehir, Kayserie, Bandirma, Erzincan, Balikesir, Afyon, and Merzifon. A rear-echelon office of the engineer group in New York procured materials and recruited personnel in the United States.[34]

On arrival in Turkey the engineer group at first was under the administrative jurisdiction of the U.S. air force group, but a later order established the separate status of the engineer group under the Joint American Military Mission for Aid to Turkey.

An immediate delay developed in getting construction equipment into operation. Most of the construction equipment and materials in Turkey were stored at the Cumoavasi Depot at Izmir, and the contractors stationed a small group of workers there to make an inventory, and to effect the transfer of property which had arrived under the aid program. But only about one-fourth of the repair parts had been unpacked and binned. The fact that all the documents were in Turkish, and that qualified storekeepers could not be found locally, complicated further the not inconsiderable task of making an inventory of this stock of some seven thousand line items. Greater delays occurred after work began in September 1950. By this time the competition of the Korean conflict for materials was becoming pronounced, but that conflict also had pointed up the urgency of the program in Turkey, and that and other considerations led to a number of revisions. A revision of the program approved in March 1951, and a further revision in the fall, as in the case of the American bases in Morocco, delayed considerably completion of the program. Revisions still were being anticipated a year later. The air force group in cooperation with the Turkish air force chose the sites, and the air force group then furnished to the engineer group the design and space criteria for each site.The engineer group then supervised the layout and planning for each project, subject to the final approval of the air force group. The design and construction of buildings, utilities, drainage, airfield pavement, and gasoline and oil storage facilities were based on Corps of Engineers and U.S. air force standards as modified by local conditions, tactical requirements, and available materials.[35] In August 1952 Secretary of the Army Pace found the construction "proceeding on schedule" and the arrangements under which it was being done "most satisfactory."[36]

Under the original Greek-Turkish Aid program, military assistance provided for Turkey was about half that granted to Greece. Under the Mutual Defense Assistance programs, the total matériel approved for Turkey for fiscal years 1950 through 1953 ($656.8 million including $38.5 million worth of surplus stocks) was greater than the Greek total by over $134 million.[37]

Iran

Long a subject of Anglo-Russian rivalry, Iran had been occupied by forces of both those countries in August 1941 in a move calculated to thwart further Axis advances in that area and as a means of consolidating a supply route for British material assistance from the Persian Gulf ports to the Soviet Union. Left no other choice, the Iranian government accepted the terms of the occupation on 9 September 1941, and the ruling pro-Axis shah abdicated a week later in favor of his twenty-one-year-old son, Mohammed Riza Pahlevi. The United States also entered the picture in September as an associate of Great Britian in delivering supplies to the Soviet Union. Arrangements for lend-lease supplies to the Russians by this route fell mainly to the U.S. Iranian Mission and its successor, the Iran-Iraq Service Command, redesignated in August 1942 the Persian Gulf Service Command. Getting supplies to the Russians had involved not only the negotiation of requirements and the submission of requests, but the planning and supervision of the construction and maintenace of port facilities, roads, railrods, and the operation of plants for assembling crated trucks and airplanes. The work had begun under civilian contractors, but after Pearl Harbor and the American entry into the war, service troops gradually took over the projects.[38]

In March 1942 Iran itself had been declared eligible for lend-lease assistance. Then the Iranian government requested the United States to furnish military missions to advise on the training and organization of the army and of the gendarmerie. A contract signed for the army mission of 3 November 1943, was retroactive to 22 March 1943, and one signed for the gendarmerie mission on 27 November 1943 was retroactive to 2 October. As contractual missions under the Iranian government, these were in a different category from the military assistance advisory groups later organized to carry out the Mutual Defense Assistance Program. American officers assigned to the missions served respectively in the Iranian Ministry of War and the Ministry of Interior. They took precedence over all Iranian officers of the same rank. The government of Iran bore all expenses of the missions, including supplementary salaries for the members. The chief of the army mission (Maj. Gen. Clarence S. Ridley) was appointed military adviser by an imperial general order. He could recommend to the shah removals, promotions, and demotions of Iranian army officers, and if requested he could offer advice on strategic and tactical planning. His activities were limited generally to improving the supply system of the Iranian army. The chief of the gendarmerie mission (Colonel H. Norman Schwarzkopf, a former chief of the New Jersey State Police) was appointed adviser to the Minister of the Interior on gendarmerie affairs, and as such, he exercised actual command over the national constabulary. This was especially important for maintaining security on the roads through Iran over which lend-lease matériel had to pass. At the end of World War II, the Iranian government asked that both missions be continued. The War Department questioned the military value of continuing the missions, but accepting the political advantages involved, agreed. A new contract for the army mission was signed 6 October 1947; a revision in 1948 prohibited advice on strategic and tactical plans, but advice and assistance on organization, training and administration continued. A revision of the gendarmerie mission contract in 1948 took away the command authority of the chief of the mission and limited him to an advisory function only.[39] The missions remained even through the convulsions of internal disorder in the period from 1951 to 1953. In mid-1953 the Department of Defense was attaching more importance than ever to the military missions. Assistant Secretary of Defense Nash told the House Committee on Foreign Affairs:

> Our military mission in Iran has been one of the real assets that we have had when that situation was so bad some months ago. . . .
> It has bolstered the morale and helped sustain the morale of the Iranian military. We think if we could get military missions such as we have in Iran in places like Syria, Iraq, and Egypt, eventually that we could bring their thinking and their sympathies around to be more oriented toward our way in the West than by other means. We have felt it would be desirable to bring the young military people from those countries over to this country for training, and not have to charge them quite the heavy cost that training involves. . . . We would like to give grant-aid training to these young military people who will go back and eventually, if it follows the pattern that is there now, be the leaders. . . .
> I would say to all of you, just as sincerely as I am capable of saying it, that there is no investment out of the whole military-aid program—with the possible exception of the amount we are asking for, for Spain—where we get more for our money than in the funds that are being asked for in the Middle East in the way of building at least the beginnings of real security in that area.[40]

Iran too got a head start on military assistance before the beginning of the general Mutual Defense Assistance Program. In 1948 the United States made an agreement with Iran for the sale of $10 million worth of surplus military equipment under the terms of the Surplus Property Act of 1944 on a credit basis. Then it developed that Iran could not raise the funds to cover handling and moving the property. In the Second Deficiency Appropriation Act of 1948, approved 26 June 1948, Congress appropriated to the president $18,300,000 for the care, handling, and disposal of surplus property abroad. About $15.5 million of this was allocated to the army for getting surplus equipment to Iran. In spite of strong Russian criticisms and protests, the program later was increased to comprise approximately $45,000,000 in surplus property assistance. The surplus equipment included fighter aircraft, light tanks, armored cars, and light artillery, defined as "non-aggression-type weapons." About 38 percent of the estimated 180,000 tons included in the total program, equal to about 58 percent of the total value, had been shipped by 30 June 1949, but the rate of shipments was increasing so that the program could be nearing completion before MDAP began.[41]

It had been demonstrated since World War II that the common pattern for communist expansion was through internal subversion. This was a particular danger in Iran, where mob violence was not uncommon. The principal aim of American military aid both under the surplus property program and under the later Mutual Defense Assistance was to strengthen the army and the gendarmerie so that they might maintain order within the country. The Iranian government did not sign the required bilateral agreement for mutual defense assistance until 23 May 1950—after protracted negotiations. Now a military assistance advisory group, in addition to the two military missions already there, went to Iran to supervise execution of the new program. Shipments did not reach sizeable proportions until early 1951, and even then of course they were on a much more modest scale than those to Greece and Turkey. Then the Mutual Security Act of 1951 required a further agreement of statement of guarantee that the matériel would be used for the stated purposes on the part of recipient countries before they could be declared eligible for additional aid. Since a bilateral agreement under the Mutual Defense Assistance Act already had been signed, Premier Mohammed Mossadegh refused to give any such further assurances. At the end of the ninety-day period permitted by the act for compliance, 8 January 1952, military aid to Iran was suspended. After American officials gave notice that the program would be cancelled and the funds reallocated, Mossadegh finally signed an innocuous statement, and shipments were effective 24 April.[42]

Within six months after his appointment as premier in April 1951, Mossadegh had nationalized the rich oil fields and the great refinery at Abadan of the Anglo-Iranian Oil Company. It was a popular move, but poverty and turmoil came in its wake. In the next two years the aging premier seemed to be depending more and more on the support of the communist Tudeh Party, and seemed to lean more and more toward friendliness with the Soviet Union. "Today it appears," Senator Homor Ferguson observed in May 1953, "that Iran is thinking much better of Russia, the Russia that took all their camels and everything else, than they are of America who has been trying to fill the gap."[43]

In April 1953 mobs sacked the office of the U.S. Technical Cooperation Administration. Yet the military missions seemed to retain their popularity. A series of uprisings in August 1953 in which Mossadegh first seized dictatorial control and the shah fled to exile, and then, with CIA intervention, Mossadegh in turn was seized and the shah returned in triumph, left a confusing situation in this strategic middle eastern country. The stakes were high. Oil production virtually had ceased after the expulsion of the British, so that the West no longer could count upon that important source of supply. It still seemed important to keep those resources out of the hands of the Russians.[44]

In addition, the touchy relations between Israel and the Arab states, and the relations of the United States and Great Britain to them both, placed further blocks in the way of military cooperation and assistance in the area.[45]

Notes

1. See Chapter 5.
2. C. L. Sulzberger, "Greeks and Turks Have Key Role in NATO Plans," *The New York Times,* 9 Mar. 1952; see also "Greece, Turkey, and NATO," *World Today* 8, 4 (Apr. 1952): 162–69.
3. *Docs Regarding the Situation in Greece,* January 1945, presented by the Secy. of State for Foreign Affairs to (the British) Parliament, Greece No. 1 (1945), London, 1945; Floyd A. Spencer, Libr. of Cong., Eur. Affairs Div., *War and Postwar Greece; an Analysis Based on Greek Writings* Washington, 1952), 64–112.
4. *Annual Rpt. of the Secretary of the Army,* 1948, 58.
5. Brief History USAGG, Procurement, 24 May 47 to 31 Aug 49, prep. by Rpts. and Records Sec. (Greece), 4–10; *First Rpt. to Congress on Assistance to Greece and Turkey,* for period ending 30 Sept. 1947, Dept. of State Publ. 2957, 2, 13.
6. Brief History of USAGG Procurement, 24 May 47 to 31 Aug 49, 5–7.
7. Brief Hist. of JUSMAPG, 1 Jan. 48 to 31 Aug. 49, 1–3; *Annual Report of the Secretary of the Army,* 1948, 58–59; Lt. Col. Edwin P. Curtin, "American Advisory Group Aids Greece in War on Guerrillas," *Armored Cavalry Jnl.,* 58 (Jan.–Feb. 1949): 8–11, 34–35.
8. Brief History of JUSMAPG, 1 Jan. 48 to 31 Aug. 49, 3; *Fifth Rpt. to Congress on Assistance to Greece and Turkey,* 10; Brief History of USAGG Procurement, 26–27.
9. Ltr., Major William Leffingwell to Col. Hayes, 27 Feb. 49, and Draft Forward to Rpt., 26 Feb. 48; Rocco M. Paone, Hist. of Foreign Military Aid, draft MS, ch 1, 24; FMA Hist., Draft MS in G-4 FMA Hist. file, ch 5; *Third Rpt. to Congress on Assistance to Greece and Turkey,* 4–5.
10. First Rtp. to Congress on Assistance to Greece and Turkey, 12–16.
11. Brief Historyof JUSMAPG, 4–6; *Assistance to Greece and Turkey,* 2d. Rpt., covering the period to 31 Dec. 47, House Doc. 534, 80th Cong., 2d Sess., 16 Feb. 1948, 4–11; *Annual Rpt. of the Secretary of the Army,* 1948, 58–59.

12. Assistance to Greece and Turkey, 2d. Rpt., to 31 Dec. 47, 7–9.
13. Brief Hist of USAGG, Procurement, 24 May 47 to 31 Aug. 49, 9–25.
14. Ibid; G–4 Rev. of the Month, January 1948, (Dec. and Jan. data), publ. 29 Feb. 48, 1, 30; G–4 Rev. of the Month, 31 May 48, 1, 25; *Annual Rpt. of the Secy. of the Army,* 1948, 60.
15. Brief Hist. of JUSMAPG, 14–15; *Annual Rpt. of the Secy. of the Army,* 1948, 60; *Third Rpt. to Cong. on Assistance to Greece and Turkey,* for period ending 30 June 1948, Dept. of State Publ. 3278, 1–7; *Fifth Rpt. to Cong. on Assistance to Greece and Turkey,* for the period ending 30 Sept. 1948, Dept. of State Publ. 3371, 4–9; *Sixth Rpt to Cong. on Assistance to Greece and Turkey,* for the period ending 31 Dec. 1948, Dept. of State Publ. 3467, 1–11.
16. The President's Letter of Transmittal, *Fifth Rpt. to Cong. on Assistance to Greece and Turkey,* for period ending 30 Sept. 1948, iii.
17. Brief Hist. of JUSMAPG, 11–13.
18. Brief Hist. of USAGG, Procurement, 24 May 47 to 31 Aug 49, 26–34; Hist. of JUSMAGG, 25 Mar. 49 to 30 June 50, prep. by Rpts. and Records Sec., JUSMAPG, 1–9, 62.
19. Brief Hist. of USAGG, Procurement, 24 May 47 to 31 Aug. 49, 33–34; *Eighth Rpt. to Cong. on Assistance to* Greece and Turkey, 10–11.
20. Brief Hist. of JUSMAPG, 16–36; *Seventh Rpt. to Congress on Assistance to Greece and Turkey,* for the period ending 31 March 1949, Dept. of State Publ. 3594, 1–15; *Eighth Rpt. to Congress on Assistance to Greece and Turkey,* for period ending 30 June 1949, Dept. of State Publ. 3674, 1–12; John C. Campbell, *The United States in World Affairs 1948–1949* (New York, 1949), 116–22; Richard P. Stebbins, *The United States in World Affairs 1949* (New York, 1950), 263–67.
21. Hist. of JUSMAGG, 156–92.
22. G–4 Review of the Month, 1 Jan. 50, 13.
23. Rpt. by Maj. Gen. Reuben E. Jenkins, Deputy Dir. JUSMAPG, 13 Oct. 49, Quoted in Hist. of JUSMAGG 25 Mar. 49 to 30 June to 50 110–22.
24. Statement by Henry F. Grady, Ambassador to Greece, Submitted to Sen. For. Rel. and Armed Services Comm. and House For. Affairs Comm. *Dept. of State Bulletin,* 22 (June 1950): 1046.
25. *Eighth Rpt. to Congress on Aid to Greece and Turkey,* 10–11.
26. Dept. of Defense Opns. Under the Mutual Security Program, May 1953, 23.
27. *The Greek Question,* Dept. of State Publ. 4568, Apr. 1952.
28. Unless otherwise noted, this section is based upon the following: *First Report to Congress on Assistance to Greece and Turkey,* 17–19; *Second Rpt. to Cong. on Assist. to Greece and Turkey,* 36–39; *Third Rpt.* 30–33; *Fourth Rpt.* 32–36; *Fifth Rpt.* 11–19; *Sixth Rpt.* 15–25; *Seventh Rpt.* 17–27; *Eighth Rpt.* 13–23; *Mutual Security Act of 1953,* Hearings before Sen. Comm. on For. Rel., 83d Cong., 1st Sess., 13 May 53, 288–90.
29. Millis, *The Forrestal Diaries,* 257.
30. See *Annual Rpt. of the Secy. of the Army,* 1948, 61–62; Under an agreement of 27 Feb. 1946 and a supplemental agreement of 6 Dec. 1946, Turkey had obtained some surplus property on a credit basis; Ltr., Chester M. Carre, consultant OFLC to Lt. Col. Chester I. Davis, SS$P, 14 Apr. 47; Lt. Col. Russell O. Fudge, "Turks' Friends and Advisors," *U.S. A. Combat Forces Jnl.*, 2, (June 1952): 30–32.
31. G–4 Review of the Month, 1 Jan. 50, 13.
32. Logistical Operations Summary, 1 July 50, 12.
33. Statement by George Wadsworth, Ambassador to Turkey, submitted to Senate For Rel. and Armed Servs. Committees and House For Affairs Comm., 9 June 50, *Dept. of State Bulletin,* 22 (June 1950): 1047–48.
34. Corps of Engrs. Hist Summary, 30 Oct. 51, covering period 25 June 50 to 8

Sept. 51, Pt. 2 B: Corps of Engrs. Field Agencies: Div. Engrs., North Atlantic Div. Sec., 1–3, 4–9.

35. Ibid.

36. Memo for Record, 2 Sept. 52, Rpt. of Trip to Europe of Secy. Pace and Party, 9, 12.

37. Dept. of Defense Ops. under MDAP, May 1953, 23.

38. T. H. Vail Motter, *The Persian Corridor and Aid to Russia,* in U.S. Army in World War II, (Washington, 1952), 1–27, 82–100.

39. Ibid., 161–73; 461–80; *Annual Rpt. of The Secy. of the Army,* 1948, 63; *Semiannual Rpt. of the Secy. of the Army,* 1 Jan. 1951 to 30 June 1951, 97; Statement of Maj. Gen. William H. Arnold, Chief JAMMAT, 31 Mar. 52, *Mutual Security Act of 1952,* Hearings before Senate Comm. on For. Rel., 82d Cong., 2d Sess., 555–56. Statement of Maj. Gen. William H. Arnold, 1 Apr. 52, *Mutual Security Act Extension,* Hearings before House Comm. on For. Affairs, 82d Cong., 2d Sess., 393.

40. Statement of Frank Nash, Asst. Secy. of Defense, 4 June 53, *Mutual Security Act Extension,* Hearings before House Comm. on For. Affairs, 83d Cong., 1st Sess., 1046.

41. *Annual Rpt. of the Secy. of the Army,* 1948, 63. *Annual Rpt. of the Secy. of the Army,* 1949, 157; G–4 Review of the Month, 30 Sept. 48, 17; G–4 Review of the Month, 1 July 49, 18; William Adams Brown, Jr., and Redvers Opie., *American Foreign Assistance,* (Washington: The Brookings Institution, 1953), 446.

42. *Third Semiannual Rpt. to Congress on the MDAP,* 6 Oct 1950 to 31 Mar. 1951, 21–22; Testimony of Maj. Gen. George C. Stewart, Dir. OMA, OSD, 26 May 53, Mutual Security Act Extension, Hearings before House Comm. on For. Affairs, 83d Cong., 1st Sess., 728; Statement by John C. Wiley, Ambassador to Iran, submitted to Senate For. Rel. and Armed Servs. Committees, and House For. Affairs Comm., 9 June 50, *Dept of State Bulletin,* 12 (June 1950): 1048; Statement of John D. Jernegan, Actg. Asst. Secy. of State for Near Eastern, South Asian, and African Affairs, 26 May 53, *Mutual Security Act Extension,* Hearings before House Comm. on For. Affairs, 83d Cong., 1st Sess., 723; Statement presented by Associate Deputy Director for Mutual Security, 29 Apr. 52, *Mutual Security Act Extension,* Hearings before House Comm. on For. Affairs, 82d Cong., 2d Sess., 1029; G–2 Defriefing by Colonel John I. Hinks, Military Attaché to Iran, Pentagon, 29 Apr. 53.

43. *Mutual Security Act of 1953,* Hearings before Senate Comm. on For. Rel., 15 May 53, 377.

44. Kennett Love, "Iran's Army Now Holds the Balance of Power," *The New York Times,* 23 Aug. 1953; "U.S. Point Four Office Sacked by Iranians," *The New York Times,* 17 Apr. 1953; *First Rpt. to Cong. on the Mutual Security Program,* 31 Dec. 1951, 25; "Political upheaval in Iran," *Air Intel. Digest* (Sept 1952) 10–13; R. S. Allen, *The New York Post,* 13 Aug. 1952; *The New York Times,* 23 Aug. 1953.; Walter Isaacson and Evan Thomas, *The Wise Men* (New York, 1986), 556n.

45. Statement of John D. Jernegan, 26 May 53, *Mutual Security Act Extension,* Hearings before House For. Affairs Comm., 720–21.

8
Military Assistance in the Far East: China and Korea

> The last act of the drama is yet to be unfolded.... The people of America will, in some form or other, extend their dominion and their power... upon the eastern shores of Asia. And I think too, that eastward and southward will her great [Russian rival] ...stretch forth her power to the coasts of China and Siam: and thus the Saxon and the Cossack will meet once more, in strife or in friendship, on another field. Will it be in friendship? I fear not! The antagonistic exponents of freedom and absolutism must thus meet at last, and then will be fought that mighty battle on which the world will look with breathless interest; for on its issue will depend the freedom or the slavery of the world.
> —Commodore Matthew C. Perry, 6 March 1856.

> Conceding the critical importance of the present moment in the history of the world, admitting that movements intellectual and political, long in progress in China, are now reaching a turning point determinative of great future issues, it is essential to the United States that her individual citizens should seriously consider... the part the country ought to play, and the preparation necessary to that part.
> —Alfred Thayer Mahan, *The Problem of Asia* (1900)

The Far East

Outside of Europe, most American military aid went to the Far East. Problems of providing military assistance in Asia and the Pacific region differed appreciably from those encountered in Europe and the Near East. In some ways they were considerably more complex. Conditions varied a great deal too from one country to another in this area.[1] The main links connecting the programs in those countries were the facts that they happened to occupy the same quarter of the globe, that mutual defense assistance was provided for them under the same title of the Mutual Defense Assistance and the Mutual Security Acts, and the common threat of communist aggression or subversion, which ran like a red thread through all these military aid programs. Programs for each of the Far Eastern countries were worked out individually.

They comprised no unified effort during this period to 1954 either among the recipient nations or in execution by the United States. Although suggestions for a Pacific pact patterned after the North Atlantic Treaty were offered from time to time, no NATO-type structure was developed during this time.[2] The United States did enter into a mutual defense treaty with the Philippine Republic on 1 September 1951, formalizing a relationship that had previously been based on executive agreements, and a treaty with Australia and New Zealand (also on 1 September 1951), commonly referred to as the ANZUS pact. In each case the parties agreed that "an armed attack on either [any] of the Parties is deemed to include an attack on the metropolitan territory of either [any] of the Parties, or the island territories under its jurisdiction in the Pacific, or on its armed forces, public vessels, or aircraft in the Pacific." But American policy thus far was opposed to establishing formal machinery for defense cooperation such as had been done for the North Atlantic area. Furthermore no mutual defense assistance program was established for Australia or New Zealand.

While sympathetic to suggestions for coordinating the aid programs in the Asian and Pacific areas, Maj. Gen. George H. Olmsted, who had been director of the Office of Military Assistance in the Department of Defense, cautioned against a policy that would seem to assign any inferior status to the Far Eastern participants in amy coordinated effort. He told the House Foreign Affairs Committee in March 1953:

> From the military standpoint the problem in Asia is one problem and the several little shooting wars are just parts of that one problem. . . .
> If we would view the area as an area, rather than a number of isolated and independent countries, we have potentially there a balanced economy that could well nigh be self-sufficient. There has been some stirring and some talk, as you know, on the political side about integration of the area. Nothing could be more fatal to our standing in the area than to popularize the expression of "Asians fight Asians."
> These people, for an understandable reason, do not like that concept and that really is not the problem. It is the free world and communism that is the issue, not Asians or Europeans or North Americans.[3]

The rivalry arising from the competition for resources between American forces in Europe and in the Far East also was manifest in the military aid programs. Doctrines of "Asia first" and "Europe first," often with little relevancy to their strategic and logistic merits, became part of American domestic politics. European fears of a "pull to the Pacific" in military aid had some justification in terms of the American support for South Korea, and in the increasing American interest in Southeast Asia after the Korean attack of June 1950.[4] But American policy in those areas was related to a global pattern. If the free world were to be held safe from communism, according to this policy, overt communist aggresssion in Korea had to be stopped.

Whether the later programs for arming a large South Korean army could be justified on the same basis was another question. The focal point of interest in Southeast Asia was Indochina. Here military aid to the French and Indochinese forces could have important results for the defense of Europe by easing the strain the French were bearing in that remote area. In the spring of 1953 the new Secretary of State, John Foster Dulles, indicated that there might be a substantial shift in American aid from Europe to the Far East.[5]

China was the principal recipient of American assistance in the Far East, and the Philippines and Korea as well as China received special consideration as beneficiaries of military aid programs developed some time before the Mutual Defense Assistance Program. In this sense the Far East had a clear priority over Europe in terms of military assistance (though not in economic aid) until 1949. But by the time the Mutual Defense Assistance Program got started, the communists had overrun continental China. Thereafter military assistance to China, including Formosa, was suspended until after the Korean War. Earlier transfers of surplus property to the Republic of Korea had been completed, but mutual defense assistance, just beginning when the attack came, was suspended for that country too. Larger programs of direct assistance out of Department of Defense funds, of course, replaced MDAP in Korea for waging the war that ensued. Then Indochina replaced China as the principal Far Eastern recipient (exclusive of support for the Korean war) of American military assistance. The increasing communist threat to Indochina also brought Thailand into the assistance program in October 1950. A mutual security survey team was refused access to Burma, but that country did receive ten coast guard patrol vessels under MDAP. In Indonesia too there were serious misgivings about accepting American assistance. The Indonesian government did sign an agreement to receive aid, but it led to the downfall of the premier. That country received small quantities of small arms, trucks, and radios under the original MDAP for its national police mobile brigade as a means for promoting internal security. Shipments under the original program continued, but there were no programs for Indonesia for fiscal years 1952 and 1953. The military assistance advisory group that had been sent to Indonesia in 1950 was withdrawn in January 1953, and the Indonesian government converted what remained of the previously approved mutual defense assistance program to a reimbursable basis.[6]

Beginning slowly in 1950, the Mutual Defense Assistance Program was building up to significant proportions in the Far East by 1952 and 1953. In the spring of 1953, the status of the total program so far, excluding the earlier aid programs for China, the Philippines, and Korea, was as shown in table 4.

China and Formosa

It had taken a considerable effort on the part of the United States to keep Chinese military forces participating effectively in World War II, but the need

Table 4. MDAP for Fiscal Years 1950–1953, as of 30 June 1953

	Limits approved by Director for mutual security for matériel programs	(millions of dollars) Programmed	End Items Shipped	Measurement tonnage Shipped (Excluding vessels and aircraft delivered under own power)
Indochina (excluding 1952 special defense support program)	$807.5	789.5	506.4	770,603
Army	533.7	509.8	353.0	
Navy	138.8	137.0	82.3	
Air force	135.0	142.7	71.1	
China (Formosa)	485.2	474.4	236.4	335,407
Army	265.7	260.8	157.4	
Navy	35.1	35.1	10.3	
Air force	184.4	178.5	68.6	
Philippines	107.9	106.6	53.9	100,783
Army	69.1	68.3	39.8	
Navy	20.2	19.8	6.7	
Air force	18.7	18.6	7.3	
Thailand	114.7	109.1	69.2	105,565
Army	55.8	54.7	36.6	
Navy	21.4	21.2	15.2	
Air force	37.5	33.2	17.4	
Indonesia	5.4	5.4	3.9	4,427
Army	5.4	5.4	3.9	
Navy	0	0	0	
Air force	0	0	0	
Korea	10.9	10.2	10.2	69[a]
Army	10.0	9.5	9.5	
Navy	.1	.1	.1	
Air force	.7	.5	.5	

SOURCE: Dept. of Defense Opns. Under MSP, June 1953, 23–24; Dept. of Defense Opns. Under MSP, July 1953, 29, 37.
[a] This does not include shipments of vehicles and other supplies from Japan

to tie down sizeable Japanese forces on the Asiatic mainland had made the effort important. According to the hopes of American leaders, China should emerge after the defeat of Japan to fill the resulting "power vacuum" in East Asia. In the postwar scheme of things the role assigned to China was that of the great power of the Far East. But it was an assignment that proved to be out of reach until some years later when a communist regime hostile to the United States would in effect achieve that status.

A troublesome complication to effective Chinese participation in World War II was the smoldering civil war that had been running off and on between the dominant Kuomintang and the Chinese communists since 1927. Fortunately the two parties shared a common hostility toward the Japanese, but even the unity of purpose this afforded was tenuous and unsteady. Often military measures taken during the war assumed more the appearance of jockeying for advantage over the rival party than of effective steps against the Japanese. In the hope of strengthening the position against Japan in China, various American officials attempted to bring the two parties together. Since the United States was cooperating with communists of the Soviet Union in the war against Germany, it did not seem illogical that communist assistance should be solicited in China against the Japanese.

In the spring of 1944 President Roosevelt sent Vice President Henry Wallace to China to see what might be done in that direction. Ambassador Clarence E. Gauss and Maj. Gen. Patrick J. Hurley, first as personal representative of the president, and then as ambassdor, worked toward conciliation between communists and Kuomintang. George Atcheson, the American chargé d'affaires at Chungking, recommended that the United States supply arms and equipment to the Chinese communist armies as a means of encouraging a settlement between the two factions, as a means of obtaining the cooperation of all forces in China in the war, and as a means of avoiding throwing the communists into the arms of the Russians—a result that otherwise, he believed, would be inevitable in the event that the Soviet Union entered the war against Japan. While hoping for conciliation and cooperation between the two factions, Hurley strongly opposed the supplying of arms to the communist forces. It remained the policy of the United States to supply matériel and financial support only to the recognized Chinese national government.[7]

After V–J Day the United States, as noted previously, continued lend–lease assistance to the national government of China in order to enable forces of that government to accept the surrender of Japanese troops in China and to complete the program begun during the war of providing equipment for a thirty-nine-division army. The actions that followed took on the aspect of a contest between nationalists and communists for control of the Japanese-held areas. In geography, the communists had an initial advantage, for many of them had been operating as guerrillas far behind Japanese lines, while most of the government troops were in south and west China beyond the limits of the Japanese advance. But immediately, Headquarters, U.S. Forces, China theater, set up an airlift under lend-lease arrangements to move Chinese forces to key sectors of north and east China. Reinforcements followed by sea until some four to five hundred thousand men had been moved to new positions. With this American assistance, the nationalist forces of Generalissimo Chiang Kai-shek were able to obtain the surrender of most of the 1,200,000 Japanese soldiers, together with their arms and equipment, stationed in those areas. However, this did not include the reoccupation of Manchuria, where Russian forces were taking the surrender of the Japanese. American policy had been not to support one side against the other in the internal struggle in China, but the effect of our assistance to the nationalists in building up their army during and immediately after the war and in deploying forces to accept the Japanese surrender had been to give to the Kuomintang forces a superiority of about five to one in combat troops and rifles over the communists, and to give to the nationalists control of the major cities and communications centers throughout China proper. A contingent of fifty thousand U.S. marines landed in north China to assist in repatriating the Japanese and in reestablishing Chinese control.[8]

Although redeployment of the approximately sixty thousand American troops in China began soon after V–J Day, Headquarters, U.S. Forces, China theater continued to assist in the movement of Chinese forces and in supervising the turnover to the Chinese of military supplies. At the same time plans went forward for establishing military advisory groups to remain after the deactivation of the China theater headquarters. The purpose would be to assist in the consolidation and reorganization of the Chinese armies under general terms that already had been agreed to by the national government and the Chinese communists. This was in accord with President Truman's statement (of 14 September 1945) that the United States was "prepared to assist China in the development of armed forces of moderate size for the maintenance of internal peace and security and the assumption of adequate control over the liberated areas of China, including Manchuria and Formosa." The president had warned, however, that "it should be clearly understood that military asistance furnished by the United States would not be diverted for use in fractricidal warfare or to support undemocratic administration."[9]

Activated on 20 February 1946, the Nanking Headquarters Command provided the interim organization for United States advisers in China. Acting on his emergency war powers, President Truman on 25 February directed the secretaries of war and the navy to establish jointly a U.S. Military Advisory Group to China. Actually two groups, army and navy, were formed. The army advisory group was the successor to the ground forces section, Nanking headquarters command, which had been organized in April. At first this group was limited to giving advice and assistance on the organization and functions of Chinese ground force headquarters, and on the operation of service schools. Recommendations on the organization and equipment of Chinese units and on their training during this period was the function of the Peiping executive headquarters, an organization set up in January to supervise the execution of the terms of a ceasefire agreement entered into between nationalists and communists as a result of General Marshall's negotiations.

As factional strife continued in China, President Truman named General Marshall as his personal representative in China, with instructions to work for a cessation of hostilities and a coalition government in which communist participation would be included. Upon his arrival in Chunking on 27 December 1945, Marshall agreed to serve as chairman of a committee of three, with a representative of the national government and one from the Chinese Communist Party, to discuss a cessation of hostilities and related matters. On 10 January, three days after the committee's first formal meeting, a ceasefire agreement was concluded, and Chiang Kai-shek and Mao Tse-tung, chairman of the Central Committee of the Chinese Communist Party, issued orders to their respective forces to cease hostilities. About a month later the two parties established a military subcommittee, with General Chang Chih-chung of the national government, General Chou En-lai of the Chinese Communist Party, and with General Marshall as adviser, to draw up plans for the integration and reorganization of the Chinese armies. Such a plan was agreed to on 25 February. Preserving the five to one ratio, it provided for a reduction in the nationalist armies to ninety divisions within twelve months, and a reduction in Chinese communist forces to eighteen divisions during the same period, and for a further reduction during the next six months to fifty nationalist and ten communist divisions of not more than fourteen thousand men each. A political consultative conference already had laid the basis for organization of a coalition government. With these bright prospects of success, General Marshall returned to Washington briefly in March, and recommended a broad program of economic reconstruction.[10]

Serious difficulties soon arose in Manchuria. In agreement with the Chinese government, the Soviet Union postponed the withdrawal of its forces from Manchuria to 1 February 1946. They were still there in March, and the Chinese then formally requested their withdrawal. The Russians agreed to a progressive withdrawal of troops during April. However, when Soviet forces did withdraw, Chinese nationalists, although they had some 137,000 troops in Manchuria by this time, were unable to move into the areas evacuated by the Russians quickly enough to forestall the occupation of many of those areas by Chinese communists. Denied access through the principal port of Dairen by the Russians, and operating over extended lines of communication, the nationalists were unable to support effectively their forces in Manchuria. On the other hand the communists were able to seize large stocks of arms and equipment that the Japanese had left in Manchuria. On 15 April, the day after the withdrawal of Russian troops from the city, Chinese communists attacked Changchun and occupied it three days later. This open violation of the cease fire agreement seemed to justify the fears of those in the government who had insisted that the communists never intended to carry out their agreement.

When General Marshall returned, the same day that Changchun fell, a new impasse had developed between the Kuomintang and the communists. After prolonged efforts and informal conversations on the part of Marshall with leaders of both sides, agreement even on the Manchurian question seemed to be within grasp. But even as negotiations proceeded, government troops in Manchuria were moving to fight back. The untimely arrival of Chiang Kai-shek at Mukden on General Marshall's plane just as government troops were about to reenter Chanchun gave the implication of a lack of faith on the nationalist side; the implication was emphasized when Chiang failed to issue a ceasefire order and permitted his forces to continue northward toward Harbin and eastward toward Kirin. Nevertheless, when Chiang returned to Nanking early in June, the communists agreed to his proposal for a truce—first set at fifteen days and then extended to thirty. Before the expiration of the truce, the committee of three was able to agree upon ceasefire terms for Manchuria. Then the communists demanded revision of the plan for military reorganization.

Soon popular antagonisms against the United States and of each side against the other began to appear. As negotiations for a permanent settlement dragged on through the summer of 1946, success became more remote. During this period the United States made several agreements with the national government for further assistance—for surplus property left at Shanghai and Tsingtao, a lend-lease "pipeline" agreement for civilian-type goods on a reimbursable basis, a military aid agreement for continuing some military lend-lease on a reimbursable basis, and the big bulk sale of surplus property in India, China, and various islands of the Pacific. But in giving this assistance, the United States was accused by the communists of supporting the Kuomintang in the civil war. This seemed to put General Marshall in an untenable position as mediator; consequently, he asked that an embargo be placed on arms shipments to China while his negotiations were in progress. In August the State Department suspended the issuing of export licenses for shipments of munitions from the United States to China, and in September shipments of combat-type items from the Pacific area were temporarily suspended.

The confidence of the Nationalists was growing, however, and this involved a corresponding reluctance on their part to accept compromises with the communists, as they extended their holdings of areas and communications lines through 1946. By this time the communists had taken over Japanese stocks in Manchuria, but government forces still enjoyed a superiority in rifles variously estimated at three or four to one. As local fighting increased, negotiations deteriorated. Convinced at last that neither side really was seeking a peaceful settlement, General Marshall gave up his attempts at mediation and returned to the United States in January 1947.

In Manchuria the nationalists were overextending themselves, but they were confident that they were in a position to settle matters by force. In March 1947 nationalist troops captured Yenan, the communist "capital," and against the advice of American observers, launched an all-out offensive to complete their control of Manchuria. The Chinese chief of staff announced that the main communist armies would be crushed within three months.[11] But within less than three months the communist tide in Manchuria was flowing in the other direction, against little or no resistance on the part of demoralized nationalist forces in many areas. On 26 May 1947 General Marshall, now secretary of state, lifted the embargo on the shipment of combat matériel to China, and approved the sale of 130,000,000 rounds of surplus rifle ammunition at 10 percent of procurement cost. The ammunition was shipped from West Coast ports on 14 July and 11 August 1947. Previously, in April and May, the U.S. marines had begun their withdrawal from north China, and had left much of their small arms and artillery ammunition for the Chinese.[12]

Now the question was whether the United States should make an all-out effort to forestall the communist advance in China, or should provide limited assistance to the government in the hope that that government, if it could not conquer the communists, at least could maintain its own position as it had been able to do for over twenty years of varying degrees of civil war, or whether a strictly hands-off policy should be maintained in order to avoid antagonizing any major Chinese group. In search of a China policy, President Truman on the advice of Marshall in July 1947 sent General Wedmeyer to China on a fact-finding mission.[13]

A veteran of Chinese affairs from his wartime service as commander of the China theater, General Wedemeyer was deeply discouraged by what he found in the course of a month's observations. He was convinced that sweeping reforms were needed in the Chinese army and in the government administration, but that the effectiveness of the nationalist army also depended upon a sound program of equipment and improved logistic support. This implied outside aid. In his report to the president, General Wedemeyer arrived at these conclusions:

> The spreading internecine struggle within China threatens world peace. Repeated American efforts to mediate have proved unavailing. It is apparent that positive steps are required to end hostilities immediately. The most logical approach to this very complex and ominous situation would be to refer the matter to the United Nations.
>
> A China dominated by Chinese Communists would be inimical to the interests of the United States, in view of their openly expressed hostility and active opposition to those principles which the United States regards as vital to the peace of the world.
>
> The Communists have the tactical initiative in the overall military situation. The Nationalist position in Manchuria is precarious, and in Shantung

and Hopei Provinces strongly disputed. Continued deterioration of the situation may result in the establishment of a Soviet satellite government in Manchuria and ultimately in the evolution of a Communist-dominated China.

China is suffering increasingly from disintegration. Her requirements for rehabilitation are large. Her most urgent needs include governmental reorganization and reforms, reduction of the military budget and external assistance.

A program of aid, if effectively employed, would bolster opposition to Communist expansion, and would contribute to gradual development of stability in China.

Due to excesses and oppressions by government police agencies basic freedoms of the people are being jeopardized. Maladministration and corruption cause a loss of confidence in the Government. Until drastic political and economic reforms are undertaken United States aid can not accomplish its purpose.

Even so, criticism of results achieved by the National Government in efforts for improvement should be tempered by a recognition of the handicaps imposed on China by eight years of war, the burden of her opposition to Communism, and her sacrifices for the Allied cause.

A United States program of assistance could best be implemented under the supervision of American advisors in specified economic and military fields. Such a program can be undertaken only if China requests advisory aid as well as material assistance.[14]

In effect General Wedemeyer was recommending that substantial aid be given nationalist China, while he warned that such aid would do no good unless drastic political and economic reforms were undertaken. Whether this could be done before the communists completely gained the upper hand remained an open question. Wedemeyer recommended that aid be made conditional on Chinese willingness to request the United Nations to seek a cease-fire in Manchuria and to agree to setting up a five-power guardianship (China, the Soviet Union, the United States, Great Britain, and France) or a United Nations trusteeship over Manchuria. Chinese acceptance of American advisers also should be made a condition of further assistance. The administration hoped to use the prospect of aid as a lever to achieve the reforms in China that would be necessary to make the aid itself effective. On the other hand it was anxious to avoid over committing itself in China at the time when the postwar demobilization of American armed forces had reached its nadir.

Even while Wedemeyer was in China, communist forces began infiltrating southward across the Lunghai and toward the Yangtze. By late 1947 a sizeable communist force had been concentrated in central China, and overextended nationalists, clinging to the northern cities, were being isolated—to be consumed in detail during the coming year.[15]

In December 1947 the Chinese signed a commercial contract for the purchase of 6,500,000 rounds of .50-caliber ammunition in the United States, and in the next five months they signed contracts for the purchase of stores of surplus ammunition and explosives in the Marianas, Hawaii, Okinawa, and other Pacific islands.[16]

By this time pressure was building up in the Congress for an extensive China aid program, and the administration was making plans for such a program to include significant economic aid as well as military assistance. In April 1947 the Chinese defense ministry had given to Lt. Gen. A. C. Gillem, then commander of the Peiping headquarters group, a list of munitions still needed to complete the thirty-nine-division program to present to General Marshall on Gillem's return to the United States later that month. In February 1948 the Chinese completed a detailed reworking of the thirty-nine-division program in anticipation of forthcoming military aid.

Meanwhile controversy was waxing strong in Congress about doing something for China. It look General Marshall three or four months to get agreement among the various government agencies concerned and the Bureau of the Budget for submitting to Congress a request for a China aid program. Two months after laying the Marshall Plan for European economic recovery before Congress in December 1947, President Truman submitted a proposed China aid program calling for the expenditure of $570 million over a fifteen-month period for economic assistance. Although the administratioin in this case argued that dollars released by American economic assistance could be put to military use by the Chinese, Congress inclined to the reasoning that as in Greece internal security was necessary before economic aid could be effective. At first the House of Representatives proposed to add a provision for Chinese military assistance to the Greek-Turkish aid bill. The State Department protested against any such procedure, which would imply that the United States was about to undertake the same type program in China—which would have to be on a vastly greater scale—as was being done in Greece. Ultimately the China Aid Act (Title Four of the Foreign Assistance Act of 1948, approved 3 April) provided for a $463 million program for a period of twelve months—$338 million for economic acid, and $125 million to be spent as the Chinese saw fit for military aid. The appropriation act, which was not passed until nearly three months later, cut the amount for economic assistance to $275 million, but retained the $125 million that would be available for military aid. In considering the appropriation measure, members of the House of Representatives made a further unsucessful attempt to require the same type of supervision over these funds as had been exercised in Greece and Turkey.[17]

A few weeks after the passage of the China Aid Act, the Chinese completed another revision of their thirty-nine-division program to scale it down to the $125 million level. In May Maj. Gen. David G. Barr, chief of the army advisory group, China, informally submitted to the foreign military aid branch of logistics division a list of requirements the Chinese Defense Ministry, with the advice of the U.S. army group, had drawn up on that basis. General objectives in overall planning were to provide a twelve-months supply of ammuni-

Military Assistance in the Far East: China and Korea 211

tion for the units actually in combat, minimum essential combat equipment (less artillery) for twelve divisions, plus a year's supply of maintenance parts, and replacements for 25 percent of the weapons together with equipment for training divisions and for operating replacement training centers.

In carrying out the China Aid Program, procedures would be quite different from those used in Greece. The $125,000,000 was to be spent as the Chinese saw fit, not as approved by the advisory group or others.[18] The initiative was to remain in their hands. Late in May the Chinese military procurement technical group arrived in Washington to take up these duties. This group would submit to the State Department from time to time requests for payment for goods or services procured. On approval, the State Department would authorize the Treasury Department to make the payment to the Chinese government. In cases where the Chinese arranged for procurement throught he army or other U.S. government agency, the State Department would transfer the necessary funds to that agency. The supply procedure for items procured through the army was for the Chinese military procurement technical group to submit requisitions to the director of logistics whose staff would number them and forward them to the technical services. The goods would be shipped on a government bill of lading to the port of embarkation (San Francisco was designated the primary port) for ocean shipment on an army-owned or army-chartered vessel to Shanghai or Tsingtao. Shipments to Shanghai would be for the custody of the U.S. army advisory group, while those destined for Tsingtao would be for the custody of the commander, naval forces, western Pacific. Title would pass to the Chinese government at the end of the ship's tackle in the Chinese port. The U.S. army advisory group would maintain in Nanking a file of manifests and "out-turn" reports signed by authorized representatives of the Chinese government on receipt of the goods.[19]

Small shipments of aircraft spare parts went to China in June, and approximately ten thousand tons of small arms and artillery ammunition in July, but it was November before the first shipment of items procured through the Department of the Army was made. The U.S.S. *Algol* carried a cargo of about five thousand measurement tons of small arms and ammunition to Shanghai, but by the time it arrived at the end of November, the military situation already had deteriorated to the extent that later ships had to be diverted. In January 1949 the Chinese military procurement technical group decided that all ships carrying supplies for the China Aid Program should be diverted to Formosa. By this time about $60,000,000 worth of equipment had been shipped—of which two-thirds had been procured through the Department of the Army. To save time, the Far East Command at the direction of the Department of the Army shipped about seven hundred measurement tons of small arms ammunition on navy shipping 7 November 1948 to Shanghai and Tsingtao. A little over a week earlier 1,360 measurement tons of surplus demolitions and explosives had been shipped from Hawaii on commercial shipping to Shanghai.[20]

Pending legislative authorization, and on the basis of an informal draft agreement with the Chinese government, army and navy advisory groups in September revised their organization to establish a Joint U.S. Military Advisory Group (JUSMAG—China) to include army, navy, and air divisions together with a combined services group and a joint advisory staff. The new JUSMAG was activated formally on 1 November 1948 with General Barr as director. The group received political guidance from the American ambassador in China and military guidance directly from Department of the Army. In case of local emergency it would come under the operational direction of the ambassador; in the event of a general emergency it would come under the control of Far East Command through the commander, U.S. naval forces, western Pacific. Members of the advisory groups were not authorized officially to give operational advice to the Chinese, nor to participate directly in the civil war, nor to accompany troops in the field.[21] In Paris for a United Nations meeting, the Chinese delegate approached General Marshall with a proposal for the United States officers actually to command Chinese army units under the pretense of acting as advisers. Apparently the position of the secretary of state on this proposal was the same as the one he expressed with regard to a proposal made about the same time to send a high-ranking American officer on a visit of inspection to China—"Even if the record of the repeated failure of the Chinese Government in the past to accept U.S. advice did not exist, it would be foolhardy for the United States, at this stage of disintegration of the Chinese Government authority in civil as well as the military sphere, to embark upon such a quixotic venture."[22]

Actually, throughout 1948 the chief of the army advisory group, and later the director of JUSMAG gave advice, informally and confidentially, to senior Chinese officers. But apparently it was with little effect. Hardly a month after it had been formally activated, JUSMAG withdrew from China to Japan.[23]

By this time the complete defeat of the nationalists in China appeared to be inevitable. Planners in the State Department considered themselves faced with these alternatives: (1) To continue to do all possible to support the nationalist government of China, and then accept the embarrassment that would accompany its disintegration; (2) to explain the inadequacies of the Kuomintang regime to the Aerican people, apparently for the purpose of softening the blow of the collapse when it came.[24] In August 1949 Secretary of State Acheson released a voluminous collection of documents with an explanation of policies toward China—a publication generally referred to as the China "White Paper." This made it clear that the administration saw no possibility of rescuing the nationalist regime by further aid.[25]

Meanwhile communist forces in China, capitalizing on the strategic gains already made, were eliminating the nationalist garrisons systematically and with little real opposition. American observers at times found it difficult to find the great battles that the nationlist forces reported to be raging. In the autumn of 1948 the communists with surprising ease occupied Weihsien,

Tsinan, Chincow, Changchun, Mukden, and Hsuchow; they captured large quantities of rifles and ammunition and virtually completed their control of all Manchuria. In January they occupied Tientsin and Peiping. In the four-and-one-half-month period from mid-September 1948 to the end of January 1949, the national government lost approximately 45 percent of its troop strength, while communist forces were growing by nearly as much. On 14 April President Truman approved an extension of the China Aid Act of 1948, but it was too late. On 20 April the communists crossed the Yangtze River against ineffective opposition and occupied Nanking. When nationalist forces failed to make a stand on the banks of that broad river, it seemed unlikely that they would make a stand anywhere. Hankow fell on 17 May, Shanghai on the 25, Tsingtao on 2 June. The nationalists abandoned Canton on 14 October, and gave up Chungking on 30 November. On 8 December the nationalists abandoned the Chinese mainland altogether, and took refuge on the island of Formosa.[26]

Whether or not greater quantities of American equipment would have made any difference to nationalist forces who began the contest with a four-or five-to-one rifle superiority over the communists is doubtful. Vice Admiral Oscar C. Badger, then commander of U. S. naval forces, western Pacific, maintained that the failure to get adequate weapons and ammunition to nationalist General Fu Tso-yi in north China led to the quick collapse of his forces, and that this was "the straw that broke the camel's back." He stated that a shipment that arrived in November, after a five months' delay in red tape, included only 10 percent of what had been requested, and even then the machine guns arrived without spare parts, and light machine guns without tripods or belt-loading machines and with insufficient clips for submachine guns.[27] General Barr, director of JUSMAG, insisted on the other hand that everything on the Chinese general's high priority list that was available was shipped, and while it was true that spare parts, clips, and tripods had not been included in the quantities needed, those shortages were made up by immediate air shipments from Japan.[28]

Colonel L. B. Moody, a retired ordnance officer who had served briefly in China earlier, after an independent study decided that the nationalist defeat could be attributed mainly to shortages of ammunition. Ruling out most of the American surplus ammunition as unserviceable, he calculated that the total usable American and Chinese-produced rifle and machinegun ammunition that the national government acquired in 1948 amounted to only sixty-three days of supply in active operations.[29] Yet sixty-three days of supply at combat rates for the size for the nationalist forces then under arms (approximately 2,723,000) was not an inconsiderable total quantity. Moreover some additional ammunition presumably was on hand from stocks acquired during World War II and during 1945, 1946, and 1947. In any case there is little evidence that nationalist resistance in 1948 was equivalent to more than sixty-three days of active operations of an entire force of more than 2,700,000 men.

According to Secretary of State Acheson, "Our military observers on the spot have reported that the Nationalist armies did not lose a single battle during the crucial year of 1948 through lack of arms or ammunition."[30] Again General Barr insisted, "So far as the actual battles I know of, there never was one that ended but what there was an abundance of ammunition still available which was captured by the communists."[31]

In November 1948 General Barr reported to the Department of the Army:

I am convinced that the military situation has degenerated to the point where only the active participation of United States troops could effect a remedy. It has been obvious to me for some time that nothing short of a United States organization with the authority and facilities available to you on V–J day including a United States fed and operated supply pipeline could remedy the situation. Military matériel and economic aid in my opinion is less important to the salvation of China than other factors. No battle has been lost since my arrival due to lack of ammunition or equipment. Their military debacles in my opinion can all be attributed to the world's worst leadership and many other morale destroying factors that lead to a complete loss of will to fight. The complete ineptness of high military leaders and the widespread corruption and dishonesty throughout the Armed Forces, could, in some measure, have been controlled and directed had the above authority and facilities been available. Chinese leaders completely lack the moral courage to issue and enforce an unpopular decision.[32]

Later, General Barr concluded:

Instead of being content with consolidating North China, the [Chinese Nationalist] Army was given the concurrent mission of seizing control of Manchuria, a task beyond its logistic capabilities. The Government, attempting to do too much with too little, found its armies scattered along thousands of miles of railroads, the possession of which was vital in view of the fact that these armies were supplied from bases in central China. In order to hold the railroads, it was also necessary to hold the large cities through which they passed. As time went on, the troops degenerated from field armies, capable of offensive combat, to garrison and lines of communication troops with an inevitable loss of offensive spirit. Communist military strength, popular support, and tactical skill were seriously under-estimated from the start. It became increasingly difficult to maintain effective control over the large sections of predominantly Communist countryside through which the lines of communication passed. . . . As the Communists grew stronger and more confident, they were able, by concentrations of superior strength, to surround, attack, and destroy Nationalist units in the field and Nationalist held cities.[33]

General Marshall's appraisal of the Nationalist failure was this:

What actually happened as I analyze the situation was that they had taken the equipment that we had given them, the munitions that we had provided

Military Assistance in the Far East: China and Korea 215

them and the airlift and fighting planes that we had provided them with, and had attempted something that we all considered was a military impossibility for them, and they had wrecked themselves on that basis together with the character of the leadership that was involved.

They had a great advantage in equipment, they had an advantage in numbers. They lacked in leadership and they lacked the general support of the Chinese public because of the character of government that had been carried on through a period of years.

Now when they had overextended themselves, particularly in the matter of capturing cities, which they had to support, and the communications which they had to cover, they fell, you might say, of their own weight.[34]

Perhaps the most eloquent testimony to the effectiveness of the supplies and equipment furnished the nationalists was the use to which they were put in the hands of the communists. General Barr stated that after the fall of Weihsien and Tsinan in the fall of 1948, "the Communists had more of our equipment than the Nationalists did."[35] Between mid-September and mid-November the American Embassy in China reported that thirty-three nationalist divisions had surrendered with all their equipment. Eight of these divisions had been 85 percent equipped with American equipment. All together these losses included some 100,000 American rifles and about 130,000 rifles of other origin. In December 1948 the military attaché at Nanking reported that seventeen divisions that had been equipped originally with American equipment had lost that equipment. In the four-and-one-half months ending with the fall of Peiping at the end of January 1949, it was estimated that nationalist forces had given up four hundred thousand rifles.[36] Another observer reported that "The Communist forces that took over Tientsin were so completely equipped with American equipment that they appeared to be American-equipped units."[37] American jeeps and two-and-a-half-ton trucks were prominent in the newsreels of the communists' triumphal entry into Peiping.

Because of different values and pricing policies used, depending upon the circumstances, any estimate of the total worth of matériel supplied to China is most difficult to figure with any accuracy. In general, reports of the military departments and of the State Department[38] indicate that total military and economic assistance given to China between V–J day and March 1949 was of the order of two billion dollars, about equally divided between economic and military aid. The total of $998.7 million authorized in military aid included $797.7 in grants and $201 million in credits.[39] This total included postwar lend-lease ($694.7 million), the transfer of vessels and ordnance by the Navy ($159 million), a credit of $20 million for the purchase of excess U.S. army stocks in west China, and the $125 million under the China Aid Act of 1948 (as of 31 December 1951, over $123 million worth of goods had been delivered to China and Formosa under this grant). That total does not include the more than 6,500 tons of ammunition left by the U.S. marines in north China, nor the sale in 1947 and 1948 of surplus ammunition, airplanes, parts, and small quantities of other military equipment having a total procurement value of $100.8 million, accepted by the Chinese at a sale price of $6.7 million. Neither does it include the bulk sale of civilian-type surplus property valued at $900 million in 1946 for a total sale price of $175 million.[40]

When it became clear that matériel assistance alone could not save the situation in China, a frequent suggestion was that the United States should go into China on the same basis that it had gone into Greece—including the complete operational direction of Chinese units in the field. Indeed this appeared to be the only alternative to a complete nationalist defeat in China, but the price of such American participation was far too great a commitment in the view of the State Department during these times when some means had to be retained for dealing with developments in other parts of the world. Some estimates suggested that an American advisory group of not less than ten thousand officers and men would have been required to do the job with any chance at all of success. Greece was a country of about fifty-one thousand square miles, with a population of 7.4 million people—about the population of Shanghai and its surrounding areas. In Greece, armed forces of between one hundred and fifty and two hundred thousand faced some twenty thousand guerrillas. China had an area greater than that of the United States with a population of approximately 450 million. There, in late 1947, nationalist armies of 2,500,000 to 3,000,000 men faced communist forces of 1,000,000 to 1,500,000 men who controlled approximately one-fourth of the area and population of China at that time. The United States was not prepared to take on the direction and full logistic support of a war of that magnitude.[41]

George F. Kennan of the State Department plans and policy staff in a conference in 1949 put the China situation in its global setting by suggesting that the United States should devote its major attention to those major aggregations of manpower, skills, and industrial strengths that were of key importance from the viewpoint of worldwide strategy. Of these he suggested there were four outside the United States itself: Japan, Great Britain, the Soviet Union, and central Europe, including Western Germany and the area adjacent to it—France, Belgium, Austria, Czechoslovakia, Silesia. "I think the greatest danger that could confront the United States security," he said, "would be a combination and working together for purposes hostile to us of the Central European and the Russian military-industrial potentials."[42] This was not to suggest that combination of the Soviet Union and China would be without grave consequences for American security, but it did suggest that what could be done to prevent such a combination had to be weighed against what might have to be done against what was considered the greater threat of a possible Russian domination of central Europe.

After the removal of the Chinese nationalist government and the half million or so men remaining of its armed forces to Formosa, that island suddenly leaped to new prominence in strategic consideration as various groups in the

United States, amidst rancor and recrimination, sought to fix the responsibility in this country for the "loss of China." Now aid to nationalist China had to be directed to Formosa, and justification for such continued assistance was sought in impassioned declarations on Formosa's strategic importance, and on the hopes of building up the nationalist forces to retake mainland China from the communists who had just expelled them. As in special pleas for aid to any area, the success of efforts to build up Formosa would detract from other places of possibly equal or even greater importance. In the realm of "emotional strategy," Formosa loomed large throughout the early 1950s. Once more the familiar appeal went up that all that was necessary was American logistic support. Clearly pleas to defend Formosa at all costs and to "unleash Chiang Kai-shek" for a return to the mainland carried unmistakable implications of further drains on United States logistic resources.

In November 1950 Senator William F. Knowland of California told representatives of the press, "If Formosa were in unfriendly hands—and Communist hands are unfriendly—our defense line would be driven back to the Pacific Coast."[43] Five months later General MacArthur, addressing a joint meeting of Congress on the occasion of his return from command in the Far East, expanded upon this theme. Expressing forcefully the profound changes in implications for American security that had come about as a result of victory over Japan, MacArthur said:

> Of more direct and immediate bearing upon our national security are the changes wrought in the strategic potential of the Pacific Ocean in the course of the past war.
> Prior thereto the western strategic frontier of the United States lay on the littoral line of the Americas, with an exposed island salient extending out through Hawaii, Midway, and Guam to the Philippines. That salient proved not an outpost of strength but an avenue of weakness along which the enemy could and did attack. The Pacific was a potential area of advance for any predatory force intent upon striking at the bordering land areas.
> All this was changed by our Pacific victory. Our strategic frontier then shifted to embrace the entire Pacific Ocean, which became a vast moat to protect us as long as we held it. Indeed, it acts as a protective shield for all of the Americas and all free lands of the Pacific Ocean area. We control it to the shores of Asia by a chain of islands extending in an arc from the Aleutians to the Mariannas, held by us and our free allies.
> From this island chain we can dominate with sea and air power every Asiatic port from Vladivostok to Singapore—with sea and air power, every port, as I said, from Vladivostok to Singapore—and prevent any hostile movement into the Pacific.
> Any predatory attack from Asia must be an amphibious effort. No amphibious force can be successful without control of the sea lanes and the air over those lanes in its avenue of advance. With naval and air supremacy and modest ground elements to defend bases, any major attack from continental Asia toward us or our friends of the Pacific would be doomed to failure.

Under such conditions, the Pacific no longer represents menacing avenues of approach for a prospective invader. It assumes, instead, the friendly aspect of a peaceful lake.

Our line of defense is a natural one and can be maintained with a minimum of military effort and expense. It envisions no attack against anyone, nor does it provide the bastions essential for offensive operations, but properly maintained, would be an invincible defense against aggression.

The holding of this littoral defense line in the western Pacific is entirely dependent upon holding all segments thereof, for any major breach of that line by an unfriendly power would render vulnerable to determined attack every other major segment. This is a military estimate as to which I have yet to find a military leader who will take exception.

For that reason, I have strongly recommended in the past, as a matter of military urgency, that under no circumstances must Formosa fall under Communist control. Such an eventuality would at once threaten the freedom of the Philippines and the loss of Japan and might well force our western frontier back to the coast of California, Oregon, and Washington.[44]

This appeared to suggest that Formosa was a key to the defense of the whole Pacific area. But if it were a question of dominating the ports of Vladivostok, Dairen, Port Arthur, and even Shanghai, that could be done better from Japan than from Formosa. The Philippines were little farther from Canton and the South China coast than was Formosa, and the coasts of Indo-china, Siam, and Burma were much more at the mercy of bases on the Philippines, at Singapore, and on Ceylon than of any bases on Formosa. The suggestion that the fall of Formosa to communists "would at once threaten the freedom of the Philippines and the loss of Japan" made no allowance for the possibility that Formosa itself would be even more vulnerable to attacks from Japan and from the Philippines—and from the new air base constructed on Okinawa. If possession of Formosa would give to the communists the power to dominate Japan and the Philippines, then surely their possession of the mainland of China already gave to them the power to dominate those places and Formosa as well.

Curiously Formosa was one of the relatively few major strategic spots of the world where the United States itself maintained no bases at all. If the views of extreme Formosa partisans were to be accepted, this meant that the fate of California, Oregon, and Washington rested in the first instance in the hands of Chiang Kai-shek and in the effectiveness of American logistic support made available to him.

Actually few people were suggesting seriously in the early 1950s that Chiang's forces were prepared for a return to the mainland in a major invasion. As a matter of fact, one of the difficulties in providing effective aid to the Chinese nationalist forces on Formosa was the lack of a clear-cut objective. Formosa would be defended, but there were no plans for supporting an invasion of the mainland in force. Chiang offered thirty-three thousand troops for service in Korea, but the political implications of transferring the Chinese civil war to Korea, and the lack of training and equipment on the part of the troops available operated against acceptance of the offer. The principal immediate objective seemed to be to keep the nationalist government in being and to prepare it to defend itself in its island refuge. Perhaps the greatest advantage of such a policy was in maintaining a government that would serve as a focal point to attract the political loyalties of millions of unassimilated overseas Chinese throughout Southeast Asia. In Thailand, Indochina, Burma, and the East Indies, these Chinese were the merchants, the bankers, and the businessmen of many of the principal cities. It was important for American policy in the whole region that they should not align themselves with the communist movement.[45]

As indicated above, military matériel that China had obtained under the $125,000,000 grant in the China aid program was diverted to Formosa after the situation became critical in China proper. Under that program the army continued to assist the Chinese national government in procuring from American industry to furnish from stocks or new procurement such matériel as was requested within the funds made available to the Department of the Army by the Chinese government, and to perform the services necessary to get those supplies to the Chinese on Formosa.[46]

Actually in late December 1949 the State Department also was willing to write off the loss of Formosa. Considering the fall of Formosa to the communists to be likely, Acheson was anxious to dissociate the United States from a futile defense of the island. Consequently he ruled against a Department of Defense proposal to send a military mission to Formosa and to give military aid beyond the $125,000,000 already provided for. The president reaffirmed this policy in January with an announcement that Chinese resources on Formosa were considered adequate for its own defense. The Korean War introduced new implications. In a move to limit that outbreak to the Korean peninsula, President Truman announced on 27 June 1950 that the U.S. Seventh Fleet was to prevent any attack against Formosa from the mainland, and also to prevent attack from Formosa against the mainland. (President Eisenhower removed the latter restriction in the spring of 1953, but this had no immediately noticeable effect on Chinese military operations.) In August 1950 a military investigation mission, headed by Maj. Gen. Alonzo P. Fox, went to Formosa to inquire into the advisability of further military assistance. In November 1950 an emergency shipment of artillery and small arms ammunition (valued at $9.7 million) went to Formosa, and under a bilateral agreement signed in February 1951, Formosa became eligible for mutual defense assistance under the provisions of Title 3 of the Mutual Defense Assistance Act of 1949 providing for emergency aid in the general area of China. A military assistance advisory group was established on Formosa effective 1 May 1951. This relieved the Chinese nationalist government of much of the initiative and final responsibility for procurement that it had exercised under the China Aid Act of 1948, and procedures were brought into line with those followed in providing assistance to other countries under the Mutual Defense Assistance Program.⁴⁷

Results of renewed military assistance to the Chinese on Formosa were not encouraging at first. Forces had to be reorganized, equipment had to be restored. A further complication was the economic burden that support of this force of half a million or more men posed for the population of Formosa, which numbered about nine million. In January 1952 Maj. Gen. William C. Chase, chief of the MAAG, advised Chiang Kai-shek that "Prompt and generous U.S. logistical support will be necessary for your NGRC [National Government of the Republic of China] Armed Forces in case of any determined invasion attempt by a common enemy."⁴⁸

Going into specific deficiencies, the MAAG chief reported that the co-operation so far received from officers of the nationalist army on matters of reorganization and related questions had been limited to words rather than action. Repair work and preventive maintenance was generally unsatisfactory in all arms and services. Food supplies were adequate, but the distribution of rations and food handling were not satisfactory. Equipment for artillery, engineer, and signal units was seriously deficient, but this was expected to improve with the arrival of increased American supplies. More serious was the continuation of the influence of the Political Department in the Army—a system analogous to the political commissars generally associated with communist armies. A rule that political officers had to countersign all orders had been rescinded, and the amount of training time allotted for the Political Department had been reduced from 25 percent of the total to 10 percent, but the Political Department was more than a propaganda agency, in that political officers performed the functions performed by chaplains, special services, Red Cross, and other welfare groups in the U.S. army. But it was an obstacle to American advisers. A proposed reorganization of the Chinese army was further delayed in 1952 for the reason that the Chinese wanted to wait until the new equipment called for in revised tables of organization and equipment had arrived before they reorganized their units along those lines.⁴⁹

Conditions improved noticeably during the next year. Though still not altogether satisfactory, the quality of maintenance in the spring of 1953 was considerably better than it had been earlier, additional supplies were arriving in quantity from the United States, and organization and training were improving. In the spring of 1953 the Chinese nationalist army numbered about 463,000 officers and men, including 49,000 in the combined service forces, and including an overhead of 39,000 in the Ministry of National Defense. It was organized into twenty-eight divisions of five thousand to eight thousand men and independent units, grouped in twelve armies. What they could do depended largely on what the United States could do for them.

On one point, at least, General MacArthur and General Marshall were agreed—the quality of the Chinese soldier. In May 1951 General MacArthur stated to the Senate Committees on Armed Services and Foreign Relations,

"I believe all those troops would be good troops with a little more supply, a little more training, a little more confidence that they are going to be supported, a little more hope that they may ultimately be successful."[50] As in 1943 it could be said, "The Chief of Staff, Gen. George C. Marshall, believed that if the Chinese were properly led, fed, trained, and equipped, they would be equal to any soldiers in the world."[51] Of the truth of that statement Americans were to learn to their sorrow in Korea. But then what people would not make good soldiers if they were "properly led, fed, trained, and equipped?"

Defense Assistance to Korea

The policy of making American military advisers available to the Government of Korea had antecedents extending all the way back to the 1880s. First of the western powers to conclude a treaty of friendship and commerce with Korea after the opening of that country to western trade by Commodore Robert W. Schufeldt of the U.S. Navy (1882), the United States received favorably overtures from the Korean Emperor to provide officers to serve as his military advisers. Both President Arthur and President Cleveland favored the project, and with the sanction of both China and Japan, an American military mission arrived in Seoul in 1888.[52] Indicating an American concern for Korean integrity that largely disappeared in the course of the next twenty years, to be revived less in words than in deeds in 1950, President Arthur stated in 1883: "We seek no monopoly of its commerce and no advantage over other nations, but as the Chosenese, in reaching for a higher civilization, have confided in this Republic, we can not regard with indifference any encroachment on their rights."[53]

American troops of the XXIV Corps landed in Korea on 8 September 1945 to begin an occupation that seemed to have as its object the denial of Russian control south of the 38th parallel no less than the liquidation of Japanese control and the maintenance of local order. Soviet forces alone doubtless would have been capable of carrying out the latter tasks. Russian troops had begun moving into North Korea four weeks before the arrival of the first Americans in South Korea.

After the final failure in September 1947 of the U.S.–U.S.S.R. Joint Commission on Korea to arrive at an agreement for the formation of a unified Korean government, the division at the 38th parallel which had begun as an expedient of military occupation by the two powers soon acquired the character of indefinite continuation. On each side of the line of demarcation the occupying power encouraged the development of a government cast in its own image. Each regime aspired to unification of the country on its own terms. Each obtained certain military assistance from its sponsor with a view to maintaining itself and possibly with a hope of achieving unification forcibly.[54]

On completion of his two-month mission in the Far East in 1947, General

American soldiers of the 32nd Infantry Division marching through Seoul, Korea, 10 September 1945.

Wedemeyer presented recommendations to the president relating to policy in Korea as well as to that in China. These recommendations called for providing American military advisers and matériel assistance for South Korea.[55]

Already, at the time of the Japanese surrender, forty thousand Japanese rifles and remaining stocks of ammunition had been turned over to South Koreans. Soon quantities of American surplus equipment also were made available, but this property was intended to bolster the civilian economy rather than the military forces. Indeed, the terms of agreements between the Office of the Foreign Liquidation Commissioner (Department of State) and the U.S. Army Military Government in Korea, acting on behalf of South Korea, provided specifically that nondemilitarized combat matériel should not be included in the surplus property transferred. This surplus property was financed through the extension of $25 million in credit to the military government—which obligation in September 1948 was assumed by the newly recognized Republic of Korea. Property involved included vessels and other equipment transferred from Navy and Marine Corps surplus as well as Army equipment. Pricing varied. Surplus property selected from stocks in Japan was charged at the same rate that applied to Japanese purchases—30 percent of procurement cost. Equipment that became surplus in Korea itself, and that moved to Korea from Iwo Jima, carried a sales price of 21 cents on the dollar—the same as had applied to the China bulk sale. Equipment selected from Hawaii, mostly in good condition, and shipped to Korea at Army expense, was transferred on the basis of 50 percent of procurement cost. Other movable goods came from the Philippines at a price equal to 40 percent of the procurement cost. All together South Korea acquired property having an original procurement value of nearly $70 million for the $25 million in credit.[56]

By the time the military occupation of Korea had extended beyond a year and a half, American leaders were looking for a way to pull out. At a Pentagon luncheon with the chiefs of staff in April 1947, Secretary of War Patterson expressed concern about the unhappy lot of soldiers assigned to duty in Korea as well as about the continuing drain on military resources that the occupation entailed in a time of seriously restricted appropriations. Five months later General Marshall, as Secretary of State, still was giving close study to the problem of withdrawing troops from Korea. An offer on the part of the Russians to withdraw their troops, he thought, might give an opportunity to withdraw without the loss of face.[57]

This opportunity came almost immediately. After the breakdown of negotiations in the U.S.–U.S.S.R. Joint Commission, the United States in September 1947 took the issue to the General Assembly of the United Nations. Immediately the Soviets proposed that both America and Russia withdraw their troops by 1 January 1948 and let the Koreans conduct their own elections. Still, Secretary of State Marshall was determined to go through with the plan of laying the problem before the United Nations. As a result of that procedure the General Assembly set up a Temporary Commission to supervise elections to be held in Korea the following spring. The Commission was permitted to function only in South Korea, but elections held there in May 1948 provided the basis for the government of the Republic of Korea which was organized that summer. This experience, however, turned the thinking of the Joint Chiefs of Staff toward the problem of reinforcing rather than relieving American forces in Korea.[58]

The new government of the Republic of Korea, with Syngman Rhee as president, took over full responsibilities for government in South Korea on 15 August 1948. Thereafter the occupational duties of U.S. Army Forces in Korea were limited to assistance in training and equipping the South Korean security forces—including a constabulary and coast guard that later would emerge as an army and navy—and to the repatriation of Japanese who still remained.[59] On 10 September 1948 the Soviet-sponsored Democratic People's Republic of Chosen began to function as the government of North Korea. Ten days later the Soviet Union announced that all Russian troops would be withdrawn by 1 January 1949. This move gave to the United States an opportunity to withdraw its own troops gracefully, but it also presented a dilemma. American withdrawal now seemed to be necessary if the appear-

Lt. Gen. John R. Hodge addresses a crowd gathered for the inauguration of a new government of the Republic of Korea, Seoul, 15 August 1948.

General MacArthur inspects Honor Guard of the 31st Infantry, Seoul, Korea, 15 August 1948.

ance of imperialistic domination of South Korea were to be avoided, but American leaders were convinced that Soviet willingness to withdraw was predicated on an assumption that the military effectiveness of the regime it was leaving behind would be superior to that of the southern republic. Syngman Rhee recognized the threat from the north. In December 1946 he had gone to Washington to urge the immediate establishment of a Korean government and the withdrawal of American troops. In August 1948, when press reports suggested that American troops would be withdrawn, the South Korean president asked that they remain a while longer. Gradual withdrawal of the 50,000 American occupation troops did begin soon thereafter, but completion of the withdrawal was delayed to June 1949. Then only the U.S. Military Advisory Group to the Republic of Korea (KMAG), numbering approximately five hundred officers and men, remained to continue assistance in training and equipping South Korean security forces. An Air Force detachment of fifty officers and men remained at Kimpo airport, near Seoul, until civil administration could take over the operation of the field.[60]

In anticipation of the departure of American forces, the United States made available further surplus military equipment for South Korea—now with the frank purpose of arming defense forces. The growing Korean constabulary had to depend almost entirely on American equipment and on some captured Japanese matériel.

All together, departing American occupation forces turned over to the Korean security forces military equipment having an original cost of $56 million—with a replacement value of approximately $110 million. This included over 100,000 rifles, pistols, and machine guns, together with about 50 million rounds of small arms ammunition; 2,000 bazookas and 40,000 rockets, over 4,900 vehicles, and 20 liaison aircraft, as well as quantities of mortars, antitank guns, 105-mm. howitzers, and about 700,000 rounds of ammunition for those weapons. After the withdrawal of American forces another million dollars' worth (at original acquisition cost) of military equipment was turned over to the South Koreans—individual and organizational equipment for fifteen thousand troops, transferred from U.S. Army stocks in Japan. All this was in addition to forty thousand Japanese rifles which had been transferred to South Korean units previously.[61]

In all these transactions American leaders studiously withheld such weapons as tanks and medium and heavy artillery which might have enabled the South Koreans to launch an attack of their own.[62] Unfortunately, the Russians failed to exercise such restraint in providing arms for their North Korean comrades. As a result the Republic of Korea found itself at a serious disadvantage. The weakening of the potential offensive strength of its security forces could not fail to weaken its defensive powers as well—with possible disastrous consequences. Yet the American caution seemed fully justified. As early as 1948 Foreign Minister Chang Taisang had declared that the government of South Korea would not hesitate to move against the traitors in the north to recover the "lost territory."

Even as plans were being completed for the withdrawal of occupation forces, the administration asked Congress to approve a $150 million program of economic assistance for Korea for fiscal year 1950.[63] The Economic Cooperation Administration already had replaced the Army in administering economic assistance, and the proposal was intended to extend that assistance. Appealing for support for the program, Secretary of State Acheson told the House Committee on Foreign Affairs:

> Now obviously we don not say that this bill will produce a situation in Korea which it is certain will increase the security of the United States. We know the security of the United States would be adversely affected by the movement of Communists into Korea because they get that much more trouble, and also because of the general situation in the Far East. For us just to quit and walk out without giving those fellows who have trusted in us any possible chance to survive is just not a decent American thing to do.[64]

The committee reported the bill favorably, but it was to the accompaniment of the vigorous dissent of five members who saw no advantage in offering economic aid when military forces were being withdrawn. The minority statement said, in part:

> Every authority who has testified before the Committee on Foreign Affairs with respect to the Korean situation has acknowledged the fact that there could be no effective defense against an armed aggression originating in the northern half of the country.
> Our forces, with the exception of an advisory mission, have been withdrawn from South Korea at the very instant when logic and common sense both demanded no retreat from the realities of the situation. With our forces on the scene of action, there might have been advanced substantial arguments in favor of economic assistance, but without the presence of an adequate force to protect delivery of, and guarantee practical utilization of the great volume of matériel and supplies, it appears folly of the highest order to embark on the program.[65]

Unquestionably, security was closely linked with economic well-being. Now the question was whether the end of overall security for the Republic of Korea would be better served by an emphasis on economic assistance or on direct military aid. It was a question generally applicable to programs of foreign assistance throughout the world. For the moment, the Administration chose to put the emphasis on economic assistance. Congress was less disposed to accept the desirability of immediate and substantial economic assistance for Korea.

The House of Representatives took no action on a $150 million Korean aid bill that the Committee on Foreign Affairs had approved, though the Senate did pass a similar bill, during the first session of the 81st Congress (1949). The supplemental appropriation bill passed on the last day of the session (19 October) did include $30 million for continuation of economic assistance through 15 February 1950. After defeating a bill providing for an additional $60 million for the period after 15 February, the House a few weeks later finally accepted, with some amendments, a Senate bill authorizing such an extension.[66]

Further military assistance was to come under the mutual defense assistance program. The bilateral agreement necessary for mutual defense assistance was signed 26 January 1950. The Korean parliament, on 20 March, ratified an additional agreement covering the status and activities of KMAG.[67] This program was barely getting started when the invasion came. The only equipment in process of shipment on 25 June 1950 consisted of about $52,000 worth of surplus communication wire and equipment. In addition the South Koreans had made cash purchases, under Section 408(e) of the Mutual Defense Assistance Act of 1949, of equipment for trainer aircraft and for naval vessels at a cost of about $253,000.[68]

Actually the Foreign Military Aid Coordinating Committee in March 1950 had approved a program for Korea amounting to $10,286,774, but combat support soon had overtaken preparations for an orderly build-up of defense forces.[69] The relative weakness of South Korean military forces was apparent. John C. Muccio, the American ambassador to Korea, reported on 9 June, "The undeniable matériel superiority of the north Korean forces would provide north Korea with the margin of victory in the event of a full-scale invasion of the Republic."[70] More time and more effort would be required before the southern republic could be made secure against a full-scale invasion from the north.

One of the immediate results of the invasion when it did come was the dissipation of a large share of the military resources which had been assembled by various means for the defense of South Korea. Neglecting the organization of their defense and supply systems in depth, the South Koreans had disposed nearly all available men and supplies close to the thirty-eighth parallel—where supplies remained vulnerable to enemy military action and available for the resupply of the invader. General MacArthur explained, "When they [the South Koreans] lost that immediate line, they lost their supplies. They were not able apparently to destroy them en masse; so that at one initial stroke this North Korean Army had a new supply base in the area between the thirty-eighth parallel and Seoul, which enabled them to press south with the full strength of their base being immediately behind them; they no longer had to rely upon the long distance from the Yalu to get their supplies down."[71] As in China the United States found itself in the ironic position of "furnishing" equipment, to some extent, to both sides in a conflict having important implications for its own security.

Only the small part of MDAP funds used for communication wire, as noted above, actually was applied under the original program. Most of the released $10,286,774 that had been approved now was for the procurement of trucks in

Japan for the South Korean Army.[72] But it was impractical to go through all the steps necessary for programming MDAP matériel in the circumstances of sudden and large-scale military operations. Otherwise all MDAP, except $294,500 for Navy items, was canceled in August 1950. American military aid to Korea thereafter came out of regular defense appropriations as a part of the support of the Korean conflict.[73] Now, in that area, the "cold war" had become a "hot war," and logistic support for that effort is another story.

In August 1953 Secretary of State John Foster Dulles went to Seoul to initial a draft of a mutual defense treaty as part of an effort to dissuade President Syngman Rhee from jeopardizing by unilateral action the uneasy truce that at last had been concluded with the communists. Conversations with the South Korean president at that time contemplated the continuation of a program to build up the armed forces of the Republic of Korea with the benefit of American assistance for an indefinite time in the future.[74]

Notes

1. See William Adams Brown and Redvers Opie, *American Foreign Assistance,* 315; *Semiannual Rpt. of the Secy. of Defense,* 1 Jan. to 30 June 1950.
2. See, for example, Thomas E. Dewey, *Journey to the Far Pacific,* (New York, 1952), 166–67, 333–35.
3. Statement of Maj. Gen. George H. Olmsted, former director OMA, OSD, 11 Mar. 53, *Mutual Security Act Extension,* Hearings before House Comm. on For. Affairs, 83d Cong., 1st Sess., 7.
4. Brown and Opie, *American Foreign Assistance,* 495.
5. "Dulles Indicates Shift in Aid from Europe to the Far East," *The New York Times,* 13 Apr. 1953.
6. Brown and Opie, *American Foreign Assistance,* 494–95; *First Rpt. to Congress on the Mutual Security Program,* 30–31; *Second Rpt. to Congress on the Mutual Security* Program, 30 June 1952, 24 n; Testimony of W. Averell Harriman, Director for Mutual Security, 13 Mar. 52, *Mutual Security Act Extension,* Hearings before House Comm. on For. Affairs, 82d Cong., 2d Sess., 41; "Indonesia Agrees to New Aid Terms," *The New York Times,* 14 Dec. 1952; Interview with Col. Carl L. Junge, FMA Div., G-4, 27 Aug. 53.
7. *United States Relations with China, with Special Reference to the Period 1944–1949,* Dept. of State Publ. 3573, Aug. 1949, 73–92; Barbara W. Tuchman, *Stilwell and the American Experience in China 1911–45* (New York, 1970), 463–66, 510–31; Charles F. Romanus and Riley Sunderland, *Time Runs Out in CBI.* (Washington, 1959), 368–96.
8. *U.S. Relations with China*, 131–32, 311–13; Brown and Opie, *American Foreign Assistance,* 317–21.
9. Oral Statement by President Truman to Dr. T. V. Soong Concerning Assistance to China, 14 Sept. 1945, printed in *U.S. Relations with China,* Annex 170, 939.
10. This and immediately succeeding paragraphs are based on *U.S. Relations with China,* 132–237, Brown and Opie, *American Foreign Assistance,* 321–26; Herbert Feis, *The China Tangle* (Princeton, 1953), 413–30.
11. Report to President Truman by Lt. Gen. Albert C. Wedemeyer, U.S. Army, 19 Sept. 47, *U.S. Relations with China,* Annex 135, 808; F. F. Liu; *A Military History of Modern China 1924–1949* (Princeton, 1956), 243–70.

12. *U.S. Relations with China,* 313–18; Testimony of Dean Acheson, Secy. of State, 5 June 1951, Senate Hearings on Relief of General MacArthur, Pt. 3, 1929.
13. *U.S. Relations with China,* 255–61; Rovere and Schlesinger, *The General and the President,* 211–12; Brown and Opie, *American Foreign Assistance,* 326–33.
14. Report to President Truman by Lt. Gen. Albert C. Wedemeyer, *U.S. Relations with China,* Annex 135, 773.
15. *U.S. Relations with China,* 317–18.
16. Testimony of Dean Acheson, Secy. of State, 5 June 1951, Senate Hearings on relief of General MacArthur, Pt. 3, 1929.
17. Chronological Hist. of Chinese Military Aid Program, 15 Oct. 48; Brown and Opie, *American Foreign Assistance,* 333–37, 345–48; Testimony of Secy. of Defense, George C. Marshall, 10 May 1951, Senate Hearings on Relief of General MacArthur, Pt. 1, 465; Testimony of Secy. of State, Dean Acheson, 2 June 1951, Senate Hearings on Relief of General MacArthur, Pt. 3, 1829, 1855.
18. Ltr., Lindsay C. Warren, Comptroller General of the U.S., to the Secretary of State, 30 Sept. 48.
19. DF CSGSP/D3 41201, Dir. Log. to Chiefs Tech. Servs., 10 Sept. 48, sub.: Interim Procedures for Furnishing Aid to the Republic of China.
20. Shipments under China Aid Program by agencies of U.S. Government and by Chinese agencies, Authorized by Sec. 404 (b), China Aid Act of 1948, as of 31 Dec. 1948, *U.S. Relations with China,* Annex 171 (17), 953–55; Chronological Hist. of China Military Aid Program, 15 Oct. 48; G-4 Review of the Month, 31 Aug. 48, 26; *Annual Rpt. of the Secy. of the Army,* FY 1949, 157; Memo, Lt. Col. A. K. Tudhope, FE Sec., Log. Div., to Col. Davis, 7 Oct. 48, sub.: Status of China Aid Program; Rpt., Chief of Transportation to Dir. Log., 9 Nov. 48, sub.: Shipping Status Rpt. on Chinese Aid Program, and memo for record thereon.
21. *U.S. Relations with China,* 340–51; *Annual Rpt. of the Secy. of the Army,* 1949, 67.
22. Msgs., Secy. of State Marshall (temporarily in Paris) to Under Secy. of State Lovett, 6 Nov. 48 and 8 Nov. 48, printed in *U.S. Relations with China,* 887.
23. "United States Advisory Groups," formal statement supplied by the State Dept. to the Senate comm. holding hearings on the Relief of General MacArthur, 19 June 51, Pt. 4, 2815; DF CSGLD/DS 6835, Dir. Log. to CofT, 15 Feb. 49, sub.: Supply Manifest Distr. for China Aid Program Shipments.
24. Millis, *The Forrestal Diaries,* 534.
25. See letter of transmittal, Dean Acheson to the President, 30 July 1949, *U.S. Relations with China,* iii–xvii.
26. *U.S. Relations with China, 318–23; Rpt. of Operational Advice Given to the Generalissimo, The Minister of National Defense, and the Chief of the Supreme Staff by Maj. Gen. David Barr, (Excerpts),* in *U.S. Relations with China,* 325–38; "Fifteen Years of U.S.–Chinese Relations," *The Reporter,* April 1952; F. F. Liu, *A Military History of Modern China* (Princeton, 1956), 243–70.
27. Testimony of Vice Adm. Oscar Charles Badger, USN, Comdr., Eastern Sea Frontier, 19 June 51, Senate Hearings on Relief of MacArthur, Pt. 4, 2746–27.
28. Testimony of Maj. Gen. David G. Barr, Former CG of Seventh Inf. Div. in Korea, 22 June 1951, Senate Hearings on Relief of MacArthur, Pt. 4, 2982.
29. Freda Utley, *The China Story* (Chicago, 1951), 34–38.
30. Ltr. of Transmittal, *U.S. Relations with China,* xiv.
31. Testimony of Maj. Gen. David G. Barr, Hearings before Senate Comm. on Relief of General MacArthur, 22 June 51, Pt. 4, 3031.
32. *U.S. Relations with China,* 358.
33. Rpt. of Operational Advice, by Maj. Gen. David Barr, *U.S. Relations with China,* 336–37.

34. Secy. of Defense George C. Marshall, 14 May 1952, Senate Hearings on Relief of General MacArthur, Pt. 1, 688.

35. Quoted in Richard H. Rovere and Arthur M. Schlesinger, Jr., *The General and the President; and the Future of American Foreign Policy,* (New York, 1951), 215n.

36. *U.S. Relations with China,* 357–58; Millis, *The Forrestal Diaries,* 532–33.

37. Statement of Colonel McCann, CIA, Cong. on Problems of U.S. Policy in China, 6 Oct. 1949, Dept. of State, Transcript of Proceedings, copy in Army Library, (unclassified), A–6.

38. Because of different presentations, there is some discrepancy between army and State Department figures. The States Department, for example, did not include surplus property sales under military aid, except where they were covered by credit grants, while the army did include surplus at first. See letter, Sprouse to Butterworth, n. d., sub.: Army Rpt. on Aid to China.

39. By resorting to some rather devious arithmetic, Freda Utley, in *The China Story,* 31–34, reduces the amount of postwar military aid extended to China to "about $360 million." First of all she ignores the $201 million in credits advanced to the Chinese for the purchase of military equipment and takes her deduction from the $797.7 million in grants. Then she refuses to count the $335.8 million of lend-lease for services and expenses in moving Chinese armies to North China after V–J Day. More seriously, she then proceeds to deduct $100 million in surplus property that is not even included in the State Department total! Ignoring the breakdown of surplus military property sales given, she apparently confuses the sale of surplus military equipment with the nonmilitary type stocks (including $900 million worth of goods sold under the bulk sale agreement of August 1946), which the State Department lists separately under economic aid. But even the sale of military type surplus is not included in the State Department totals, except insofar as they may be included in some of the credits. But credit extended covered only a part of the surplus sales; moreover, credit would be based on the sale price to the Chinese (about six cents on the dollar) rather than upon the procurement value of the goods.

Far from deducting $335.8 million in services and expenses from postwar lend-lease given to China, Miss Utley might have been better advised to have added some of the $825.7 million (net grants) in wartime lend-lease given to China, if her intention was to give a true picture of the American contribution to the Chinese military establishment. Presumably in the Chinese as in other armies, a certain amount of this matériel should have been left over when the war ended.

40. Summary of U.S. Government Economic, Financial, and Military Aid Authorized for China since 1937, 21 Mar. 37, in *U.S. Relations with China,* Annex 185, 1042–53; See also U.S. Economic, Financial, and Military Aid to China since 1 April 1941, prep. by OSD, Off. of Progress Rpts. and Statistics, China Aid Rpt. No. 2, also reprinted (except for statement seven) in *Mutual Security Act Extension,* Hearings before House Comm. on For. Affairs, 83d Cong., 1st Sess., 735–44; Detailed analysis and breakdown of U.S. Military Aid to China from V–J Day until March 1949, (formal statement presented by State Dept. to Senate Comm. holding hearings on Relief of General MacArthur, submitted 19 June 51), Senate Hearings on Relief of General MacArthur, Pt. 4, 2815–24; United States Govt. Military Aid to China Since 1941, (formal statement to Senate Comm. holding hearings on Relief of General MacArthur, submitted by State Dept., 19 June 51), Senate Hearings on Relief of General MacArthur, Pt. 4, 2813–14; Testimony of Dean Acheson, Secy. of State, 4 June 1951, Senate Hearings on Relief of General MacArthur, Pt. 3, 1857; Study of American Military Matériel and Services Provided to the Chinese Government since V–J Day, in *U.S. Relations with China,* Annex 171, 940–69.

41. Freda Utley, *The China Story,* (Chicago, 1951), 40–41; *U.S. Relations with Chi-*

na, 351–53; Testimony of Secy. of Defense, George C. Marshall, 3 May 1951, Senate Hearings on Relief of General MacArthur, Pt. 1, 465.

42. Statement of George F. Kennan, Plans and Policy Div., Dept. of State, Conf. on Problems of U.S. Policy in China, Dept. of State, 6 Oct. 1949, Transcript of Proceedings, copy in Army Library, 20–22.

43. *The New York Times*, 24 Nov. 1950, quoted in Utley, *The China Story,* 85.

44. *General of the Army Douglas MacArthur's Address to Congress,* 19 Apr. 1951, (Chicago, 1951), 13–17.

45. Testimony of Maj. Gen. George Olmsted, Dir., Off. of Mil. Asst., Dept. of Defense, 1 Apr. 52, *Mutual Security Act of 1952,* Hearings before Senate Comm. on For. Rel., 82d Cong., 2d Sess., 603–5; Statement of Maj. Gen. George Olmsted, 24 Apr. 52, *Mutual Security Act Extension,* Hearings before House Comm. on For Affairs, 82d Cong., 2d Sess., 801–2.

46. Supply Supplement, Pt. 2 of The Troop Program and Troop List, 1 Jan. 51, 64–65.

47. Brown and Opie, *American Foreign Assistance,* 348–51; Semiannual Rpt. of the Secy. of Defense, 1 Jan. to 30 June 1951, 68; Statement of General J. Lawton Collins, CofS, 26 May 51, Senate Hearings on Relief of General MacArthur, Pt. 2, 1345; *The Mutual Security Program,* First Rpt. to Congress, December 1951, 31.

48. Year End Rpt., incl. with ltr., Maj. Gen. William C. Chase, chief MAAG, Formosa, to Generalissimo Chiang Kai-shek, President NGRC, through General Chow Chih-jou, Chief of General Staff, 10 Jan. 52.

49. Ibid; Foreign Service Despatch 588, AMEMBASSY, Taipei to Dept. of State, 19 June 52, sub.: MDAP General Rpt., Apr.–May 1952.

50. General Douglas MacArthur, 5 May 1951, Senate Hearings of Relief of MacArthur, *Military Situation in Far East,* Pt. 1, 268.

51. Charles F. Romanus and Riley Sunderland, *Stilwell's Mission to China,* in U.S. Army in World War II (Washington, 1953), 386.

52. Louis Martin Sears, *A History of American Foreign Relations,* 3d ed., (New York, 1936), 380–83; Special Message, President Chester A. Arthur to the Senate and House of Representatives, 30 Jan. 1885, in James D. Richardson, ed., *A Compilation of the Messages and Papers of the Presidents* (Bureau of National Literature edition), Vol. 10, 4856; First Annual Message, President Grover Cleveland to the Congress, 8 Dec. 1885, in Richardson, Vol. 10, 4915; George M. McCune and John A. Harrison, ed., *Korean-American Relations: Documents Pertaining to the Far Eastern Diplomacy of the United States,* Vol. 1, (*The Initial Period*, 1883–86), Berkeley and Los Angeles, 1951), 53–65; Frederick Foo Chien, *The Opening of Korea: A Study of Chinese Diplomacy, 1876–1885* (New York, 1967), 72–93.

53. Third Annual Message, President Chester A. Arthur to Congress, 4 Dec. 1883, in Richardson, Vol. 10, 4761.

54. See George M. McCune, *Korea Today,* 47–51, 72: *Annual Report of the Secretary of the Army, 1948,* 66.

55. Korea: Report to the President Submitted by Lt Gen A. C. Wedemeyer, September 1947 (Washington, 1951), 27 pp., U.S. Senate Comm. on Armed Services, Committee Print.

56. History of the Office of the Foreign Liquidation Commissioner, Field Commissioner for Japan and Korea, Tokyo, 8–9, 14–16, 52–74; Testimony of Dean Acheson, Secy. of State, 6 June 1951, Senate Hearings on Relief of MacArthur, pt. 3, 1993.

57. Millis, *The Forrestal Diaries,* 265, 321–22, 375.

58. McCune, *Korea Today,* 67, 71; see also *Annual Report of the Secretary of the Army,* 1948, 66; Millis, *The Forrestal Diaries,* 375.

59. For the activities of KMAG in the training and equipping of ROK military

forces, see Robert K. Sawyer, *Military Advisors in Korea: KMAG in Peace and War* (Washington, 1962), 34–95.

60. McCune, *Korea Today,* 221, 244–45, 267–68; *Annual Report of the Secretary of the Army, 1948,* 66, 156; Stebbins, *The United States in World Affairs, 1949,* 458.

61. Testimony of Dean Acheson, Secy. of State, Senate Hearings, Relief of General MacArthur, pt. 3, 1993: Semiannual Report of the Secretary of Defense, 1 Jan. to 30 June 1950, 15; Press Branch Fact Sheet No. 136–50S, Dept. of Def., OPI, 6 July 50, Mil. Asst. to ROK; *Foreign Aid by the U.S. Govt. 1940–1951* (Supplement to *Survey of Current Business*), 31.

62. Draft Report of Sec. of Def. on Opns. in Korea, pt. 1, 9–10; McCune, *orea Today,* 267n.

63. An economic aid agreement with the Republic of Korea under the Economic Cooperation Program had been signed on 10 December 1948. In the agreement the United States undertook to assist the Korean government in financing a long-range economic rehabilitation program. McCune, *Korea Today,* 251–52.

64. Quoted in House Rpt. 962, 81st Cong., 1st Sess., 26 July 1949, 46–47.

65. House Report 962, pt. 2, 81st Cong., 1st Sess., 26 July 1949, 2.

66. Richard P. Stebbins, *The United States in World Affairs, 1949,* (New York, 1950), 62, 87–88; McCune, *Korea Today,* 254–57; Testimony of Dean Acheson, Secy. of State, 4 June 1952, Senate Hearings on Relief of General MacArthur, pt. 3, 1837; Charles M. Dobbs, "Limiting Room to Maneuver: The Korean Assistance Act of 1949," *The Historian,* vol. 48, August 1986, 528–36.

67. *Semiannual Report of the Secretary of Defense,* 1 Jan. to 30 June 1950, 15.

68. Testimony of Dean Acheson, Secy. of State, 6 June 1951, Senate Hearings on Relief of MacArthur, pt. 3, 1993.

69. G–4 Hist Summary, 13 Dec. 51, Supply Div.: For. Mil. Aid, 1; Sawyer, *Military Advisors in Korea,* 96–104.

70. Statement by John C. Muccio, Ambassador to Korea submitted to Senate For. Rel. and Armed Svcs. Committee and House For. Aff. Committee, 9 June 50, *Dept. of State Bulletin* 22 (26 June 1950), 1048–49.

71. General Douglas MacArthur, 5 May 1951, Senate Hearings on the Relief of General MacArthur, pt. 1, 231.

72. Foreign Military Aid, prep. by Supply Planning Br., Supply Div., G–4, July 1953.

73. G–4 Memo of Imp Actns, 25 Aug 50, 1.

74. Texts of U.S.–Korea Mutual Defense Treaty and Dulles-Rhee Statements, *The New York Times,* 8 Aug. 1953, c3.

9
Defense Assistance to the Philippines, Indochina, Japan

> No nation, however powerful, may with safety rely exclusively upon its own defense potentiality. . . . Defense is no longer national; it has become international.
> —General of the Army Douglas MacArthur, Address before the Philippine Congress, 1945

Aid to the Philippines

It was to be expected that the United States would maintain an active interest in the defense of the Philippines after granting independence to that republic. Shortly after the passage of the Tydings-McDuffie Act in 1934 establishing the Commonwealth of the Philippines and providing for complete independence by 1946, Manuel Quezon, first president of the commonwealth, formally requested the War Department to send a military mission to the Philippines. Of course regular United States forces continued to be stationed in the Philippines, but the purpose of this mission was to assist the Philippine government to develop its own armed forces to the point that they could effectively support independence when that finally came. In 1935 General MacArthur, upon completion of five years as army chief of staff, went to the Philippines as chief military adviser. A year later he was made a field marshal in the Philippine army. Although World War II intervened, independence came to the Philippines on schedule, 4 July 1946.

Concurrently with the independence of the Philippines, a U.S. advisory group was established there to continue advice on training and to administer the grant-aid military program for the new republic. Already (in May 1945) the president had concluded an executive agreement providing for full military cooperation with the Philippine government. By an agreement signed 14 March 1947 the United States obtained the free use of military bases in the Philippines, and a complementary agreement signed a week later provided for the continuation of American military assistance. The latter agreement provided specifically for building up reserves of American military equipment for the Philippines as well as supplies for active Philippine forces. It also provided for the continuation of the U.S. advisory group—later redesignated the

Joint U.S. Military Advisory Group, Philippines. The advisory group was assigned for administrative purposes to the Far East Command, but it was under the direct operational control of the Joint Chiefs of Staff.[1]

The agreement for military assistance to the Philippines was based on the Republic of the Philippines Military Assistance Act passed the previous year. The act authorized the president, for a five-year period from 4 July 1946 to provide for training Filipino personnel, to send advisory missions to the Philippines, to maintain and repair military equipment, and to transfer munitions to the Philippine government, provided only that such actions be consistent with United States military requirements and "in the national interest." The president could provide this assistance "by sale, loan, exchange, lease, gift, or transfer for cash, credit or other property with or without warranty and upon such other terms and conditions" as he should "find proper."[2] Actually this formed the basis for the first postwar program of military assistance. It should be noted that this was supplementary to the provisions in the Philippine Rehabilitation Act of 1946 for the disposal of up to $100,000,000 worth at "fair value" of surplus property to the Philippines.[3] The Military Assistance Act carried an open authorization fro the appropriation of funds. Actually no new funds were appropriated for carrying out the act. Congress transferred

High Commissioner and Mrs. Paul V. McNutt greet General of the Army and Mrs. Douglas MacArthur at a reception in Manila on the eve of Philippine independence, 3 July 1946.

$19,700,000 from appropriations already made to the army for other purposes.[4] About 90 percent of the matériel transferred under the act was in fact drawn from surplus stocks. Holding that it was not in the national interest to support the armed forces of another nation at the expense of U.S. forces, the Joint Chiefs of Staff discouraged the practice of transferring appropriated army funds to military assistance programs. Only about $10 million of the amount transferred for the original Philippine program was used.[5]

Execution of the Philippine military assistance program was held up until conclusion of the agreement, which in turn was delayed until the base agreement had been concluded. Most of the initial supplies and equipment for the Philippine army and air force were available from surplus stocks, and for the most part they already were in the hands of the Philippine forces on a custodial basis pending completionof the agreement. Surplus equipment was not available, however, to fill the needs for the Philippine army war reserve.

The procurement cost of surplus army (including air forces) supplies and equipment transferred to the Philippines under both the Philippine Rehabilitation Act of 1946 and the Republic of the Philippines Military Assistance Act reached a total of $1.135 billion by 30 September 1948.[6]

In approving the Philippine military assistance program, the Joint Chiefs of Staff considered the purposes of the United States in undertaking it to be these: (1) To fulfill a moral obligation of the United States to ensure the stability and safety of its former dependency: (2) to preclude the Philippine government's turning to other powers for military assistance; (3) to develop the military manpower potential of the Philippines; (4) to support the objectives of the United Nations by contributing to the stability of the Far East, and (5) to maintain the prestige of the United States in the Orient. The Joint Chiefs saw the more specific objectives as building up the Philippine armed forces for these major tasks, in order of priority: (1) maintenance of internal law and order; (2) defense against minor raids and sabotage; (3) assistance in receiving and deploying U.S. forces in the event of combined operations against a common enemy; (4) development of organization, personnel, and facilities for the mobilization of the largest possible force in the least possible time for national emergencies. This order of priority was not misplaced, for the first task of Philippine forces was to deal with the communist-led guerrilla forces known as the Huks.

As in many countries that were the victims of hostile occupation during World War II, guerrilla activities that had begun as a counteraction to foreign occupation continued to some extent after the war in defiance of all government. The life of the guerrilla was attractive to some people. Apparently some of them preferred fighting to working. Again, clandestine meetings, secret plans, the risk of danger, the spoils of plunder, and the thrill of importance in being a part of causes and activities thought to be of great moment could not be lightly traded for the quiet tending of a rose garden, or the routine tasks of a merchant, or the unpicturesque work of a farmer. Yet other people, willing enough to work peacefully for a living, but finding no way to do so, turned to the guerrillas as a means of overcoming their economic handicaps. In the Philippines unhappy rural economic conditions in relatively overcrowded central Luzon swelled the ranks of the communist-inspired Huks. One of the objectives of economic and technical assistance under the Mutual Security Program was to relieve the crowded conditions on Luzon by transferring a number of farm families to the relatively undeveloped southern island of Mindanao. But in the meantime the Huk menace had to be met by direct military action.[7]

As in Greece, guerrilla raids in the rural areas drove refugees to the cities. In 1951 an estimated 150,000 refugees had been driven into already overcrowded Manila. American military equipment continuing to the Philippines under the Mutual Defense Assistance Program after 1949 went to direct use for combat purposes. The nature of the fighting in mountains and swamps, and the long periods of heavy rainfall, made steady resupply necessary. Shipments between June 1949 and May 1951 included $3 million worth of new equipment. Effective 1 April 1951 an additional ten battalion combat teams, equipped with American assistance, were organized in the Philippine army, and as soon as they could be trained they went into action against the guerrillas. The number of active guerrillas, estimated at about fifteen thousand was cut by perhaps one-third during the year. By mid-1953 the Huk insurrection had been suppressed in large part, though final elimination of armed defiance apparently depended upon improved economic conditions in rural areas.[8] Between 1 April 1950 and 30 June 1953, the Philippine armed forces reported 4,119 encounters with the Huks, during which 5,475 of the insurrectionists had been reported killed and 7,641 taken prisoner. In addition there had been some eighty small-scale encounters with Moro bandits.[9]

The Problem of Indochina

In the sequence of events that led to American involvement against Japan in the Far Eastern extension of World War II, about the "last straw" was the movement of Japanese troops into French Indochina in 1940 and 1941. American diplomats interpreted the Japanese movement into southern Indochina in July 1941 as an overt act directly menacing the security of the United States. This further deployment of Japanese forces appeared to American officials as a first step toward moving into the rich East Indies, as a menace to trade in the area, and as an encircling movement threatening the Philippines. It was at this point that the United States adopted a policy to discontinue trade with Japan. Further Japanese troop movements into Indochina in November 1941 gave substance to general assumptions that war was imminent. The Indochina question was one of the principal subjects discussed in the pre–Pearl Harbor conversations between Secretary of State Cordell Hull and the special Japanese emissaries.[10]

So far as the United States was concerned the strategic significance of Indochina in the late 1940s and 1950s was hardly less than it had been on the eve of American involvement in World War II. Extending a thousand miles, north to south, and comprising a total area greater than that of Texas or of France itself, Indochina included the central areas of the great "rice bowl" of Southeast Asia. The total population of about 28 million was concentrated—to the extent of five-sixths—in the coastal states of Tonkin, Annam, and Cochin-China—those joined in the new republic of Vietnam.[11]

While guerilla warfare occasionally flared in the neighboring states of Laos and Cambodia, Vietnam was the scene of most of the long and bitter warfare in which the French found themselves involved almost without interruption from the end of World War II into the 1950s.

By this time the revolutionary society known as Viet Minh had acquired a decidedly communist complexion, though this had not always been the case. Outbreaks of violence had disturbed French rule as early as 1908, and other incidents provoked by nationalist, revolutionary, and communist elements occurred in 1929 and 1930. The Communist Party of Indochina reached its greatest strength in 1931 with a claimed membership of 100,000 under the leadership of Nguyen Ai Quoc, who later changed his name to Ho Chi Minh. Through a vigorous campaign of mass arrests and imprisonments and executions of leaders, the French by 1933 had driven the communists underground. But Ho Chi Minh's organization continued to function. In 1939 some of the communists and their associates formed a new party they called Viet Minh, or the League for the Independence of Vietnam. In 1942 the other important parties—the Annamese Nationalists, the Association of Revolutionary Annamese Youth, and the Indochinese Communist Party—joined with the Viet Minh to fight for Vietnamese independence against both the French and the Japanese. The Japanese retained collaborating French in administrative positions until 1945, when they assumed direct control. The Japanese then declared Cambodia and Laos to be independent under their respective kings, and they established a nominally independent puppet government in Annam, Tonkin, and Cochin-China—brought together under the designation "Vietnam"—with the young Annamese emperor, Bao Dai at its head. Assisting allied operations with effective guerila warfare, Viet Minh would have nothing to do with the Japanese puppet governments. Upon the surrender of Japan, Viet Minh proclaimed the Republic of Vietnam. Bao Dai stepped down from his throne, and gave his blessing to the new republic after elections held early in 1946. Ho Chi Minh became president. The ex-emperor, Bao Dai, took a seat in the constituent assembly.[12]

Previously in March 1945 the provisional government of France in Paris had announced plans for an "Indochinese Federation" as a part of the proposed French union under the new constitution for the Fourth Republic. Indochinese states under the plan would enjoy a degree of local autonomy. This was insufficient to satisfy leaders of the Vietnamese republic. Since

French forces were not available for disarming the Japanese and restoring order in Indochina after the Japanese surrender, those tasks fell to the Chinese in the north and to the British in the south. Using some Japanese to reinforce their own contingents, made up largely of Indian elements, the British remained until some fifty thousand French troops arrived. The Chinese withdrew from Tonkin in the north upon the arrival of French forces in that area early in 1946.

The French were able to reach agreement quickly on their plan for an Indochinese federation within the French union in Cambodia and Laos, but Vietnam presented a problem. In March 1946 the French did sign an agreement with Vietnam, which appeared for a time to put an end to the war that had broken out. In the agreement the French recognized the republic as a free state with its own government, parliament, army, and control over finances, forming a part of the Indochinese federation and the French union. Vietnamese leaders assumed that Cochin-China was included in the republic under this arrangement. But the French acted otherwise in establishing an autonomous republic of Cochin-China under close French supervision. Here, where the chief city of Saigon was located and French interests were most deeply involved but where the population appeared to be overwhelmingly in favor of joining Vietnam, a peaceable settlement seemed remote.

In 1947 the French sought another approach. They encouraged anti–Viet Minh groups in Vietnam to persuade Bao Dai, then living in Hong Kong, to return as leader of a movement against Viet Minh, but the ex-emperor was reluctant to compete with Ho Chi Minh for pupular support unless the French were prepared to make further concessions. In June 1948 the French set up a rival provisional government of Vietnam. General Xuan, an Annamite officer with long experience in the French army, was made premier. It was intended that Bao Dai should head the new government. At last he agreed in a treaty signed in March 1949. Effective 30 December, the treaty provided for an independent Vietnam within the French union with control of foreign affairs and defense remaining in the hands of the French. Collectively Vietnam (including Tonkin, Annam, and Cochin-China), Cambodia, and Laos now were referred to as the Associated States of Indochina.

Meanwhile, war had broken out anew with the Viet Minh of Ho Chi Minh. The March 1946 truce had ended with a surprise attack by Viet Minh forces against the French garrison and population of Hanoi in the Tonkin delta area in December of the same year. The war soon spread to much of Annam and to parts of Cochin-China, where the countryside was subject to the terror of Viet Minh guerrilla operations. In the ensuing months the war assumed the features of a chronic disturbance. It was difficult to describe precisely the areas held by French and Vietnamese forces and those under Viet Minh control. In many areas it was Vietnam by day and Viet Minh by night. The Tonkin delta area continued to be the area of the most critical fighting.[13]

With the consolidation of communist control in China, the United States

Defense Assistance to the Philippines, Indochina, Japan 239

began to share the French concern that Chinese communist forces might overflow into Indochina. At once the struggle against Viet Minh took on new significance in the general effort to hold back communist expansion in Asia.

A month before the attack in Korea the United States announced a decision to provide military equipment as well as economic aid for the support of the French and their local allies in Indochina. The decision was based upon the recommendations of a special United States mission that visited Indoina in May 1950 and upon discussions between Secretary of State Acheson and Robert Schuman, the French foreign minister. Acheson said in his statement:

> The United States Government, convinced that neither national independence nor democratic evolution exists in any area dominated by Soviet imperialism, considers the situation to be such as to warrant its according economic aid and military equipment to the associated states of Indo-China and to France in order to assist them in restoring stability and permitting these states to pursue their peaceful and democratic development.[14]

In order to make this new program of military assistance effective promptly, the initial financing would come out of the president's emergency fund. Thereafter Indochina would be included in the regular Mutual Defense Assistance Program.[15] Eight C-47 transport planes, flown across the Pacific by the U.S. air force, comprised the first delivery of equipment under the program. Other early shipments included small arms, artillery, ammunition, trucks, and jungle-fighting equipment. In a further effort to save time, the Department of the Army in October 1950 directed Far East Command to ship from reserve supplies equipment needed quickly in Indochina. Other items, such as ten thousand tons of barbed wire requested in November, Far East Command obtained from Japanese sources. In some cases it was necessary to substitute items for those requested—such as M2A1 howitzers for the M3. To coordinate these substitutions so that unusable equipment would not be shipped, Brig. Gen. Francis Brink, chief of the military assistance advisory group that had recently been established in Saigon, went to Tokyo to meet with Far East Command staff officers.[16]

The MAAG that General Brink headed in Saigon included at the start thirty-five officers and fifty enlisted men. Later the group expanded to a total strength of 109. As in other areas, difficulties in preparing programs and accounting for property arose almost immediately. The French were supposed to make up the initial programs, but in working with American standard nomenclature lists they ran into trouble at once. It was up to members of the MAAG then to do much of this work. Special teams went out to set up property accounting procedures. A "pentalateral agreement" to which Vietnam, Laos, and Cambodia as well as France and the United States were parties, governed the military aid program. Actually the title to the equipment passed to the French upon arrival in Indochina. Thus France was the recipient of military equipment under two separate provisions of the Mutual Defense Assistance Act—for the build-up of defenses in Europe, (Title 1), and for defense of Indochina (Title 3). There was an understandable tendency on the part of French officials at times to seek approval for certain policies or for modified allowances through the "backdoor" of Paris and Washington rather than directly through the MAAG in Saigon. This was a situation demanding the closest possible coordination in Washington.[17]

Equipment delivered to Indochina in the last half of 1950 probably was the most immediately effective of all of MDAP contributions. The timely arrival of aircraft, artillery, ammunition, and vehicles was a major factor in enabling French and Vietnamese troops to turn back a dangerous communist offensive in January 1951.[18]

Through 1950 the French were losing one supposedly strong position after another. During four years of war the French position had become increasingly difficult. They continued to hold the main cities and most of the coastal strip of Vietnam in late 1950, but their positions were far from secure. In the northern delta area (Tonkin) the communist Viet Minh forces had driven the French and their Vietnamese allies into a pocket around Hanoi, and hostile forces stood ready for an assault against that key city itself. The Viet Minh had established good communication lines to their supply and training centers in communist China, and the French appeared to be in danger of losing all of northern Vietnam. It was at this point that General Jean de Lattre de Tassigny arrived from France to take command. Commander of the French First Army in World War II—an organization that probably was as important as any other single factor in rejuvenating France after bitter defeat and four years of German occupation—General de Lattre now brought experience and enthusiasm to the task of rejuvenating French forces in Indochina. By applying a rare military *savoir faire*, by the skillful use of American equipment, and by sheer force of personality, General de Lattre was able to restore morale and effectiveness to French and Vietnamese Soldiers alike. Bringing up reinforcements from the south, he met the Viet Minh assault against Hanoi in January 1951 head-on and straitaway broke it up. Other local victories followed. He organized mobile units to meet the hit-and-run attacks of Viet Minh guerillas. Yet much remained to be dome. When General de Lattre died unexpectedly a year later, the outcome of the war still remained in doubt.[19]

By mid-1952 evidences of American military aid were to be found in virtually every part of Vietnam. American equipment was especially noticeable in the area of the Red River delta in the north (Tonkin) where most of the fighting had taken place. At Haiphong, near one of the mouths of the Red River, freighters lined the quays stern to bow. American military material was stored in a big depot that had been set up at the city's race track and at other large depots in the area.[20] On 29 January 1952 American and French leaders and officials from each of the associated states participated in a ceremony at Saigon on the occasion of the arrival of the one hundredth ship bearing MDAP supplies for Indochina;[21] on 28 May 1952 a similar ceremony recognized the arrival of the 150th shipload of American military supplies to reach a port of Indochina.[22]

Inevitably delays arose. Reports of impressive totals of tonnages shipped did not reveal the serious shortages of particular items that had developed. When, early in 1951, the French expressed concern over the tardy arrival of certain promised items, General Brink indicated that the increasing rate of deliveries would soon lay to rest the French fears.[23] Yet at the end of the year 1951, the French still considered the rate of shipment inadequate for operational requirements. Now the U.S. military assistance advisory group in Indochina agreed with that view. Transport vehicles, shop trucks, and engineer trailer-type tractors were especially sought after at that time. Inadequate port facilities in Indochina were as much a bottle neck to some deliveries as were delays of various kinds in shipment. Even the port of Saigon could accommodate only three liberty ships simultaneously discharging their cargoes directly onto the wharves.

Under the leadership of General de Lattre, the French set about training Vietnamese units to take over an increasing share of the war effort in Indochina. The program showed quick results. The French furnished most of the individual equipment for these units, while the United States provided most of the combat matériel. This included infantry weapons, some artillery, light armored vehicles, and signal, medical, engineering, and ordnance-maintenance equipment. Reporting the training of Vietnamese units to be excellent, American observers late in 1951 noted that the combat efficiency of the units was affected more by the amount of equipment received than by the amount of training received. All units that had received their full allotment of American equipment were rated excellent.[24]

Further reports in mid-1952 indicated generally good use being made of MDAP materiel. The ever-present problem of maintenance could not be avoided. While the scale of maintenance equipment and spare parts available to units gave a general impression of austerity, and the maintenance provided by French forces generally was not up to United States standards, it was in most cases satisfactory. Individual units varied from unsatisfactory with respect to the maintenance of certain items to general excellence. In many cases the lack of tools and spare parts frustrated commendable efforts at proper maintenance.[25]

Nowhere were the close relationships between events and conditions in widely separated areas of the world more clearly demonstrated than in the seemingly inescapable conflict that held the French in Indochina. While the Indochinese war continued, about one-third of French armed forces were committed to that action. This included some 235,000 men—colonial troops and foreign legionnaires as well as regular French officers and men—and a somewhat greater number of Indochinese. With another third of the French army generally en route from one station to another, this left only one-third for the defense of France and French Africa and for carrying on training activities in the home country. Casualties were heavy. After six years of warfare, casualties among French union forces included an estimated thirty thousand killed and missing—as many as the United States lost in three years of fighting in Korea. Vietnam had suffered a like number of casualties. Especially serious for France was the toll among young officers and noncommissioned officers. French leaders had to be furnished for Vietnamese units—until indigenous units could develop capable leaders—as well as for their own units. At least a third of France's regular officers and noncommissioned officers were on duty in Indochina—at a time when they were badly needed to help build up France's part of Western European defenses. It was said that France was losing each year in Indochina the equivalent of the graduating class of the French military academy, St. Cyr.[26]

The financial burden was hardly less severe. Annual expenditures by the French in Indochina were between $1 billion and $1.5 billion—about one-fourth of the total French military budget.[27] The total outlay amounted to more than all the aid France had received from the United States during the same period.[28] By 1953 the United States was carrying about one-third of the financial burden in Indochina.[29] Still the drain on French resources that Indochina posed continued to have grave consequences for the economic stability of France. The economic well-being of France at the same time was highly significant for Western European defense.

The policy of Congress after the outbreak of the conflict in Korea in cutting economic assistance in favor of military aid came at a time when the French economy itself was reaching the point where it threatened to impair the military effort. After a series of visits to the United States by Jules Moch and Jean Monnet, the minister of defense and commissioner general of economic planning, respectively, Secretary of State Acheson was willing to look toward a special program of military assistance that might ease the economic situation in France while making a contribution to military preparedness in Indochina. The project encountered some opposition in the United States Department of Defense, but soon American officials were able to present a united front in accepting what came to be known as the Lisbon defense support program for Indochina.[30]

It was at Lisbon, where officials had gathered in January 1952 for the meeting of the North Atlantic Council, that a Franco-American agreement was concluded to put the program into effect. This provided for the procurement by the United States for transfer to the French of up to $200 million worth of military supplies and equipment. The agreement was couched in the language of the mutual security program. In practice the arrangement amounted largely to the assumption of financial responsibility on the part of the United States for orders the French already had placed. The program was a two-edged weapon aimed at strengthening the French economy by relieving France of an important financial burden, while also stimulating French industry, and making available much-needed supplies and equipment for shipment to Indochina.[31]

As a first step the secretary of defense requested that $132,435,000 be transferred from Title 1 countries under the Mutual Security Act to Title 3 countries. These funds still would be expended in France, but it would be for the purpose of military assistance in Indochina.[32]

The program as then worked out set down over $70 million for the air force and navy parts, which included some items for use in France as well as for Indochina. The army's share, $120 million, was entirely for matériel to be used in Indochina. This included $23 million for the purchase of items in the United States, $43 million for items already contracted for in French arsenals, and $54 million for items from French private industries—all for shipment to Indochina. Recognizing that it would be impractical for American contracting officers in Europe to make "normal" inspections of French-type goods, the secretary of defense authorized the military departments to direct acceptance of certification by the French government respecting conformity of items to contract standards and specifications. Spot checks might be made in specific cases, but in general French acceptance would be tantamount to American acceptance.[33] Through June 1953 total shipments to Indochina under the special Lisbon support program amounted to $91.4 million.[34]

As communism displayed greater strength in China and Korea, Indochina loomed ever larger in the strategy of the free world against the communist threat.[35] What the United States had regarded in earlier years as a war of French imperialism and prestige now became identified as a major theater of operations against communist expansion. As Frenchmen became weary of the unceasing conflict and its drain on their manpower and resources, Americans became more anxious to keep the French in the fight as a part of a common struggle. Secretary of State Dulles in 1953 expressed the American appraisal of the strategic situation as follows:

The Soviet Russians are making a drive to get Japan, not only through what they are doing in northern areas of the islands and in Korea but also through what they are doing in Indochina. If they could get this peninsula of Indochina, Siam, Burma, Malaya, they would have what is called the rice bowl of Asia. That's the area from which the great peoples of Asia, great countries of Asia such as Japan and India, get, in large measure, their food. And you can see that, if the Soviet Union had control of the rice bowl of Asia, that would be another weapon which would tend to expand their control into Japan and into India. That is a growing danger; it is not only a bad situation because of the threat in the Asian countries that I refer to but also because the French, who are doing much of the fighting there, are making great effort; and that effort subtracts just that much from the capacity of their building a European Army and making the countribution which otherwise they could be expected to make.[36]

A communist thrust into Laos in 1953 indicated that the Viet Minh had not lost its aggressive character. Although improvements in the situation could be reported from time to time, it still remained through mid-1953 a situation of near stalemate. If that stalemate could not be broken up by vigorous French and Vietnamese military efforts, backed by sound economic policies, there was a danger that serious military and political deterioration might set in throughout Southeast Asia. As in the Philippines and Greece, the insecurity and political stalemate confronting the newly established governments of Vietnam, Cambodia, and Laos tended to operate in a vicious circle as both the cause and the effect of the long continuing hostilities. As long as defense efforts consumed their resources, those governments were unable to provide the public services that might have attracted popular support; yet without winning popular support they could not win the war.[37]

A noticeable inertia appeared among French forces after the loss of General de Lattre. The French now based their military policy on building up a series of fortifications that would serve as centers of defense against the marauding Viet Minh. To garrison these strong points, and to provide mobile units for meeting guerilla attacks, the French organized their forces generally into independent battalions. Such dispositions were undoubtedly of some help in providing local security, but they could not get at the real problem of destroying the communist forces. This left the initiative largely in the hands of the Viet Minh. The best this system could be expected to do was to maintain the stalemate without eliminating the cause of the trouble. Such an approach ran counter to the whole American view of the situation. American advisers urged that complete divisions be organized so that major offensive operations could be undertaken to clear the country of the communist forces. French leaders agreed that this would be desirable, and they pointed out that offensive action would be expensive—and would require more American aid.[38]

In the spring of 1952 General Raoul Salan, the successor to General de Lattre as commander in chief, had predicted hopefully that barring Chinese intervention the situation could be brought under control by mid-1953. American observers were unable to share this optimism. Donald Reade Heath, United States minister to Vietnam, Cambodia, and Laos, gave as his own prediction that it would take at least a year longer to rid the associated states of the communist menace. Indeed it seemed for a time that the old lethargy would settle once more over the French forces in Indochina. But once again an energetic commander arrived on the scene with a promise of offensive action—General Henri Eugene Navarre.[39] His first major action was an airborne attack against the Viet Minh supply base at Langson, just eleven miles from the Chinese border.[40]

Discussions among political and military leaders in Washington, Paris, and Saigon looked toward increased American assistance and French plans for offensive action. In December 1952 the North Atlantic Council declared the war in Indochina to be a matter of common concern deserving the support of the western allies. Rene Mayer, the French premier, and Georges Bidault, French foreign minister, on a visit to Washington in the spring of 1953 raised the question of increased American assistance. The position of the Eisenhower administration was that the question would be taken under study, but that new strategic plans then being prepared should be submitted to form a basis for this study. In June 1953 Lt. Gen. John W. O'Daniel, commanding general of U.S. army, Pacific, headed a mission to inspect conditions in Indochina. This group joined the members of the military advisory group in urging the organization of full divisions and the development of offensive plans. General Navarre came up with a plan for launching of offensive operations during the year—but to carry it out he would need more men and equipment. Bidault returned to Washington in July for a big three foreign ministers' conference, and at that time Secretary of State Dulles expressed satisfaction with General Navarre's plan.[41]

Almost at the same time the Senate was cutting the amount for military assistance to Indochina that the Eisenhower administration already had requested. The Senate cut the $400,000,000 that had been included in the fiscal year 1954 Mutual Security Program for Indochina to $300,00,000. General O'Daniel returned from his tour of inspection a few days later, and on the basis of his recommendations a Senate-House conference restored the full $400,000,000.[42]

Then in September 1953 the National Security Council approved a recommendation for an additional $385,000,000 for military assistance in Indochina.[43] Committed to a policy of giving greater attention to the Far East in general, the new administration put Indochina high on its priority list for military aid. Actually Secretary of State Acheson over a year earlier had put the war in Indochina on a par with the Korean conflict as a part of the fight against communist aggression.[44] Both President Eisenhower[45] and Secretary of State Dulles publicly declared the keen American interest in Indochina. Plans for increased military aid and public announcements of the interest of the United States in seeking a complete victory in Indochina proved to be no occasion for general enthusiasm in France. Weary of the years of struggle and the loss of life and resources, large elements of the French population were anxious to abandon the whole thing if a way could be found to do it. Now the renewed interest of the United States implied that victory would have to be won—at the price of even greater sacrifice—before any relief could be expected. Noting that new plans called for the French to send out more officers while the United States provided additional equipment, some Paris newspapers saw it as a "blood versus dollars" proposition.[46]

Moreover the new activity and the new interest inevitably raised the question of possible Chinese reactions. Earlier American leaders had expressed concern about a possible intervention by Chinese communists. It was no secret that the Viet Minh forces were being supplied from bases in China,[47] but so far no active participation on the part of Chinese communists had been noted. Secretary of Defense Robert A. Lovett had intimated that a Chinese intervention might lead to the involvement of the United States in another war on the Korean pattern.[48] With the conclusion of the armistice in Korea in July 1953, Chinese communist forces were released for further action in Indochina, if communist leaders should adopt a policy of intervention.[49]

An urgent request from Thailand in the spring of 1953 for an increased supply of ammunition under the MDAP being developed for that country had to be turned down because of the lack of satisfactory ammunition reserves in the United States.[50] This came at the very moment when the increased American assistance and the new French offensives might serve to incite the Chinese communists to just such a course. In order to forestall such a development, Secretary of State Dulles made explicit what previously had been only intimated—that the United States would intervene in force should the Chinese communists do so. This made it clear. Either the Chinese would not intervene to oppose the stepped-up French and Vietnamese campaigns, or the United States would indeed be involved in another war of the Korean kind.[51] As a matter of fact the United States had been planning for such an eventuality since the spring of 1951. The Chinese intervention in Korea in November 1950 had indicated to American leaders the possibility of a similar intervention in Indochina. Considering anticipatory planning to be essential, G–4 proceeded to prepare a logistic study on supporting possible military operations in Indochina. The initial study was completed in May 1951, and then was kept up to date in keeping with further developments.

While touring the Far East in November 1953, Vice President Richard Nixon voiced the sentiment of the Eisenhower administration when he said, "We must see to it that no supplies are lacking for the Indo-China war, which is at present a world front. In principle, all supplies that can be absorbed in the Indo-China war will be furnished."[52] Yet in France itself rumbles of discontent were growing. They would not be stilled until someone could find a way at last to stop the fighting in Indochina—even if it meant giving up northern Vietnam, including the rich Tonkin delta area—to the communists. In the sequel this is precisely what happened. An armistice agreement signed at Geneva in July 1954—from which the United States dissociated itself—provided for the division of Vietnam at the seventeenth parallel.

Japan

The United States in the 1950s ironically turned to a policy of rearming a reluctant Japan. Much to the disappointment of Americans who saw in "total victory" and "unconditional surrender" the solution for all the international problems that troubled them, the removal of one threatening power only paved the way for the rise of another, no less troublesome and no less threatening. Such an extreme disturbance to the balance of power in the Far East as the defeat of Japan entailed required extreme concern for the security of

American interests in that area, for the inevitable result was the extension of Soviet influence into the so-called "power vacuum" thus created. Indeed it was this that gave to the Korean conflict itself its special strategic significance. Apart from its importance as a symbol of United Nations collective action and as an indication of determination on the part of the United States to fight if necessary to contain communism, the Korean War was for the United States a primary step in maintaining the security of Japan. This—the defense of Japan—had by that time become the principal mission of the Far East Command. Communist seizure of South Korean—the traditional "dagger aimed at Japan"—would have had grave consquences for the Japanese security position. Now with China under communist rule, the security of the United States in the Pacific was bound irrevocably with that of Japan. It already had become clear that, failing the build-up of nationalist China to the status of a great power in the Far East, the only alternative to complete Soviet domination was the rebuilding of Japanese strength. Just as a possible hostile combination of Soviet and German strength in Europe was in the view of American policy makers the most serious eventuality for American security in Europe, so Soviet control of Japan, with East Asia's greatest industrial plant, would have been the most serious development for American security in the Pacific.

As the State Department noted in June 1953:

Of all the Far East Nations, Japan possesses the most advanced industry and the greatest reservoir of technical skills and commercial experience. Thus, she is in position to contribute positively and substantially not only to the strengthening of the security of the free nations of the Pacific but also to the raising of living standards in that area. United States policies with respect to Japan are directed toward the following objectives: An independent Japan, politically stable, economically viable, and capable of contributing to its own defense and that of other free nations of the Pacific.[53]

This hope that the Japanese might be able to contribute to the defense of other free nations in the Pacific as well as to their own was a long way from the demilitarization policies of five and six years earlier. In the early days of the occupation the assumption apparently had prevailed that the question of defense would not arise, or that the United States should undertake altogether the defense of Japan for an indefinite time in the future.

In 1948 a Japanese police force armed with American pistols and other light equipment had been organized for local protection. But it was the Korean conflict that gave birth to postwar Japanese military forces. The deployment of American divisions to Korea practically denuded Japan of effective defense forces. Concerned about this situation, General MacArthur in July 1950 took action to activate four Japanese divisions, with a total of seventy-five thousand men, and cabled the Joint Chiefs of Staff for confirming authority. With equipment furnished by the United States, this force would be orga-

Lt. Col. C. E. Hutchens of the War Department, Lt. Gen. Albert C. Wedemeyer, and Col. F. L. Huff and General D. L. Farman of the Army Air Forces, meet in Japan.

nized as the equivalent of American "light divisions." In American planning the force was referred to as "special FECOM reserve"; locally it was given euphemistic designations, first as the "Japanese national rural police reserves," later as the "Japanese national police reserve" and still later as the "national safety force." In December 1950 the U.S. army added requirements for heavy equipment for the Japanese force, and already American plans anticipated the expansion of that force ultimately to ten divisions with a total strength of 250,000 men.[54]

Even after the Chinese communist intervention in Korea, General MacArthur did not lose sight of his primary mission. When the Joint Chiefs of Staff early in January 1951 sought his views on a program they were considering for rearming the army of the Republic of Korea, MacArthur replied, "The over-all interests of the United States will be better served by making these weapons available to increase the security of Japan rather than arming additional ROK forces."[55] Subsequently the continued fighting against the Chinese and considerations of domestic politics in the United States served to alter that emphasis. Indeed MacArthur himself professed to be at a loss to understand why the arming of South Korean draftees was being delayed.[56] By

1952 and 1953 nearly the whole emphasis was being placed on doubling the South Korean forces even at the expense of the local defense in Japan, and even though the defense of Japan remained the primary mission of the Far East Command.

At the time of the signing of the Japanese peace treaty in San Francisco on 8 September 1951, the United States also concluded a security treaty with Japan. Noting the threat of possible aggression against Japan, together with Japan's inability at that time to provide adequately for its own defense, this treaty formed the legal basis for stationing American forces in Japan after the termination of the occupation with the coming into force of the peace treaty. But the security treaty also carried the expectation that Japan would "increasingly assume responsibility for its own defense."[57]

In a conference in Washington in February 1952, officers of Far East Command and Department of the Army headquarters agreed upon a troop basis and equipment program for expanding the Japanese national police reserve from the original four-division, seventy-five-thousand-man force to six divisions with 180,000 men by 31 March 1953, and ten divisions with 325,000 men by 31 March 1954. Neither the mutual security agency budget nor the army budget for fiscal year 1953 contained any provision for equipping Japanese units as such. But in December 1951 the secretary of defense had directed the army to include $300,000,000 in its own budget items for logistic support of the Japanese. Thus while this was not identifiable in the army's budget, it brought the total of logistic support authorized for the Japanese national police reserve, when added to issue availabilities of $150 million in fiscal year 1952 and $78,556,000 in fiscal year 1951, to $528,556,000. In August 1952 the president authorized the transfer of tanks, artillery, and other heavy equipment to the Japanese national safety force on a loan basis. In addition the Far East Command received an allotment of $72 million for offshore procurement in Japan for the national safety force—a program that would serve further to stimulate Japanese defense industries while also providing necessary equipment for the safety force. It was expected that matériel now being "loaned" to the Japanese later would be given to them, and that a regular mutual defense assistance program would be set up for Japan within the next year or so.[58]

In October 1952, after obtaining the approval of the Japanese Diet, the Japanese government established the national safety agency. Amounting to a rudimentary department of defense, the new agency brought under centralized control the national safety force (with an authorized strength at that time of 110,000 men), the coastal safety force, and the maritime safety board. The Japanese budget for the fiscal year ending 30 March 1953 included the equivalent of $500 million for defense, but only about 60 percent of those funds were obligated during the year. Most of the remaining unobligated funds were for facilities for the use of American troops. The Japanese House of Representatives cut the defense appropriations for the next fiscal year ending 31 March

1954 to the equivalent of $353 million—nearly half of which again was for Japan's share of the expenses of supporting American forces stationed in Japan under the terms of the security treaty.[59]

Clearly the Japanese budgets indicated that the expansion program that the United States had developed was not going to be met. The Japanese government had provided only for a four-division force in fiscal year 1953, with expansion in the indefinite future. In June 1953 the national safety force still numbered only slightly more than 100,000 men, and then the budget adopted in July indicated a cut rather than an expansion in defense expenditures.[60]

Concerned about the Japanese tendency to "drag their feet" in building up defense forces, Secretary of State Dulles during a visit to the Far East in August 1953 obtained a personal interview with the Japanese Premier, Shigeru Yoshida. Indicating the American interest in Japanese rearmament, Dulles pointed out that Japan was spending only about two-and-a-half percent of its national income on defense, while such a country as Italy—in a less exposed position—was spending 7 percent. Yoshida insisted, however, that Japan for the time being could not go beyond the four divisions then being maintained in the national safety force. Dulles reportedly answered that it was strange that South Korea, with a population less than a quarter as great as Japan's, had raised seventeen divisions and now was trying to increase this to twenty.[61]

But Yoshida was responding to the political climate in Japan. Rearmament had become a hot domestic issue, and as in Germany a large segment of the population in this once-militaristic state openly opposed rearmament. Of course this anti-military attitude had had the full encouragement of the United States only a few years before. With American blessings, the Japanese had included in their new constitution (promulgated 3 November 1946, effective 3 May 1947) a chapter on the renunciation of war that remained in force in 1953. Article 9 read as follows:

> Aspiring sincerely to an international peace based on justice and order, the Japanese people forever renounce war as a sovereign right of the nation and the threat or use of force as a means of settling disputes.
> In order to accomplish the aim of the preceding paragraph, land, sea, and air forces, as well as other war potential, will never be maintained. The right of belligerancy of the state will not be recognized.[62]

In the treaty of peace the allied powers recognized that Japan "as a sovereign nation" had "the inherent right of individual or collective self-defense referred to in Article 51 of the Charter of the United Nations,[63] and they agreed specifically that Japan might voluntarily enter into collective security arrangements. On the same day that the peace treaty was signed (8 September 1951) Japan entered into the security treaty with the United States referred to above. By an exchange of notes with the American secretary of state, also on the same day, the Japanese government furthermore agreed to permit and facilitate forces of United Nations members in and about Japan while those forces were engaged in United Nations actions.[64]

But cooperation with other forces did not mean that the Japanese people necessarily welcomed foreign troops in their midst, nor that they themselves were ready to rearm. About 47 percent of the people questioned in a nationwide poll conducted by the Japanese newspaper *Asahi Shimoun* in the summer of 1953 were opposed to the continued presence of American troops in Japan. Of the remainder, 26 percent had no opinion, and only 27 percent would say that the Americans should remain. Sentiment for Japanese rearmament appeared to be even less than that in favor of having American troops stationed in Japan. The only major political party espousing rearmament, the Progressive Party, had lost heavily in the most recent election. There was little prospect in mid-1953 that the constitutional restrictions against armed forces would be amended soon. By the terms of the constitution, a national referendum was necessary for amendments. Furthermore, the constitution had given the vote to the women—a group generally pacifistic and strongly opposed to rearmament. Government officials might admit privately that Japan would have to rearm, but they considered that it would be highly unpopular for a political party to say so.[65]

These sentiments made it highly important in the Japanese view to avoid any references to a new Japanese army by resorting to such euphemisms as "national police reserve" and "national safety force."[66] For its part the United States risked criticism for rearming an ex-enemy on its own responsibility, so that euphemistic expressions also served its purpose well.

The Liberal Party of Premier Yoshida was opposed to a constitutional amendment to permit rearming. About as far as Yoshida was willing to go in making concessions to his rival party, the Progressive Party, on this point was to join in a statement with the leader of that party, Mamoru Shigemitsu, in September 1953 in proposing to change the name of the national safety force to the national defense force and to authorize that force to oppose any foreign invasion of Japan.[67]

This announcement seemed to be aimed at justifying grants of American military aid under the Mutual Defense Assistance Program. Negotiations on a bilateral agreement as required under the Mutual Security Act had been dragging on for months. There already was an American military advisory group in Japan. This security advisory group, which had been organized under Far East Command to train the Japanese in the use of American equipment, would become a military assistance advisory group (MAAG) as soon as the bilateral agreement became effective, and from that item military aid to Japan would become a regular MDAP such as that found in other countries around the world. Thereafter too funds for military aid to Japan would be provided in the mutual security program budget rather than included in regular appropriations for the army. Thus the United States would bring to full tide a policy of collaborating with another erstwhile enemy in order to curb the aggressive designs of a former ally.[68]

Notes

1. Basic Policies of the Dept. of the Army, C 11, May 1953, 29–32; *Annual Rpt. of the Secy. of the Army,* 1948, 67.
2. Republic of the Philippines Military Assistance Act, P. L. 454, 79th Cong., 60 Stat. 315.
3. Philippine Rehabilitation Act of 1946, P. L. 370, 79th Cong., Title 2, 60 Stat. 134–35; see Chapter 1.
4. First Supplemental Appropriation Act, 1947, P. L. 663, 79th Gong., 60 Stat. 916.
5. Brown and Opie, *American Foreign Assistance,* 440–41.
6. G–4 Review of the Month, 30 Sept. 48, 19.
7. "U.S. Technical and Economic Assistance in the Far East," reprinted in *Mutual Security Act Extension,* Hearings before House Comm. on For. Affairs, 82d Cong., 2d Sess., 832.
8. *First Rpt. to Congress on The Mutual Security Program,* 31; *Third Semiannual Rpt. to Congress on the Mutual Defense Assistance Program,* 6 Oct. 1950 to 31 Mar. 1951, 24–25; *Rpt. to Congress on the Mutual Security Program,* 30 June 1953, House Doc. 226, 83d Cong., 1st Sess., 41–42; Statement of General J. Lawton Collins, CofS, 26 May 51, Senate Hearings on Relief of MacArthur, Pt. 2, 1345; Testimony of Secy. of State, Dean Acheson, 2 June 1951, Senate Hearings on Relief of General MacArthur, Pt. 3, 1772; Thomas E. Dewey, *Journey to the Far Pacific,* (New York, 1952), 153–56.
9. Letter, Chief Adviser JUSMAG to CinC Pacific, 9 July 53, sub.: Monthly Summary of Activities for June 1953.
10. Papers Relating to the Foreign Relations of the United States, Japan: 1931–1941, 2:340–792; Samuel Flagg Bemis, 2 vols. *A Diplomatic History of the United States,* 3d ed., (New York, 1950), 869–73.
11. "The War in Indochina," *Armed Forces Talk* 439, 2–3; David Douglas Duncan, "The Year of the Snake," *Life,* 3 Aug. 1953, 73–75; Charles A. Fisher, *South-East Asia: A Social, Economic and Political Geography* (London, 1964), 529–75.
12. Raymond Kennedy, "Southeast Asia and Indonesia," in *Most of the World,* edited by Ralph Linton, (New York, 1949), 699–710; W. Robert Moore, "Strife-torn Indochina," *The National Geographic Magazine* 98 (Oct 1950): 499–501.
13. *Major Problems of U.S. Foreign Policy 1950–1951,* (Brookings Institution), 311–15, 349–50; Linton, *Most of the World,* 700–710; Moore, "Strife-torn Indochina," 503; "The War in Indochina," *Armed Forces Talk* 4–8.
14. Quoted in *Major Problems of U.S. Foreign Policy 1950–1951,* 313; see also Dean Acheson, *Present at the Creation* (New York, 1969), 671–73.
15. *Major Problems in U.S. Foreign Policy 1950–1951,* 313.
16. *Semiannual Report of the Secretary of Defense,* 1 Jan. to 30 June 1950, 16; Comd. Rpt., G–4, FEC, 1–30 Nov 50, 13–14; Jap. Log. Comd. Rpt., Nov. 1950, Hq. JLCOM, Narrative Summary, 90.
17. Interview with Col. Emons B. Whisner, formerly exec. officer, MAAG Indochina, 27 July 1953.
18. *Semiannual Report of the Secretary of Defense,* 1 Jan. to 30 June 1951, 68; see also *Third Semiannual Rpt. to Congress on MDAP,* 6 Oct. 1950 to 31 Mar. 1951, House Doc. 179, 82d Cong., 1st Sess., D/S Publ. 4291, Gen'l. For. Pol. Ser. 59, released July 1951, 23.
19. "The War in Indochina," *Armed Forces Talk,* 8–12; George W. Long, "Indochina Faces the Dragon," *The National Geographic Magazine* 52 (Sept. 1952): 287–94.

Defense Assistance to the Philippines, Indochina, Japan 253

20. Long, "Indochina Faces the Dragon," *The National Geographic Magazine,* 317–18.
21. NATO Notebook Series, D-4, 10 Mar. 52, Chronology of Events, 30.
22. "Indo-Chinese Get 150th U.S. Aid Cargo," *The New York Times,* 29 May 1952.
23. "U.S. Aide Sees Rise in Indo-China Help," *The New York Times,* 12 January 1951.
24. See testimony of General J. Lawton Collins, Chief of Staff, USA, Senate Hearings on Relief of MacArthur, 26 May 1951, Pt. 2, 1345.
25. Report of Field Visit by Field Svc. Sec., OMA, OSD, 1 July 52 to 6 Aug. 52, Rpt. by army members of SE Asia Surbey Mission; Monthly Activities Rpt. for Mar. 1953, MAAG Indochina, 25 Apr. 53, copy in G-4 FMA Div., Control Sec.
26. Statement of General Alfred M. Gruenther, CofS, SHAPE, 25 Mar. 52, *Mutual Security Act Extension, Hearings* before House Comm. on For. Affairs, 82d Cong., 2d Sess., 242–43; Statement of Robert A. Lovett, Sec. Def., 13 Mar. 52, Hearings before House Comm. on For. Affairs, 22; Remarks of Maj. Gen. George G. Richards, formerly Chief, MAAG France, Dept. of Defense, 30 Jan. 53; Hanson W. Baldwin, *The New York Times,* 25 Nov. 1952; "The War in Indochina," *Armed Forecs Talk* 9; Duncan, "The Year of the Snake," *Life,* 75; Statement of Harold E. Stassen, Dir. for Mutual Security, 25 Mar. 53, Hearings before House Comm. on For. Affairs, 83d Cong., 1st Sess., *Mutual Security Act Extension,* 67.
27. Remarks of General Richards, 30 Jan 53.
28. Total net foreign aid to France during the six fiscal years from 1946 to1951 inclusive, including credits as well as grants, was $4.188 billion, or an average of $698 million a year. Dept. of State, *Foreign Aid by the U.S. Government,* 1940–51, (Washington, D. C., 1952), 82.
29. See Duncan, "The Year of the Snake," *Life,* 3 Aug. 1953, 80–81.
30. Interview with Brig. Gen. D. L. Van Syckle, formerly Chief Procurement Div., OMA, OSD, 11 Sept. 53; Acheson, *Present at the Creation,* 675–77.
31. Bilateral Agreement between Government of France and Government of the United States, Dept. of State, *United States Treaties and Other International Agreements,* 1952 (Washington, D. C. 1953).
32. Memo, OSD for Secretaries of Army, Navy, Air Force, sub.: FY 1952 MDA "Lisbon Programs"—Indochina and France.
33. Draft ltr. G4/E5, DA to CG EUCOM, n. d. (prep. 22 Apr. 52), sub.: Implementation of FY 1952 MDA "Lisbon Programs"—Indochina and France, copy in OMA, OSD; Memo, OSD for Secretaries of Army, Navy, Air Force, n. d., sub.: FY 1952 MDA "Lisbon Programs"—Indochina and France, copy in OMA, OSD.
34. MDAP, D/D Opns. Under the Mutual Security Program, prep. by Mil. Asst. Off. of Secy. of Def. (July 1953), 29.
35. See Jacques Soustelle, "Indo-China and Korea: One Front," *Foreign Affairs* 27 (Oct 1950); Hamilton Fish Armstrong, "The World Is Round," *Foreign Affairs* 31 (Jan 1953): 185–89; Woodrow Wyatt, "Of Equal Importance—Asia's Second Front," *The New York Times Magazine,* 26 July 1953.; Acheson, *Present at the Creation,* 675–77.
36. Statement of Secy. of State, John Foster Dulles, quoted in *Army Talk,* 11.
37. Statement submitted by Mutual Security Agency on defense support program in Indochina, Hearings before House Comm. on For. Affairs, 83d Cong., 1st Sess., *Mutual Security Act Extension,* 768–71.
38. Remarks of Lt. Gen. John W. O'Daniel (CG USARPAC) 20 July 53; Duncan, "The Year of the Snake," *Life,* 3 Aug 1953, 74–79.
39. Hanson W. Baldwin, "Indo-China War Enters New and Critical Phase," *The New York Times,* 20 Sept. 1953.

254   *Defense Assistance to the Philippines, Indochina, Japan*

40. See Tillman Durdin in *The New York Times*, 18 July 1953.
41. Harold Callendar, "Paris Debate on Indo-China Shows Differences with U.S.," *The New York Times*, 24 July 1953.
42. *The New York Times*, 11 Sept. 1953.
43. "U.S. to Double Aid in Indo-China War," *The New York Times*, 11 Sept. 1953.
44. "If Indo-China is Invaded—U.S. to Aid by Sea and Air," *U.S. News and World Report*, 4 Apr. 1952.
45. See text of talk by President Eisenhower at Governors' Conf., Seattle, 4 Aug. 53, in *The New York Times*, 5 Aug. 1953.
46. Harold Callendar, "Paris Debate on Indo-China Shows Differences with U.S.," *The New York Times*, 24 July 1953.
47. *The New York Times*, 25 Nov. 1952.
48. "If Indo-China is Invaded—U.S. to Aid by Sea and Air," *U.S. News and World Report*, 4 Apr. 1952, 44; *The New York Times*, 25 Nov. 1952.
49. See Hanson W. Baldwin, "Indo-China War Enters New and Critical Phase," *The New York Times*, 20 Sept. 1953; Ben L. M. Chassin, "Guerre en Indochine," *Revue de Defense Nationale* (Juillet 1953): 3–22.
50. Memo, Lt. Col. H. R. Low, Secy. Allocations Committee (Army), for Chairman Allocations Committee, 6 May 53, sub.: Allocation of Ordnance Matériel to Thailand, and DF, Chief FMA Br., to DACofS G–4 FMA, 8 June 53, MDAP Shipments to Thailand.
51. *The New York Times*, 5 August 1953.
52. *The New York Times*, 5 Nov. 1953.; Acheson, *Present at the Creation*, 677–74.
53. Statement submitted by the Dept. of State, June 1953, *Mutual Security Act Extension*, Hearings before House Comm. on For. Affairs, 83d Cong., 1st Sess., 1050.
54. G–4 Hist. Summary, Plans Office, 3–4; Statement submitted by Dept. of State, June 1953, *Mutual Security Act Extension*, Hearings before House Comm. on For. Affairs, 83d Cong., 1st Sess., 1050–51.
55. Quoted in Rovere and Schlesinger, *The General and the President*, 172.
56. Ibid; *Situation in the Far East*, Hearings before Senate For Relations and Armed Services Committees concerning the Relief of General MacArthur, Pt. 2, 1032.
57. Statement submitted by Dept. of State, June 1953, *Mutual Security Act Extension*, Hearings before House Comm. on For. Affairs, 83d Cong., 1st Sess., 1050.
58. Statement submitted by Dept. of State, June 1953, *Mutual Security Act Extension*, Hearings before House Comm. on Foreign Affairs, 83d Cong., 1st Sess. 1050–51.
59. Statement submitted by the Dept. of State, June 1953, *Mutual Security Act Extension*, Hearings before House Committee on For. Affairs, 83d Cong., 1st Sess., 1050.
60. William J. Jordan in *The New York Times*, 18 July 1953; Statement of Frank Nash, Asst. Sec. of Def., 4 June 53, *Mutual Security Act Extension*, Hearings before House Comm. on For. Affairs, 83d Cong., 1st Sess., 1047–49; DA G–4 Hist. Summary, 1951–52, Plans Off., 6–7.
61. James Reston in *The New York Times*, 10 Aug. 1953; see also "Fallen Hopes Engulf the Land of the Rising Sun," *Newsweek*, 17 Aug. 1953, 34–36.
62. The Constitution of Japan, printed in Department of State Publ. 2836.
63. Treaty of Peace with Japan, Treaties and Other International Acts, series 2490, Dept. of State 4613, Article 5.
64. Exchange of Notes between the Secretary of State and the Japanese Prime Minister, 8 Sept. 1951, printed in *Treaty of Peace with Japan*, Department of State publ. 4613, 170–73.
65. James Reston, "Earlier Policies Plague U.S. in Moves to Rearm Japan," *The

New York Times, 7 Aug. 1953.

66. Statement of Kenneth T. Young, Officer of Near Eastern Affairs, Dept. of State, 4 June 1953, *Mutual Security Act Extension,* Hearings before House Comm. on For. Affairs, 83d Cong., 1st Sess., 1049; Statement of Frank Wash, Asst. Sec. Def., 4 June 53, *Mutual Security Act Extension,* Hearings before House Comm. on For. Affairs, 83d Cong., 1st Sess., 1051–52.

67. *The New York Times,* 4 Oct. 1953.

68. Statement of Maj. Gen. George H. Olmsted, formerly director OMA, 11 Mar. 53, *Mutual Security Act Extension,* Hearings before House Committee on For. Affairs, 83d Cong., 1st Sess., 2–3; DA G–4 Hist. Summary, 1951–52, Plans Office, 7.

10
Western Hemisphere Defense

> We in the Americas are no longer a far away continent, to which the eddies of controversies beyond the seas could bring no interest or harm. Instead, we in the Americas have become a consideration to every propaganda office and to every general staff beyond the seas. The vast amount of our commerce and the strength of our men have made us vital factors in world peace whether we choose it or not.
> —Franklin D. Roosevelt, 18 August 1938

Defense of the Panama Canal

Probably to nothing else in the world was American reaction more sensitive than to any hostile threat to the Panama Canal throughout the period from its construction to the mid-1950s. The canal made possible not only the crucial shifting of naval forces in time of war, but it also contributed to the logistic support of land forces in Europe and Asia by making it possible for Atlantic and Gulf ports to assume a share of the burden of shipping men and supplies to the Pacific or for Pacific ports to relieve Atlantic and Gulf ports in supplying Europe during critical times. The fact that land forces and matériel—and supplies and equipment for air forces as well—could be shifted from one ocean to another rapidly was hardly less important for security than was the shifting of naval forces. The importance of the canal for national security had made of the whole Caribbean-Central American region an area of "vital interest" to the United States. In general each new communist threat that characterized the "Cold War," and in particular every indication of communist activities in neighboring Latin American countries, was a matter of concern to military commanders in this mid-American sector. The Korean conflict itself brought added responsibilities in the shipment of the Puerto Rican regiment to the Far East, in the coordination of troop movements through the canal, and in the coordination of local support for Colombian forces participating in the Korean action. Rising demands for petroleum products from this area to meet Far East Command and other needs emphasized anew the importance of coordinating with British, Venezuelan, and Dutch authorities in the protection of the oil fields in Venezuela and Trinidad and of the refineries in Aruba, Curacao, and Trinidad against possible sabotage.

The aircraft carrier, U.S.S. *Shangrila* in the Pedro Miguel lock, Panama Canal, March 1946.

The U.S. naval transport *Gaffey,* with troops of the 45th Infantry Division aboard, passing through the Panama Canal, bound for Korea, April 1951.

The defense of this critical area during this period was entrusted to the Caribbean Command, another unified command for which the chief of staff of the army was executive agent, and which accordingly was organized under an army commander.

In the unified structure of the Caribbean Command, the commander in chief, Lt. Gen. W. H. H. Morris, Jr., with headquarters at Quarry Heights, Canal Zone, exercised command through the commanders of three service components—U.S. army, Caribbean sea frontier, with headquarters at San Juan, Puerto Rico, and the Caribbean Air Command, with headquarters at Albrook Air Force Base, Canal Zone. Actual administrative and operational control was broken down into two area commands—the Panama area, which remained under the direct command of the commander in chief, and the Antilles area, where the commander of the Caribbean sea frontier Rear Adm. M. R. Greer as the senior officer was in command. U.S. army forces Antilles, with headquarters at Fort Brooke, Puerto Rico, was the army component of the Antilles area. The air force did not as yet have any active units in this area. In January 1952 the chief of staff of the army asked G–3 to make a study of the desirability of establishing the army commands in the Panama and Antilles areas as completely independent of each other, so that there would be in effect two theater army commands in the Caribbean Command. As might have been anticipated, the commanding general, U.S. army, Caribbean, opposed any such change, while the commanding general, U.S. army forces, Antilles strongly recommended it. General Morris himself also recommended that the command structure not be modified. When Lt. Gen. Horace L. McBride became commander in chief, Caribbean (April 1952), he concluded that it did not make a great deal of difference either way, though the balance of advantages seemed to him to lay on the side of separating the army commands. The Department of the Army G–3 considering that operational disadvantages would outweigh administrative advantages in June recommended against the proposal. In December 1952 the commanding general, Antilles was authorized direct communication with Department of the Army agencies and army field forces on certain intelligence reports, school quotas, reserve component matters, and burials and cemeteries.[1]

Principal troop housing and training areas in the Canal Zone were at Fort Amador, Fort Clayton, Fort Davis, Fort Gulick, Fort Kobbe, the post of Corozal, and Empire Range. Storage facilities for the area included the Balboa general depot, and an ordnance depot at Corozal. There was a general hospital at Fort Clayton. All together, military and naval reservations as of 30 June 1951 took up 102.47 square miles of the total of 372.49 square miles of land area in the Canal Zone. In Puerto Rico a replacement training center operated at Camp Tortuguero, and other troop housing and training facilities were to be found that Fort Buchanan—where general hospitalization also was provided at Rodriguez Army Hospital—at Fort Bundy, Camp Losey (home station for the 296th Infantry, the Puerto Rican national guard regiment then in Federal Service), Henry Barracks, and Camp Salinas.[2]

In addition to its local defense mission and area responsibilities, the Caribbean Command exercised some administrative supervision over the U.S. army section of the Joint Brazil–U.S. Military Commission in Rio de Janeiro, and over the U.S. army missions in thirteen other Latin American countries.[3]

In the interest of interservice logistic coordination the Caribbean Command had set up a number of boards and committees made up of representatives of army, navy, and air force commands, and frequently including represention from the Canal Zone government. Under a memorandum that Secretary of Defense Johnson issued in November 1949, the command organized the Panama Area Joint Committee to make site studies at the request of boards and offices of the Department of Defense and the military departments in Washington as well as of local field commanders to determine ways of eliminating duplication and improving cross-servicing and joint action among the military services in the field. A joint cross-servicing committee established on 15 May 1950 coordinated the delivery of supplies and services among the service components at the operational level. Other joint committees whose activities were of special interest to the Logistics Division of Caribbean Command included the joint civil defense committee, established in August 1950 to include representatives of the Canal Zone government, U.S. Embassy, and the Republic of Panama; the military sea transportation joint space assignment committee, organized in June 1951; the Panama area air transportation board, organized in August 1951; the Canal Zone public transportation committee, established in October 1951; the joint medical advisory committee, established in August 1948, and the joint fire fighting board, established in August 1950.[4]

One item of supply receiving special attention during this period was perishable foodstuffs. The assumption was that forces in the Caribbean area would depend largely on local production for perishable foods in time of emergency, but in the early 1950s even the peacetime needs of the army forces in the area could not be met. In the Panama area the Caribbean Command cooperated closely with the embassy in efforts to encourage local agriculture to increase the production of foods desired by the armed forces. The quartermaster looked hopefully to the technical cooperation administration program ("point four") being introduced in 1952 to improve both the quality and quantity of agricultural production in Panama.[5]

Another problem that troubled army planners was the lack of army storage for motor gasoline in this oil-rich area. In Panama the Panama Canal Company could supply military needs for motor gasoline, but in the Antilles area gasoline was purchased locally, and commercial companies had to be depended upon to maintain the necessary mobilization reserve levels.[6]

At the direction of the Department of the Army the Caribbean Command developed a replacement and evacuation plan for the Colombian infantry battalion in Korea. Most of the details were worked out in a conference with

Colombian officers in August 1951. Both the first and second increments of replacements, making a total of seven officers and 206 enlisted men, departed from Cartegena 19 November. Other increments followed as required and as shipping became available. Upon completion of their period of service in Korea, Colombian troops returned home with similar groups of Puerto Ricans. The return of hospital patients was handled by the transportation officer of Brooks Army Hospital, San Antonio, Texas, whence military air transport service planes flew the patients to a Colombian airport.[7]

A mission that was normal for Caribbean Command almost every year was cooperation with the Red Cross and other agencies in furnishing tentage, bedding, and medical supplies for disaster relief. During 1951, for example, disaster relief operations included cooperation with those agencies in relieving distress at St. Kitts-Nevis in the Lesser Antilles after an earthquake hit on 31 December 1950, in El Salvador where a series of earthquake shocks hit on 6 May 1951, and in Jamaica and at Tampico, Mexico, where a hurricane struck on 18 and 19 August.[8]

Until 1 July 1951 the name, "Panama Canal" referred to two different things. The first of course was to the big ditch itself. But the name also referred to the agency charged with the operation of the canal and with administering the Canal Zone. The title of the chief executive was "governor of the Panama Canal." Also until 1 July 1951 a major adjunct of the Panama Canal was the Panama Railroad Company. Originally organized as a private corporation in 1849 under the laws of the State of New York to operate a transisthmian railroad in support of the gold rush to California, the United States government acquired ownership of the company in 1904 when work on digging the canal was beginning. The company was incorporated 1 July 1948 as a federal corporation. Ranging far beyond the operation of a railroad across the isthmus, activities of the Panama Railroad Company also included the operation of a steamship line (the Panama Line) between New York and Cristobal, harbor terminals and fueling facilities, two hotels, commissary plants and stores, printing plants, and a telephone system. By direction of the president the secretary of the army was sole stockholder of the company. As such he appointed the board of directors, except that the governor of the Panama Canal (appointed by the president) was *ex officio* a director and president of the company.[9]

Under an act of Congress approved 26 September 1950 and an executive order of the president issued 29 June 1951, this set-up was rearranged completely as of 1 July 1951. The Panama Railroad Company became the Panama Canal Company, and its activities related to the canal as well as those that the railroad company had previously been carrying on. At the same time the agency that had been known as "the Panama Canal" became the Canal Zone government to continue the discharge of the duties of civil administration that that agency had been performing in addition to its responsibilities for operating the canal. The organization of the new Panama Canal Company remained essentially what it had been as the Panama Railroad Company. The secretary of the army now was designated sole stockholder of the Panama Canal Company, and the governor of the Canal Zone was *ex officio* a director and president of the company. The under secretary of the army was designated by the secretary as chairman of the board of directors.[10]

The secretary of the army and the governor of the Canal Zone held their positions in the Panama Canal Company by reason of their official positions. The other members of the board of directors (usually eleven in addition to the secretary and the governor) were appointed as individuals. Thus Karl Bendetsen, who had been assistant secretary and under secretary of the army, remained as a member of the board of directors even after he returned to private business. Other members of the board in early 1953 included two former chiefs of engineers, two former governors, another representative from the Office of the Secretary of the Army, and a number of men prominent in private business.[11]

Operation of the Panama Canal and the civil administration in the Canal Zone were quite distinct from the military command in the area. Yet the civil government bore a distinctly military complexion. By tradition an officer of the Corps of Engineers was appointed governor. (In June 1951 Brig. Gen. John S. Seybold succeeded Brig. Gen. F. K. Newcomer as Governor; General Newcomer continued as governor after retiring from the regular army in 1949.) Of eleven major officials of the Panama Canal in June 1949, four including the governor, were active army officers, and two were navy officers. The situation was about the same two years later. Then of fifteen major officials, the governor and the civil affairs director were retired army officers, the lieutenant governor and the health director were active army officers, and the marine director and industrial director were navy officers.[12]

It was of the utmost importance for the defense of this critical area that the responsibilities of the military and civil authorities be clearly defined. The fact that the governor happened to be an army officer in no way placed him under the authority of the commander in chief, Caribbean. The governor was responsible to the president through the secretary of the army. The secretary of the army in his civil capacity also was charged with the operation of the Panama Canal. But this alone did not assure cooperation between local officials and military authorities in their day-to-day operations or in emergency plans for defense of the canal.

Under the Panama Canal Act of 1912, the president could in time of war or when he considered war to be imminent designate the commander of army troops as the senior authority in the Canal Zone. The act provided that when so designated the army commander in the area would "assume and have exclusive jurisdiction over the operations of the Panama Canal and all its adjuncts . . . , including the entire control and government of the Canal Zone, . . . and . . . the Governor . . . shall . . . be subject to the order and direction of such officer of the Army."[13] Shortly after the German invasion of Poland in September 1939, President Roosevelt issued an executive order giving effect to those provisions.[14] This remained in effect, with the governor subject to the authority of the commander, first of the Caribbean Defense Command, and later of the Caribbean Command, until 8 February 1950.[15] The effect was to return to "normal peacetime" relationships less than five months before the outbreak of the Korean conflict. Then the question arose as to what arrangements were necessary to clarify responsibilities for protection of the canal during this emergency. The question went back and forth among the secretary of the army, the general staff, and the Joint Chiefs of Staff in Washington, and the Caribbean Command and the governor of the Canal Zone in the Panama area for several months. Finally in September 1952 the president approved a new executive order. This did not go as far as the executive order of 1939 in giving the army commander complete jurisdiction, but it did state that as between the commander in chief and the governor, the views of the former would prevail in determining whether any aspect of the protection of the Canal Zone related to its military security. If the governor disagreed on any point he could appeal through the secretary of the army or through the board of directors of the Panama Canal Company to the president, but while the appeal was pending the decision of the commander in chief would continue to be binding. The order also revoked an executive order that had been issued in 1916 that charged the governor with responsibility for protection of the canal in peacetime in cooperation with the military forces. The new executive order was to remain in force until the termination of the emergency that the President had proclaimed on 16 December 1950.

Not only security plans, but ordinary day-to-day activities of military forces in the Panama area called for close cooperation with the Panama Canal Company, for the military was dependent upon the company for a great many facilities and services. During fiscal year 1951 the armed services received services from what was to become the Panama Canal Company valued at $4,284,000. Over 25 percent of this was for maintenance and construction services. Late in 1951 the Panama Canal Company agreed to handle the disposal of scrap for all three services. The Panama Canal Company also agreed to assume responsibility for the maintenance of the Transisthmian highway. In this case the Department of the Army continued to budget for the costs involved, and then transferred the necessary funds to the company.[17]

As in practically all command areas, family housing was short in the Caribbean. In October 1950 the Panama Canal, with an appropriation of $2,500,000, began a housing program estimated to have a total cost of approximately $80,000,000. After the reorganization of 1951, the Panama Canal Company took over the program. But it was only for employees of the Panama Canal Company and the Canal Zone government. Assistant Secretary of the Army Bendetsen called a meeting of representatives of the Panama Canal Company, the Canal Zone government, and the armed forces in Washington in November 1951. The result was a recommendation for the Caribbean Command to prepare a family housing program of its own. In drawing up their requirements, the services in the Caribbean divided them into three phases. The first was to meet the needs arising from the fact that Panama Canal Company housing then occupied by military families no longer would be available to them, the second, to overcome additional shortages based on peacetime strengths, and the third phase was to include the replacement of all wooden and temporary housing that was requiring excessive maintenance. However, the necessary congressional appropriations were not forthcoming, and at the end of 1952 requirements for military family housing in the Panama area remained unsatisfied.[18]

For other services it was necessary to go to the Canal Zone government. The local government had to be reimbursed for such services as schools, hospitalization, and certain board of health laboratory work. Liaison had to be maintained with the Republic of Panama for such problems as controlling post exchange sales, arranging for the use of additional training areas in Panama territory, and highway transit and maintenance.[19]

A great deal of effort went into the preparation of emergency plans for the defense of the Caribbean area. The whole effort was focused principally upon protecting a fifty-mile ditch—but it was about the most important ditch in the world for American security.

Military Assistance to Latin America

Military assistance and international cooperation for Western Hemisphere defense were continuations mainly of policies brought to fruition during the course of World War II. This was the kind of policy to which isolationists and internationalists alike could give warm support. The Monroe Doctrine itself had been an isolationist statement—noting the lack of American interest in European affairs and insisting that European powers maintain a similar aloofness toward affairs on the American continents. As World War II approached, the movement for "hemisphere solidarity" provided a convenient rationalization for isolationists who were determined not to become involved in Europe and yet who were troubled by thoughts that something ought to be done to contribute toward international cooperation. Subscribing to a curious "emotional geography" that put all of South America into the "backyard" of the United States and that created a great barrier between the Old World and the New, many of the same people who watched the fall of France in 1940 with seeming indifference—at least as far as action by the United States was concerned—were willing to send their troops anywhere in the Americas that Axis forces might threaten. The acts of Congress in 1940 authorizing the mobilization of the national guard and providing for conscription carried the proviso that men brought into the armed forces thereby would be available for service only in the "Western Hemisphere."[20] Thus a German landing in Argentina would have been opposed with all possible force—even though Buenos Aires, or even Rio de Janeiro, were farther from New York than was Moscow. A German landing at Natal, on the "bulge" of Brazil would have caused great alarm and swift reaction as an intolerable threat to the Panama Canal; yet Germans in Brittany already were closer to New York than they would have been to Panama had they landed at Natal.[21]

On the other hand, people who recognized fully the importance of France and Britain for the security of the United States faced the dim prospect in the summer of 1940 of having to build up defenses in the Americas as a last stronghold against Nazi conquest. Notably less optimistic than their civil chiefs at this point, army planners themselves recommended that the United States take no action that might involve military commitments outside the Western Hemisphere. The fall of France had had an immediate impact on war plans in the United States. Suspending plans for fighting a war across the Pacific or across the Atlantic, the army planning staff turned to the preparation of plans for major operations in the Western Hemisphere.[22]

In any case the course of prudence in such critical times was to "seek for allies wherever they can be found." Moreover the mineral and agricultural resources of the other American states loomed larger in war mobilization plans for the United States as European and Asian resources came under German and Japanese control.

Weak European defenses and insecurity in the Far East invited similar prospects as communist domination spread across much of Europe and Asia in the wake of World War II. Now men cool toward an Atlantic alliance and aid to Europe or the Far East could seize again upon Latin America as the object of a display of international cooperation. But in the critical days of the "Cold War," as in World War II, the administration resisted efforts to divert large amounts of military resources from Europe and Asia to Latin America. There was no denying that Latin America held an important security position for the United States. The need for resources and for solidarity was as important in the current struggle for power against communist Russia as it had been against Nazi Germany and imperialist Japan. But as long as the possibility remained for a successful defense of such critical areas as Western Europe, Japan, and Indochina, Latin America was bound to be relegated to a position of secondary importance in programs of military assistance.

THE RIO TREATY AND THE ORGANIZATION OF AMERICAN STATES

Simon Bolivar's original conception of a union of the American republics had been one devoted mainly to the building of defenses against possible European encroachments. With the passing of the threat of the holy alliance, however, that notion had faded as later interAmerican conferences met from time to time. When the United States at last began to participate actively in this idea with the calling of the First International Conference of American States (the beginning of the modern series of "Pan American Conferences") in 1889 at Washington, the delegates concerned themselves almost wholly with economic questions. After World War I the inter-American conferences turned to problems of peaceful settlement of disputes among American republics. Then in the 1930s the Pan American system began a gradual but certain evolution in the direction of collective security and military collaboration.[23]

At the special Inter-American Conference for the Maintenance of Peace, which met at the suggestion of President Roosevelt in Buenos Aires in December 1936, the American republics adopted the first of a series of declarations expressing "continental" solidarity in opposing aggression. Actually the declaration as adopted—Declaration 27: Principles of Inter-American Solidarity and Cooperation—was a collection of innocuous statements that remained after concessions were made to Argentine opposition to a strongly worded treaty proposed by the Central American delegations.[24] Anticipating the position the American republics would be willing to take a decade later, Article 2 of the proposed treaty stated: "All of the American nations will consider as an attack upon themselves individually an attack which may be made by any nation upon the rights of another, and such a situation shall give rise to an agreement or consultation between the foreign offices with the object of determining what position is to be taken or, it may be, the rules of concerted neutrality."[25] This was too strong for the Argentines. In the interest of gaining unanimous support, the treaty was reduced to a declaration, and Article 2 reduced to this statement in the declaration: "That each act susceptible of disturbing the peace of America affects each and every one of them and justifies the initiation of the procedure of consultation provided for in the Convention for the Maintenance, Preservation and Re-establishment of Peace, signed at this Conference."[26]

The next step on the path toward collective security come in 1938 at the Eighth International Conference of American States at Lima, Peru. Once more it was necessary to water down the statement in order to gain the support of reluctant Argentina, and once again the delays and controversies that tended to arise in the process of ratifying treaties was avoided by making the statement in the form of a declaration rather than a treaty.[27] Reaffirming their "continental solidarity," the American governments in the Declaration of Lima agreed:

> And in case the peace, security or territorial integrity of any American Republic is thus threatened by acts of any nature that may impair them, they proclaim their common concern and their determination to make effective their solidarity, coordinating their respective sovereign wills by means of the procedure of consultation, established by conventions in force and by declarations of the Inter-American Conferences, using the measures which in each case the circumstances may make advisable. It is understood that the Governments of the American Republics will act independently

in their individual capacity, recognizing fully their juridical equality as sovereign states.[28]

The declaration further provided that ministers for foreign affairs of the American republics should meet in consultation at the initiative of any of them to discuss measures of joint action in emergencies.

Soon after the outbreak of World War II, the foreign ministers of the American republics held their first meeting of consultation at Panama. There they sought to adopt common policies of neutrality and to insulate the American continents from the war in Europe.[29]

At a second meeting of consultation at Havana in 1940, the foreign ministers reaffirmed the no-transfer principle regarding European colonies in the Western Hemisphere—a principle that had been a policy of the United States since 1811—and further adopted a far-reaching Declaration of Reciprocal Assistance and Cooperation for the Defense of the Nations of the Americas, which stated: "That any attempt on the part of a non-American state against the integrity or inviolability of the territory, the sovereignty or political independence of an American state shall be considered as an act of agression against the states which sign this declaration."[30]

In case of actual or threatened aggression the American nations were to consult on what countermeasures should be taken. Further the signatories agreed to proceed with the negotiation of complementary agreements for the purposes of organizing cooperation for defense and mutual assistance.

Several of the Latin American states followed the United States into active participation in World War II after Pearl Harbor, and others broke off diplomatic relations with the Axis powers. Before the end of the war all the American states had declared war—though Argentina, Chile, Paraguay, Peru, Uruguay, and Venezuela waited until 1945 to do so.[31] The United States sought closer inter-American collaboration in order to obtain the use of military bases, to curtail subversive activities, and to obtain indispensable strategic raw materials. Countries making bases available to the United States included Brazil, Cuba, Ecuador, Mexico, Nicaragua, and Panama. The Emergency Advisory Committee for Political Defense was established at Montevideo to pool information on subversive agents and their activities. The third meeting of the foreign ministers at Rio de Janeiro in January 1942 provided for the establishment of the Inter-American Defense Board. In addition the United States entered into bilateral arrangements with various of the states for direct military cooperation and for financial assistance in return for making strategic materials available.[32]

As had been the case with Canada, it generally was assumed that the measures of military collaboration that the United States had developed with Latin American countries should be continued and improved upon in the postwar period. Moreover World War II had served to stimulate general acceptance of the principle of collective security in the Americas. Argentina had remained recalcitrant during most of the war, and not until March 1945 did that state yield to pressure to declare war in order to become eligible for participation in the forthcoming United Nations Conference at San Franciso. Most of the American states had thus far withheld recognition from the government of Argentina, so that that government, and that of El Salvador as well, were absent when the special Inter-American Conference on Problems of War and Peace assembled at historic Chapultepec Castle on the outskirts of Mexico City in February 1945. The "Act of Chapultepec" that came out of that conference extended the principles of the declaration given at Havana to include attacks from within as well as from without the Americas.[33] "Every attack of a State against the integrity or the inviolability of the territory, or against the sovereignty or political independence of an American State," it said, "shall . . . be considered as an act of aggression against the other States which sign this Act."[34] More significantly, the act included a recommendation that a treaty be drawn up to establish procedures whereby threats or acts of aggression against any American republic would be met by the application as necessary of diplomatic, commercial, economic, financial, communications, or military sanctions.

Two-and-one-half years later all the American republics joined in signing the Inter-American Treaty of Reciprocal Assistance commonly referred to as the "Rio Treaty."[35] The treaty reaffirmed the principles of the act of Chapultepec with the provision, "The High Contracting Parties agree that an armed attack by any State against an American State shall be considered as an attack against all the American States and, consequently, each one of the said Contracting Parties undertakes to assist in meeting the attack in the exercise of the inherent right of individual or collective self-defense recognized by Article 51 of the Charter of the United Nations."[36] Succeeding articles spelled out procedures for enforcement actions, as had been recommended in the act of Chapultepec. Ratification followed relatively promptly—perhaps with some persuasion being exercised by the communist attack in Korea. By the end of November 1950 all of the American republics except Guatemala had deposited their instruments of ratification with the Pan American Union.[37]

The Rio Treaty marked the completion of the long evolutionary process toward general acceptance of collective security in the Americas. Then all that remained was to bring about a permanent organic structure for the various treaties and agencies that had been developing into a Pan American system since 1889. This came with the acceptance of a constitution at the Ninth International Conference of American States at Bogota, Colombia, in the spring of 1948. The "Bogota Charter"[38] established the Organization of American States as a regional organization under the United Nations. This brought together all the machinery for the peaceful settlement of disputes, for economic and cultural relations, for diplomatic consultation, and for enforcement actions, which had been set up by the inter-American conferences over the years.[39]

The Inter-American Defense Board remained a permanent autonomous agency "within the framework of the Organization of American States." During World War II the defense board had recommended from time to time the continuation of inter-American military collaboration in peacetime to cover such matters as tactical cooperation, communications, transportation, antisubmarine and antiaircraft defenses, military bases, local security and sabotage, standardization in the organization and training of armed forces, the use of manpower, production of strategic materials, and standardization of matériel. After the conclusion of the Rio Treaty the defense board reviewed and extended the scope of its studies in the light of the changing international conditions.[40]

After President Truman's proclamation of a national emergency in December 1950, the United States requested the Organization of American States to convoke a meeting of consultation of foreign ministers. Meeting in Washington in March and April 1951, the foreign ministers reviewed the problems of inter-American cooperation to meet the threat of communist aggression. The United States government hoped to win general political support for its policy of resisting communist expansion, to promote a stabilization of economic relations, and to promote effective military collaboration. This military collaboration would have as its object the development of additional military strength that might be put at the service of the United Nations, and, in particular, that might relieve the United States of the necessity of assuming responsibility for defense of Latin American areas. During World War II the commitment of United States troops in Latin America rose to 140,000 men. Afterward each country accepted the responsibility for its own defense and for cooperating in the defense of the Western Hemisphere as recommended by the Inter-American Defense Board. The question was whether Latin American defense forces could be developed to the point where this concept would be effective—and whether that could be done without stimulating military dictatorships in certain of the Latin American countries.[41]

MILITARY MISSIONS

A highly significant development in United States military collaboration with Latin American states that came with World War II was the establishment of U.S. military missions in these countries. Congress had authorized such missions in 1926,[42] but only a few—mostly naval missions—actually had been established by 1939. One major exception was Brazil where a four-man U.S. army mission had been advising and instructing the Brazilian army in coastal defense, chemical warfare, and ordnance since 1934. Otherwise most Latin American states had been depending for years on German, French, and Italian military missions. Thus the first requirement for United States leaders was to convince the Latin Americans that European armies were not necessarily the finest in the world.[43]

As relations with the axis powers approached open hostilities, the continuation of German and Italian military missions in Latin America became intolerable for the United States. Fortunately the Latin American governments proved to be receptive to the idea of accepting United States military missions, and presently all the southern republics except Uruguay had received such missions.[44]

In a somewhat different category were the commissions that were established in Mexico and Brazil. After the Declaration of Reciprocal Assistance and Cooperation for the Defense of the Nations of America at Havana in 1940 had prepared the way, the United States had proceeded to enter into mutual defense agreements with various of the Latin American states. Conversations began with Mexico in March 1941, which led to the establishment early in 1942 of the Joint Mexican-United States Defense Commission, modeled after a similar arrangement with Canada. A military agreement was signed with Brazil in May 1942, and the Joint Brazil-United States Defense Commission was established in Washington in August 1942. A counterpart to this commission was established in Rio de Janeiro in December 1942—the Joint Brazil-United States Military Commission. In effect this commission absorbed the personnel and functions of the previous military missions in Brazil. But now it was a matter of more direct participation by the United States in preparing studies on common defense problems and in providing assistance in training and procurement. Both the Brazilian and Mexican commissions continued their activities after the conclusion of World War II.[45]

The military missions (as distinct from the commissions) operated under contracts with the host governments. Those governments retained them for the purposes of advising and instructing the local military forces. Members of the missions received compensation from the host government amounting to about $1,000 to $2,000 a year (in addition to their army pay) and ordinarily including payment for transportation of the members of the mission their dependents, household goods, and private automobiles. Contracts usually ran for a four-year period with an option for renewal. During the operation of the contract, the host government accepted an obligation to employ no other foreign military personnel for the instruction of its forces. In June 1948 United States military missions or sections of commissions remained in thirteen of the Latin American republics. A total of 114 officers and 112 enlisted men of the United States were assigned to this duty. During the year 1947-48 seven contracts were renewed and negotiations were undertaken for the establishment of additional missions. In 1953 military missions or commissions (one or more, army, navy, air force) were operating in all twenty of the Latin American republics. Army missions were serving in twelve of the republics (in additon to the commissions in Brazil and Mexico). U.S. Army, Caribbean, had the responsibility for supervising and coordinating the activities of the army missions in Latin America.[46]

MATÉRIEL ASSISTANCE

Occupying an area where the danger of a major direct attack from the outside was relatively remote, Latin America during the period of the "Cold War" remained a secondary priority for receiving arms and equipment from the United States. Yet Latin American requirements could not be ignored. Aside from strategic considerations of defending the approaches to the Panama Canal, it was essential to keep U.S. access to critical raw materials in Latin America. But American officials could expect that any program of military assistance would be fraught with the same kind of difficulties that had attended lend-lease operations in World War II.

Just before World War II Germany and Italy had been the principal sources of military equipment for Latin America, and, faced with a huge mobilization program of its own while furnishing aid to hard-pressed allies in Europe and Asia, the United States had found it most difficult to replace the Axis powers as Latin America's arsenal. Some months before the passage of lend-lease, Congress had approved a resolution to permit the secretaries of war and the navy to sell or procure military equipment and ammunition for Latin American republics for coastal and antiaircraft defense.[47] But this had to be on a cash payment basis. The Lend-Lease Act of March 1941 provided the authority for transferring matériel, but little equipment could be spared for Latin America. For a time it was virtually impossible for the United States to make even token shipments of the newer weapons to Latin America. Secretary of War Stimson observed that the Latin American nations "not unnaturally . . . conceive of us as a huge arsenal well-stocked with all kinds of weapons, and when we tell them of our real condition they don't believe us. Being non-industrial nations, they have no conception of the time necessary for the manufacture of munitions. The consequent result is that they doubt our sincerity."[48]

Continuing German and Italian influence in some ares made the question of supplying arms both more urgent and more difficult. Internal instability in a number of the states made more doubtful the wisdom of supplying arms.[49] Moreover, the rivalries among nations added to the doubts regarding the efficacy of assistance programs of any kind. As an army historian of the period noted:

> Every individual allotment had to be calculated in the light of jealousies and rivalries between each state and its neighbors. Nor could the United States expect that the supply of arms would serve to purchase the good will of the Latin Americans. It was far more likely that the allocations to any particular state would arouse the envy and distrust of its neighbors.[50]

By the end of 1945 the dollar value of army aid furnished to Latin America under lend-lease arrangements had reached a total of $324 million. Yet this represented only 1 percent of all lend-lease assistance, and nearly 71 percent of the Latin American total was for Brazil, though all Latin American states except Argentina received some lend-lease aid. Nevertheless it appeared that lend-lease assistance made a significant contribution, in spite of the rivalries that sometimes greeted it, toward inter-American collaboration both during and after World War II.[51]

In the spring of 1946 the War Department joined with the navy in supporting an Inter-American Military Cooperation Bill. Intended to give effect to the sentiments expressed in the act of Chapultepec, the bill would have provided for the transfer of equipment to Latin American states as well as for assistance in the training of their forces under specific agreements to be concluded with each cooperating government. General Eisenhower, then chief of staff, told the House Foreign Affairs Committee that he considered it essential to continue sending military missions to Latin America whenever requested, to allot quotas in United States service schools for Latin Americans, and to transfer necessary equipment to Latin American countries for their peacetime establishments. He suggested that emphasis would be on providing the basic equipment necessary for training. Thus for the time being relatively few actual weapons would be needed.[52]

Considering that it lacked the general authority to do so, the War Department had not developed comprehensive plans for a broad program of military cooperation with any of the Latin American countries. The proposed act would give the department that authority.[53]

The Inter-American Military Cooperation Bill won a generally favorable response on the part of the House Committee on Foreign Affairs, and on 7 June 1946 that group reported the bill favorably with only minor amendments and recommended passage.[54] The response in the Senate was much less enthusiastic. The Senators were doubtful about taking up such a meausre so late in the session, and when it became clear that delays in submitting the bill had been due to differences within the State Department, some of the earlier support dwindled. The bill was allowed to die without ever coming to a vote.[55]

In the next Congress President Truman again tried to get passage of an Inter-American Military Cooperation Bill.[56] But once more opposition in the State Department interposed a delay. General Marshall, then secretary of state, continued to give his support to the plan, as he had while chief of staff. He joined with Secretary of War Patterson in June 1947 in urging passage of a military aid program for the Latin American countries in order to prevent their seeking weapons and training elsewhere. But Marshall did not have a united State Department behind him. Spruille Braden, assistant secretary of state for American republics affairs, opposed the program on the ground that it was likely to lead to an unfortunate armaments race within Latin America. Under Secretary of State Dean Acheson prepared a letter at the direction of Marshall to give a consensus of opinion of certain officials within the department. The letter indicated a belief that an armaments program would run counter to the department's considered policy of economic cooperation with Latin America with the objective of raising the standard of living in that area. Once more Congress let the bill die without acting upon it.[57]

Anticipating the passage of the Inter-American Military Cooperation Bill, the War Department by the spring of 1946 had prepared a comprehensive Western Hemisphere Defense Program. The program was to be based upon the transfer of surplus World War II property to Latin American military forces. No new procurements would be authorized. As it was ultimately worked out, the overall program called for the equipping of twenty-four Latin American divisions and sixty-seven air squadrons with about 1,530 aircraft. These forces were to receive complete initial organizational and individual equipment, less clothing (but including M-1 steel helmets) and less certain items that had been screened from the tables of allowances to apply to Western Hemisphere defense units. Five years' replacements for purely military-type items (excepting aircraft) on the basis of peacetime use rates in continental United States, and five years' allowance of training ammunition were to be provided. Equipment for the program appeared as an established War Department requirement, but no action to transfer it was to be taken until the Inter-American Military Cooperation Bill had been passed.[58]

Meanwhile the War Department undertook a program of interim allocations to make available surplus equipment for the equivalent of three divisions and thirty air squadrons. This would include vehicles to the extent of about 2,550 trucks, jeeps, and motor cars, and about 900 trailers. The State Department encouraged those allocations. In fact Secretary of State James F. Byrnes in July 1946 asked the War Department "to give every assistance possible" to representatives of other American governments in locating matériel needed to satisfy commitments under the Western Hemisphere Defense Program. He further suggested that responsible army officers in the Pacific area be advised of possible visits of representatives of the American republics. The War Assets Administration—the agency established to dispose of most of the surplus property in the continental United States—followed a policy of "freezing" property to meet veterans' priority requirements. In order to get around the difficulties and delays thus created, the War Department sought to obtain as much as possible of the needed equipment from overseas areas through the Office of the Foreign Liquidation Commissioner (Department of State)—the agency charged with disposing of most of the surplus property outside the continental United States.[59]

Actually a large share of the equipment made available to Latin American countries under the Western Hemisphere Defense Program Interim Allocation did come from overseas theaters. Failing to obtain passage of any legislation such as the proposed Inter-American Military Cooperation Act, the administration proceeded to make available surplus property under the authority of surplus property legislation and the act of 1940 authorizing the sale of weapons, equipment, and ammunition to American countries for the purpose of coastal and antiaircraft defense. The Office of the Foreign Liquidation Commissioner extended credits amounting to approximately $11,188,000—$10,017,000 in fiscal year 1947 and $1,161,000 in fiscal year 1948.[60] In addition the Export-Import Bank loans to Latin American countries, totalling $362,075,000 for the five fiscal years from 1946 to 1950 would be of indirect assistance in surplus property purchases.[61]

Direct appropriations for military cooperation with Latin American countries during the 1945 to 1951 period were limited to relatively small amounts ($400,000 to $1,000,000) each year "For all expenses necessary to enable the Secretary of War to adopt such measures, appropriate to the functions and activities of the War Department, as he may deem advisable, to promote better relations with the other American countries, including transportation and subsistence expenses, while traveling in the Western Hemisphere, of Army officers and students of other American countries and Army officers of the United States."[62]

Declarations of surplus property under the Interim Allocation Western Hemisphere Defense Program reached a total of over $98,126,000 at the original procurement cost of the property by the end of 1947. Slightly over half of this was for ground forces. In addition to items listed in the original interim allocation program, this included one year's maintenance spare parts and three years' training ammunition for the equipment that had been transferred previously under lend-lease.[63] After the immediate threat of war in the Western Hemisphere had passed, Argentina came in for a share of surplus military equipment with an initial declaration of $5,600,000 worth of property for that country in February 1948.[64] Initial declarations for the Dominican Republic and Honduras in August 1948 brought the number of American republics participating in the program to seventeen.[65] With the completion of the interim allocation program in 1949, nearly $120,000,000 worth (at original cost) of surplus equipment had been shipped to the Latin American republics.[66]

After the expiration of lend-lease and war surplus disposal legislation, the army had no legal authority to turn over military equipment to the Latin American countries except for the cash sale of equipment or the giving of assistance in procurement under the act of 1940. Limited assistance in procurement from current production for cash payment was the extent of the army's matériel assistance to American republics until they came under the Mutual Defense Assistance Program in 1951.[67]

After the countries accepted the principle of an integrated defense for the Americas at the meeting of foreign ministers in March 1951, immediate demands arose for equipment and training that would enable Latin American forces to take in effective part in common defense plans. By June 1951 requests for over $100 million worth of military equipment for Latin American forces were pending. If a program of collective defense in the Americas was to amount to anything more than hopes on paper, it was clear that the United

States would have to make available substantial assistance. Without such assistance it was doubtful that several Latin American countries could make any contribution to common defense missions at all. The support of even one regimental combat team would take the entire national budget of some of these countries. But, as in World War II, demands for equipment for Latin America were coming at a time when little could be spared from active operations in the Far East and from the build-up of forces in the potentially decisive area of Europe. Nevertheless, Latin America was added to the Mutual Defense Assistance Program by the Mutual Security Act of 1951 with a military assistance program of $38 million for fiscal year 1952.[68]

From the point of view of the United States, the objectives of providing military aid for Latin America were the same essentially that they had been a decade before—to secure sources of strategic materials in Latin America; to keep open the lines of access to those materials; to have armed forces in the Latin American countries prepared to act against air and submarine attacks, and to reduce the call on United States forces for defense in those countries.[69] Here was where United States military leaders hoped to gain over the situation that had prevailed during World War II by developing an effective program of collective defense whereby an important part of the more than one hundred thousand troops the United States had maintained in Latin America during World War II might be replaced by Latin American forces.

While few would have questioned the general desirability of building up an integrated inter-American defense or of furnishing United States equipment in order to do so, any program of assistance to Latin America had to be considered in relation to the worldwide interests and commitments of the United States. A most important consideration was the effect that military assistance to Latin America would have on the support of operations in Korea and on mutual defense assistance to the North Atlantic treaty countries— where most of MDAP was scheduled to go.[70] The warning that Henry L. Stimson had given shortly after assuming his duties as secretary of war in 1940 might have reapplication: "We should refrain from being fooled by the evident bluff of Hitler's so-called fifth-column movements in South America. On the face of them, they are attempts to frighten us from sending help where it will be most effective."[71]

As was the case with other countries receiving grant aid under the mutual defense assistance program, the Latin American countries each had to sign a bilateral agreement with the United States in order to become eligible for assistance. The Joint Chiefs of Staff approved programs for particular countries on the basis of the willingness and capability of the country to carry out certain missions under the common defense scheme prepared by the Inter-American Defense Board. The mutual defense asistance program for Latin America was on a much more limited scale than the program for European and other countries. Whereas assistance in other countries was given on the basis of support for all or a major part of the armed forces concerned, in Latin

America it was restricted to certain small segments having specific missions to perform in hemispheric defense plans.[72]

A provision of the Mutual Security Act prohibited anyone in the pay of a foreign government from serving on a military assistance advisory group (MAAG). This at once made the members of United States military missions in Latin America ineligible for such an assignment as long as they received additional pay from their host governments. Yet it would have appeared strange and inefficient to send a MAAG to a place where a military mission already was serving—and such a step might have impaired the prestige and the effectiveness of the original mission. The solution to the dilemma finally adopted was to appoint one officer, responsible for the property involved, and two or three enlisted men to be the "MAAG," and then for the existing military missions to carry out most of the activities of a MAAG.[73]

Existing military missions assumed mutual defense assistance program functions in Colombia, Cuba, Ecuador, and Peru, as soon as the required bilateral agreements had become effective with those countries. The American section of the Joint Brazil-United States Military Commission at Rio de Janeiro assumed mutual defense assistance functions in Brazil. Shipments of equipment to Chile, Uruguay, and the Dominican Republic had to await the arrival of military assistance advisory groups, since there were no military missions in those countries. No other Latin American countries had concluded bilateral agreements with the United States by June 1953. Negotiations had been proceeding for several months with Mexico, but so far no agreement had been concluded and that country had not asked formally for arms assistance. All the agreements were based on the Rio Treaty, and all contained the declaration required by the law that the assistance to be given was in the interest of the security of the United States. Communist and nationalist opposition delayed acceptance of many of the agreements. The first of the agreements to become effective was the one with Ecuador on 20 February 1952. The agreement with Cuba became effective on 7 March 1952, with Peru on 8 April 1952, with Colombia on 17 April 1952, with Chile on 10 July 1952, with Brazil on 19 May 1953, with the Dominican Republic on 10 June 1953, and with Uruguay on 11 June 1953.[74]

When the mutual defense assistance program for Latin America was being set up in 1951, the Caribbean Command recommended that the headquarters be made the coordinating agency for the program, but in the spring of 1953 responsibilities for coordinating MDAP in Latin America remained obscure. There was no central agency for either the interservice coordination of MDAP activities or for the coordination of the army's assistance program in Latin America below the Washington level. Although exercising general supervision over the army missions in Latin America that were responsible for a large part of the MDAP activities, U.S. Army, Caribbean, still had received no definite assignment of responsibilities for the mutual defense assistance program. The Caribbean Air Command, at the same time, exercised control over the air force portion of MDAP as well as over the air force sections of the military missions.[75]

When shipments of arms to Latin America under MDAP begin, little progress had been made toward developing effective armed forces in the American republics. It was clear that for some time to come the United States would have to rely chiefly on its own resources for the defense of the southern parts of the Western Hemisphere.[76]

By May 1953 generally satisfactory progress could be reported in the equipping of an antiaircraft battalion in Peru and another in Colombia—where about one-third of the equipment had been received, but only enough uncrated for the detachment of 630 men that had been organized up to that time. Efforts to organize an antiaircraft battalion in Ecuador were less satisfactory. Indeed the United States ambassador to Quito questioned the ability of Ecuador to operate the equipment of an antiaircraft battalion, even though officers of the military mission suggested that the technical difficulties involved were no greater than those encountered in regard to the signal, air force, and navy equipment that Ecuadorians already were operating.[77]

The Latin American countries came into the mutual defense assistance program late, and then they remained in a relatively minor position in receiving assistance. The total of all MDAP funds allocated to Latin America as of 30 April 1953 amounted to $68.6 million ($35.7 million for army equipment and assistance, $13.7 million for the navy, and $19.2 million for the air force). This represented less than one-half of 1 percent of overall MDAP allocations.[78] In the program proposed for fiscal year 1954, the share for Latin America amounted to $20 million—again one half of 1 percent of the total.[79] In addition to grant assistance, most of the Latin American countries continued to buy excess matériel at about 10 percent of procurement cost and to purchase other equipment from current production under the "reimbursable aid" provisions of the Mutual Security Act. By 30 June 1953 Latin American countries had spent something over $26.4 million for these purchases of property having an original cost of nearly $140 million.[80]

In times of world troubles, Latin America had for the United States an importance that could not be ignored. But the interests of th United States in Latin America were admittedly secondary to some of those elsewhere, and when Congress called for economy cuts the modest assistance program for that area could be cut at the least immediate peril to American security. Pleading for a continuation of the Latin American program for fiscal year, 1954, John M. Cabot, assistant secretary of state for inter-American affairs stated his case in this way:

> This program is only one of the many things we are doing to assure maximum military, economic, and political cooperation from Latin American countries in the event of global war. Under bilateral agreements, Latin American countries participating in the program have agreed to prepare units

of their armed forces for specific hemisphere defense missions. They are contributing money, manpower, and equipment for the creation of these units, and we in turn are providing them with training and equipment to meet their deficiencies. By agreeing to prepare these units, the countries believe—and rightly so—that they have made an important new commitment to the United States. In fact, Communist and extreme nationalist elements in Latin America have charged that the local governments have committed themselves too far, that they have entered into agreements which are not really reciprocal at all, but consist mainly of unilateral concessions to the United States. Latin American governments have found it difficult to persuade even non-Communist elements that the agreements are two-sided, that they provide for a significant contribution of assistance from the United States. Failure to appropriate money for the program this year would very likely play into the hands of these Communists and extreme nationalists, who would charge the United States with lack of interest in the program. Moreover, our failure to appropriate funds for the program might cause the governments themselves to wonder whether we have a genuine interest in continuing the program. . . .

It would appear to me to be both poor economy and poor inter-American politics not to continue the program. Considering the difficulties that have had to be overcome, I believe that great progress has been made during the eighteen months since Congress first authorized this program of increased inter-American cooperation in the military field.[81]

Whether the military aid program to Latin America was making any really significant contribution to the actual defense of the Americas only the future could tell. But in some ways the hemispheric defense programs had a significance extending far beyond what local defenses actually had been improved. This was in helping to pave the way toward general support of broader programs. Though the whole concept of hemispheric defense rested in part on the support of people anxious to rationalize their fundamentally isolationist outlook, this support tended at times to lead out of isolationism to broader fields of international cooperation. The American Republics Act of 1940—the law authorizing the sale by the government and assistance in procurement of equipment for coastal and antiaircraft defense to the latin American countries was a precedent for the "reimbursable aid" provisions that appeared in the Lend-Lease Act of 1941 and then reappeared in the Mutual Defense Assistance Act of 1949. Though the proposed Inter-American Military Cooperation Act (1946 and 1947) never became law, it was one of the forerunners, in a sense, of the much broader Mutual Defense Assistance Act of 1949, and specifically it helped pave the way of adding Title 4, Latin America, to the Mutual Security Act of 1951. With the Rio Treaty of 1947 the United States broke with its traditional policy of avoiding peacetime alliances, and provided for this country an important precedent for accepting another regional arrangement for collective defense in the North Atlantic Treaty two years later.

Defense of the Northern Approaches

COOPERATION WITH CANADA

Though it remained outside the Pan American system and the Organization of American States—presumably because of its traditional ties with the British Commonwealth and an unwillingness to accept any appearance of hemispheric isolation—Canada held an area of greatest strategic importance for the American republics. As doubts began to arise in 1940 about Britain's capability of holding out against the Axis powers, Canada almost instinctively drew closer to the United States. Strong economic ties—Canada was the most important country in terms of foreign trade of the United States—common political and cultural traditions, and above all, a sense of common danger inevitably brought Canada into intimate association with the United States in preparing for the defense of North America.[82]

President Roosevelt had anticipated this over a year before the outbreak of the war in an address at Kingston, Ontario, 18 August 1938, when he said, "The Dominion of Canada is part of the sisterhood of the British Empire. I give to you assurance that the people of the United States will not stand idly by if domination of Canadian soil is threatened by any other Empire."[83]

More significant was the conference between President Roosevelt and Prime Minister Mackenzie King of Canada at Ogdenburg, New York, in August 1940. Following hard upon the disquieting news of the capitulation of France, the conference met in an atmosphere of apprehension concerning whether Britain would be able to hold out through the coming winter. An immediate result was the creation of the Permanent Joint Board on Defense. Charged with coordinating general plans for the defense of North America, the board was to study questions of matériel and personnel as well as tactical and strategic problems relating to the conduct of military operations by land, sea, and air.[84]

The Permanent Joint Board on Defense was but the first of a series of joint agencies set up between Canada and the United States for defense cooperation while the latter was yet technically a neutral country. Others were the Matériel Coordinating Committee, the Joint Economic Committees, and the Joint War Production Board. After the Pearl Harbor attack these agencies continued to function, and cooperation between the two countries increased. At this point, however, considerations of global strategy and logistics, treated principally through joint boards set up by the United States and Great Britain, superseded what previously had been restricted largely to matters relating to the defense of the Western Hemisphere.[85]

With the ending of World War II hostilities in 1945, the Permanent Joint Board on Defense turned its attention to peacetime problems. It was taken for granted that defense collaboration would continue indefinitely in the postwar period. The Permanent Joint Board truly became a permanent agency.[86]

Delivery of U.S. Army supplies on Baffin Bay, Canada.

In addition the two countries maintained a Joint United States–Canada Industrial Mobilization Planning Committee. After the outbreak of the Korean conflict they concluded agreements on the standardization of weapons and equipment. This made possible reciprocal purchasing agreements that worked to the advantage of both countries in their rearmament programs.[87] Developments in air power, and possibility of air attack by way of the Arctic regions made close cooperation with Canada indispensable for the air defense of the United States.

As it had developed in World War II, so it was afterward—military collaboration with the United States was much broader than Western Hemispheric defense as such. Canada was not a part of the Pan American system, but it was an active member of the North Atlantic Treaty Organization. After the absorption of the four other regional planning groups of NATO by Supreme Headquarters Allied Powers Europe, the Canada–United States Regional Planning Group continued its functions of operational planning for the North American area.[88]

In spite of its close military collaboration, Canada was almost unique among the active allies of the United States in maintaining itself virtually free of grants of American matériel. In the eleven-year period from 1940 to 1951, Canada received credits from the United States totalling about $175 million; by 30 June 1951 less than $8 million of this remained outstanding.[89] Canada obtained no outright grants during this time. On the contrary, Canada was the largest cash purchaser under the mutual defense assistance program—as it had been under the lend-lease program during World War II. Purchases through MDAP machinery, in which United States military procurement agencies handled the purchasing on a reimburseable basis, gave to this foreign country the advantages of this procurement machinery while making possible better coordination of the overall military procurement programs in the United States. Canada itself adopted a policy of furnishing mutual aid. When it undertook its large-scale program of standardization and of converting its equipment from British to American types, it released the British-type equipment for other NATO units in Europe.[90]

ALASKA

Americans in the 1950s were turning their attention more and more to what currently was being considered a region of increasing importance for American security—the frozen lands and seas of the north that lay on the shortest routes between North America and Eurasia, and over which any effective air attacks against the United States itself seemed most likely to come. As seemed logical under the circumstances, the unified commands charged with the defense of the northern reaches of North America were organized under the executive agency of the air force.

In the 1920s General "Billy" Mitchell had seen Alaska as the key to the control of the North Pacific. By the 1950s the wisdom of this observation seemed more apparent than ever. Alaska was being regarded more and more as a guardian over the Arctic air routes from the Soviet Union. Impressed with the importance of Alaska's location after a visit to the region, Secretary of the Army Royall told a congressional committee in March 1949:

> When I found out that the shortest route from Washington, D. C., to western Australia was by way of northern Alaska, it further opened my eyes to the geography of the world. When I realized that you can leave Washington— as our schedule provided, but we did not quite make it— after lunch and eat supper in Anchorage; and leave Anchorage the next morning in a Constellation, and eat supper in Japan, I realized how close neighbors we now are to both sides of the world. There is a great necessity for Army troops to hold and protect those fields, in the event of war. We would need them in that event for the defense of Alaska and for the interception of an air attack against the United States, if any attacks came over our extreme north (western) boundaries. We probably need them for offensive or retaliatory action if war should come. I believe we should increase the forces in Alaska, as soon as we have facilities to do so.[91]

The dominant factor affecting military activities in Alaska was, of course, the climate. Extremes of heat and cold, rain and snow, and fog and high winds in various places combined with rugged or swampy terrain to make operations on the ground most difficult. Almost continuous heavy fog in summer and violent recurring storms in winter hampered operations in the Aleutian Islands area. Along the coast of the Gulf of Alaska, winds and heavy precipitation were big problems. The military port of Whittier on occasion had been covered by as much as ninety-six inches of snow in four days; at such times virtually all other activities came to a standstill, while all available manpower turned to clearing snow from rooftops to prevent their collapse. Snowslides were frequent along the Alaska Railroad; at times the tracks were covered to depths of five feet for distances of a thousand feet. In some areas it was dangerous for trains to cross wooden trestles in high winds. Protected from strong winds and heavy snowfall by surrounding mountain ranges, the area of Anchorage and the Matanuska Valley had a relatively temperate climate.

Temperatures were most extreme in the vast Yukon Valley north of the Alaska Range. A record summer temperature of a hundred degrees had been recorded at Fort Yukon, and days of ninety-degree temperatures were not uncommon. During the long winter nights in central Alaska, temperatures frequently fell to fifty and sixty degrees below zero. But precipitation was much lighter, and the winds less severe, than in the areas along the coast. Temperatures in winter were not as low on the northern Arctic slope, north of the Brooks Range, but the higher winds made sensible temperatures lower; high winds in low temperatures exposed men to the effects of wind-chill.

North of the Alaska Range permanently frozen subsoil, the permafrost, added immeasurably to problems of construction, sanitation and military operations. Under a campfire the ground would thaw and drown the fire in a mass of soggy mud. It took dynamite to dig fox holes and trenches in this rock-hard ground. In summer, travel was exhausting over the waterlogged layer of soil that thawed above the permafrost. Individual equipment had to be designed not only to protect men against the cold of winter but also against the annoyances of insects and flies in summer. In lake or swampy regions as many as 100 to 125 mosquitoes would alight on a man's hand in less than a minute. Big horseflies, deerflies, and mooseflies, and small blackflies and midges as well, pestered anyone frequenting marshy or wooded areas in summer.[92]

After the fashion of air force usage, the joint staff of the Alaskan Command was organized in six "directorates," but the division of functions and the designations were those common in joint headquarters. In addition to the J–1, J–2, J–3 and J–4 ordinarily found in joint headquarters, the Alaskan Command had a J–5 for communications, and J–6 for weather. Army officers headed those directorates representing areas of the army's greatest responsibilities—J–4, logistics, and J–5, communications. The U.S. Army,

Unloading supplies and equipment at Galema airport, Alaska, January 1948.

Alaska, with headquarters at Elmendorf Air Force Base (near Anchorage), close to Alaskan Command headquarters, was responsible for the logistic support of army units and of the air force above station level for common use, army-purchased supplies, including both supply and depot maintenance; for the operation of mainland ports, and for rail and highway transportation. The Alaskan Air Command was responsible for base-level support of air force units and for certain common support of army troops located on air bases, for the supply of all air-force-type equipment, and for air transportation within the theater. The naval component of the command, the Alaskan sea frontier, was responsible for logistic operations at naval bases, for furnishing gasoline and oil and shipping for the other services in the Aleutian, Bering Sea, and Arctic Ocean areas, and for all construction contracting in the Aleutians. The army operated the Alaskan Communications System, for civilian as well as military service, directly under the chief signal officer. Major military construction was the responsibility of the Alaska district engineer. The Alaska district was one of four districts under the North Pacific division—with headquarters in Portland, Oregon—of the Office of the Chief of Engineers.[93]

Plans approved by the Joint Chiefs of Staff for the defense of Alaska anticipated the holding of certain critical areas and dependence upon air and naval

Soldiers build snow huts, or igloos, during a training exercise near Big Delta, Alaska, 1948.

action or mobile ground forces to attempt to defend other areas. No preparations were being made for the ground defense of the Seward Peninsula and of other areas close to Siberia, which, it was assumed, would fall quickly in the event of a Russian invasion. Military commanders in Alaska hoped that enemy use of these areas could be denied by bombing, though this was a plan highly unpopular with the local residents. During World War II most of the military effort in Alaska had been on the Aleutian Islands, in the direction of Japan. In the 1950s emphasis had shifted to bases on the mainland to offer defense against attacks—particularly air attacks—from the west and northwest.[94]

The principal installations during this period were the Port of Whittier; Elmendorf Air Force Base and Fort Richarson, near Anchorage; Ladd Air Force Base and Eilson Air Force Base, near Fairbanks; the army's Arctic indoctrination and test center at Big Delta, and the naval base at Kodiak. Army supply, construction, and services generally fell into two categories—for forces south of the Alaska Range, and for those north of the range.[95]

As a part of the deployment of forces to strategic areas overseas during the emergency precipitated by the attack in Korea, an additional 120-mm. gun antiaircraft battalion went to Alaska in the summer of 1952. But forces available to defend such a vast territory remained relatively small. An Alaskan National Guard with logistic support from army installations in the territory was organized in 1949, but in early 1951 it had developed to the extend of only two scant battalions and cadres for two other battalions. No large reserve forces from a total population numbering less than 130,000 people could be expected. At this time the total strength of all reserve components in Alaska was less than one thousand men.[96]

The shortage of troops in Alaska in proportion to the military tasks to be done was especially noticeable with respect to service troops. Officers of the army general staff had learned to expect criticism from Congress generally aimed at cutting down on the number of service troops being used, but members of the Senate preparedness subcommittee who visited Alaska in September and October 1950 reported as follows:

> There does not appear to be an adequate logistical support organization to meet the requirements of the theater. In the Anchorage area it is a regular practice to use infantry troops to perform duties for the supply department. This is curtailing their training and they would not be available, in the event of attack, for such duties. No military organization can function efficiently unless its logistical system is adequate to support the troops operating within its area. Based on subcommittee investigations it is believed that the number of service troops allocated for this purpose and the facilities available to them are inadequate to meet even the requirements of the present forces in the theater. In the event of war there are other commitments to the theater which would have to be supported out of stocks on hand and through normal supply channels. If they are submarginal (as indicated) in

relation to present requirements it is probable that they will fail completely in the event of wartime operations in the theater.[97]

One of the things limiting the number of troops being stationed in Alaska was the lack of facilities— particularly of troop and family housing—to accommodate them. After his visit to Alaska early in 1949, Secretary of the Army Royall declared that troop conditions there were "deplorable." He reported unsatisfactory and inadequate barracks for many enlisted men as well as an acute lack of housing for married enlisted men and junior officers. Recreational facilities were, he said, uniformly insufficient. He noted that spirits were high where housing for soldiers and dependents was adequate, but where housing was poor, morale was also.[98]

Matériel as well as men had to have protection from the elements. Lack of covered storage made it necessary to store most supplies in Kivora huts (tarpaulin-covered wooden frames)—the roofs of which had to be cleared after every snowfall to prevent collapse—or in the open where equipment would be covered with snow all winter but then would deteriorate rapidly with the coming of the spring thaws.[99]

The cold weather, deep snows, heavy rains, and high winds that made construction urgent also made it difficult and costly. The great distances that materials had to be moved and the sparse population from which to draw construction workers added further to the costs. A warehouse worth $100,000 in Seattle could be expected to cost $250,000 in the Anchorage area, and $300,000 in the area north of the Alaska Range. Even before the increase of prices had set in fully after the Korean attack, a unit of cement that cost $17.75 in Seattle cost $48.77 in Anchorage, or $58.57 in Fairbanks. Prefabricated steel delivered to Ladd Air Force Base cost 2.41 times as much as it did in Seattle. Wages in Alaska were approximately 65 percent higher than in Seattle.[100]

Construction projects themselves were subject to the delays of weather, the relatively short season for outdoor construction work, and all the administrative delays common to public construction in remote places. Special precautions were necessary in putting up buildings to withstand winds and snow. In the area north of the Alaska Range special care had to be taken not to disturb the permafrost. Permafrost itself was as hard as rock, and would support great weights, but water pipes or masonry foundations set in it would cause it to thaw and the foundations to crumble. This made it necessary to provide for insulation beneath buildings; for large buildings it was necessary to excavate permafrost and replace it with gravel or other materials before foundations could be laid.[101]

Time-consuming legislative and executive procedures awaited the development of any plans for new military construction. Delays arising from local conditions were in addition to those relating to approval of the project in Washington before construction work could begin. The ordinary procedures for giving effect to a construction project included the following steps:

1. Item included in master plan.
2. Item submitted on Form 726.
3. Item approved by Logistics Division (G–4).
4. Price approved by Office of the Chief of Engineers.
5. Item submitted to Secretary of the Army.
6. Item approved by Secretary of the Army.
7. Item submitted in program to Secretary of Defense.
8. Program approved by Munitions Board.
9. Program approved by Secretary of Defense.
10. Legislation submitted to Bureau of the Budget.
11. Legislation approved by Bureau of the Budget.
12. Legislation reviewed by House Armed Services Committee.
13. Legislation approved by House Armed Services Committee.
14. Legislation passed by House of Representatives.
15. Legislation reviewed by Senate Armed Services Committee.
16. Legislation approved by Senate Armed Serivces Committee.
17. Legislation passed by Senate.
18. Conference between House and Senate to resolve differences, if necessary.
19. Conference report adopted by House and Senate.
20. Enrolled enactment report to the President prepared by (Department of Defense).
21. Legislation signed by the President and becomes law.
22. Budget directive issued by Army Comptroller to commands.
23. Stations prepare budget items for projects included in legislation.
24. Item included in command budget submitted to Army Comptroller.
25. Item reviewed by Office of the Chief of Engineers and placed in Military Construction, Army Budget.
26. Budget, reviewed by Budget Advisory Committee, Department of the Army.
27. Budget approved by Chief of Staff.
28. Budget approved by Joint Chiefs of Staff.
29. Budget approved by Secretary of Defense.
30. Budget submitted to Bureau of Budget.
31. Budget approved by Bureau of Budget.
32. Appropriation bill reviewed by House Appropriations Committee.
33. Appropriation bill approved by House Appropriations Committee.
34. Appropriation bill passed by House of Representatives.
35. Appropriation bill reviewed by Senate Appropriations Committee.
36. Appropriation bill approved by Senate Committee.
37. Appropriation bill passed by Senate.
38. Conference between House and Senate to resolve differences, if necessary.
39. Conference report adopted by House and Senate.
40. Appropriation bill signed by President.
41. Construction program approved by Secretary of Defense.
42. Funds apportioned by Bureau of the Budget to Army Comptroller.
43. Funds allotted by Army Comptroller to Office, Chief of Engineers.

44. Design Directive issued to district engineer by Office of Chief of Engineers.
45. Control estimate submitted by District Engineer.
46. Construction directive issued to district engineer by Office, Chief of Engineers.[102]

It yet remained for the district engineer to advertise for bids or to undertake contract negotiations, award the contract, and then supervise the execution of the contract.

Before World War II Chilcoot Barracks in southeast Alaska was the only permanent army post in the territory. It had facilities for three hundred men. Buildings erected under a permanent construction program begun in 1939 and 1940 at Elmendorf Field and Ladd Field, changed after the Pearl Harbor attack to one of temporary structures, had deteriorated beyond use. Early in 1946 the Joint Chiefs of Staff approved a long-range program for construction to meet the requirements of a permanent peacetime garrison. Previously it had been the practice for troops allocated for the defense of Alaska to remain in the continental United States during the winter months. In 1947 the joint chiefs revised their concept of operations in Alaska to shift the emphasis to the Anchorage and Fairbanks areas. The revised construction program was intended to provide necessary facilities for all forces allocated to Alaska by the end of 1952. Actually by 1951 practically all forces allocated for Alaska, including the increases resulting from the critical international situation, were located there—in what permanent housing had been completed and in temporary structures that still were usable.[103]

Because of the uncertain price and wage conditions prevailing in 1946, the reluctance of competent contractors to bid on jobs in Alaska unless protected by escalator clauses, and because of the very short time available to them, the initial contracts were made on a cost-plus-a-fixed-fee basis. Work hardly had begun when cost estimates began to be revised upward. One group of items estimated to cost $58,900,000 at the date of the contract later were reestimated at $164,500,000. Engineering officers attributed the increases to the rising costs of labor and materials, to an unusually severe winter in 1946–47, to a shipping strike, to the shortage of skilled labor willing to remain in Alaska, to the lack of information relative to site conditions, the lack of plans and specifications sufficient for accurate estimating, and to the speeding up on construction of certain facilities, and to the heavy costs of contractors' facilities. In 1948 and 1949 the district engineer was able to change to competitive-bid, lump-sum contracts. In order to assure competition in bidding by reducing unknown factors for the contractors, the district engineer undertook the operation of messes for the construction workers, the operation of a concrete batch plant at Fort Richardson, the listing of government-owned equipment and materials that would be available to the contractors, and the preparation of a comprehensive brochure describing the geography, climate, economic conditions, and other factors affecting construction in Alaska. In addition the district engineer, Colonel William E. Potter, personally appeared before groups of contractors in the continental United States in order to interest them in the Alaska work. Bids on the work for the summer of 1949 resulted in lower unit prices than had previously been obtained. However, the expansion of the program and additional rises in the general price level after the Korean attack soon promised to reverse that trend toward lower construction costs.[104]

By the end of 1950 Congress had appropriated over $290,000,000—virtually all that had been asked—for army and air force construction in Alaska. Another $100,000,000 had been authorized. To complete the then-planned consolidated developmental program it would take an estimated $543,300,000 in addition to the funds already appropriated or authorized. Congress authorized $109,453,730 for army construction and $213,838,000 for air force construction in Alaska during 1952, but the authorizing legislation was not approved until 28 September 1951, and the appropriation act to finance it was not approved until 1 November. This left too little time to permit the completion of the contracts as planned, and in Alaska when major outdoor construction work was not finished before the onset of winter, it simply had to be carried over until the next season.

Facilities and labor at this time were sufficient for the Alaskan Command to place and have carried out approximately $225,000,000 in construction a year, so that it was not likely that this $323,000,000 program could be carried out in a single season, but every day lost in awarding contracts and beginning work would mean many days lost in the completion dates of the projects. The delay in the Alaska 1952 program was one of the major factors in the overall balance of $1.1 billion in unobligated army construction funds shown on 31 March 1953. As a result of this unobligated balance, the army requested appropriations neither for fiscal year 1953 nor 1954. The army did request a supplementary appropriation for fiscal year 1953 that included $71,900,000 for continuation of the construction program in Alaska. This represented about 36 percent of the program then remaining to be financed. The plan was to have it all financed by fiscal year 1956, and to have the construction essentially completed by 1958. Total military construction completed or programmed through fiscal year 1953 represented outlays of approximately $750 million. In July 1952 the district engineer estimated that another $400 million of work remained to be programmed. Thus it seemed clear that the total cost of the current postwar military construction program ultimately would reach well over a billion dollars.[105]

An outstanding feature of the new construction program for the army was a $5,900,000 composite building at Whittier—a six-story, concrete frame building with concrete block curtain walls, which included squad rooms for 750 men, bachelor officers quarters, mess hall, administrative offices, classrooms, a theater, service club, bowling alleys, post exchange, and infirmary. Begun in 1951, the building was ready for occupancy in the spring of 1953.[106] A thing that distressed members of a House armed services special subcommittee visiting Alaska in September 1951 was failure to carry out such coordination in other places where army and air force units were involved. Although many activities were to be operating under a single roof at Whittier, headquarters facilities for air force and army units were to be in two separate buildings at Eilson Air Force Base, two service clubs were being built for enlisted men, and more unexplainable still was a plan for building two three- hundred-man chapels—one for army and one for air force—within about six hundred feet of each other.[107]

Nearly a year and a half after Secretary of the Army Royall had reported that troop conditions in Alaska were "deplorable" and that there was an acute shortage of family housing, a "task force" from the Preparedness Subcommittee of the Senate Committee on Armed Services reported, "The housing for dependents in the Alaskan theater is shocking. There appears to be no justification for the Federal Government not realizing its obligation to the families of military personnel permanently assigned to Alaska and supplying adequate shelter for them."[108]

A year after that in September 1951 a special subcommittee of the House Armed Services Committee reported:

> Housing accommodations in Alaska for military personnel. . . are still shocking, still exorbitant. Military personnel, officers as well as enlisted men, with their families, are living in huts, trailers, tents, substandard and deplorably deficient quarters of all types and descriptions, and many are paying rents that would be considered ridiculously high in the United States. Sanitary and bathing facilities, in many of these areas, are as far as a half mile from the families' dwellings, in regions where the wintertime temperature drops as low as 50° to 60° below zero.[109]

Again, with time, conditions began to improve. In spite of delays and difficulties, barracks and headquarters and housing units eventually did appear. A notable saving in the construction of family units resulted from the competitive bidding in 1950. On 21 March the district engineer issued invitations to bid on the construction of four hundred dwelling units at Fort Richardson. The invitations called for bids on five optional sets of specifications, including a design recommended by the Defense Housing Commission, which had made an inspection trip to Alaska a few months earlier. Eighteen contractors submitted bids. They indicated that a three-bedroom house with basement could be built at Richardson for even less than the ceiling price recommended by the commission for a house without a basement. The low bid was at $14,772 a unit for substantially the same house that cost $35,630 under the 1949 construction program at Fort Richardson. Bids taken for family housing at Eilson Air Force Base resulted in a low bid of $17,389 for a three-bedroom unit with a basement, where a similar unit had cost $42,650 under the 1949 program. Still the House armed services special subcommittee that investigated construction in Alaska in October 1951 concluded that a great deal of unjustifiable expense was going into the construction of family housing. This was because of a policy under which all family units were being constructed with three bedrooms even though over half of the married officers and nearly two-thirds of the enlisted men entitled to family quarters had a wife only or a wife and only one child. Moreover the limitation that Congress had set in the permissible floor space for family units—1,080 square feet—was being used as the minimum as well as the maximum size for the housing designs.[110]

By the end of the 1952 construction season, dependent housing comparable to that found at military installations in the continental United States generally was available at the four principal posts—Fort Richardson and Elmendorf, Ladd Field, and Eilson Air Force Base—and to a more limited extent at Whittier and Big Delta.[111] From 1946 to the summer of 1952 a total of 2,496 family units costing about $57 million had been completed; 977, representing an outlay of $22 million, were under construction, and 1,623 units had been programmed and $37 million funded but had not yet been placed under contract. This total of 5,096 family units (2,583 for army and 2,513 for air force personnel) represented perhaps 55 to 65 percent of the total planned program.[112]

A special subcommittee of the House Committee on Expenditures in the Executive Departments (Committee on Government Operations), headed by Representative Chet Holifield of California, had some sharp criticisms for certain aspects of the housing construction program in Alaska. While recognizing the serious difficulties of construction in Alaska, and the difficulties under which the Office of the Chief of Engineers operated in performing its tasks with the limited personnel available, the subcommittee reported:

> The subcommittee's attention was drawn to military housing construction in Alaska by reports of poor performance by contractors and lax supervision on the part of the district office of the Corps of Engineers. An investigation was undertaken by the General Accounting Office and the subcommittee held hearings in Alaska. . . .
>
> From a review of the background developments in Alaska housing, the subcommittee observes that this program is marked by trial and error and considerable lack of expert knowledge as to the most suitable housing design, materials and construction methods to meet economy demands and military needs. Certain materials specified in the design, lagging construction of utilities, possible excessive excavation in the permafrost area, and failure to take exact account of family needs and available private housing, add up to an uneven approach to economy in Alaska housing.
>
> Examination of specific housing contracts leads the sub-committee to observe that the district engineer tends to rely too heavily on the contractors' formal responsibility, to be too casual in acceptance of shop drawings which omit pertinent details, and to be overgenerous in approving modifications, which add to the cost of contract administration. In part the shortcomings lie with the technical divisions within the district office, and in

part with the inspections system in the field.[113]

Accessibility was one of the biggest problems of construction in Alaska, as it was of all military operations in that area. If transportation set the limits to logistics in Korea, it was much more of a limiting factor in Alaska where rugged or frequently marshy terrain had to be overcome in covering the great distances between bases.

The principal ports of Alaska were Seward, a commercially operated port on the Kenai Peninsula where most civilian goods intended for mainland destinations arrived, and Whittier, a completely military port north of Seward on Prince William Sound. An ice-free, year-round port, Whittier had deep-water berthing for four ships. An annual rainfall of close to 180 inches, an annual snowfall of about 200 inches, and winter winds reaching a velocity of fifty miles an hour made conditions for handling ships and cargo there something less than ideal, but its situation was convenient to the military operations for which it was used. Here the mountains came down practically to the water's edge in such a way as to leave little room for the expansion of port facilities. Only a railroad line provided egress from the port to the interior. Development of the port began in 1942 for the purpose of supporting World War II activities and it began operations upon the completion of connecting railroad tunnels in 1943. The army turned the port over to the Alaska Railroad and the Department of the Interior in December 1945, and five months later it was closed down altogether. Then the army reopened it as a military port in September 1946. Seward had the advantage of an airport and an all-weather highway connection as well as a railroad connection. Separated from Whittier by high mountains, but with room for expansion near the water front, Seward was valuable as an auxiliary to Whittier in receiving the greater quantities of supplies that would be necessary in wartime, and it was located where it could be used as an alternate port if Whittier should be disabled.[114] The need for an alternate port became very real in June 1953 when fire swept through the Whittier port area. In less than four hours wind-blown flames destroyed the main pier, the warehouse, and other facilities and left the port virtually useless for the time being. The port commander estimated the total damage at $20,000,000.[115]

Several smaller ports supplemented Seward and Whittier. Anchorage itself was a port city on Cook Inlet, but it was free of ice floes only four or five months of the year, and its tidal variation of about thirty-eight feet was among the most extreme in the world. Another commercial port, Valdez, lay across Prince William Sound from Whittier, and paved highways connected it both with the Anchorage and the Fairbanks areas. The military port of Haines stood at the break in transportation between the inside passage route and an extension of the Alaska Highway that together provided an alternative route from Seattle to the Fairbanks area—a route likely to be most important in time of war.

Access to Anchorage and to the Fairbanks area from the ports of Seward and Whittier was mainly by means of the Alaska Railroad. In fact the 470 miles of track from Seward to Fairbanks and a spur to Eilson Air Force Base was the entire extent of the Alaska Railroad. Over 62 percent of the traffic (in 1951) was for military support. In 1912 the government had purchased the privately operated Alaska Northern Railroad that then extended only seventy miles north of Seward, and had completed it to Fairbanks in 1923. It was operated by the Department of the Interior. Another private line, the Copper River and Northwestern Railway extending from Cordova on Prince William Sound 195 miles northward and eastward to Kennicott copper mine had been abandoned in 1938.[116] Before the outbreak of the Korean conflict, the Department of the Interior had intended to abandon the part of the rail line from Seward to Portage as soon as the new highway to Seward was open. The route was a tortuous, if scenic, one that depended on a system of tunnels and trestles through the mountainous areas that were expensive to keep in good repair. After the Korean attack the army was anxious that this line as well as the one to Whittier be maintained. Visiting Congressmen agreed with that view, and the Department of the Interior agreed that rail lines should be kept open to both ports. But by this time the Seward line had deteriorated to the point where it would take an estimated $15,000,000 to restore it completely. However, Congress failed to approve a request made by the Department of the Interior, with the full support of the Defense Department, for funds to rehabilitate and maintain the line. The Department of the Interior did indicate that the Seward-Portage line of the Alaska Railroad would be kept in operation during the winter of 1952–53 with the qualification that the line could not be restored to service soon in the event of a major landslide or similar catastrophe. At the end of 1952 the Bureau of the Budget had approved the inclusion of funds for rehabilitation of the line in the president's fiscal year 1954 budget, but the army would continue to consider the problem a critical one until such funds actually had been appropriated.[117]

The only other railroad in Alaska was a twenty-mile stretch of the privately operated White Pass and Yukon route from Skagway to the Canadian border where it continued on for another ninety-one miles to Whitehorse in Yukon Territory.[118]

The Alaska highway, built by army engineers during World War II to connect Dawson Creek, terminus for the Alberta Northern Railroad in eastern British Columbia, to Big Delta, where it joined the Richardson highway to Fairbanks, still was the major highway for the area. Other principal roads were the Richardson highway, running from Valdez to Fairbanks (a distance of 366 miles), the Glenn highway between Anchorage and Glenallen (189 miles) on the Richardson highway, the Tok junction cut-off linking the Alaska and Richardson highways between Gulkana and Tanacross, and the previously mentioned highway between the port of Haines and the Alaska highway, and the one linking Anchorage and Seward (127 miles). Other roads radiated from towns, mines, and military posts, but the great expanse of country west of the Alaska Railroad and north of the Yukon River practically was without connecting roads or railroads. In that area the rivers were the main highways—for small tugs or stern-wheel steamers or small boats in summer, and for sleds or crosscountry vehicles in winter. Tractor trains had practically replaced dog teams for the transportation of military supplies across snowfields. Alaska was a place where air transportation was especially significant. After the pioneer air mail flights of Colonel Carl Ben Eilson in 1922, 1927, and 1928 scores of "bush pilots" appeared on the scene to operate small planes from landing strips or from lakes between the principal towns and mining camps. With the benefit of 270 airports and landing strips, many of them built during World War II, and thirty seaplane bases, commercial air lines were serving many parts of Alaska in the 1950s. The Military Air Transport Service carried supplies as well as personnel to military installations throughout the territory.[119]

For the transportation of bulk petroleum products construction of an eight-inch pipeline from Haines to Fairbanks began late in 1951. Congress appropriated $20,000,000 for the project on fiscal year 1952 funds, but then an overall command reduction and reprogramming required by the Department of the Army resulted in a reduction of available funds to $10,000,000. The only other pipelines serving the interior of Alaska were Canol No. 2, a four-inch line from Skagway (near Haines) to Whitehorse, Yukon, and a three-inch line from Whitehorse to Ladd Air Force Base. This pipeline followed the railroad from Skagway to Whitehorse and used the railroad tunnels; for this reason it was not used for the pumping of volatile fuels, but was useful for getting highly important supplies of diesel fuel to the area.[120]

Logistics studies indicated that if necessary it would be possible to supply installations on the Arctic Ocean by a combination of rail, highway, and river routes, but the normal procedure was to send joint expeditions by sea each summer to supply stations above the ice line with stocks sufficient for the entire year. Navigation on the Arctic Ocean was possible only during the month of August, and during the first few days of that month, the annual "BAREX" expedition made its dash to supply Point Barrow and Barter Island. Resupply expeditions to posts on the Bering Sea could begin late in May to Naknek (on the north side of the Alaska Peninsula on Bristol Bay) but the other calls were between the middle of June and the middle of August. These included voyages by landing ships and army landing craft in the summer of 1952, for example, to Nakenk, Tin City (on Cape Prince of Wales), Cape Newenham, Cape Romanzof, Cape Lisburne, Northeast Cape and Gambell on St. Lawrence Island, Kotzebue, St. Matthew Island, and Skull Cliff. In some places it was possible for landing ships and oil barges to discharge their cargoes directly onto the beaches; in most places smaller landing craft had to be used as lighters to get the supplies ashore. At Naknek, getting chilled and frozen food to storage quickly was accomplished by putting trucks on the lighters and then unloading the food supplies directly from the ship into the trucks, which, on reaching the shore, drove off the landing craft to the storage site.[121]

Supplying fresh and frozen foods to military forces in Alaska required special efforts. Stations submitted monthly requisitions on a sixty-day cycle to the Seattle Port of Embarkation, which in turn called upon the Seattle market center, a part of the quartermaster market center system, to get the required perishables. These included fresh fruits and vegetables, eggs, and frozen milk as well as meat, poultry, and sea food (including salmon!). The food then was shipped out by special transportation. One method was by refrigerator ships from Seattle to Whittier, a voyage of about five days. At Whittier the food supplies had to be sorted on the pier and loaded into refrigerator cars of the Alaska Railroad—cooled in summer and heated in winter—for movement by rail to the destinations. It took ten days or longer ordinarily for the foodstuffs to reach their destinations by this method, and the handling involved in transshipment, and the difficulties of keeping the refrigerator cars at the proper temperature either in winter or summer added to the drawbacks of this method of transportation. A second method was to send these supplies by barge, pulled by a sea-going tug, from Tacoma by way of the inside passage route and the Gulf of Alaska to Valdez to be picked up by trucks. This route was most expeditious when big semitrailer vans were loaded with frozen food, packed with dry ice, and then the whole thing lifted aboard barges. One of the barges could carry eighteen of the vans crosswise on the deck. Tractor trucks called for the vans at Valdez, and after refrigerating units had been installed, moved them by highway to the destinations. By this method the time from Tacoma to points of destination was about eight days. Finally, highly perishable fresh fruits and vegetables went from Seattle to Alaska by air. Begun in April 1949, the airlift by the summer of 1951 included fourteen planes of the Military Air Transport Service and three commercial planes that were flying seventy-five tons of perishable foods to Alaska weekly.[122]

Arctic and subarctic climates meant that special individual and unit clothing and equipment had to be made available if military activities were to be carried on in all kinds of weather. The most serious shortages of supplies in September 1951 were in those very specialized items—Arctic tents, Arctic clothing, Yukon stoves, and winterization kits for motor vehicles. Additional shipments of these items, other than the vehicle winterization kits, arrived that same month, so that after that the overall supply situation appeared to be good aside from the lack of storage and maintenance facilities. The search for improved types of clothing and equipment went on in testing activities at Fort Churchill, Manitoba, and at Big Delta, and in winter exercises such as the WARM WIND exercises of the 503d Airborne Regimental Combat Team in November 1952.[123]

An especially difficult problem was the maintenance of vehicles in Alaska. Lack of covered and heated shop space, and the perennial shortage of spare parts for World War II–type vehicles in particular limited the effective work that could be done in 1951. A special aspect of this problem was the maintenance of army-procured vehicles for the air force. By standard procedure, it was the responsibility of the army to repair those vehicles, but the army in Alaska did not have the facilities and equipment necessary to do a complete job of depot maintenance. It appeared that the air force did have facilities of its own that could be used for vehicle maintenance, but for several months the two commands seemed to be unable to get together on procedures. At last in September 1951 U.S. Army, Alaska, and the Alaskan Air Command arrived at an agreement by which the thirty-ninth Air Depot Wing at Elmendorf Air Force Base would perform necessary depot maintenance on army-procured air force-owned vehicles on a reimbursable basis. The army general depot at Fort Richardson would provide necessary parts, and U.S. Army, Alaska, would continue to fund for depot maintenance and supply support for all ordnance-procured vehicles. For base maintenance, vehicles either were returned to the continental United States or were repaired under local contracts with civilian garages. The U.S. Army, Alaska, G–4 considered the second method to be quicker and cheaper in spite of labor costs of $5.50 an hour.[124]

In overcoming the time and space factors incident to military operations in the Alaska region, an effective system of signal communications was indispensible. Communication for civilian uses as well as military uses to and from as well as within the territory was the responsibility of the army. Its agency for carrying out this mission was the Alaska Communication System, which operated directly under the Chief of the Signal Corps apart from the Alaskan Command. Tactical military communications were integrated with those of this system. The Alaska communications system had its headquarters in Seattle, and subheadquarters at Juneau, Anchorage, Fairbanks, and Adak. Primary radio telephone and radio teletype channels connected the subheadquarters with Seattle. A submarine cable extended from Unalaska in the Aleutians to Seattle with terminal points at Cold Bay, Kodiak, Whittier, and Ketchikan. Landlines from Anchorage to Fairbanks were jointly maintained and operated by the Signal Corps and the Alaska Railroad. Landline connections with the continental United States extended from Fairbanks along the Alaska highway to Edmonton, Alberta, and thence over the facilities of the American Telephone and Telegraph Company. In 1948 the signal corps began a five-year construction program to provide minimum housing for troops and technical housing for equipment. A major difficulty developed in attempts to improve facilities between Anchorage and Fairbanks—along the axis of major military activities. Surveys indicated that a microwave system would be impractical because of the rugged terrain and heavy icing at high altitudes. Proposals for a coaxial cable system seemed to be out of the question because of the damaging effects of extreme temperature variations and the action of permafrost. Technicians from the American Telephone and Telegraph Company were called in, and their recommendation was to put up a pole line from Anchorage to connect with the line along the Alaska highway at Tok Junction. In August 1950 Department of the Army G-4 granted authority to the chief signal officer to issue a letter order in the amount of $600,000 to commence work on the 345-mile, four-pair open wire pole line between those points. The total amount of the proposed contract was estimated at $3,717,000. An important supplement to the army's communications facilities in Alaska was a network of several hundred amateur radio stations that extended to practically all parts of the territory.[125]

As possibilities of a future air war impressed themselves on American military planners and the public alike, the demands for adequate facilities and forces in Alaska were bound to be given attention. But attention to Arctic air routes showed that likely routes of approach to the North American continent could not be confined to the Alaska area alone. Aircraft from northern Europe would be more likely to come in over Greenland.

THULE AIR BASE

Back in 1927 Bernt Balchen, an Arctic flyer who had served on the Byrd polar expeditions, heard with interest the comments of a Danish explorer friend, Knud Rasmussen, who insisted that a place called Thule, on Hayes Peninsula in the northwest of Greenland, had good possibilities for an Arctic air base. Twenty-three years later, as a colonel in the U.S. air force in Washington, Balchen pushed the idea of establishing an air force base at that place. In 1946 the United States had made an agreement with Denmark (Greenland was a Danish colony) to establish a joint weather station in the area. Since that time the installation had consisted of eight small buildings, where some eighteen weather observers lived and did their work, and a small, gravel-topped airstrip. Now the question was whether it could be developed into a base from which modern jet fighters and heavy bombers could operate. Lt. Gen. Lewis A. Pick, chief of engineers, opined that it could be done. It would be an air force base, but the construction would be the responsibility of the army's corps of engineers; the loading and unloading of equipment that would be needed in developing and maintaining the base would be the work of the army transportation corps, and the job of sea transportation would be the navy's.[126]

The location of Thule was, as Balchen put it, "In the center of the world of the ice age."[127] The distance from Thule to Murmansk, the main northern port of Soviet Russia, was about eighteen hundred miles—about the distance that B-29s flew from Saipan to Tokyo in World War II. To Moscow it was about 2,750 miles; to Kiev, in the Ukraine, 3,150 miles; to Stalingrad, 3,200 miles, to Sverdlovsk, in the Ural industrial area, 3,000 miles; to Stalinsk, in the Kuznetsk industrial region, 3,400 miles, to Irkutsk, 3,600 miles, to Vladivostok, 4,200 miles. It was about 2,500 miles to Berlin, 2,320 miles to London, 2,330 miles to New York, 2,360 miles to Detroit. Thule was only 930 miles from the North Pole, and it had the rigorous climate to be expected in the Arctic. Yet it was considerably milder than other points in Greenland much farther south. Extreme winter temperatures of sixty degrees below zero, and wind velocities as high as 150 miles an hour had been recorded, but the average temperatures on the coldest days was about twenty-five to thirty degrees below zero, and it averaged about fifty degrees in summer. Annual snowfall was only about fifteen inches. Situated at the mouth of Wolstenholme Fjord, on North Star Bay, Thule occupied one of the rare sizeable flat areas to be found along Greenland's jagged west coast. Ten to twelve miles inland was the edge of the Greenland icecap; the largest in the world, it rose to a thickness of ten thousand feet.

Beginning 1 January 1951 Colonel Clarence Renshaw began assembling a staff and negotiating for contracts for Project Robin, later to be known as Blue Jay. Then operating under the New York district of the corps of engineers, Colonel Renshaw became district engineer of the Northeast district (also under the North Atlantic division) when that new command was activated effective 1 April. By this time contracts already had been let. The engineering firm of Metcalf and Eddy of Boston and the architectural firm of Alfred Hopkins and Associates of New York received the contracts for preparing the designs. The construction contract went to the North Atlantic Constructors, a joint enterprise that had been formed by Peter Kiewit Sons' Company and Condon-Cunningham of Omaha, Nebraska, and S. J. Groves and Sons and the Al Johnson Construction Company of Minneapolis, Minnesota.

Since ocean shipping could reach Thule only about three months of the year and the outdoor working season was not more than five to six months, it was necessary to have everything ready to go by May and June.

In March the northeast district and the North Atlantic Constructors set up a base at Rosemount, near St. Paul, Minnesota in the "cold states" area to recruit workers, and they set up a base at Norfolk, Virginia, to receive materials and equipment to be shipped out by sea. When hiring began at Rosemount in April, applicants were told only that they would be going overseas and to a very cold climate. After special physical, mental, and trade tests—including such requirements as making carpenters put up an Arctic barracks building, just as they would have to do in Greenland—approximately five thousand workers were chosen from over fifteen thousand applicants. With the cooperation of various engineer districts and divisions, the transportation section of the northeast district supervised the movement of over 150,000 tons of equipment and materials at Norfolk.

In order that work could begin at the earliest possible moment, an advance party with heavy equipment including a 29,000-pound shovel and prefabricated shelters, began arriving at the Thule airstrip from Westover Air Force Base in planes of the Military Air Transport Service. By the end of June the

Camp at site of air base construction at Thule, Greenland, July 1951.

Army engineers assemble steel frames for construction of hangars at Thule Air Base, August 1951.

advance party had prepared the beaches for the landings. By the end of July over 1,200 men and 3,385 tons of supplies and equipment had been airlifted to the site.

Delayed for two weeks by unusually heavy ice in Baffin Bay, the sea expedition, carrying about seventy-five hundred men—military and civilian—and thousands of tons of engineering equipment, prefabricated units, building materials, vehicles, and individual supplies and equipment began arriving 11 July. Trucks and heavy engineering equipment moved directly from beached landing ships to the shore. Work began immediately on the runway, hangars, barracks, warehouse, and a thousand-foot pier. In order to cut down on the secondary logistical problems of housing the workers, Colonel Renshaw had decided that the workers should live on board the ships until permanent buildings ashore could be occupied. They commuted by landing craft between the barracks ships and their jobs.

Taking advantage of the midnight sun, construction crews worked in two ten-hour shifts seven days a week. Actually the average work week for individuals was eighty-four hours, which gave each worker forty-four hours of overtime. The average base pay rate was $4.25 an hour, which meant that workers on the average would draw over $450 a week.[128] Secretary of the Army Pace anticipated some criticism of the high wage rates, but the rates had been set by the Department of Labor and he believed that under the prevailing working conditions they were fully justified. It is possible that some of the army men who were working under the same conditions diasgreed, but apparently no major difficulties developed on that score.

As in central Alaska the eternal problem of permafrost had to be met by special methods for insulating buildings and piles to preserve the permafrost footing. In the absence of heating utilidors, water and sewage had to be moved to and from buildings in heated trucks.

By the middle of August six barracks had been completed and the transfer of men from the ships to living quarters on shore could begin; twenty-four more barracks were occupied within the next three weeks. The thousand-foot pier was completed in time for the unloading of the last ships to arrive during the season on 21 August. Floating ice crowded the ships into small anchorage areas, and damage to ships' propellers was frequent, but port companies unloaded an average of 3,386 tons of supplies and equipment for forty-four days. In measurement tons the total cargo unloaded by 30 August amounted to nearly three hundred thousand tons. By that time, fifty-two days after the arrival of the first ships, an additional 1,874 tons of cargo had arrived by air. Military and civilian personnel at the site totalled 4,435 men. A tank farm of 55,000-barrel tanks had been completed, and three-fourths of its tanks filled with fuel from tankers accompanying the expedition. Warehouses as well as barracks and other installations were being completed on schedule. The largest of the structures included two maintenance hangars, three saltwater distillation plants, and six heating and power plants. On 11 September a loaded C-124 heavy transport plane took off from the new asphalt-surfaced runway.

Leaving behind a party of four hundred men to man the base through the long, dark winter, most of the workers and troops departed in September to return to the United States. During the winter months the base depended entirely on the airlift for the transportation of personnel, fresh foods, and key items of equipment.

Completion of the major part of the project remained for the 1952 season. By September 1952 most parts of the base were finished, including the ten thousand-foot runway, and four hundred and eighty acres of barracks, warehouses, fuel tanks, and service installations. But now the air force wanted to change its original specifications for the runway to increase its width by fifty feet. Completion of the entire project was estimated for September 1953. The total cost would be approximately $183,000,000.

Thule was one of a series of air bases in Labrador, Newfoundland, and Greenland that came under the operational control of the newly established unified command, U.S. Northeast Command. Like the Alaskan Command, the Northeast Command was under the executive direction of the chief of staff of the air force. But in contrast with the joint structure of the Alaskan Command, its headquarters organization was almost entirely air force; one navy captain and one army lieutenant colonel in the plans and requirements directorate was the extent of the representation of other services in the joint headquarters.[129]

ICELAND

Whether Iceland should be considered a part of the North American or the European sphere depended upon one's point of view or the map one happened to be using. Strictly speaking it lay not quite within the Arctic, but the problems of maintaining forces there were closely akin to those relating to Alaska. The importance of Iceland to American security closely paralleled in certain ways the importance of Alaska itself, for the location of Iceland with respect to the North Atlantic shipping routes was analogous to the role of Alaska with respect to the North Pacific. In addition Iceland was close to the strategic areas of Europe, and not a great deal farther from New York and Washington than was Thule. It was an important way station for air transportation—military and civil—between North America and Europe.

After the German occupation of Denmark and Norway in the Spring of 1940, the British had sent a sizeable garrison to hold Iceland, then under the Danish crown, against attempts of the Germans to extend their control in that direction. Concerned with Hitler's inclusion of Iceland within the war zone where neutral shipping would be sunk on sight, President Roosevelt a year later had responded favorably to British proposals for Americans to take over the defense of Iceland in order to relieve British troops for duty elsewhere.

American marines had arrived at Reykjavik on 7 July 1941—just a few hours after the Icelandic prime minister had been persuaded to issue the formal invitation for American forces to participate in the country's defense. Later, elements of the Fifth Infantry Division arrived to reinforce and then to relieve the marines, though the total force was not yet large enough to permit the withdrawal of most of the British.[130]

After World War II the new Republic of Iceland agreed to permit the United States to continue to operate the airport that had been built on the Keflavik peninsula (some distance to the west of the capital city of Reykjavik), provided the operation would be in the hands of civilians. In January 1947 American Overseas Airlines signed a contract to undertake the operation of the airport, and that company assigned the actual operations to a subsidiary, the Iceland Airport Corporation. Eighteen months later the Lockheed Aircraft Overseas Corporation assumed the airport responsibilities under a contract renewed annually until 31 August 1951. By that time American military forces had returned to that North Atlantic island. Iceland had become a member of the North Atlantic Treaty Organization in 1949, but at that time it had not been contemplated that foreign troops would be stationed there in peacetime. After the deterioration in the international situation in 1950, and with the support of North Atlantic Treaty Organization members, the United States raised the subject of reestablishing military bases there. Negotiations with the Icelandic Foreign Office by a U.S. State Department—Armed Forces negotiating group in Iceland led to the conclusion of a formal agreement that was signed on 5 May 1951. Within forty-eight hours of the signing, the first elements of the Iceland Defense Force (designated Joint Task Force 109 until 6 July) arrived by air at the Keflavik Airport. Threats of a general strike in Iceland had developed as the diplomatic negotiations neared completion, and officials of Iceland and the United States alike were anxious that the forces arrive before rather than after the calling of a strike, in order to forestall possible violence or sabotage on the part of communist elements opposed to the arrangement. On 24 May the Althing, Iceland's parliament, passed a provisional law to give legal effect temporarily to the defense agreement pending formal ratification. Formal ratification did not come until 11 December 1951.[131]

The Iceland Defense Force was a joint command with officers of all three services represented on its joint staff under the jurisdiction of the Atlantic Command. The commander was an army officer, Brig. Gen. Edward J. McGaw, until 20 June 1952 when he was succeeded by Brig. Gen. Ralph O. Brownfield of the air force. The Atlantic Command, with headquarters at Norfolk, Virginia, had been established by the Joint Chiefs of Staff as one of the unified commands for which the chief of naval operations was executive agent, but so far its headquarters had not been separated from that of the navy's Atlantic fleet. Lines of authority for the Iceland Defense Force were not always clear, particularly with respect to air units that were assigned to the Military Air Transport Service. The army element of the headquarters was assigned to the Department of the Navy. Principal army units were a headquarters detachment and two companies of the 278th Infantry until April 1952 when the remainder of the battalion combat team arrived.

The sending of the full forces as planned had to await the erection of housing. Many of the Quonset huts that had been set up during World War II either had been removed for use as barns or warehouses or had deteriorated beyond the point that they could be used. Unfortunately delays in arriving at plans, in getting materials, in contract negotiations, and in obtaining funds caused much of the 1951 construction season to be lost. Negotiations in Iceland and in the United States resulted in the signing of a contract in the United States with an association of thirty-nine Icelandic contractors on 23 August 1951. Work on the first building began three days later.

A number of factors operated to delay seriously the whole construction program in Iceland. In the first place the tremendous distances separating the various headquarters having a direct interest in construction projects made it practically impossible to obtain quick coordination. In addition to the Iceland government and the Iceland Defense Force in Iceland, construction matters in whole or in part had to be referred to the commander in chief, Atlantic, at Norfolk, to the Atlantic district of the corps of engineers in New York, and to U. S. air force and Military Air Transport Service headquarters in Washington. Another drawback was the failure of the navy and air force to get together on a master plan upon which detailed on-the-ground planning could be based. Delays on agreeing on the location of the four permanent barracks and a mess hall held back the beginning of work on those buildings several months. This was closely related to another factor common to the northern lands—the short working season, generally from May to October. Severe storms and cold temperatures interfered with work at other times of the year. Finally, the difficulty of obtaining funds seemed to interfere with beginning or continuing construction projects throughout the year. This may have been due to difficulties of reprogramming funds when none had been provided for in the original fiscal year 1952 budget for undertaking any base development in Iceland.

But as in other outlying bases, if the crises could wait, the construction would get done sooner or later. During the first year barracks, a mess hall, theater, post office, dental unit, shoe shop, and a hospital extension appeared. In October 1952 the district engineer of the north district, a newly organized district of the corps of engineers at Keflavik, signed a contract with the Association of Icelandic Contractors for eight new barracks. Amounting to over fifty three million Icelandic Kronur (equivalent to about $3,260,000), it was the largest single contract for building construction ever signed in Iceland. American contractors would supervise the work of the Icelandic contractors. The project was scheduled to be completed during the 1953 building season.

The problem of general logistic support for the elements of the Iceland Defense Force was not worked out until October 1952. Under the arrangement then agreed to by the three services, the air force would provide all common logistic support for army units, while the army would provide only the supplies and services peculiar to the army itself. The Iceland Defense Force commander was responsible for coordinating logistic support for the components of his command, but these depended upon their individual services for the supplies and services for which they were respectively responsible, and for coordinating the budgeting and reimbursement of the other departments for support that they furnished.

Hawaii

The army element of the Pacific Command, a unified command under the executive authority of the chief of naval operations, was U.S. Army, Pacific (USARPAC), located in Hawaii with headquarters at Fort Shafter. Its functions mainly related to furnishing certain logistic support for Far East Command, the training of replacements and assigned units, and as a component of the joint Hawaiian Defense Command providing forces and services for local defense. Here where the movement for armed forces unification probably had received its greatest impetus when the apparent lack of interservice coordination had contributed to the Pearl Harbor disaster in 1941, coordination after World War II had reached the point where the defense of Hawaii was entrusted to a joint defense command operating under an overall unified command.[132]

Shortly after assuming command in April 1949, Lt. Gen. H. S. Aurand introduced the "one-post concept" into the organization of U.S. Army, Pacific. Under this system all posts, such as Schofield Barracks and Fort Shafter, were consolidated administratively into the single post of Oahu. Technical service units were organized into operating groups, and each was supposed to perform all the functions of its specialty for all other army units. The signal operations group, for example, was to perform all signal functions; no other groups or units were to perform any signal functions at all. All transportation was consolidated under the control of the Hawaiian land transportation group, and other group commanders had to obtain transportation from the central motor pool.[133] As General Aurand explained it, "Every time one of these groups performs for itself a function which another group should perform for it [the purpose of] the one-post concept is lost."[134]

After he succeeded to the command of USARPAC on 10 Sept 52 Lt. Gen. John W. O'Daniel returned to the old system. In March 1953 the 8250th AU became Hq. and Hq. Co., USARPAC, and the 8285th AU, which had been Hq. and Hq. Co., USARPAC and Post of Oahu, became the designation for the station complement of Ft Shafter.[135]

The outbreak of hostilities in Korea immediately created demands for emergency logistic support from Hawaii. Some supplies already available on the islands were sent out, and the "crossroads of the Pacific" soon became an important way station in the line of supply and evacuation to and from Korea. In particular, shipments of ammunition from Hawaii were important during the early months of the Korean conflict. Scarce equipment withdrawn from national guard units for shipment to the Far East included those withdrawn from national guard units in Hawaii. Various kinds of supplies and equipment in excess of the needs of U.S. Army, Pacific, continued to be shipped to Japan and Korea in the months that followed. In October 1951 Department of the Army G–4 asked U.S. Army, Pacific, to list all World War II–type vehicles over and above what would be needed for minimum requirements through June 1952 so that they could be shipped to the Far East.[136]

The level of supply maintained in Hawaii included operating and safety levels (with a stockage objective of sixty days of supply) for the Pacific Division of Military Air Transport Service as well as for element of U.S. Army, Pacific, itself. In addition USARPAC supply requirements included a "retention level" of sixty days of supply at combat rates plus an additional basic load of ammunition for units to be mobilized or staged in Hawaii in the event of war. Actual supplies on hand on 1 January 1951, while not completely in balance, included some forty-four thousand tons in excess of both the normal level of supply and the reserve retention level. During the year most of these excess stocks were shipped out to the Far East or, if they were not needed there, returned to the continental United States. By 31 December 1951 excess supplies in USARPAC had been reduced to about sixty-five hundred tons—about half of which was ammunition being held at the direction of the Department of the Army. With the exception of a few items of equipment that were short, the supply situation in Hawaii continued to be healthy at the end of 1952. As of 30 September 1952 some weapons, vehicles, and radios that had been withdrawn from the Hawaiian national guard had not yet been replaced, but the quantities involved were relatively small.[139]

Under a rewarehousing plan drawn up in July 1950 and revised in February 1951, general warehousing and industrial areas were established for each of three technical services—ordnance, engineer, and quartermaster—at Schofield Barracks during 1951. The purpose was to locate maintenance and supply facilities close together, to minimize supply movements, and to reduce guard requirements for storage areas. In addition ammunition was moved out of facilities at Waikakalus and at Upper and Lower Kipapa and consolidated in the Aliamanu Crater area. In 1952 the adjutant general depot at Fort Kamehameha was relocated in the signal corps area at Fort Shater. Later the quartermaster depot, leaving a detachment at Schofield Barracks, moved to Sand Island. Army–air force exchange and Hawaiian medical depot supplies remained in temporary storage facilities at Hickam Air Force Base.[138]

During 1951 an average of more than two vessels a day arrived or departed with military cargo. Honolulu army port received over 194,000 measurement tons of supplies and equipment during that year, and shipped out more than 246,000 measurement tons. In addition nearly 135,000 military passengers—about 65,000 of them en route to other commands—passed through the port during the same period. In August 1951 a detachment of Honolulu army port established a subport on Johnston Island, about nine hundred miles southwest of Honolulu, to serve the air force base located there.[139]

Military cargoes depended upon regular civilian dock workers for handling at Honolulu. Labor difficulities interfered with commercial shipments from time to time, but not until June 1953 had striking stevedores refused to handle military cargoes. Then stevedores joining in a strike called by the International Longshoremen's and Warehousemen's Union—called in protest against a court conviction of the union leader and six others of plotting to teach and advocate the violent overthrow of the government—refused to handle military cargo. Army and navy men then had to take over the work of loading five ships bound for Korea.[140]

As previously noted, Hawaii also was an important stop-over point for aircraft operating on the Pacific airlift. Effective 2 January 1952, U.S. Army, Pacific, at the request of the commander in chief, Far East, assumed responsibility for issuing air movement priorities for all army traffic on the air routes from Honolulu to Japan, Okinawa, and Manila.[141]

Tripler army hospital at Moanolua (just outside Honolulu) provided hospitalization for all three of the armed forces in the Hawaiian area. In fact the navy had over twice as many patients in the hospital as did the army. In addition patients being evacuated by air from the Far East to the continental United States stopped here—usually for about twenty-four hours—for rest and a checkup. They took up on the average about one hundred beds during 1951. The total number of patients in the hospitals rose from an average of 981 in December 1950 to 1,265 in December 1951.[142]

Other than providing logistic support for the Far East and maintaining mobilization reserves, the activity in Hawaii that claimed the greatest attention for logistic support during this period was the operation of the Hawaiian infantry training center at Schofield Barracks. In March 1951 the Department of the Army approved plans for sending five thousand recruits from the mainland to Hawaii to receive their basic training at the Hawaiian infantry training center. At the end of that month 1,700 recruits and 680 men who had completed their basic training and were to serve as trainers were to leave from Camp Stoneman, California. The plan then was that beginning 14 July an additional increment of 1,760 recruits was to be shipped every two weeks until the peak load of the center should reach approximately 13,320 trainees. Actually the number of trainees never got much above five thousand.[143]

General Aurand extended his one-post system to include the training center. It operated as an activity of the post of Oahu and not as a separate USARPAC activity, and post technical service operations groups provided all logistic services and supplies. Battalion messes operated under the supervision of the USARPAC quartermaster, and mess stewards received their supplies directly from the quartermaster operations group. Company supply sergeants dealt directly with the various technical service operations groups without going through any Hawaiian infantry training center staff officers. There were no technical staff officers on the training center's staff. All personnel records were kept by the post of Oahu.[144] The commanding officer of the Hawaiian infantry training center, said General Aurand, "Cannot set up any office or officer to do any job that the various operating groups and the rest of the Post of Oahu are supposed to do for him."[145]

The purpose was to permit the training center to carry on its training activities without having to concern itself with administrative details and supply responsibilities. The members of an inspecting team from army field forces in July 1951 observed that the system had merit, but they expressed a fear that it might give to trainees the impression that army equipment was handed out "on a golden platter."[146]

For a time the infantry training center had difficulty in obtaining badly needed equipment. Through an administrative oversight it was included within the supply priority category of U.S. Army, Pacific, which was 1–K, while other replacement training centers in the continental United States enjoyed a higher priority, 1–G. After this was called to the attention of visiting G–4 staff officers in September 1951, the error was corrected. But the change would not affect actual supply shipments fully until December. By this time questions were being raised about the continuation of the Hawaiian infantry training center itself.[147]

Discontent and opposition to the operation of the center had arisen in Congress both on the grounds of the leave policy for trainees and of economy. It was a policy of the army to grant to all trainees a seven-day leave at their homes upon the completion of their basic training. This included the Hawaiian infantry center. But there of course a special problem arose because of the distance to the mainland. The army permitted the trainees to return to the continental United States for their leaves if they did so at their own expense; otherwise they could take seven days leave in Hawaii. Inevitably this led to complaints and congressional reaction. Senator Lyndon Johnson, chairman of the preparedness subcommittee of the Senate Armed Services Committee, was interested particularly in economy of operations. Questioning the wisdom of operating a replacement training center in Hawaii, he asked for a comparative cost analysis. The analysis showed the yearly cost of training in Hawaii to be $3,059,339 in comparison with a cost of $1,957,852 for similar training being given at a comparable replacement training center in the continental United States. This practically sealed the fate of the Hawaiian infantry training center. In March 1952 the army discontinued the shipment of mainland recruits to Hawaii. Soon the number of trainees dropped from the 6,370 of December 1951 to about 1,760—men from the Pacific area and Alaska.[148]

Another problem that created some furor in Congress and the press about the same time was the removal of wooden crosses from the National Memorial Cemetery of the Pacific in the Punchbowl above Honolulu. An opinion survey conducted by U.S. Army, Pacific, among citizens of Honolulu in April 1948 indicated that a majority were in favor of using a flat marker instead of the cross, which was common to other American cemeteries. This was in line with plans to develop a memorial park type of cemetery where lawn, shrubs, and flowers would contribute toward a coordinated appeal of beauty and dignity. The Korean conflict made it necessary to hasten the completion of the cemetery layout in order to receive some twelve thousand remains for which the cemetery had been chosen as the final resting place. Following earlier plans, U. S. Army, Pacific, let a contract for flat granite markers for the graves. But the large number required and the delays resulting from the checking of data with next of kin before inscribing the markers meant that it would be some time before the permanent markers would be in place. There happened to be stored in Hawaii a number of wooden crosses designed as temporary markers for use in overseas cemeteries. General Aurand decided to set these up pending the availability of the permanent markers. The rows of white crosses set in the green grass in this crater overlooking Honolulu created such a spectacle that popular sentiment began to develop in favor of retaining them permanently. On 20 September 1951 General Aurand wrote to local newspaper editors, veterans organizations, and civic leaders to explain that the wooden crosses by this time were deteriorating badly, funds were not available for maintaining them, and that the permanent markers now were in place. Four days later USARPAC closed the cemetery for one afternoon while all the wooden crosses were removed. The next day a storm of protest arose in Honolulu, and it soon reached the halls of Congress and newspapers in the continental United States. Actually it appeared that a majority of those concerned still favored the new type of marker, but the pressure was strong in the other direction. But the army could do nothing without special funds, and the expense of installing double markers did not seem to be justified. At the end of 1952 it appeared that no special legislation would be forthcoming, and therefore it was likely that the development of the National Memorial Cemetery of the Pacific would continue as planned.[149]

Most Americans seemed to agree for varying reasons on the need for giving attention to the defense of American outposts and of the Western Hemisphere. Hostile encroachments in these areas could not be tolerated under any circumstances. But in the post–World War II years, other areas of the world were competing for consideration as essential to American security with an authority that could not be ignored. Though possibly more remote in ordinary thinking, if not in geography and commerce, Europe was the area where the main effort of maintaining a military establishment and providing military assistance was to be made. The central importance of Europe in grand strategy had not been lost with the coming of the uneasy peace after World War II.

Conclusions

With the end of combat operations in 1945, many logistic problems remained for the U.S. Army which, if anything, were greater than before. The Army had been deployed over the globe during the course of four years. People demanded its return in a few months. Rapid demobilization had a special impact on the handling of the vast quantities of matériel that remained. At war's end, the residue of the American "miracle of production," which had loomed so large in winning the conflict, lay in supply rooms, warehouses, and outdoor dumps scattered the world over—largely unwanted by those who had it, but wanted very much by many who had it not.

The immediate postwar years were years of turmoil when Army leaders must have felt that they indeed were trying to "ride off in all directions at the same time." Even as troops were being rushed home from the war, others were being put in motion to replace them and to man distant outposts against new threats to national and world security.

The maintenance of relatively large forces overseas on a more or less permanent basis was a new role for the U.S. Army. True, the Army had maintained overseas garrisons since the turn of the century, but these had been limited generally to China and to the possessions of the United States in the Pacific, Alaska, and the Canal Zone. Now what had begun primarily as occupation missions in Europe and the Far East gave way to concern for security against possible aggression by the Soveit Union. The years between V–E Day and the Japanese peace treaty saw perhaps the greatest demobilization *and* the greatest "peace-time" build-up in history. In 1951, largely as a consequence of the Chinese intervention in Korea, the United States returned four divisions to Europe.

Again, the nature and extent of foreign military assistance during this period was altogether without precedent. To be sure, the United States had cooperated with the Allies in sharing munitions during the First World War and had provided Lend-Lease during the Second, but now paralleling the rebuilding of its own forces, the United States was contributing to the matériel support of other forces around the world. Aside from the transfer of surplus property to several nations, this began essentially in the programs of aid to Greece and Turkey in response to the enunciation of the "Truman Doctrine" in 1947. In addition there were special programs of assistance to China, to the Philippines, to the French in Indochina, and to Latin America. And there was a beginning of efforts to make of Iran a viable military power in the

Middle East. Then came the vastly expanded and regularized Mutual Defense Assistance Program to include Western Europe and all the others.

Though the United States now was involved in worldwide commitments and worldwide programs of logistic support and assistance—even to the extent of a shooting war in Korea—the primacy of Europe remained paramount. As a result of attack in Korea and the intervention of the Chinese there, four additional divisions went to Europe. Then that force became the irreducible minimum. Why? What calculators showed this to be the right troop strength to defend or promote American interests in that quarter?

In a way, it appeared that the United States might be making its greatest efforts toward preparing for the wars least likely to happen—either nuclear exchanges or massive land battles in Europe—at the expense of those most likely to happen, extensive, long-range infantry action in the jungles and rice fields of Southeast Asia or singular strikes in the Indian Ocean or in the Caribbean Sea. According to some, if the purpose of keeping American forces in Europe was to contain a determined ground attack from the east, they were insufficient to do that. If, on the other hand, their primary purpose was to serve as a "trip-wire" to guarantee American involvement in the event of an attack of any kind against Western Europe, they were too numerous in terms of what was needed for that.

At the same time, if a massive European war was the least likely, perhaps it was the visible American presence there that made that so. It was conceivable that a nuclear stalemate might make a conventional war in Europe more likely, on the ground that antagonists on each side might assume that the other would avoid the use of nuclear weapons in the face of certainty of capability for retaliation by the other side.

In the years to come the United States would face continuing questions about the nature and extent of its national security policies and programs. Previously the question had been whether the United States would respond at all against threats to world order and international security. Now the question would be whether the United States might overextend itself in temptations to police the world. And the balance of commitments and forces, the matching of requirements and resources, indeed the definition of overextension is essentially a question of logistics.

Notes

1. Comd. Rpt., Caribbean Comd., 1951, 10–12; DA G–3 His Summary, 1951–52, Latin American Br., par. 5.
2. Rpt. by JLPC, 17 June 53, U.S. Base Rqmts. outside CONUS, Incl. B., 118–19, 126; Annual Rpt. of the Governor of the Panama Canal for Fiscal Year 1951, House Doc. 290, 82d Cong., 2d Sess., 61; Directory and Station List of U.S. Army, 1 Nov. 51, 469–72; Directory and Station List of U.S. Army, 15 Apr. 53, 470–74.
3. The number of U.S. Army missions in Latin American countries rose to fourteen briefly when a new mission was established in Cuba in Austust 1952, but then in

October the mission in Argentina closed out. DA G-3 Hist. Summary, 1951-1952, Latin American Br., par. 23-28.

4. Comd. Rpt., Caribbean Comd., 1951, 98-99, 111-15.

5. Ibid., 99.

6. Ibid., 128-39.

7. Ibid., 120

8. Ibid., 109-11; *Semiannual Rpt. of Secy. of Army, 1 Jan. 1951 to 30 June 1951,* (included with *Semiannual Rpt. of Sec. Def.*).

9. Rpt. on Audit of Panama Railroad Company, 28 Jan. 52, House Doc. 336, 82d Cong., 2d Sess., 1.

10. P. L. 841, 81st Cong., 2d Sess., 26 Sept. 1950, 64 Stat. 1038-43; Exec. Order 10263, 29 June 51; Annual Rpt. of the Governor of the Panama Canal for Fiscal Year 1951, 3, 48; Rpt. on Audit of Panama Railroad Company, 28 Jan. 52, House Doc. 336, 82d Cong., 2d Sess., 2.

11. Interview with Peter Beasley, Special Consultant (Panama Canal) to US/A, 26 June 53; Tp. conv. with William M. Whitman, Secy. Panama Canal Co., 26 June 53.

12. Annual Rpt. of the Governor of the Panama Canal for FY 1949, House Doc. 410, 81st Cong., 2d Sess., v; Annual Rpt. of the Governor of the Panama Canal for FY 1951, House Doc. 290, 82 Cong., 2d Sess., v.

13. 48 U.S.C. par. 1306, 1946 ed.

14. Exec. Order 8232, 5 Sept. 39.

15. Exec. Order 10107, 8 Feb. 50.

16. Comd. Rpt. Caribbean Comd., 1951, 23-25; DA G-3 Hist. Summary, 1951-52, Latin American Br; Exec. Order 2382, 17 May 1916; Exec. Order 10398, 30 Sept. 1952.

17. Comd. Rpt., Caribbean Comd., 1951, 99-100; DA G-3 Hist. Summary, 1951-52, Latin American Br., par. 13; DA G-4 Hist. Summary 1951-52, Tab. E, Service Div., Logistics Services Br.

18. Report on Audit of Panama Railroad Company, 28 Jan. 52, 2-3; Comd. Rpt., Caribbean Comd., 1951, 105, 122; Tp. Conv. with Peter Beasely, Special Consultant to US/A (Panama Canal), 29 June 53; Tp. Conv. with Lt. Col. R. F. Toomey, Chief Family Housing Sec., Facilities Br., Serv. Div., OACofS G-4, 29 June 53.

19. Comd. Rpt., Caribbean Comd., 1951, 115-21.

20. Pub. Res. No. 96, 76th Cong., 3d Sess., 27 Aug. 1940, 54 Stat. 859; Selective Training and Service Act of 1940, P. L. 783, 76th Cong., 3d Sess., 54 Stat. 886.

21. See Eugene Staley, "The Myth of the Continents," *Foreign Affairs* 19 (Apr. 1941): 481-94.

22. Maurice Matloff and Edwin M. Snell, *Strategic Planning for Coalition Warfare 1941-1942,* in U.S. Army in World War II, (Washington, 1953) 12-13.

23. See Samuel Guy Inman, *Latin America: Its Place in World Life,* rev. ed., (New York, 1942), 389-97.

24. Samuel Flagg Bemis, *The Latin American Policy of the United States,* (New York, 1943), 284-93.

25. Quoted in Ibid., 290.

26. Text given in James W. Gautenbein, ed., *The Evolution of Our Latin American Policy,* (New York, 1950), 773.

27. Inman, *Latin America,* 405.

28. Text given in Gantenbein, ed, *The Evolution of Our Latin American Policy,* 787.

29. Bemis, *Latin American Policy of the United States,* 361-66.

30. Text given in Gantenbein, ed, *The Evolution of Our Latin American Policy,* 799.

31. *The World Almanac and Book of Facts for 1946*, 40–42.
32. Stetson Conn and Byron Fairchild, *The Framework of Hemisphere Defense* (Washington, 1960), 172–99; Brookings Institution, *Major Problems of United States Foreign Policy 1951–1952*. (Washington, 1951), 340; *U.S. Government Organization Manual 1950–1951*, 469.
33. Arthur P. Whitaker, *Inter-American Affairs*, Annual Survey, No. 5, (New York, 1946), 2–19.
34. Text given in Gantenbein, *The Evolution of Our Latin American Policy*, 818.
35. *Major Problems of U.S. Foreign Policy 1949–1950*, 262–69; *Annual Report of the Secretary of the Army*, 1948, 69–70.
36. Text given in Gantenbein, *The Evolution of Our Latin American Policy*, 823–24.
37. Guatemala had ratified the treaty on 26 Sept. 1950, but the deposit of its instrument of ratification awaited the approval by the other parties of a reservation that had been attached. Honduras and Nicaragua also had attached reservations to their ratifications.
38. Text given in Gantenbein, *The Evolution of Our Latin American Policy*, 855–71.
39. *Major Problems of U.S. Foreign Policy 1949–1950*, 186–91; *Major Problems of U.S. Foreign Policy 1950–1951*, 317–21, 140–47.
40. Brookings Institution, *Major Problems of U.S. Foreign Policy 1949–1950*, 267; *U.S. Government Organization Manual 1950–1951*, 469.
41. Brookings Institution, *Major Problems of U.S. Foreign Policy 1951–1952*. 340–45; Basic Policies of the Department of the Army, C 7, Jan. 1952; *Armed Forces Talk* 437, *Inter-American Defense*.
42. Pl. 247, 69th Cong. 44 Stat. 565.
43. Conn and Fairchild, *The Framework of Hemisphere Defense*, 173–92; 245–68; Statement of Gen. Dwight D. Eisenhower, CofS, 28 May 1946, Hearings before House Comm. on For. Affairs, 79th Cong., 2d Sess., *Inter-American Military Cooperation Act*, 14; *Annual Report of the Sectetary of the Army*, 1948, 70; Inman, *Latin America*, 11–12.
44. *Annual Report of the Secretary of the Army*, 1948, 70.
45. Conn and Fairchild, *The Framework of Hemisphere Defense*, 329–30, 338–44; Bemis, *The Latin American Policy of the United States*, 370; *Annual Report of the Secretary of the Army*, 1948, 70; *U.S. Government Organization Manual 1950–1951*, 480–81.
46. Statement of Robert M. Sayre, Office of Regional American Affairs, Dept. of State, 28 May 53, Hearings before House Comm. on For. Aff., *Mutual Security Act Extension*, 849–50; *Annual Report of the Secretary of the Army, 1948*, 70; Directory and Station List of the U.S. Army, 15 Apr. 1953, 56–57; Basic Policies of the Dept. of the Army, C 7, Jan 1952, 32b.
47. Pub. Res. 83, 76th Cong., 54 Stat. 396–97.
48. Quoted in Conn and Fairchild, *The Framework of Hemisphere Defense*, 220.
49. Ibid., 208–9.
50. Ibid., 218.
51. Ibid., 236.
52. House Report No. 2230, 7 June 1946, 79th Cong., 2d Sess., Rpt. of Comm. on For. Aff., *The Inter-American Military Cooperation Act;* Statement of General Eisenhower, 28 May 46, Hearings before House Comm. on For. Aff., *Inter-American Military Cooperation Act*, 16.
53. Statement of General Eisenhower, 28 May 1946, Hearings before House Comm. on For. Affairs, *Inter-American Military Cooperation Act*, 16.

54. House Report No. 2230, 79th Cong., 2d Sess., 7 June 46, *The Inter-American Military Cooperation Act.*

55. C. P. Trussell in *The New York Times*, 24 June 1947; Thomas J. Hamilton in *The New York Times*, 9 June 1946.

56. Message of the President to Congress, 26 May 1947, *Congressional Record*, 93: 5780.

57. C. P. Trussell, in *The New York Times*, 24 June 1947; Bertram D. Hulen, "Move to Arm Americas Has a Double Motive," *The New York Times*, 1 June 1947.

58. Summary Sheet, prep. by C. M. Ankcorn, sgnd. Lt. Gen. Le R. Lutes for CofS and SW, 27 July 46, sub.: Supply of Automotive Equipment to Other American Countries under Provisions of Surplus Property Act as Amended, carbon, CofS 400.703; Supply Supplement to the War Department Troop Deployment, 1 May 1946, 16–25; Supply Supplement, Pt. 3 of the U.S. Army Troop Program, 1 Dec. 1946, 367–97; Supply Supplement, Pt. 3, of the U.S. Army Troop Program, 1 Feb. 48, 36–38.

59. Summary Sheet, prep. by C. M. Ankcorn, sgnd. Lt. Gen. LeR. Lutes for CofS and SW, 27 July 46, sub.: Supply of Automotive Equipment to other American Countries under Provision of Surplus Property Act as Amended, carbon, CofS 400.703; Memo, WDG SP/O 435, Brig. Gen. T. M. Osborne, Ch. Supply Grp., SS&P, 20 Sept. 46, sub.: Unresolved Surplus Property Problems, Carbon, CofS 400.703; Supply Supplement, Pt. 3 of the U.S. Army Troop Program, 1 Dec. 46, 389; Supply Supplement, Pt. 3 of the U.S. Army Troop Program, 1 Feb. 48, 36–38; FMA History, Draft MS in G–14 FMH Hist. file, Ch. 4.

60. In addition, Brazil had received a loan of $1,965,000 from the Reconstruction Finance Corporation in 1946 for the purchase of U.S. surplus property located in Brazil. The War Assets Administration extended credits to Haiti of $15,000 in fiscal year 1948 and $135,000 in fiscal year 1949 for the purchase of surplus property in the United States—*Foreign Aid by the U.S. Government, 1940–1951*, Supplement to the Survey of Current Business, 78, 92, 96–97.

61. Ibid., 96–97.

62. Military Appropriation Act, 1947, PL. 490, 79th Cong., 5 July 46, 60 Stat. 560; Military Appropriation Act, 1948, PL. 267, 80th Cong., 9 July 47, 61 Stat. 286; Military Appropriation Act, 1949, (Army) PL. 766, 80th Cong., 24 June 48, 62 Stat. 650; National Military Establishment Appropriation Act, 1950 (Army), PL, 434, 81st Cong., 29 Oct. 49, 63 Stat. 989; General Appropriation Act, 1951 (Army) PL. 759, 81st Cong., 6 Sept. 50, 64 Stat. 732.

63. G–4 Rev. of the Month, Jan. 1948, publ. 29 Feb. 48, 31.

64. G–4 Rev. of the Month, 1 Apr. 48, 1, 25–26.

65. G–4 Rev. of the Month, 31 Aug. 48, 27.

66. G–4 Rev. of the Month, 1 July 49, 18; A few items earmarked for Argentina that had not yet been shipped were returned to stock after the outbreak of the Korean conflict.—G–4 Memo G4/Bl 44171, 25 Aug. 50, 2; The Troop Program, Pt. 3, Supply Supplement, 1 Feb. 49, 1:54.

67. Statement of Edward G. Miller, Jr., Asst. Sec. State for Inter-American Affairs, 6 Aug. 51, Hearings before Senate Comm. on For. Rel., 82d Cong., 1st Sess., *Mutual Security Act of 1951*, 393–94; Also testimony of General Bolte, 405–8; Supply Supplement, Pt. 3 of The U.S. Army Troop Program, 1 Feb. 1948, 38.

68. Senate Report 403, 83d Cong., 1st Sess., Rpt. of the Senate Comm. on For. Rel., *The Mutual Security Act of 1953*, 13 June 53, 47; Statement of Lt. Gen. Charles L. Bolte, DCofS and Chairman, Inter-Amercan Defense Bd., 25 July 51, Hearings before House Comm. on For. Aff., 82d Cong., 1st Sess., *The Mutual Security Program*, 1048–90; *Semiannual Report of the Secretary of Defense*, 1 Jan. to 30 June 1951, 58–59.

69. Statement of Edward G. Miller, Jr., Asst. Sec. State for Inter-American Affairs, 6 Aug. 51, Hearings before Sen. Comm. on For. Rel., 82d Cong., 1st Sess., *Mutual Security Act of 1951,* 394.

70. See *Major Problems of U.S. For. Policy 1949–1950,* 268–69.

71. Henry L. Stimson and McGeorge Bundy, *On Active Service in Peace and War,* (New York, 1949), 319.

72. Statement of Lt. Gen. Charles Bolte, DCofS and Chairman, Inter-American Defense Bd., 6 Aug. 51, Hearings before Sen. Comm. on For. Rel., 82d Cong., 1st Sess., *Mutual Security Act of 1951,* 396–400; Testimony of C. Tyler Wood, Deputy to Dir. for Mutual Security, 28 May 53, Hearings before House Comm. on For. Aff., 83d Cong., 1st Sess., *Mutual Security Act Extension,* 853–54.

73. Testimony of Maj. Gen. George C. Stewart, 28 May 1953, Hearings before House Comm. on For. Affairs, 83d Cong., 1st Sess., *Mutual Security Act Extension,* 848–50; Statement of Robert M. Sayre, Office of Regional American AFF, Dept. of State, 28 May 53, Hearings before House Comm. on For. Affairs, 83d Cong., 1st Sess., *Mutual Security Act Extension,* 850.

74. *The Mutual Security Program,* Second Report to Congress, 30 June 1952, 35; Operation M–DAP, DACofS G–4, FMA, Feb. 1953, U.S. Groups Performing MDAP Functions; Testimony of Maj. Gen. George C. Stewart, Dir. OMA, 28 May 53, Hearings before House Comm. on For. Aff., 83d Cong., 1 Sess., *Mutual Security Act Extension,* 847–48, 851; House Report No. 569 (Union Calendar No. 201), 83d Cong., 1st Sess., Rpt. of Comm. on For. Aff., *Mutual Security Act of 1953,* 16 June 1953, 32; Sydney Gruson, "Mexico Talks Set on U.S. Arms Help," *The New York Times,* 4 Feb. 1952; *The New York Times,* 15 Mar. 1952; Sam Pope Brewer, "U.S., Brazil Sign Military Aid Pact," *The New York Times,* 16 Mar. 1952; Tp. Conv., Off. of Mil. Asst., Off. of Sec. of Def., 29 Dec. 53.

75. Comd. Rtp., Caribbean Comd., 1951, 122; memo, Colonel William Massello, Jr., for Chief Ops. Div., OACofS, G–3, 12 May 53, sub.: Rpt. of Visit ... to Canal Zone, Colombia, Ecuador, and Peru to Appraise and Assist MDAP in those countries, copy in G–4 FMA Hist. files No. 400, Title, 4.

76. "Latin America's Military Effort in 1951," G–2 *Intelligence Review* No. 189, Feb. 1952, 84–89.

77. Memo, Col. William Massello, Jr, for Chief Ops. Div., OACof S, G–3, 12 May 53, sub.: Rpt. of Visit to Canal Zone, Colombia, Ecuador, and Peru to Appraise and Assist MDAP in Those Countries.

78. MDAP Allocations of Available Funds, 30 Apr. 1953, Hearings before House Comm. on For. Affairs, 83d Cong., 1st Sess., *Mutual Security Act Extension,* 324; Statement of Harold E. Stassen, Dir. for Mutual Security, 5 May 53, Hearings before House Comm. on For. Aff., 83d Cong., 1st Sess., *Mutual Security Act Extension,* 150.

79. Statement of Maj. Gen. George C. Stewart, Dir. OMA, 14 May 53, Hearings before Sen. Comm. on For. Rel., 83d Cong., 1st Sess., *Mutual Security Act of 1953,* 370–71.

80. MDAP—Dept. of Def. Ops. Under the Mutual Security Program, July 1953, 41.

81. Statement of John M. Cabot, Asst. Sec. of State for Inter-American Aff., 4 June 53, Hearings before House Comm. on For Affairs, 83d Cong., 1st Sess., *Mutual Security Act Extension,* 1081; See also Statement of John M. Cabot, Asst. Sec. State, 14 May 53, Hearings before Senate Comm. on For. Rel., 83d Cong., 1st Sess., Mutual Security Act of 1953, 367–68; and Statement of Robert A. Lovett, Sec. Def., 13 Mar. 52, Hearings before House Comm. on For. Aff., 82d Cong., 2nd Sess., 22.

82. Brookings Institution, *Major Problems of U.S. Foreign Policy 1950–1951,* 316; James R. Donal, "Canadian Industrial Potential for War," transcript of ICAF lecture, 1949–50, L50–118.

83. Text in Franklin D. Roosevelt, *The Public Papers and Addresses of Franklin D. Roosevelt,* 1938 Volume: *The Continuing Struggle for Liberation,* (New York, 1941), 493.

84. Conn and Fairchild, *The Framework of Hemisphere Defense,* 365–77; *U.S. Government Organization Manual 1950–1951,* 484.

85. John P. Humphrey, "Canada," in Arthur P. Whitaker, ed., *Inter-American Affairs, 1942: An Annual Survey,* No. 2, (New York, 1953), 46–52.

86. Conn and Fairchild, *The Framwork of Hemisphere Defense,* 376–77; *Annual Report of the Secretary of the Army,* 1948, 70.

87. *Semiannual Report of the Secretary of Defense,* 1 Jan. to 30 June 1951, 63; See also *Department of Defense Directory of Boards and Committees,* Admins. Off., Off. of Sec. Def., Apr. 1952.

88. Testimony of Frank Nash, Asst. Secy. Def., 19 Mar. 1953, Hearings before House Comm. on For. Aff., *Mutual Security Act Extension,* 83d Cong., 1st Sess., 27; *The NATO Handbook,* 1 Jan. 1953, 28.

89. *Foreign Aid by the United States Government 1940–1951, A Supplement to the Survey of Current Business,* 1952, Tables C and G, 84, 93.

90. Ibid., 68.

91. Statement of Kenneth C. Royall, Sec/Army, 7 Mar. 49, Hearings before House Subcommittee on National Military Establishment Appropriations Bill for 1950, Pt. 4, 81st Cong., 1st Sess., 4.

92. Draft FM 31–70, Basic Arctic Manual, Feb. 1951, 1–9, 102–3; Rpt. of the Alaskan Task Force, Seventh Rpt. of Preparedness Subcommittee of Committee on Armed Services, U.S. Senate, 1 Mar. 1951, Sen. Doc. No. 10, 82d Cong., 1st Sess., 1–4; Remarks of Brig. Gen. Elmer J. Roberts, Rpt. of Alaskan Task Force, Appendix A, 40–46; Palmer W. Roberts, "Cold Weather Engineering," *The Military Engineer* 45 (Jan–Feb 1953): 3; Palmer W. Roberts, "Effects on Materials in Arctic Cold," *The Military Engineer,* 42 (1950), 176–78; Colonel Walter K. Wilson, Jr., "The Problem of Permafrost," *The Military Engineer,* 40 (Apr. 1948): 162–64; Kirk Bryan, "The Study of Permanently Frozen Ground and Intensive Frost Action," *The Military Engineer,* 40 (July 1948) 304–8; "Operation Alspost," *The Quartermaster Review,* 28 (Jan–Feb 1949): 69–70, 98.

93. Remarks of Brig. Gen. Elmer J. Roberts, Jr., USAF, Dir Plans and Ops., ALCOM, Rpt. of Alaskan Task Force, Appendix A, 46–48; Lt. Col. Claude W. White, Chem. Off., USARAL, and Capt. Eugene E. Monk, "The Chemical Corps in Alaska," *Armed Forces Chemical Jnl.* 6 (Oct 1952): 5–6; Questions and Answers from Address by Maj. Gen. C. D. Eddleman, Army War College, 4 Feb. 53, 9; 22d Intermediate Rpt., Comm. on Expenditures in the Exec. Depts., 30 Dec. 52, Military Housing Construction in Alaska, House Rpt. 2507, (Union Calendar No. 794), 82d Cong., 2d Sess., 3–4.

94. Rpt. of the Alaskan Task Force, Senate Preparedness Subcomm., 1 Mar. 1951, 4–5, 35.

95. Rpt. of the Alaskan Task Force, 1 Mar. 1951, 4–5; Rpt. by Joint Logistics Plans Committee on Survey of Current U.S. Base Rqmts. outside Continental U.S. (JCS 570/283), 17 June 53, Incl. B, 1 Jan. 53, 1–2, 22.

96. DA G–3 Hist. Summary, 1951–1952, North American Br., par. 7; Rpt. of the Alaskan Task Force, Sen. Prep. Subcomm. 1 Mar. 1951, 27–29; Annual Report of the Chief, National Guard Bureau, Fiscal Year Ending 30 June 49, 40.

97. Rpt. of the Alaskan Task Force, Senate Prep. Subcommittee, 1 Mar. 1951, 6.

98. Statement of Kenneth Royall, Sec/Army, 7 Mar. 49, Hearings before House Subcommittee on National Military Establishment Appropriation Bill for 1950, Pt. 4, 81st Cong., 1st Sess., 5.

99. Rpt. of Staff Visit by G-4 Representatives, Colonel A. M. Parsons and Lt. Col. J. F. Guerin to USARAL, FECOM, and USARPAC, Sept-Oct 1951, Sec. 2, USARAL, 3.

100. Remarks of Brig. Gen. Elmer J. Roberts, Rpt. of Alaskan Task Force, Appendix A, 42; Rpt. of Alaskan Task Force, Sen. Prep. Subcomm., 1 Mar. 1951, 10.

101. See Twenty-second Intermediate Rpt., Comm. on Expenditures in the Exec. Depts., 30 Dec. 52, Military Housing Construction in Alaska, House Rpt. 2507 (union Calendar No. 794) 82d Cong., 2d Sess., 9-10; Roverts, "Cold Weather Engineering," *The Military Engineer,* 45 (Mar.-Apr. 1953): 114-17; Colonel Bernt Balchen, "Engineering Problems in the Arctic," *The Military Engineer,* 44 (Nov.-Dec. 1952): 426-28.

102. Rpt. of Alaskan Task Force, Appendix E, 59-60.

103. Rpt. of the Alaskan Task Force, Senate Prep. Subcommittee, 1 Mar. 1951, 6-12.

104. Rpt. prep. by OCofEngrs, 19 Sept. 50, on Contractual Methods used on Military Construction in Alaska, in Rpt. of Alaskan Task Force, Appendix C, 57-59.

105. Rpt. of the Alaskan Task Force, Sen. Prep. Subcommittee, 1 Mar. 1951, 8, 32, Appendix D, 59; PL. 155, 82d Cong., 1st Sess., 28 Sept. 51, 65 Stat. 342; Second Supplemental Approp. Act, 1952, PL. 254, 82 Cong., 1st Sess., 1 Nov. 51, 65 Stat. 764; PL. 534, 82d Cong., 2d Sess., 14 July 52, 66 Stat. 608-9; Rpt. of Staff Visit by Colonel Parsons and Lt. Col. Guerin to USARAL, Sept.-Oct. 1951, 1, 6-7; Twenty-second Intermediate Rpt., Common Expenditures in the Executive Depts., 30 Dec. 52, Mil. Housing Constr. in Alaska, House Rpt. 2507 (Union Calendar No. 794), 82d Cong., 2d Sess., 3; Statement of the Under Sec/Army, Hearings before the Committee on Approp., U.S. Senate, Supplement Approp. Bill, 1953, 565; Statement of Lt. Gen. George Decker, and Maj. Gen. George Honnen, Chief Budget Div., OCA, 27 May 53, Hearings before the Subcommittee of the Committee on Approp., 83d Cong., 1st Sess., D/A Approp. for 1954, 101-2, 119; Rpt. of the Special Subcommittee on Public Works in Alaska of the Armed Services Comm., House of Representatives, Following an investigation 31 Aug. 1951 to 10 Sept. 1951, 9-10, 11-13.

106. Military Structures, *Architectural Record,* CX, (Sept. 1951), 107-125; *The New York Times,* 8 Feb. 1953.

107. Rpt. of the Special Subcommittee on Public Works in Alaska of the Armed Services Committee, House of Representatives, Following an Investigation 31 Aug. 1951 to 10 Sept. 1951, 10-11.

108. Rpt. of the Alaskan Task Force, Sen. Prep. Subcomm., 1 Mar. 1951, 31.

109. Rpt. of the Special Subcommittee on Public Works in Alaska, Sept.-Oct. 1951, 11.

110. Final Rpt. and Recommendations, D/D, Housing Commission, 15 Jan. 51; Rpt. of the Special Subcommittee on Public Works in Alaska, Sept.-Oct 1951, 11-16; PL. 564, 81st Cong., 2d Sess., 17 June 50, 64 Stat. 244-45.

111. Claude W. White and Eugene E. Monk, "The Chemical Corps in Alaska," *Armed Forces Chemical Jnl.* 6 (Oct 1952): 7.

112. Military Housing Construction in Alaska, House Rpt. 2507, 3.

113. Ibid., 19.

114. Rpt. of the Special Subcommittee on Public Works in Alaska, Armed Serv. Comm., House of Representatives, 31 Aug. to 10 Sept. 1951, 23-24; Rpt. of the Alaskan Task Force, Sen. Prep. Subcomm., 1 Mar. 1951, 12-16; Rpt. by Joint Logistics Plans Committee on Survey of Current U.S. Base Rqmts. Outside Continental U.S., (JCS 570/283,) 17 June 53, Incl. B, 1 Jan. 53, 1-2, 22; Transportation Corps Notes, 28 Mar. 52, 1-2; Rpt. of Critical Problems, G-4-27, 30 Nov. 51.

115. Press Releases, Office Chief of Information, USARAL, 18 June 53, in

OCMH; *The Washington Post,* 19 June 1953.

116. Colonel John R. Noyes, "Transportation in Alaska," *The Military Engineer* 45 (Mar.-Apr. 1953): 99-103; U.S. Dept. of the Interior, *Mid-Century Alaska,* (Washington, 1952), 24-26.

117. Rpt. of Special Subcomm. on Public Works in Alaska, Aug.-Sept. 1951, 23-24; Rpt. by the Alaskan Task Force, Sen. Prep. Subcomm., 1 Mar. 1951, 16-18; Rpt. of Critical Problems, 24 Dec. 52, Problem No. G4-27, Development of Military Port of Whittier, Alaska, and Seward-Portage Link.

118. Dept of the Interior, *Mid-Century Alaska,* 27.

119. Ibid., 13-27; Lt. Col. Thomas O. blakeney, "The Security of Alaska and the Tundra Army," *Military Review* 32 (Sept. 1952): 4-7; Noyes, "Transportation in Alaska," 103; White and Monk, "The Chemical Corps in Alaska," *Armed Forces Chemical Jnl.,* 4-5; Draft FM 31-70, Basic Arctic Manual, Feb. 1951, 137-39; Rpt. of Staff Visit by Colonel Parsons and Lt. Col. Guerin to USARAL, Sept.-Oct 1951, 4-5, 7.

120. Cmd. Rpt., USARAL, 1951, 11; Rpt. of the Alaskan Task Force, Sen. Prep. Subcomm., 1 Mar., 1951, 16.

121. Rpt. of the Alaskan Task Force, Sen. Prep. Subcomm., 1 Mar. 1951, 15; Remarks by Brig. Gen. Elmer J. Rogers, Jr, Rpt. of the Alaskan Task Force, Sen. Prep. Subcomm., 1 Mar. 1951, 48; Bering Sea Resupply, Beachmaster Rpt., 1952 Season, 22 Aug. 52, in OCMH.

122. W. H. Montaron, "Supplying Perishables to the Alaskan Theater," *The Quartermaster Review* 30 (Jan.-Feb. 1951): 8-10; News Release, OCofT, 1 Aug. 51, 11; Major Stanley S. Lane, "Perishables in Alaska," *The Quartermaster Review,* 27 (May-June 1948): 13, 105-6.

123. Draft FM 31-70, Basic Arctic Manual, Feb. 1951, 12-32; Rpt. of Staff Visit by G-4 Representatives, Colonel A. M. Parsons and Lt. Col. J. F. Guerin to USARAL, FECOM, and USARPAC, Sept.-Oct 1951, Sec. 2, USARAL, 2; Hist. Summary, Global Mission of the Quartermaster Corps, Sept. 1951 to Dec. 1952, copy in OCMH, 484-90; Min, G-4-Tech Serv. Conf., 1 Feb. 51, 3.

124. DF G4/D7, Chief Maint. Br., G-4 to Chief Rqmts. Br., 12 Sept. 51, sub.: G-3, G-4 Staff Visit to USARAL, FECOM, and USARPAC, in Rpt. of Staff Visit by Colonel Parsons and Lt. Col. Guerin, annex 22; Ltr., ARGSLi2 E 451 and AAMDA 451, Hq. USARAL and AAC to CO's 17 Sept. 51, sub.: Depot Maintenance of Air Force Owned Ordnance Procured Vehicles, copy attchd. to rpt. of Staff Visit by Colonel Parsons and Lt. Col. Guerin to USARAL, Sept.-Oct 1951, 3-4; Rpt. of Critical Problems, G-4-17, 30 Nov. 51.

125. Rpt. of the Alaskan Task Force, Sen. Prep. Subcomm., 1 Mar. 1951, 29-30; Remarks of Brig. Gen. Elmer J. Roberts, Rpt. of Alaskan Task Force, Appendix A, 46-47; G-4 Memo of Important Actions, G4/B1 41620, 14 Aug. 50, 1; Blakeney, "The Security of Alaska and the Tundra Army," *Military Review* (Sept. 1952): 7.

126. Unless otherwise indicated, this section is based upon the following: History of Northeast District, Corps of Engineers, Dec. 1950 to Sept. 1951, by Major James D. T. Hamilton, Incl. to Hist. of North Atlantic Div., Corps of Engrs. Hist Summary, 25 June 50 to 8 Sept. 51, in OCMH, Pt. 2-D; "Birth of a Base," *Life,* 22 Sept. 1952, 130-39; "Greenland's Global Gateway," *Military Review* 32 (Mar. 1953): 27-32; Austin Stevens, "Base Created in Greenland for U.S.-Danish Air Defense," *The New York Times,* 19 Sept. 1952. For an account of U.S. military construction and defense activities in Greenland during World War II, see Stetson Conn, Rose C. Engelman, and Byron Fairchild, *Guarding the United States and Its Outposts* (Washington, 1964), 451-58.

127. *The New York Times,* 19 Sept. 1952.

128. Memo for Record, 2 Sept. 52, sub.: Rpt. of trip to Europe of Secy. of the

Army Pace and Party.

129. JCS Unified Command Plan, revised to 23 Jan. 52; Organization Chart, n.d., Northeast Comd., in Doctrines and Procedures Br., Orgn. and Tng. Div., OACofS, G–3; Questions and Answers from Address by Maj. Gen. C. D. Eddleman, Army War College, 4 Feb. 63, 9.

130. Mark Skinner Watson, *Chief of Staff: Prewar Plans and Preparations,* (Washington, 1950), 487–90; Conn, Engelman, and Fairchild, *Defending the United States and Its Outposts,* 459–531.

131. This section is based upon the following: History of Iceland Defense Force Headquarters, narrative and documentary annexes in four vols, 1 May 51 to 31 Oct 52, copy in OCMH; DA G–4 Hist. Summary, 1951–1952, Tab. B, Plans Off., Matters of World-Wide Interest; Rpt. by JLPC, 17 June 53, U.S. Base Rqmts. outside CONUS Incl. B, 71–72; DA G–3 Hist. Summary, North American Br., par. 8.

132. Comd. Rpt., USARPAC, 1951, Vol. 1, Pt. 1, 1–5.

133. Ibid., 6–8.

134. Ibid., 8.

135. GO 13, USARPAC, 12 Mar. 53.

136. Memo of Important Actions, G4/B1 6407 (SF), 5 Oct. 50; Study prep. in Supply Div., G–4, 17 Nov. 50, sub.: The Job of Supplying Korea, Tab. B, Ammo. Supply; G–4 Hist. Summary, 1950–51, Tab. 28, Rqmts. Div.

137. Rpt. of Staff Visit by G–4 Representatives, Colonel A. M. Parsons and Lt. Col. J. F. Guerin, to USARAL, FECOM, USARPAC, 14 Sept. 51 to 3 Oct. 51, copy in G–4 Rqmts. Div., Allowances Br., Sec. 3, 5–6; Comd. Rpt., USARPAC, 1951, Vol. 1, Pt. 2, 115–16; Ltr. GPSUP, 400/150, CG USARPAC to TAG, 24 Oct. 52, sub.: Rpt. of Critical Logistics Deficiencies, RCS CSGLD–524 in G–4 Plans Off., Theaters Br., Rpts. of Critical Logistics Deficiencies.

138. Comd. Rpt., USARPAC, 1951, Vol. 1, Pt. 2, 117–19; Directory and Station List of U.S. Army, 15 Apr. 53, 570; Rpt. by Joint Logistics Plans Comm., 17 June 53, U.S. Base Rqmts. outside CONUS, (JCS 570/283) Incl. B, 1 Jan. 53, 66–67.

139. Comd. Rpt., USARPAC, 1951, Vol. 1, pt. 2, 128.

140. *The New York Herald Tribune,* 23 June 1953, *Time,* Vol. 61, no. 26, 29 June 1953, 12–13.

141. Comd. Rpt., USARPAC, 1951, Vol. 1, pt. 2, 129.

142. Ibid., 119–21.

143. Memo, Col. Chafee, Chief G–3 Far East and Pacific Br., for General Gaither, 9 Mar. 51, sub.: Training of Recruits in USARPAC, copy in G–3 Far East Pacific Br; Comd. Rpt., USARPAC, 1951, Vol. 1, Pt. 1, 11–13; Pt. 2, 89–96.

144. Comd. Rpt., USARPAC, 1951, Vol. 1, pt. 1, 12.

145. Commanding General's Presentation, USARPAC Comd. and Staff Conf., 19 Mar. 51, quoted in Comd. Rpt., USARPAC, 1951, Vol. 1, Pt. 1, 12.

146. Comd. Rpt., USARPCA, 1951, Vol. 1, pt. 2, 117–19.

147. Rpt. of Staff Visit, Colonel Parsons and Lt. Col. Guerin to USARAL, FECOM, USARPAC, 14 Sept. to 3 Oct. 51, Sec. 3, 6–7.

148. Comd. Rpt., USARPAC, 1951, Vol. 1, pt. 2, 96; Memo, G–3, 323.3 (23 Sept. 52), ACofS G–3 for CofS, Attn. VCofS, 3 Oct 52, sub.: ReExpansion of Trng. Center at Schofield Barracks, Hawaii, copy in G–3 Records, 323.3 (Sec. 2) Case 31; Replacement and Reorganization Training Plan (n.d., 1953), copy in G–3 Trng. Br., Orgn. and Planning File.

149. Comd. Rpt., USARPAC, 1951, Vol. 1, pt. 1, 45–47; Tp. conv. with Helen McDonald, Liaison Off., Memorial Div., OQMG, 25 June 53.

Glossary of Terms and Abbreviations

AAF. Army Air Forces.
ACofS. Assistant Chief of Staff.
AFMIDPAC. Air Forces Mid-Pacific.
AFWESPAC. Air Fores Western Pacific.
AGF. Army Ground Forces.
AGO. Adjutant General's Office.
AGWAR. Adjutant General, War Department.
ANZUS. Australia–New Zealand–United States.
AR. Army Regulations.
Army service area. The territory between the Corps rear boundary and the Combat Zone rear boundary. Most of the Army administrative establishment and service troops are usually located in this area.
ASF. Army Service Forces.
Basic load (ammunition). That Quantity of ammunition which is authorized and required by each nation to be on hand within a unit or formation at all times. It is expressed in terms of rounds for ammunition items fired by weapons, and in other units of measure for bulk allotment and other ammunition items.
Br. Branch.
CBI. China–Burma–India theater.
Chfs. Chiefs.
CG. Commanding General.
Ch. Chairman, Chief.
CINCAFPAC. Commander in Chief, Air Forces Pacific.
CinCAFWESPAC. Commander in Chief, Air Forces Western Pacific.
CINCPAC. Commander in Chief, Pacific Command.
CINCEUR. Commander in Chief, Europe.
CINCUSAREUR Commander in Chief, U.S. Army, Europe.
Cir. Circular.
CM-OUT. Classified Message, Out.
CofS. Chief of Staff.
Comd. Command.
COMGENUSFA. Commanding General, U.S. Forces, Austria.
Commercial loading. The loading of personnel and/or equipment and supplies for maximum use of space. Sometimes called "administrative loading."
Commodity loading. A method of loading in which various types of cargoes are loaded together, such as ammunition, rations, or boxed vehicles, in order that each commodity can be discharged without disturbing the other.

Glossary of Terms and Abbreviations

Common infrastructure. Infrastructure essential to the training of NATO forces or to the implementation of NATO operational plans that, owing to its degree of common use or interest and its compliance with criteria laid down from time to time by the North Atlantic Council, is commonly financed by NATO members.

Communications zone. Rear part of theater of operations (behind but contiguous to the combat zone) that contains the lines of communication, establishments for supply and evacuation, and other agencies required for the immediate support and maintenance of the field forces.

CONUS. Continental United States.

Cross-servicing. That servicing performed by one service or national element for other services or national elements and for which the other services or national elements may be charged.

DA. Department of the Army.

DCofS. Deputy Chief of Staff.

DELWU. (Delegation to Western Union). U.S. delegation to the military committee of the five powers.

DF. Disposition form.

Di. Directive.

DoD. Department of Defense.

Economic mobilation. The process of preparing for and carrying out such changes in the organization and functioning of the national economy as are necessary to provide the most effective use of resources in a national emergency.

ECA. Economic Cooperation Administration: the agency set up to administer the Marshall Plan.

ETO. European Theater of Operations.

EUCOM. European Command.

FACC. Foreign Assistance Coordination Committee.

FAFLO. French–American Fiscal Liaison Office.

FECOM. Far East Command.

FLC. Foreign Liquidation Commissioner.

FM. Field manual.

FSR. Field Service Regulation.

G–1. Personnel section of division or higher staff.

G–2 Intelligence section of division or higher staff.

G–3. Operations and training section of division or higher staff.

G–4. Supply section of division or higher staff.

GHQ. General headquarters.

GSP. General Staff, Personnel.

GSUSA. General Staff, United States Army.

Hist. Historical.

ICAF. Industrial College of the Armed Forces (Fort McNair, Washington, D.C.)

Infrastructure. A term used in NATO generally applicable to all fixed and permanent installations, fabrications, or facilities for the support and control of military forces.

Inventory control. That phase of military logistics which includes managing, cataloging, requirements determination, procurement, distribution, overhaul, and disposal of matériel. Synonymous with Matériel Control, Matériel Management, Inventory Management and Supply Management.

JAAF. Joint Action Armed Forces.
JAMAG. Joint American Military Advisory Group.
JAMMAT. Joint American Military Mission for Assistance to Turkey.
JCS. Joint Chiefs of Staff.
Joint staff. A staff formed of two or more of the services of the same country.
JUSMAGG. Joint U.S. Military Advisory Group, Greece.
JUSMAPG. Joint United States Military Advisory and Planning Group.
KMAG. U.S. Military Advisory Group to the Republic of Korea.
KPC. Koblenz Procurement Center.
Level of supply. The quantity of supplies or materials authorized of directed to be held in anticipation of future demands.
LOC. Line of communication, a principal supply line.
Log. Logistics.
Logistics. The science of planning and carrying out the movement and maintenance of forces. In its most comprehensive sense, those aspects of military operations that deal with (1) design and development, acquisition, storage, movement, distribution, maintenance, evacuation, and disposition of matériel; (2) movement, evacuation, and hospitalization of personnel; (3) acquisition or construction, maintenance, operation, and disposition of facilities; (4) acquisition or furnishing of services.
Log. Div. Logistics Division (General Staff).
Ltr. Letter.
MAAG. Military Assistance Advisory Group.
Marshall Plan. Program of United States for European economic recovery after World War II.
Materials handling. The movement of materials (raw materials, scrap, semifinished) to, through, and from productive processes; in warehouses and storage; and in receiving and shipping areas.
MATS. Military Air Transport Service.
MDAP. Mutual Defense Assistance Program.
MEE. Minimum essential equipment.
MFNG. Military Facilities Negotiating Group.
MRS. Memorandum routing slip.
MSA. Mutual Security Agency.
MSP. Mutual Security Program.
MSTS. Military Sea Transportation Service.
NSC. National Security Council.
MTO. Mediterranean Theater of Operations.
NATO. North Atlantic Treaty Organization.
NGUS. National Guard of the United States.
Ocean manifest. A detailed listing of the entire cargo loaded into any one ship showing all pertinent data that will readily identify such cargo.
OCMH. Office of the Chief of Military History.
OEEC. Organization for European Economic Cooperation.
OFLC. Office of the Foreign Liquidation Commissioner.
OPD. Operations Division (General Staff).
ORC. Organized Reserve Corps.

Glossary of Terms and Abbreviations

Ord. Ordnance.
PTT. Postes, Téléphones, et Télégraphs (France).
QMC. Quartermaster Corps.
Rad. Radio.
Req. Requisition.
ROK. Republic of Korea.
ROTC. Reserve Officers Training Corps.
Rpt. Report.
S/A. Secretary of the Army.
SAC. Strategic Air Command.
SACEUR. Supreme Allied Commander Europe.
SEAC. Southeast Asia Command.
Sec. Def. Secretary of Defense.
Sgd. Signed.
SHAPE. Supreme Headquarters, Allied Powers, Europe.
Slice (Division). Total strength of a combat division, together with its appropriate share of supporting forces.
Slice (Infrastructure). Program for a given year of development of NATO's common infrastructure.
SNCF. Société Nationale des Chemins de Fer (French national railroads).
SOP. Standing operating procedure.
SOS. Services of Supply.
Spl. Special.
SPOPP. Surplus Property Office, Plans and Policies.
SS&P. Service, Supply, and Procurement.
STEG. Staatliche Erfassungsgesellshaft für offentliches Gut m.b.H. (a German public corporation).
Sup. Supply.
SW. Secretary of War.
SWPA. Southwest Pacific Area.
TAG. The Adjutant General.
TCC. Temporary Council Committee.
Tech. Servs. Technical services.
TIG. The Inspector General.
TM. Technical manual.
Tp. Telephone.
Tp. Conv. Telephone conversation.
TRAPIL. Société des Transports Pietroliers par Pipeline (a French semipublic corporation).
TRUST. Trieste United States Troops.
TWX. Teletypewriter exchange.
UNRRA. United Nations Relief and Rehabilitation Administration.
USAFFE. U.S. Army Forces, Far East.
USAGG. U.S. Army Group, Greece.
USARAL. U.S. Army, Alaska.

USAREUR. U.S. Army, Europe.
USARPAC. U.S. Army, Pacific.
USARWESPAC. U.S. Army, Western Pacific.
USCA. United States Code Annotated.
USCINCEUR. U.S. Commander in Chief, Europe.
USEUCOM. U.S. European Command (successor to EUCOM).
USFA. U.S. Forces in Austria.
USFET. U.S. Forces, European Theater.
USP&DO. United States Property and Disbursing Officer.
USW. Under Secretary of War.
VITTLES. Berlin airlift.
V–E Day. Victory in Europe.
V–J Day. Victory in Japan.
WAA. War Assets Administration.
WARX. War Exercise.
WD. War Department.
WDGS. War Department General Staff.
WDCSA. War Department, Chief of Staff of the Army.
WDGSP. War Department General Staff, Personnel.
Western Union. The organization developed by the five powers (Belgium, France, Luxembourg, the Netherlands, and the United Kingdom) who had signed the Brussels Pact in 1948.
WEU. Western European Union. The redesignation of Western Union with the adherence of Germany and Italy to the Brussels Pact.
ZI. Zone of the Interior.

Bibliography

U.S. Government Documents and Publications

THE PRESIDENT

Executive Orders, 1945–1953.
Governor of the Panama Canal Zone Annual Reports
Memoranda to the Joint Chiefs of Staff
Commission on Organization of the Executive Branch of the Government
  Task Force Report on National Security Organization, January 1949.

NATIONAL MILITARY ESTABLISHMENT/DEPARTMENT OF DEFENSE

Secretary of Defense
  Annual and Semiannual Reports, 1948–1953.
  Basic Regulations for Military Supply Systems Directive 4000.8, 17 November 1952.
  Joint Termination Regulation
  Letters to the President
  Memorandum for Secretaries of the Army, Navy, and Air Force; the Joint Chiefs of Staff; Chairman, Munitions Boards; Chairman, Research and Development Board. Subject: Department of Defense Supply System, 17 November 1949.
  Messages
  Special Regulations 795–200 series. General Procedures for Furnishing Military Assistance to Foreign Governments
  Operations under the Mutual Defense Assistance Program
  Operations under the Mutual Security Program
Director of Defense Mobilization Quarterly Reports
Industrial College of the Armed Forces
  Lectures
    Bell, John O. 13 February 1950. L50–91.
    Booth, Donald P. "The Roles of JCS in the Generation of Matériel Requirements." 13 October 1948. L49–29.
    Donald, James R. "Canadian Industrial Potential for War. 1949–1950. L50–118.
    Lutes, LeR. "The Munitions Board." 27 October 1948. L49–33.
    Reeder, W. O. "Supply Management." 1 April 1952. L52–135.
    Watkins, Ralph T. "The National Security Resources Board." 15 October 1948. L49.
  Seminar. 17 December 1951.

Student Committee Report. "Organization for the Determination of Matériel Requirements under the National Security Act of 1947."
Joint Chiefs of Staff
    Memoranda, 1948–1953.
    Joint Logistics Plans Committee. Survey of Current U.S. Base Requirements outside the Continental United States, 17 June 1952.
Munitions Board
    Committee on Facilities. Report to the Secretary of Defense on Elimination of Duplication and Overlapping of Facilities and Services. 1949
National Security Resources Board
    Readiness for Mobilization, A Report on the Role and Activities of the National Security Resources Board 1947–1952. January 1953.
Research and Development Board. 1 January 1949.
Weapons Systems Evaluation Group. Handbook. May 1952.

WAR DEPARTMENT/DEPARTMENT OF THE ARMY

Secretary of the Army
    Annual Reports, 1949–1953.
    Report of Trip to Europe of Secretary of the Army Pace and Party. Memo for the Record, 2 September 1952.
    NATO Notebooks
    Directory of Boards and Committees on Which Headquarters, Department of the Army Has Representation. 5 May 1949.
Undersecretary of the Army
    Alexander, Archibald. Orientation Lecture, 8 November 1951.
Assistant Secretary of War/Assistant Secretary of the Army
    Memoranda, 1946.
    Memo for the Record. Conference in Office of the Assistant Secretary of the Army. 3 November 1949.
Chief of Staff
    Biennial Report of the Chief of Staff of the United States Army, 1 July 1943 to 30 June 1945, to the Secretary of War.
    Final Report of the Chief of Staff, United States Army to the Secretary of the Army, 7 February 1948.
Assistant Chief of Staff, G–2
    Debriefing by Colonel John I. Hinke, Military Attache to Iran. The Pentagon, 29 April 1953.
    "Latin America's Military Effort in 1951," *Intelligence Review* 189 (February 1952): 84–89.
Assistant Chief of Staff, G–3
    Historical Summary. Deployments Branch, 1951–1952.
    Historical Summary. Europe and Middle East Branch, 1951–1952.
    Historical Summary. Latin American Branch, 1951–1952.
    Historical Summary. North American Branch, 1951–1952.

Memorandum, Colonel Chaffee for General Gaither, Training of Recruits in U.S. Army Pacific. Far East-Pacific Branch.

Memorandum, Assistant Chief of Staff, G-3, for Chief of Staff, 3 October 1952, Subject: "Re-Expansion of Training Center at Schofield Barracks, Hawaii."

Replacement and Reorganization Training Plan, 1953. Training Branch.

Assistant Chief of Staff, G-4/Service, Supply, and Procurement Division/Logistics Division
Disposition Forms
Historical Summaries
Letters
Logistics Division History, 1948.
Logistics Operations Summaries, 1950–1953.
Logistics Policies and Priorities, 1 November 1952.
Memoranda
Memoranda of Important Actions, 1950–1953.
Messages
Monthly Progress Reports
Reports of Critical Logistics Deficiences. Theaters Branch.
Reports of Critical Problems, 1951–1953.
Review of the Month, 1950.
Report of Staff Visit by G-4 Representatives, Colonel A. M. Parsons and Lt. Col. T. F. Guerin to U.S. Army Alaska, Far East Command, and U.S. Army Pacific, September–October 1951.
Report of Visit by Colonel William Massello, Jr., to Canal Zone, Colombia, Ecuador, and Peru to Appraise and Assist Mutual Defense Assistance Program in Those Countries. 12 May 1953.
"Army Foreign Military Aid," Supply Planning Branch, 1 June 1953.
Correspondence, Foreign Military Aid Branch
Documents on the French Line of Communication. Plans Office, Theater Branch, 1950–1951.
"Foreign Procurement." Historical Summary, Procurement Division, 13 December 1951. Purchases Branch, Procurement Division, 1951–1953.
Supply Supplement to the War Department Troop Deployment, 1 May 1946.
Supply Supplement of the U.S. Army Troop Program, 1 December 1946.
Supply Supplement to the Troop Program and Troop List, 1 August 1950.

Operations Division
Correspondence of Secretary of State, Secretary of War, State-War-Navy Coordinating Committee, Joint Chiefs of Staff, Commanding General Forces, European Theater, Assistant Chief of Staff, Operations Division. August–December 1945.
Disposition Forms
Memoranda, 1945.

Army Field Forces
Inspection of European Command, October 1951.

Army Service Forces
Logistics in World War II, Final Report of the Army Service Forces. 1 July 1947.
Letters, 1945.

Memoranda, 1945.

History of International Division, with Supplements, 1945.

International Division. Report on Lend-Lease Operations, 1 January–10 June 1946.

Chief of Finance

Your Army Dollar, Review and Analysis of Department of the Army Statement of Funds as of 30 June 1951.

Monthly Financial Reports

Chief of Military History

The Army Almanac, 1950.

Chronology of the War Department Views on Coordination or Unification of the Armed Forces, prepared by P. M. Robinett, 1948.

Paone, Rocco M. History of Foreign Military Aid, draft MS.

Peculiarities of Russian Warfare, German Report Series, MS T–22, January 1949.

Chief of Transportation

Data on Monthly Cargo Shipments from Ports of Embarkation, 25 February 1952.

Transportation Corps Notes, March 1951.

Comptroller of the Army

Historical Summaries

Organization of the Department of the Army Staff Study by Management Division, 15 July 1948.

Report, Measures and Recommendations of Major Importance to the Improvement of the Army, 1 July 1950 to 30 December 1952, prepared in response to instructions from outgoing Secretary of the Army Frank Pace.

Quartermaster Corps

"Global Mission of the Quartermaster Corps," Historical Summary, September 1951–December 1952.

Corps of Engineers

Hamilton, James D. T. "History of Northeast District, Corps of Engineers, December 1950 to September 1951."

———. "History of North Atlantic Division." Historical Summary, 25 June 1950 to 8 September 1951.

Army War College

Address by Maj. Gen. C. D. Eddleman, 4 February 1953.

Command and General Staff College

Army Logistics—Continental Armies. Subcourse 29, 1 August 1948 (Revised 1 July 1950).

Logistics (Army)—Theater of Operations. Subcourse 60–27.

Army Regulations, 1948.

Field Manual 31–70. Basic Arctic Manual.

Field Manual 100–10. Field Service Regulations, Administration. September 1949.

Field Manual 110–10. Joint Logistics Policy and Guidance. June 1952.

Special Regulations

140–420–1, "Organized Reserve Corps, Supply and Accounting Procedures, 18 May 1949.

145–420–10, "Reserve Officers Training Corps, Requisitioning and Distribution of Quartermaster Items for ROTC Instruction," 13 May 1949.

Bibliography

725–10–2, "Issues of Supplies and Equipment, Processing Requisitions," 8 June 1949.

730–5–1, "Oversea Supply, Distribution," 15 July 1949.

Technical Manual 38–420, February 1946.

War Department Circular 379. "Property." 19 September 1944.

War Department Memorandum 700–45. "Determination for Surplus Property." 14 September 1945.

War Department Press Releases

Report of Board of Officers on the Reorganization of the War Department, 18 October 1945.

Directory and Station List of the U.S. Army, 15 April 1953.

Handbook on Soviet and Satellite Armies. Department of the Army Pamphlet 30–50–1, March 1953.

U.S. MILITARY COMMANDS

Caribbean Command
 Command Report 1951.
European Command
 Annual Narrative Reports
 Command Reports
 Chart, Army and Air Force Logistic Relationship in European Area, 13 October 1952.
 Directory and Station List. Historical Division, Occupation Forces in Europe Series.
 Disposal of Surplus Property, 1 July 1946–30 June 1947. Occupation Forces in Europe Series.
 "Establishment of Communications through France, 1950–1951." Historical Summary.
 Lay, Elizabeth S. "Berlin Airlift, 1 January–30 September 1949." Occupation Forces in Europe Series.
 Lucas, Joanne M. "Exchange of Troops and Facilities, United States and French Zones, 1950–1951." Historical Division, U.S. Army Europe.
Far East Command
 Selected Data on Occupation of Japan
Iceland Defense Force
 History of Iceland Defense Force Headquarters, Narrative and Documentary Annexes, 1 May 1951–31 October 1952.
U.S. Army Alaska
 Bering Sea Resupply. Beachmaster Report 1952 Season. 22 August 1953.
 Command Reports
 Press Releases
U.S. Advisory Group, Greece
 Brief History, Joint U.S. Military Advisory and Planning Group, Greece. 1 January 1948–31 August 1949.
 Brief History, U.S. Army Group, Greece. 24 May 1949–31 August 1949.
U.S. Forces European Theater

Occupation. Printed in Germany c. 1947.

U.S. Forces Mediterranean Theater of Operations
Messages, Commanding General

U.S. Military Government, Austria
"Military Government, Austria." Report of the U.S. Commissioner, 16 February 1947.

U.S. Military Government, Germany
"Military Government of Germany." Monthly Reports of Military Governor.
Quarterly Report on Germany. Office of the U.S. High Commissioner for Germany, September–December 1949.

U.S. Army Pacific
Command Reports

DEPARTMENT OF STATE

Aid to Greece and Turkey: A Collection of State Papers. Supplement to the *Department of State Bulletin*, 16, 409A, 4 May 1947.

Constitution of Japan. Printed in State Department Publication 2836.

Department of State Bulletin, 1945–1953.

Bradshaw, Mary E. "Military Control of Zone A in Venezia Biulia," *Department of State Bulletin* 16 (June 1947): 1257–72.

Foreign Aid by the United States Government, 1940–1951.

Germany 1947–1949. The Story in Documents. Publication No. 3556, March 1950.

Howard, Harry N. "Some Recent Developments in the Problems of the Turkish Straits, 1945–1946," *Department of State Bulletin* 16 (January 1946): 143–151, 167.

Korea 1945 to 1948. October 1948. Publication 3305.

Mill, Edward W. "One Year of the Philippine Republic," *Department of State Bulletin* 16 (June 1947): 1280ff.

Occupation of Germany, Policy and Progress. Publication No. 2783, August 1947.

Occupation of Japan, Policy and Progress. Publication No. 2671.

Office of Foreign Liquidation Commission. History, Field Commissioner for Japan and Korea, Tokyo. Prepared by Lt. Col. A. K. Akin.

Report to Congress on Foreign Surplus Disposal. January 1947.

Press releases

Reports to Congress on Assistance to Greece and Turkey

Semiannual Reports to Congress on the Mutual Defense Assistance Program

Statement by George Wadsworth, Ambassador to Turkey, submitted to Senate Foreign Relations and Armed Services Committees, 9 June 1950. *Department of State Bulletin* 22 (June 1950): 1047–48.

Statement by John C. Wiley, Ambassador to Iran, submitted to Senate Foreign Relations and Armed Services Committees, and House Foreign Affairs Committee, 9 June 1950. *Department of State Bulletin* 12 (June 1950): 1048.

The United States and the United Nations. 1946. Report, series 7.

United States Relations with China, with Special Reference to Period 1944–1949. Publication 3573.

United States Treaties and Other International Agreements. 1945–1953.

DEPARTMENT OF COMMERCE

Foreign Aid by the United States Government, 1940–1951. A Supplement to the *Survey of Current Business,* 1952.
Foreign Aid by the United States Government; Basic Data through 31 December 1952.

DEPARTMENT OF THE INTERIOR

Mid-century Alaska. 1952

DEPARTMENT OF THE TREASURY

A History of Contract Terminations and Settlements. Office of Contract Settlement. July 1947.
Hearings, War Contract Hardship Claims Board, 1947–1948.
Report by the Director of Contract Settlement to the Congress. Seventh Report. April 1946.
War Contract Terminations and Settlements. Report of the Office of Contract Settlement. Tenth Report. January 1947.

PERSONAL INTERVIEWS

Archibald S. Alexander, Under Secretary of the Army, 17 April 1952.
Peter Beasely, Special Consultant (Panama Canal) to Under Secretary of the Army, 26 June 1953.
Colonel D. L. Coates, Executive Officer, Supply Division, G–4, 27 November 1952.
Colonel Samuel F. Cohn, Army Contract Adjustment Board, Office of Assistant Secretary of the Army, 11 June 1952.
Colonel Dean E. Coonley, Office of Assistant Chief of Staff, G–4, 3 September 1952.
Colonel C. O. Frake, Chief of Disposals Section, Office of Assistant Chief of Staff, G–4, 19 May 1952.
William M. Gray, Issues Section, Distribution Division, Office of Assistant Chief of Staff, G–4, 20 November 1952.
Lt. Col. C. G. Hailey, Weapons Systems Evaluation Group, 8 July 1952.
Colonel Carl L. Junge, Foreign Military Assistance Division, 27 August 1953.
Lt. Gen. Thomas B. Larkin, Assistant Chief of Staff, G–4, 4 April 1952.
Lt. Col. E. Carroll McHenry, Supply Division, Office of Assistant Chief of Staff, G–4, 27 November 1952.
Carroll Meigs, Lend-Lease and Surplus Property Office, Department of State, 20 May 1952.
Office of Military Assistance, Office of Secretary of Defense, 29 December 1953.
Lt. Col. Victor H. Moore, Deputy Executive, Armed Services Petroleum Purchasing Agency, 5 February 1953.

Lt. Col. Larry J. O'Neil, European-Mediterranean-Middle East Section, Theaters Branch, Office of Assistant Chief of Staff, G–4, 26 May 1953.

Maj. Gen. William O. Reeder, Deputy Assistant Chief of Staff, G–4, 16 December 1952.

Lt. Col. R. F. Toomey, Chief, Family Housing Section, Facilities Branch, Assistant Chief of Staff, G–4, 26 June 1953.

William M. Whitman, Secretary of the Panama Canal Company, 26 June 1953.

Lt. Col. Oliver C. Wood, Control Office, Office of Assistant Chief of Staff, G–4, 28 July 1952.

Brig. Gen. Paul F. Yount, Chief of Engineers, 15 December 1952.

Colonel George J. Zimmerman, Chief, Technical Liaison Division, Office of the Chief of Engineers (formerly Comptroller, U.S. Army Europe Communications Zone), 3 June 1953.

CONGRESSIONAL DOCUMENTS

Congressional Record. 1945–1953.

Public Laws
   247, 69th Congress
   457, 78th Congress
   395, 79th Congress
   271, 80th Congress
   253, 80th Congress
   216, 81st Congress
   434, 81st Congress
   581, 81st Congress
   759, 81st Congress
   841, 81st Congress
   165, 82nd Congress
   254, 82nd Congress
   400, 82nd Congress

Public Resolution 83, 76th Congress

United States Code Annotated

House of Representatives
   Report to Congress on Lend-Lease Operations. 20th Report, 5 September 1945. House Doc. 279, 79th Congress, 1st session.
      21st Report, 31 January 1946. House Doc. 432.
      22nd Report, 14 June 1946. House Doc. 663.
      23rd Report, 3 January 1947. House Doc. 41.
      24th Report, 17 November 1947. House Doc. 437.
      27th Report, 14 February 1949. House Doc. 75.
      28th Report, 18 July 1949. House Doc. 263.
      30th Report, 27 April 1950.
      32th Report, 3 October 1951. House Doc. 227.
   Special Committee on Postwar Economic Policy and Planning, Final Report, *Re-*

Bibliography 331

conversion Experience and Current Economic Problems, December 1946. House Report 2729, 79th Congress, 2nd session.

Inter-American Military Cooperation Act. Hearings before House Committee on Foreign Affairs, 79th Congress, 2d session.

Hearings, *National Security Act of 1947*, Committee on Armed Services, House of Representatives. 80th Congress, 1st session.

Report on Public Works in Alaska, Special Subcommittee of House Committee on Armed Services, 31 August–10 September 1951.

The National Defense Program, Unification and Strategy. Hearings before House Committee on Armed Services, 6–21 October 1949. 81st Congress, 1st session.

Department of Defense Appropriations for 1951, Hearings before Subcommittee of House Committee on Appropriations, 81st Congress, 1st session.

Hearings before the Committee on Appropriations, 82nd Congress, 1st session.

Hearings before a Subcommittee of the Committee on Expenditures in the Executive Departments, House of Representatives, 82nd Congress, 1st session.

Report on Audit of Panama Railroad Company, 28 January 1952. House Doc. 336, 82nd Congress, 2nd session.

Hearings before Subcommittee of House Committee on Armed Services Inquiring into Military Supply Policies and Practices, 82nd Congress, 2nd session.

Hearings before Subcommittee on Procurement of House Armed Services Committee, 82nd Congress, 2nd session.

Twenty-second Intermediate Report, Committee on Expenditures in the Executive Departments, 30 December 1952, Military Housing Construction in Alaska. House Report 2507, 82nd Congress, 2nd session.

Hearings on Mutual Security Act Extension, before House Committee on Foreign Affairs, 83rd Congress, 1st session.

Mutual Security Act Extension. Hearings before House Committee on Foreign Affairs, 83rd Congress, 1st session.

Senate

Hearings before the Special Committee Investigating the National Defense Program, Senate, 79th Congress, 1st session.

Additional Report of the Special Committee Investigating the National Defense Program (Mead Committee), 22 March 1946, Investigations Overseas—Surplus Property Abroad, Senate Report 110, Part 5, 79th Congress, 2nd session.

Senate Report 239. 80th Congress, 1st session.

Hearings before the Committee on Armed Services and the Committee on Foreign Relations, U.S. Senate to Conduct an Inquiry into the Military Situation in the Far East and the Facts Surrounding the Relief of General of the Army Douglas MacArthur from his Assignments in that Area, 82nd Congress, 1st session.

Hearings before the Senate Committee on Armed Services and the Committee on Foreign Relations, 82nd Congress, 1st session.

Reports of Preparedness Subcommittee of Senate Committee on Armed Services. Senate Document No. 10, 82nd Congress, 1st session.

Hearings before Senate Committee on Foreign Relations, 82nd Congress, 2nd session.

LIBRARY OF CONGRESS

Spencer, Floyd A. *War and Postwar Greece; an Analysis Based on Greek Writings.* 1952. European Affairs Division.

International Documents and Publications

NORTH ATLANTIC TREATY ORGANIZATION

North Atlantic Council. Communiqués.
NATO Publications
  Periodicals
    NATO Background and Information Notes
    NATO: Facts about the North Atlantic Treaty Organization (Annual)
    NATO Facts and Figures (Annual)
    NATO Handbook (Annual)
    NATO Letter (Monthly)
    NATO Review (Monthly)
  Articles and Monographs
    Lord Ismay. *NATO's First Five Years.* 1955.
    Madre, Jean de. "SHAPE's Fifteen Years at Rocquencourt," *NATO Letter,* April 1967, 17–23.
    Parker, T. W. "NATO Military Development, 1949–1959," *NATO Letter,* April 1959, 5–9.
Supreme Allied Commander, Europe
  Annual Reports

CHINA

Chinese Ministry of information. *China Handbook–1950.*

UNITED KINGDOM

Documents Regarding the Situation in Greece, January 1945. Presented by the Secretary of State for Foreign Affairs to Parliament. Greece No. 1 (1945). London, 1945.

UNITED NATIONS RELIEF AND REHABILITATION ADMINISTRATION

Woodbridge, George and Staff. *UNRRA, The History of the United Nations Relief and Rehabilitation Administration.* New York, 1950.

Books and Monographs

Acheson, Dean. Address. Adelphi Papers no. 5. London: Institute for Strategic Studies, 1963.

———. *Present at the Creation*. New York: W. W. Norton, 1969.

Alexander, R. P., and Avery E. Kolg. "A New Concept in Military Railroad Service," *National Defense Transportation Journal* (March–April, 1951): 55.

Baya, G. Emery. "Army Organization Act of 1950," *Army Digest* 4 (August, 1950).

———. An Explanation of the Army Organization Act of 1950. Prepared in the Management Division, Office of the Comptroller of the Army. Copy in Office, Chief of Military History.

Bemis, Samuel Flagg. *The Latin American Policy of the United States*. New York: Harcout, Brace and Company, 1943.

Boleyn, Paul T. "Logistical Organization for an Overseas Theater," *Military Review* 31 (May 1951): 36–40.

Boll, Michael M., ed. *American Military Mission in the Allied Control Commission for Bulgaria*. East European Monographs, Boulder. New York: Columbia University Press, 1985.

Botting, Douglas. *From the Ruins of the Reich, Germany 1945–1949*. New York: Crown Publishers, 1985.

Brodie, Bernard. "Stragegic Implications of the North Atlantic Pact," *Yale Review* 39 (Winter 1950): 193–208.

Brookings Institution, *Major Problems in U.S. Foreign Policy, 1947*. Washington, D.C. 1947.

———. *Major Problems of United States Foreign Policy, 1949–1950*. Prepared by the International Studies Group. Washington, D.C.: The Brookings Institution, 1949.

Brown, William Adams, and Redvers Opie. *American Foreign Assistance*. Washington: Brookings Institution, 1953.

Cameron, Meribeth E., Thomas H. D. Mahoney, and George E. McReynolds. *China, Japan and the Powers*. New Haven, Conn: Yale University Press, 1948.

Campbell, John C. *The U.S. in World Affairs, 1945–1947*. Published for the Council on Foreign Relations. New York: Harper & Brothers, 1947.

Carlton, William G. *Revolution in American Foreign Policy*. New York: Random House, 1965.

Chester, Edward W. *The United States and Six Atlantic Outposts, The Military and Economic Considerations*. National University Publications. Port Washington, N.Y.: Kennikat Press, 1980.

Clay, Lucius D. *Decision in Germany*. New York: Doubleday, 1950.

Conn, Stetson, Rose C, Engelman, and Byron Fairchild. *Guarding the United States and Its Outposts*. (*United States Army in World War II*) Washington: Office of the Chief of Military History, 1964.

Conn, Stetson, and Byron Fairchild. *The Framework of Hemisphere Defense*. (*United States Army in World War II*). Washington: Office of the Chief of Military History, 1960.

Cressey, George B. *Asia's Lands and Peoples*. 2nd ed. New York: McGraw-Hill, 1951.

Dallin, David J. *Soviet Russia and the Far East*. New Haven, Conn: Yale University Press, 1948.

Deutsch, Karl. *Political Community and the North Atlantic Area*. Princeton, N.J.: Princeton University Press, 1957.

Dewey, Thomas E. *Journey to the Far Pacific*. New York: Doubleday 1952.

Dobb, Maurice. *Soviet Economic Development Since 1917*. London: Routledge & Regan Paul, 1948.

Donovan, Robert J. *Conflict and Crisis; The Presidency of Harry S. Truman, 1945–1948*. New York: W. W. Norton and Company, 1977.

Eccles, Henry E. *European Logistics, 1956*. George Washington University Logistics Research Project No. ONR 41904. Washington, D.C.: George Washington University, 1956.

Ely, Louis B. *Red Army Today*. Harrisburg, Pa: Stackpole Co., 1951.

Feis, Herbert. *The China, Tangle; the American Effort in China from Pearl Harbor to the Marshall Mission*. Princeton: Princeton University Press, 1953.

Fisher, Charles A. *Sound-East Asia: A Social, Economic and Political Geography*. London: Methuen & Co., 1964.

Foo Chien, Frederick, *The Opening of Korea: A Study of Chinese Diplomacy, 1876–1885*. New York: The Shoestring Press, 1967.

Gantenbein, James W., ed. *The Evolution of our Latin American Policy*. New York: Columbia University Press, 1950.

Kaplan, Lawrence S. *Recent American Foreign Policy*. Homewood, Il.: The Dorsey Press, 1968.

Kennan, George F. *Memoirs, 1925–1950*. New York: Atlantic/Little, Brown, and Co., 1967.

Lasser, J. K. *How to Speed up Settlement of Your Terminated War Contract*. New York: McGraw-Hill, 1945.

Lauterback, Richard E. *Through Russia's Back Door*. New York: Harper and Brothers, 1946.

Légère, Lawence J., Jr. "Unification of the Armed Forces." Ph.D. Dissertation, Harvard University, 1950. Copy in Office, Chief of Military History.

Leahy, William D. *I was There*. New York: Whittlesey House, 1950.

Liddell Hart, B. H. *Deterrent or Defense*. New York: Praeger, 1960.

Lippmann, Walter. *Cold War: A Study in U.S. Foreign Policy*, New York: Harper and Brothers, 1947.

Liu, F. F. *A Military History of China: 1924–1949*. Princeton: Princeton University Press, 1956.

Mako, William P. *U.S. Ground Forces and the Defense of Western Europe*. Washington: The Brookings Institution, 1983.

Marshall, S. L. A. *The Soldier's Load and the Mobility of a Nation*. Washington: Combat Forces Press, 1952.

McCune, George M., and Arthur L. Grey, Jr. *Korea Today*. Cambridge, Ma: Harvard University Press, 1950.

Meade, E. Grant. *American Military Government in Korea*. New York: King's Crown Press, 1951.

Mikhailov, Nicholas. *Soviet Russia, The Land and Its People*. New York: Sheridan House, 1948.

Millis, Walter, ed. *Forrestal Diaries*. New York: The Viking Press, 1951.

The Military Balance, 1967–1968. London: Institute of Strategic Studies, 1967.

Murphy, Robert. *Diplomat Among Warriors.* New York: Doubleday, 1964; New York: Pyramid Books, 1965.

Nelson, Otto L. *National Security and the General Staff.* Washington: Infantry Journal Press, 1946.

New York University Conference on Problems of Termination and Reconversion, 1944.

Perkins, Dexter. *The Diplomacy of a New Age: Major Issues in U.S. Policy Since 1945.* Bloomington: Indiana University Press, 1967.

Pollock, James K., and James H. Meisel. *Germany under Occupation: Illustrative Materials and Documents.* Ann Arbor: University of Michigan Press, 1947.

Reitzel, William, Mortan A. Kaplan and Constance G. Coblenz. *United States Foreign Policy, 1945–1955.* Washington: The Brookings Institution, 1956.

Rigg, Robert B. *Red China's Fighting Hordes.* Harrisburg, Pa.: Military Services Publishing Co., 1951.

Romanus, Charles F., and Riley Sunderland. *Stilwell's Mission to China* [*U.S. Army in World War II*]. Washington: Office of the Chief of Military History, 1953.

———. *Stilwell's Command Problems* [*U.S. Army in World War II*]. Washington: Office of the Chief of Military History, 1956.

———. *Time Runs out in CBI* [*U.S. Army in World War II*]. Washington: Office of the Chief of Military History, 1959.

Rovere, Richard and Arthur M. Schesinger, Jr. *The General and the President, The Future of American Foreign Policy.* New York: Farrar, Straus, and Young, 1951. Republished as *The MacArthur Controversy and American Foreign Policy,* New York: Farrar, Strous and Giroux, 1965.

Royal Institute of Internationl Affairs. *Defense in the Cold War: The Task for the Free World.* London, 1950.

Sawyer, Robert K. *Military Advisors in Korea: KMAG in Peace and War, (Army Historical Series).* Washington: Office of the Chief of Military History, 1962.

Schmitt, Hans A., ed. *U.S. Occupation in Europe After World War II. Papers and Reminiscences from the 23–24 April 1976 Conference Held at the George C. Marshall Research Foundation, Lexington, Virginia.* Lawrence, Ks.: Regents Press of Kansas, 1978.

Schwartz, Harry. *Red Phoenix: Russia Since World War II.* New York: Praeger, 1961.

———. *Russia's Soviet Economy.* New York: Prentice-Hall, 1951.

Shabad, Theodore. *Geography of the USSR: A Regional Survey.* New York: Columbia University Press, 1951.

Shlaim, Avi. *The United States and the Berlin Blockade, 1948–1949.* Berkeley and Los Angeles: University of California Press, 1983.

Somers, Herman Miles. *Presidential Agency; The Office of War Mobilization and Reconversion.* Cambridge: Harvard University Press, 1951.

Sparrow, John C. *History of Personnel Demobilization in the United States Army.* Washington, D. C.: Office of the Chief of Military History, 1951.

Spector, Ivar. *Soviet Strength and Strategy in Asia.* Seattle: University of Washington Press, 1950.

Stebbins, Richard B. *The United States in World Affairs, 1954.* New York: Harper and Brothers for the Council on Foreign Relations, 1956.

Stimson, Henry L. and McGeorge Bundy. *On Active Service in Peace and War.* New York: Harper and Brothers, 1947.

Tansill, Charles Callan. *America Goes to War.* Boston: Little, Brown & Co., 1938.
Taylor, Maxwell. *The Uncertain Trumpet.* New York: Harper and Brothers, 1960.
Truman, Harry S. *Memoirs.* 2 vols. Garden City, N.Y.: Doubleday, 1956.
Tuchman, Barbara W. *Stilwell and the American Experience in China, 1911-45.* New York: The Macmillan Company, 1971.
Utley, Freda. *The China Story.* Chicago: H. Regnery Co., 1951.
Vail Motter, T. H. *The Persian Corridor and Aid to Russia,* in *U.S. Army in World War II.* Washington, D.C.: Office of the Chief of Military History, 1952.
Vinacke, Harold M. *Far Eastern Politics in the Postwar Period.* New York: Appleton-Century-Crofts, 1956.
Whitnah, Donald R. and Edgar L. Erickson. *Occupation of Austria, Planning and Early Years.* Washington, Ct.: Greenwood Press, 1985.
Wolfe, Roy I. *Transportation and Politics.* New York: D. Van Nostrand Co., 1963.
Zink, Harold. *American Military Government in Germany.* New York: Macmillan Co., 1947.
Ziemke, Earl F. *The U.S. Army in the Occupation of Germany 1944-1946. (Army Historical Series).* Washington: Center of Military History, United States Army, 1975.

Articles and Periodicals

NEWSPAPERS AND NEWS MAGAZINES

Christian Science Monitor
Daily Telegraph (London)
Diplomat (Geneva)
The Economist (London)
Financial Times (London)
Frankfurter Allgemeine Zeitung
Le Monde
Lloyds Daily List
Manchester Guardian
New Orleans Times—Picayune
Newsweek
The New York Herald Tribune
The New York Herald Tribune (European edition)
The New York Journal American
The New York Times
Paris-Match
The Philadelphia Inquirer
The Reporter
Time Magazine
The Times (London)
U.S. News and World Report

The Washington Post
The Washington Star

ARTICLES

Acheson, Dean. Text of Speech hefore the National Press Club, Washington, D.C. 12 January 1950. *Vital Speeches of the Day,* 16 (Feburary 1950): 238–44.

Allen, Frederick Lewis. "This Time and Last Time." *Harper's Magazine,* March 1947, 195 ff.

Balchen, Bernt. "Engineering Problems in the Arctic," *The Military Engineer* 44 (November–December 1952): 426–28.

Baldwin, Hanson W. "French Defenses Thin," *The New York Times,* 22 November 1952.

Baldwin, Hanson W. "North Atlantic Treaty Powers Face a Crisis in European Defense," *New Work Times,* 14 December 1952.

Besson, Frank S., Jr. "Logistics and Transportation in the Defense of Western Europe." *National Transportation Journal 12* (March–April 1956): 54–57, 64–65.

Birrenbach, Kurt. "Partnership and Consultation in NATO." *Atlantic Community Quarterly* 2 (Spring 1964): 62–71.

"Birth of a Base." *Life,* 22 September 1952.

Bissell, Richard M. "Foreign Aid. What Sort? How Much? How Long?" *Foreign Affairs* 31 (October 1952): 15–28.

Blakeney, Thomas O. "The Security of Alaska and the Tundra Army," *Military Review* 32 (September 1952): 4–7.

Boleyn, Paul T. "Logistical Organization for an Overseas Theaters," *Military Review* 31 (May 1951): 36–40.

Brewer, Sam Pope. "U.S., Brazil Sign Military Aid Pact," *New York Times,* 16 March 1952.

Brodie, Bernard. "Strategic Implications of the North Atlantic Pact." *Yale Review* 39 (Winter 1950): 193–208.

Bryan, Kirk. "The Study of Permanently Frozen Ground and Intensive Frost Action," *The Military Engineer* 40 (July 1948): 304–8.

Callendar, Harold. "Most NATO Nations Lift Arms Outlay," *The New York Times,* 21 December 1952.

———. "Slight Arms Rise Seen in '53 in NATO," *The New York Times,* 26 November 1952.

Coats, James G. "The Supply Distribution Cycle," *Military Review* 32, 1 (April 1952): 44–52.

Curtin, Edwin P. "American Advisory Group Aids Greece in War on Guerrillas," *Armored Cavalry Journal* 58 (January–February 1949): 8–11, 34–35.

Denniston, Alfred B. "Some Accomplishments of Unification in the Field of Logistics," *Military Review* (April 1951): 38ff.

Deutscher, Isaac. "Stalin's Stake in Mao's Army," *Reporter* 6 (May 1952): 27–29.

Dobbs, Charles M. "Limiting Room to Mancuver: The Korea Assistance Act of 1949," *Historian,* 48 (August 1986): 525–38.

"Dulles Indicates Shift in Aid from Europe to the Far East," *The New York Times,* 13 April 1953.

Dyhrmann, Fred P. "'Detroit on the Isar,'" *Ordnance,* 37 (July–Aug. 1952): 5–7.
"Fallen Hopes Engulf the Land of the Rising Sun," *Newsweek,* 17 August 1953, 34–36.
Feldman, Herman. "Logistic Support for the Unified Command and Overseas Theater," *Military Review* 31 (July 1951): 3–10.
Franks, H. George, "The Great Achievement of Infrastructure," *NATO's Fifteen Nations* 4 (April 1959): 130–42: 5 (1960): 24–33.
Fudge, Russell O. "Turks' Friends and Advisors," *U.S. Army Combat Forces Journal* 2 (June 1952): 30–32.
"Germans Go Ahead on Army Planning," *The New York Times,* 19 April 1953.
Gordon, Lincoln. "NATO in the Nuclear Age," *Yale Review* 48 (March 1959): 321–35.
Hamilton, James W. "Operation Reverse," *Army Transportation Journal,* 2 (September 1946): 20–21.
Hargrave, Thomas J. "Agency of Preparedness," *The Quartermaster Review* 27 (March–April 1948): 10–13.
―――. "Security Through Planning," *Ordnance* 32 (January–February 1948): 238–39.
Hoffman, Michael L. "2-Year U.S. Budget on Arms Aid Urged," *New York Times,* 30 November 1952.
Howard, R. A., Jr. "The Munitions Board," *Quartermaster Review* 30 (March–April 1951): 10–11, 134–41.
Hulen, Bertram D. "Move to Arm Americas Was a Double Motive," *The New York Times,* 1 June 1947.
"Indonesia Agrees to New Aid Terms," *The New York Times,* 14 December 1952.
Jacques, Philippe G. "The Joint Chiefs of Staff," *The Quartermaster Review* 29 (Janunary–Feburary 1950): 10–11, 129.
Johnston, Kilbourne. "Department of the Army Reorganized," *Army Information Digest* (December 1948): 31–34.
Kaplan, Jacob J. "United States Aid Programs: Post Perspectives and Future Needs," World Politics, 3 (October 1950): 55–71.
Kluttz, Jerry. "If War Comes Again," *Nation's Business* 26 (July 1948): 29–31, 72–73.
Larkin, Thomas B. "The Logistics Division," *The Quartermaster Review* 29 (March–April 1950): 2–3.
Liddell Hart, B. H. "Is Western Europe Defensible?" *New Republic* 121 (August 1950): 14–16.
Love, Kennett, "Iran's Army Now Holds the Balance of Power," *The New York Times,* 23 August 1953.
Marston, Col. Anson D. "Doctrine and Reserve Components," *Quartermaster Review* 30 (March–April 1950): 21–33.
Maynard, Lemuel. "Mobilizing Munitions," *The Quartermaster Review* 30 (May-June 1951): 22–23, 115–16.
Mays, Donald. "Pilgrims of 1946," *Army Transportation Journal,* 2 (May 1946): 2–4.
Middleton, Drew. "Soviet Army Loses Big Lead in Europe," *The New York Times,* 4 September 1952.
―――. "Soviet Re-Equips Force in Germany," *The New York Times,* 11 September 1952.

Noyes, John R. "Transportation in Alaska," *The Military Engineer* 45 (March–April 1953): 99–103.

O'Donnell, James P. "We're All Fouled up in France," *Saturday Evening Post* 11 (April 1953): 40–41.

"Operation Alspost," *Quartermaster Review* 28 (January–February 1949): 69–70, 98.

Pleven, Rene. "France in the Atlantic Community," *Foreign Affairs* 39 (October 1959): 29–30.

Reinhardt, George C. "How Do We Get the Word?" *Military Review* 32 (August 1952): 34–36.

Richards, George. "Procurement of Defense Matériel," *Quartermaster Review* 29 (January-February 1950): 16–17, 124–128.

Roberts, Palmer W. "Effects on Materials in Arctic Cold," *Military Engineer* 42 (1950): 176–78, 272–73, 366–69, 452–55.

———. "Cold Weather Engineering," *The Military Engineer,* 45 (January-February 1953): 1–5.

Roper, Elmo. "Who Blocked Preparedness?" *Freedom and Union* 5 (September 1951): 29–30.

Scholin, Allan R. "Science: Key to Defense Progress," *The Quartermaster Review* 29 (January-February 1950): 12–15.

Schen, "The Return of our War Dead," *The Quartermaster Review* 26 (July–August 1946): 16, 18, 86.

Scott, Stanley L. "The Military Aid Program," *Annals of the American Academy of Political and Social Science* 278 (November 1951).

Smith, Kingsbury. "NATO Lags," *New York Journal American,* 10 August 1952.

Somers, Herman Miles. "Civil-Military relations in Mutual Security," *Annals of the American Academy of Political and Social Science* 288 (July 1953): 27–35.

Staley, Eugene. "The Myth of the Continents," *Foreign Affairs* 19 (April 1941): 481–94.

Stern, Michael. "How Back-Door Dawson Got $100,000,000." *True*, May 1952.

Stevens, Austin. "Base Created in Greenland for U.S.–Danish Defense," *New York Times,* 19 September 1952.

Strum, W. C. "Disposition of Surplus Property," *The Quartermaster Review* 26 (May–June 1947): 35 ff.

Sulzberger, C. L. "NATO Goals in Sight Despite Some Setbacks," *The New York Times* 10 August 1952.

"U.S. Point Four Office Sacked by Iranians," *The New York Times,* 17 April 1953.

"U.S. Will Help Arm Bonn After Europe Implements Pace," *The New York Times,* 10 April 1953.

Welles, Benjamin. "Ridgway Sees Progress in a Vast Defense Job," *New York Times,* 16 November 1952.

White, Claude W. and Eugene E. Monk. "The Chemical Corps in Alaska," *Armed Forces Chemical Journal* 6 (October 1952): 4–5.

Wilmot, Chester. "If NATO Had to Fight," *Foreign Affairs* 31 (January 1953): 201–03.

Wilson, Walter K., Jr. "The Problem of Permafrost," *The Military Engineer* 40 (April 1948): 114–17, 162–64.

Yount, Mason J. "Our New European Supply Line," *Army Information Digest* 6 (October 1951): 56.

Index

Acheson, Dean, 37, 172, 214, 226, 239, 242, 271
Act for International Development ("Point Four"), 146
Act of Chapultepec, 267
Advisory Board of Liquidation (1918), 18
Afyon, Turkey, 193
Alaska, 280–96
Alaska Highway, 291–92, 295
Alaskan Air Command, 283, 295
Alaskan Command, 282, 288
Alaskan Communications System, 283–94
Alaska Railroad, 291–95
Albania, 181, 183–84
Air Force supply system in Europe, 99–100
Albrook Air Force Base, Canal Zone, 258
Aleutian Islands, 284
Alfred Hopkins and Associates, 297
Aliamanu Crater area, Hawaii, 304
Al Johnson Construction Company, 297
Allied Command Atlantic (NATO), 163
Allied Command Europe (NATO), 163
Allied Maritime Transport Council (World War I), 163
American Battle Monuments Commission, 93
American Expeditionary Force (World War I), 18
American Mission for Aid to Greece, 170–79
American Mission for Aid to Turkey, 192
American Overseas Airlines, 301
American Telephone and Telegraph Company, 295
Anchorage, Alaska, 281, 291
Anglo-Iranian Oil Company, 132, 196
Annam, 237
Arctic Indoctrination and Test Center, Big Delta, Alaska, 284
Arctic Ocean, 293

Argentina, 265, 266–67
Armed forces procurement, 81–83
Armed Forces Procurement Act of 1947, 81–82
Army Air Forces, 21, 57
Army Service Forces, 21, 37, 57, 59–62
Arnold, Maj. Gen. William H., 191
Arthur, Chester A., 221
Asphalt Institute, 119
Associated States of Indochina, 238
Association of Icelandic Contractors, 302
Atcheson, George, 204
Atlantic Command, 301
Atlas Constructors, 116–23
Atomic explosion in Soviet Union (1949), 161
Attlee, Clement, 59
Aurand, Lt. Gen. Henry S., 41, 303, 305
Australia, 32–33, 201
Austria, 95, 102, 113–15

Badger, Vice Adm. Oscar C., 213
Baffin Bay, 279
Balboa general depot, Canal Zone, 258
Balchen, Bernt, 296
Balikesir, Turkey, 193
Bandirma, Turkey, 193
Bao Dai, 237–38
BAREX supply expeditions, Alaska, 293
Barr, Maj. Gen. David G., 213–14
Barter Island, Alaska, 293
Baruch-Hancock Report on War and Post-War Adjustment Policy (1944), 18
Bates and Rogers Construction Corporation, 116
Bayerne Motor Werke, 107
Beadle, Lt. Col. W. L., 118
Belgium, 146
Bendetsen, Karl R., 262
Ben Guerir, Morocco, 117
Berlin, blockade of, 87–91
Bidault, Georges, 245
Big Delta, Alaska, 283, 290, 294

341

Bipartite Control Office, 89
Bizonal Economic Council, 29
Blue Jay project, Greenland, 297
Blythe Brothers Company, 116
Bogota charter (1948), 267
Bolivar, Simon, 264
Bomb shelters, 71–72
Bonner, Herbert C., 109
Bordeaux, 92
Borders, Carl, 30
Boulhait, Morocco, 118
Braden, Spruille, 271
Brazil, 37, 266, 268–69, 275
Bremerhaven Port of Embarkation, 92
Brink, Brig. Gen. Francis, 239, 241
British Military Mission in Greece, 179
Brooks Army Hospital, San Antonio, 260
Brownfield, Brig. Gen. Ralph O., 301
Bruce, David, 92
Brussels Pact, 160
Budget Advisory Committee, War Department, 83
Build-up of forces in Europe, 103–13
Bureau of the Budget, 83
Burma, 33
Butler, R. A., 168
Byrnes, James F., 272

Cabot, John M., 276
Cambodia, 238–39, 244
Camp Drum Storage Depot, Innsbruck, 95
Camp Stoneman, California, 305
Camp Tortuquero, Puerto Rico, 258
Canada, 278–80
Canada–United States Regional Planning Group (NATO), 280
Cannon, Clarence, 153
Canterbury Corporation, 31
Captieux, 94
Caribbean Air Command, 275–76
Caribbean Command, 145, 258, 275
Carney, Adm. R. D., 189
Casablanca, 117
Caserne Coligny, Orleans, 93
Chamberlin, Lt. Gen. Stephen J., 87
Chang Chih-chung, General, 206
Chang Taisang, 225
Channel Committee (NATO), 163
Chase, Maj. Gen. William C., 220
Chevrolet Shell Plant, 74
Chiang Kai-sheck, Generalissimo, 62, 207, 217–18

Chilcoot Barracks, Alaska, 287
Chile, 146, 275
China, 14, 32–35, 62–63, 130, 136, 202–16; "loss of," 215–17
China Aid Act (1948), 210, 213, 219
China Aid Program, 210–13
China "White Paper," 212
Chinese Nationalists, 207–9, 214–15, 219
Chosen, Democratic People's Republic of (North Korea), 223
Chou En-lai, General, 206
Churchill, Winston, 130
Claremont Terminal, Jersey City, 119–20
Clay, Lt. Gen. Lucius D., 28, 87–91
Clayton, W. L., 33
Cleveland, Grover, 221
Cochin-China, 237–38
Collins, Gen. J. Lawton, 106
Colombia, 146, 275
Colombian infantry battalion, 259
Communications Zone, European Command, 94
Communist Party: in China, 204, 206, 208–9, 245–46; in Indochina, 237; in Western Europe, 173
Condon-Cunningham of Omaha, 297
Connoly, Maj. Gen. Donald H., 19
Construction procedures, Alaska, 285–87
Continental Motors Trust, 109
Convention for the Maintenance, Preservation and Re-establishment of Peace, Buenos Aires, 1936, 265
Cook Inlet, 291
Corinth Canal, 181
Corozal ordnance depot, Canal Zone, 258
Corps of Engineers: Alaska District, 283; East Atlantic District, 116; New York District, 297; Mediterranean Division, 121; North Atlantic Division, 116; North District, Iceland, 302
Critical materials, 75–78
Cuba, 146, 266, 275
Cumoavasi Depot at Izmir, Turkey, 193

Dade Bros, Inc., 119–20
Daimler-Benz plant, near Stuttgart, 107
Dairen, 206
Dawes, Brig. Gen. Charles G., 18
Dawson, George, 109
Dawson Creek, Alaska, 292
Declaration of Lima (1938), 265–66
Declaration of Reciprocal Assistance and

Index

Cooperation for the Defense of the Nations of the Americas (Havana, 1940), 266
Defense Housing Commission, 289
de Lattre de Tassigny, Gen. Jean, 240–42, 244
Demobilization after World War II, 14–18
Demobilization, men and matériel, 16–18
Denmark, 146, 296, 300
Department of Defense, 143–56, 242
Department of Labor, 299
Department of the Interior, 291
Derby, Col. George T., 115
Director for Mutual Security, 144, 147–56
Disposal of surplus property overseas, 18–38
Diyarbakir, Turkey, 193
Djema Sahim, Morocco, 118
Dominican Republic, 275
Dulles, John Foster, 172–73, 228, 243, 245–46, 250
Dunkirk, 130

Economic Cooperation Act of 1948, 171
Eden, Anthony, 173
Edmonton, Alberta, 295
Eighth Army, 105
Eighty-fourth Ordnance Battalion, 107
Eilson Air Force Base, Alaska, 289
Eisenhower, General of the Army Dwight D. (president), 15, 41–42, 100, 163, 245, 271
Elmendorf Air Force Base, Alaska, 283, 295
El Salvador, 260
Emergency Advisory Committee for Political Defense (Montevideo), 266
Erzincan, Turkey, 193
Eskisehir, Turkey, 193
Euboea, 181
European Command, 29, 97–101
European Defense Community: proposed, 172–73
European Recovery Program (Marshall Plan), 31
European Theater of Operations, 17
Export-Import Bank, 129, 170

Fairbanks, Alaska, 291
Family housing, 69–71
Far East, 174, 200–255; military assistance in, 200–202
Far East Command, 32, 101, 155, 211–12, 239, 248, 303
Farman, Gen. D. L., 248
Federal Bureau of Supply, Department of the Treasury, 76
Federal Housing Administration (FHA), 70–76
Federal Property and Administrative Services Act of 1949, 44
Ferguson, Homer, 197
First Infantry Division, 105
Fifth Infantry Division, 301
503d Airborne Regimental Combat Team, 294
Foreign Economic Administration, 55
Foreign military aid, 128–56
Foreign Military Assistance Coordinating Committee, 143, 227
Formosa (Taiwan), 146, 211, 216–21
Forrestal, James V., 88
Fort Brooke, Puerto Rico, 258
Fort Buchanan, Puerto Rico, 258
Fort Churchill, Manitoba, 294
Fort Clayton, Canal Zone, 258
Fort Kamehameha, Hawaii, 304
Fort Richardson, Alaska, 284, 287, 289–90
Fort Shafter, Hawaii, 303
Fort Yukon, Alaska, 281
Fourth Infantry Division, 105
Fourth Logistical Command, 114
Forty-third Infantry Division, 105
France, 23–25, 60, 92–96, 111–13, 140, 146, 172–73, 237–46
Franco, Generalissimo Francisco, 170
Frankford Arsenal, 72
French, Col. F. F., 122
French Public Health Service, 38
Fu Tso-yi General, 213

Galema airport, Alaska, 282
Gauss, Clarence E., 204
General Accounting Office, 153, 290
General Commodities Corporation, 35
General Services Administration, 74–75
George Committee (U.S. Senate), 18
Germany, 25–31, 55, 71–72, 91–92, 129; Federal Republic of, 172–73
Gilbert Islands, 32
Gillem, Lt. Gen. A. C., 210
Gordon Hamilton Contracting Company, 192

Grady, Henry F., 180, 182
Grammos Mountains (Greece), 181, 183–84
Greece, 132–35, 146, 162, 178–90
Greenland, 296–300
Greer, Rear Adm. M. R., 258
Griffith, John M., 119
Griswold, Dwight P., 178
Grove, Shepherd, Wilson and Kruge, Inc., 193
Guam, 32, 34–35

Haines, Alaska, 291, 293
Haiphong, 240
Hamilton, Brig. Gen. P. M., 117
Hanau Engineer Depot, 107
Handy, Gen. Thomas, 101
Hankow, 213
Hanoi, 238, 240
Harriman, Averill, 143, 168
Hawaii, 32, 303–8
Hawaiian Defense Command, 303
Hawaiian Infantry Training Center, 305–6
Hayes Peninsula, Greenland, 296
Heath, Donald Reade, 244
Henschel and Sohn locomotive factory, Kassel, 109
Hickman Air Force Base, Hawaii, 304
Ho Chi Minh, 237–38
Hodge, Lt. Gen. John R., 224
Hoffman, Paul G., 31
Holifield, Chet, 290
Honolulu Army Port, 304–5
Hopkins, Harry, 60
Housing: family, 69–71; in Alaska, 289
Huff, Col. F. L., 248
Huks, Philippine guerillas, 236
Hull, Cordell, 236
Hurley, Maj. Gen. Patrick, 204
Hutchens, Lt. Col. C. E., 248
H. V. Grosch Company, 37–38

Iceland, 300–303
Iceland Airport Corporation, 301
Iceland Defense Force, 301–3
Inchon landing, 162
India, 32–33, 156
Indochina, 146, 155, 173, 236–46
Indochina Armistice Agreement (Geneva, 1954), 246
Indochinese Federation, 237–38
Indonesia, 146

Industrial facilities reserves, 73–75
Infrastructure program (NATO), 165–68
Installations, 68–69
Inter-American Conference for the Maintenance of Peace (Buenos Aires, 1936), 265
Inter-American Conference on Problems of War and Peace (Chapultepec, Mexico, 1945), 267
Inter-American Defense Board, 266, 274
Inter-American Military Cooperation Bill (1946), 271–72
Inter-American Treaty of Reciprocal Assistance (Rio Treaty, 1947), 267–68
International Conferences of American States, 264–65
International Security Affairs Committee, 143
Iran, 132–33, 146; military aid to, 194–97
Iran-Iraq Service Command (World War II), 194
Israel, 197
Italy, 31, 140, 146, 173
Iwo Jima, 32

Jamaica, 260
Japan, 36, 55, 63, 156, 227–28, 243, 246–51; surrender of (World War II), 17; treaty of peace, 15
Jenkins, Brig. Gen. Reuben E., 180, 182, 189
Johnson, Louis A., 259
Johnson, Lyndon B., 119, 122, 306
Johnson Committee (U.S. Senate), 123
Johnston Island, 305
Joint American Military Advisory Group (JAMAG) (London), 145
Joint American Military Mission for Aid to Turkey, 192
Joint Army-Navy Machine Tool program (JANMAT), 74–75
Joint Brazil–United States Military Commission, 259, 269, 275
Joint Chiefs of Staff, 96, 100–101, 115, 144–45, 147–56, 164, 223, 235, 274, 283, 287, 301
Joint Logistics Plans Committee, 142
Joint Mexican–United States Defense Commission, 269
Joint Mobilization Plan, 153
Joint Munitions Allocations Committee, 151, 154–55
Joint Strategic Plans Committee, 142

Index

Joint Task Force 109, Iceland, 301
Joint U.S. Military Advisory and Planning Group (Greece), 179, 184–85, 187
Joint U.S. Military Advisory Group, China, 212–13
Joint U.S. Military Advisory Group, Philippines, 234
Joint U.S. Military Group, Spain, 171
Joint War Production Board (U.S. and Canada, World War II), 278
Jones, Herbert A., 38
J. P. Morgan and Company, 128

Kankakee Ordnance Works, 74
Kanzler, Ernest, 18
Karachi, India, 33
Karlsfeld Ordnance Center, 107
Kayserie, Turkey, 193
Keflavik airport, Iceland, 301
Kennan, George F., 216
Keynes, John Maynard, 59
Kimpo airfield, Korea, 225
Kipapa, Hawaii, 304
KMAG (Military Advisory Group to the Republic of Korea), 145, 225, 227
Knowland, William F., 217
Kodiak, Alaska, 284
Korea, 36, 90, 105, 146; defense assistance to, 221–28; Republic of, 222, 228
Korean Aid Bill (1949), 226–27
Korean War, 90, 108–13, 137, 161–62, 190, 219, 242, 246–49, 256, 303, 308–9
Krauthaff, Brig. Gen. Charles R., 18
Kuomintang, 204, 207

Labrador, 300
Ladd Air Force Base, Alaska, 284–85, 290
Lake City Arsenal, 74
Langson, Viet Minh supply base, 244
Laos, 238–39, 244
La Pallice, 92
Larkin, Maj. Gen. Thomas B., 137
La Rochelle, 93–94
Latin America, 37–38, 136; military assistance to, 263–77
Lawson, Alfred W., 38
Leahy, Fleet Adm. William O., 59
Leghorn, 95, 113–14
Lehner, Col. Charles R., 179
LeMay, Lt. Gen. Curtis E., 88–89
Lend-Lease, 131, 194, 204, 270, 273, 277; termination of, 54–63
Lend-Lease Act: extension of, 57
Liberal Party of Japan, 251
Lines of communication: to Austria, 95; across France, 92–95, 167; in Germany, 91–92; across Italy, 95–96, 167
Lipsett Pacific Corporation, 35
Lisbon goals for expansion of NATO military forces, 169, 173, 242
Livesay, Maj. Gen. William, 179
Lockheed Aircraft Overseas Corporation, 301
Logistics: definition of, 7
London Logistics Group, 180–81, 185
Lovett, Robert A., 141, 246
Lutes, Lt. Gen. LeRoy, 39
Luxembourg, 146
Luzon, 236

MacArthur, General of the Army Douglas, 36, 190, 217–18, 220, 224, 227, 233–34, 247
McBride, Lt. Gen. Horace L., 258
McCabe, Thomas B., 19
McCormick, Adm. Lynde D., 163
McGaw, Brig. Gen. Edward J., 301
Machinenfabrik-Augsburg-Nurnberg plant, 107
McNarney, Gen. Joseph T., 28, 36
McNutt, Paul V., 234
Magruder, Maj. Gen. Carter B., 28
Manchuria, 63, 206–9, 212–13
Manila, the Philippines, 34
Mantanuska Valley, Alaska, 281
Mao Tse-tung, 206
"Markos," General, 182
Marrakech, Morocco, 117
Marshall, General of the Army George C., 35, 134, 206–7, 212, 214, 220–21, 223, 271
Marshall Islands, 32
Marshall Plan, 76, 137, 164, 171
Maxon, Glen, 121
Mayer, Rene, 245
Mead Committee (U.S. Senate), 33, 42
Mechra bel Ksiri, Morocco, 117
Mediterranean Theater of Operations, 17
Meknes, Morocco, 117
Merzifon, Turkey, 193
Metcalf and Eddy of Boston, 297
Mexico, 266, 269
Military Air Transport Service (MATS), 294, 297, 302, 304–5

Military Assistance Advisory Groups (MAAGs), 134, 145–56, 220, 239, 251, 275
Military Assistance Advisory Group to the Republic of Korea (KMAG), 145
Military Housing Insurance Fund, 70
Military Missions in Latin America, 146, 268–70, 275
Mitchell, Brig. Gen. William, 280
Moch, Jules, 172, 242
Monnet, Jean, 168, 242
Monroe Doctrine, 263
Moody, Col. L. B., 213
Morocco, 115–23, 173
Morris, Lt. Gen. W. H. H., Jr., 258
Morrison-Knudson Company, 116
Mossadegh, Mohammed, 196–97
Mount Olympus, 183
Muccio, John C., 227
Mukden, 207
Munitions allocations and priorities, 154–56
Munitions Board, 76–78, 144
Murphy, Robert, 88, 90
Mutual Assistance Advisory Committee, 144
Mutual Defense Assistance Act of 1951, 137
Mutual Defense Assistance Program (MDAP), 136–43, 162, 170–72, 188, 193–97, 200–201, 203, 219, 220, 227–28, 236, 239–42, 246, 251, 273–74
Mutual Security Act of 1951, 137, 274
Mutual Security Act of 1952, 138, 149, 243
Mutual Security Agency, 144, 153
Mutual Security Appropriation Act (1953), 149
Mutual Security Appropriations (1951), 137
Mutual Security Program, 101, 137, 139, 236

Nakenk, Alaska, 293
Nanking, 211, 213
Nanking Headquarters Command, 205
Nash, Frank, 195
National Guard, 78–80, 155, 284, 304
National Industrial Plant Reserve, 73–75
National Memorial Cemetery for the Pacific, in the Punchbowl, Hawaii, 307
Naval Forces, Eastern Atlantic and Mediterranean, 97

Navarre, Gen. Henri Eugene, 244–45
Near East: U.S. military aid in the, 177–97
Nello L. Teer Company, 116
Nelson, Donald, 18
Netherlands, 146
Neutrality Act of 1939, 130
New Caledonia, 32
Newcomer, Brig. Gen. F. K., 261
Newfoundland, 300
New Orleans Port of Embarkation, 113
New York Port of Embarkation, 151
New Zealand, 201
Niagara Falls Chemical Plant, 72
Nicaragua, 266
Nixon, Richard, 246
Norfolk, Virginia, 297, 301
North African Air Bases, 115–23
North America: defense of the northern approaches, 278–303
North Atlantic Constructors, 297
North Atlantic Treaty, 36, 161, 277
North Atlantic Treaty Organization (NATO), 143, 160–74, 242, 244–45, 280, 301
North Korea, 221, 227
Norway, 145
Nouasseur, Morocco, 117

Oahu, Hawaii, 303
Oceanic Trading Company, 35
O'Daniel, Lt. Gen. John W., 245, 303
Office of the Army-Navy Liquidation Commissioner, 19
Office of the Foreign Liquidation Commissioner, 19, 20–38, 222, 272–73
Office of Lend-Lease Administration, 152
Office of War Mobilization and Reconversion, 35
Offshore procurement, 140–41
Ogdenburg, N.Y., 278
Okinawa, 34
Old, Maj. Gen. Archie, 118
Olmsted, Maj. Gen. George H., 201
"One-post concept," Hawaii, 303
Ordnance rebuilding program in Germany, 106
"Operation VITTLES," 89–90
Organization for foreign military aid, 143–46
Organization of American States (OAS), 267–68

Index

Organized Reserve Corps (ORC), 78–80, 155

Pace, Frank, 109, 120–23, 299
Pacific Command, 303
Pahlevi, Mohammed Riza, 194
Pakistan, 156
Panama, Republic of, 263
Panama Area Joint Committee, 259
Panama Canal, defense of, 256–63
Panama Canal Act of 1912, 261
Panama Canal Company, 259–63
Panama Railroad Company, 260
Pan American Union, 267
Papagos, Gen. Alexander, 185
Parodi, Alexandre, 92
Patterson, Robert P., 30, 191, 223, 271
Peace Observation Commission (United Nations in Greece), 190
Pedro Miguel lock, Panama Canal, 257
Peloponnesus, 185
Pentagon Building, 69
Permafrost, 282, 299
Permanent Joint Board on Defense (U.S. and Canada, World War II), 278
Persian Gulf, 194
Persian Gulf Service Command (World War II), 194
Peru, 146, 275
Peter Kiewit Sons' Company of Omaha, 297
Petroleum Planning Committee (NATO), 163
Philippine Rehabilitation Act of 1946, 35, 234–35
Philippines, 32–33, 146; agreement for U.S. military bases (1947), 233; defense assistance to, 233–36; independence of, 233
Pick, Lt. Gen. Lewis A., 68, 121–22, 296
Planning Board for European Inland Surface Transport (NATO), 163
Planning Board for Ocean Shipping (NATO), 163
Plowden, Edwin, 168
Point Barrow, Alaska, 293
Porter-Urquhart, Associated, 116
Portugal, 146
Post of Oahu, Hawaii, 303–6
Potter, Col. William I., 288
Preparedness Investigating Subcommittee, U.S. Senate Committee on Armed Services, 119

Prince William Sound, 291
Progressive Party of Japan, 251
Project Robin (Blue Jay), Greenland, 297
Puerto Rico, 258
Purdy Company, 31

Quezon, Manuel, 233

Ralph E. Mills Company, 116
Rasmussen, Knud, 296
Reconstruction Finance Corporation (RFC), 74, 76
Redeployment, Europe to the Pacific, in World War II, 16
Redeployment of U.S. forces from China, 205
Red tape, 8
Remington Arms Company, 74
Renshaw, Col. Clarence, 297, 299
Republic of the Philippines Military Assistance Act (1946), 234
Research and Development Board, 144
Reserve Components: support for, 78–81
Reserve Officers' Training Corps (ROTC), 78, 80
Rhee, Syngman, 223, 228
Rhein-Main Air Force Base, 89
Richards, Maj. Gen. G. J., 69
Ridgway, Gen. Matthew B., 101, 163
Ridley, Maj. Gen. Clarence S., 195
Rio Treaty (1947), 267, 277
Rodriguez Army Hospital, Puerto Rico, 258
Roosevelt, Franklin D. (president), 54, 56, 130–31, 204, 262, 278, 300
Rosemount, Minn., 297
Rothschild Frères of Paris, 129
Royall, Kenneth C., 37, 281, 285, 289

Saigon, 241
Saipan, 32, 34
Salan, Gen. Raoul, 244
Sale, Morocco, 117
Sand Island quartermaster depot, Hawaii, 304
San Francisco Port of Embarkation, 151
Schofield Barracks, Hawaii, 303–4
Schufeldt, Commodore Robert W., 221
Schwarzkopf, Col. H. Norman, 195
Seattle Port of Embarkation, 294
Second Armored Division, 105
Seoul, 224

Seventeenth parallel (Indochina), 246
Seventh Fleet, 219
Seward, Alaska, 291
Seybold, Brig. Gen. John S., 261
Shanghai, 207, 211, 213
Siberia, 61
Sidi Slimane, Morocco, 117
Sixth Infantry Regiment, 105
Skagway, Alaska, 292
S. J. Groves and Sons, 297
Soong, T. V., 33
South Pacific, 32
Spain, 170–72
Staatliche Erfassungs-Gessellschaft fur offentliches Gut m.b.H. (STEG), 28–29, 108–9
State Department, 76, 216, 219, 247, 301
Stimson, Henry L., 56, 270, 274
Strategic Air Command, 97, 115–16
Strategic and critical materials stockpiles, 75–78
Strategic and Critical Materials Stockpiling Act of 1939, 76; amendments of 1946, 76–78
Supply and industrial reserves, 72–78
Supply stocks, 72–73
Supreme Headquarters Allied Powers Europe (SHAPE-NATO), 163, 165–69, 280
Surplus property, disposal of: in the European Theater, 32; in Latin America, 37–38; in the Pacific and Far East, 32–37; overseas, 18–38; in the United States, 38–43
Surplus property, sales of: sales to China, 207; sales to Korea, 222–23; sales to Latin America, 272–73
Surplus Property Act of 1944, 19, 28, 44, 62, 196
Surplus Property Board, 19
Surplus Property Division, Department of the Interior, 32

Tacoma, Wash., 294
Taft, Robert A., 135
Taiwan (Formosa), 216–21
Tampico, 260
Technical Cooperation Administration, Department of State, 146, 259
Tempelhof Airfield, 89
Temporary commission to supervise elections in Korea (United Nations), 223

Temporary Council Committee (NATO), 163
Thailand, 146, 246
Thirty-first Infantry Regiment, 224
Thirty-second Infantry Division, 222
38th parallel (Korea), 221
"Three Wise Men" (NATO Temporary Council Committee), 168–69
Thule Air Base, Greenland, 296–300
Tinian, 34
Tito, Marshal Josip, 170, 184
Thorson, Brig. Gen. Truman C., 179
Tok Junction, Alaska, 296
Tonkin, 237, 240
Tonkin delta, 238
Treaty of Alliance and Mutual Assistance, Dunkirk (1947), 160
Treaty of Economic, Social, and Cultural Collaboration and Collective Self-Defence, Brussels (1948), 160
Trieste, 95, 173
Trieste U.S. Troops, 97
Tripler Army Hospital, Moanolua, Hawaii, 305
Trucks and Spares, 109
Truman, Harry S., 13, 55, 89, 131, 134, 137, 205–6, 208, 213, 219, 268, 271
Truman Committee (U.S. Senate), 18
Truman Doctrine, 132–36, 177–78, 308
Tsingtao, 207, 211, 213
Tudeh Party, Iran, 196–97
Turkey, 135–36, 146, 162; military aid to, 190–94
Twenty-fourth Corps, 221
Twenty-eighth Infantry Division, 105
296th Infantry Regiment, 258
Tydings-McDuffie Act (1934), 233

Ukrainian S.S.R., 133
Union of Soviet Socialist Republics, 60–63, 87–90, 132–33, 161, 173–74, 190–91, 206, 221, 243
United Kingdom, 25–26, 55, 56–60, 132–34, 140, 146, 150, 177–79, 194, 300
United Nations, 63, 132–33, 160, 190, 209, 223, 250
United Nations Command (Far East), 101
United Nations Relief and Rehabilitation Commission (UNRRA), 30, 36, 181
United States Forces, European Theater (USFET), 28, 97

Index

United States Liquidation Commission (1919), 18–19
United States Maritime Commission, 44
United States Property and Disbursing Officer (USP & DO), 79–80
United States Steel Corporation, 31
United States Steel Export Corporation, 130
"Uniting for Peace Resolution" (United Nations General Assembly, 1950), 190
"University of Lawsonomy," 38
Uruguay, 146, 275
U.S. Air Forces in Europe, 97
U.S. Army, Alaska, 282–83, 295
U.S. Army, Caribbean, 275
U.S. Army, Caribbean Sea Frontier, 258
U.S. Army, Europe, 101–2
U.S. Army, Pacific, 303–4
U.S. Army Group, Greece, 179
U.S. Army Military Government in Korea, 222
U.S. Army Missions in Latin America, 259
U.S. Engineer Group, Ankara, 193
U.S. European Command, 101–3, 145, 148
U.S. Forces, China theater, 205
U.S. Forces in Austria, 95, 97, 113–15
U.S. Forces in Europe, 96–115
U.S. Iranian Mission (World War II), 194
U.S. Military Advisory Group to China, 205
U.S. Northeast Command, 300
U.S. Public Roads Administration (Federal Works Agency), 192
U.S. Rubber Company, 74
U.S.-U.S.S.R. Joint Commission on Korea (1947), 221

Valdez, Alaska, 294

Vandenberg, Arthur H., 135
VanFleet, Lt. Gen. James A., 180, 186
Varkiza agreement in Greece, 178
Verona, 114
Vienna, 114
Viet Minh, 237–46
Vietnam, 237–46
Vinnell Company, 35
Vitsi Mountain area (Greece), 181, 183, 186

Wadsworth, George, 192
Waikakalus, Hawaii, 304
Wallace, Henry, 204
War Assets Administration (WAA), 38–45, 74
War Assets Corporation, 38
Wedemeyer, Lt. Gen. Albert, 89, 208, 221–22, 248
Weisbaden Air Force Base, 89
Western Europe: military aid to, 160–74
Western Hemisphere defense, 256–309
Western Hemisphere Defense Program, 272–73
Western Union, 160–61, 164
Western Union Defense Organization, 160–61
Westover Air Force Base, 297
Wheeler, Lt. Gen. R. A., 68
Wherry Act, 70–71
Whitehorse, Yukon Territory, Canada, 292
Whittier, Alaska, 281, 288, 290–91, 294
Wilson, Edwin C., 192
Wolfe, Glenn, 44
World War II: termination of, 15

Yangtze river, 209, 213
Yoshida shigeru, 250
Yugoslavia, 170–72, 184

RAYMOND H. FOGLER LIBRARY
DATE DUE

BOOKS ARE SUBJECT TO RECALL AFTER TWO WEEKS